Happily Made

HAPPILY MADE

Lillian Good

Library of Congress Control Number:		2017900050
ISBN:	Hardcover	978-1-5245-2128-8
	Softcover	978-1-5245-2127-1
	eBook	978-1-5245-2129-5

Names are changed to protect the identity of real people.

Print information available on the last page.

Rev. date: 01/16/2017

To order additional copies of this book, contact:
Xlibris
1-800-455-039
www.Xlibris.com.au
Orders@Xlibris.com.au
751131

Contents

Three things cannot be long hidden:
the sun, the moon and the truth.

Buddha

Acknowledgements

My absolute thanks to Martel Carter and Naina Knoess for assisting me in making this book possible.

Also my four children. This book is not for the masses, it's for you. In knowing my story you will come to know your own.

And to Jon who made me question, search and believe in 'stuff'.

1

In the Beginning

In the late autumn of 1974 I was born in a quaint university town in the southern tip of Sweden. My parents had only recently returned after trying to make a life for themselves in the United States where my father was from.

Legend has it, and to this day my mother claims this is truth, a strange event took place right after my birth. I was two days old. My mother was still in hospital with me, recovering from the birth, and possibly delaying returning home to a demanding four year old daughter and two year old son.

It was All Saints Day, a day to remember the dead and pray for their souls. The maternity ward was quiet and my mother was looking out the window at the massive cathedral next door to the hospital. She could hear the bells ringing for the Sunday service. As she stood there she noticed a woman entering the ward. She came on her own and looked out of place. The only way my mother can describe her appearance is that her skin had a very unusual tone to it, a greenish hue that gave the woman an eerie appearance. My mother kept looking at the woman wondering who she was there to visit. As she wandered down the hall past the rooms with new babies, my mother decided to follow and see where this very unusual lady was going. Much to my mother's surprise the woman walked into the nurse's kitchenette, opened a drawer and pulled out a knife. My mother froze. How could this possibly be happening? She instinctively started running for help, hoping to find someone who could stop this lady. As she ran down the hall she passed my room, and quickly turned to check that I was still safely in my crib. My mother was shocked to see that there were four beings in the room. Four giant beings. So giant their proportions didn't fit in with the dimensions of the room. They seemed taller than the ceiling. There was one on each corner of my crib. They were radiating light and, despite the crisis unfolding, my mother felt an instant sense of calm and knew I was safe.

As it turns out, my mother found someone to help, and the woman was immediately removed from the hospital grounds. Serenity was restored. Most of the mothers on the ward hadn't even realised what had taken place.

I grew up hearing this story. It was so familiar, and it was never really made a big deal of. Of course I had had four giant beings protecting me. There was no drama in it. Nothing spectacular. It just was.

It would probably help to explain that my parents had recently stepped into the Christian faith, and angels and demons were very much part of their world. It's not that they had any encounters with them as such, but if the Bible says there are angels, then so it is. And having four of them rock up to protect their daughter on All Saints Day didn't seem that far-fetched.

When I say that my parents had recently 'stepped into the Christian faith', I don't think I'm doing justice to what actually took place. I feel I need to share the background to their story.

My mother was the firstborn child and only daughter in her very typical Swedish family. Her father was a proud Atheist. An academic. He was a school principal as well as a teacher of seven languages. He had high hopes for his very bright daughter who was the apple of his eye. She was the top student in her class for all of her schooling life and well ahead of her peers in academics. Once she finished school she moved to Lund, the quaint little university town where I was born. She was working hard on her law degree and very much following on the path her parents had set for her.

My father was also the firstborn child and the only son in his Jewish family. He was born in New York to hard working parents. His father was away serving in the war so for the first two years of his life he lived with his mother and her parents. His grandfather worked in the synagogue and my father, being the only grandson, had very high expectations placed on him. When my grandfather returned from the war I can only assume that he was traumatised by it. Of course there was no help for young men like him, he was expected to assimilate back into society and put the memories behind him. I've never been given many details except that my grandfather would take out his trauma on his two oldest children. My father and his sister were on the receiving end of a lot of anger.

My father's escape was his guitar, and he would play it for hours every day. His hard work paid off when he was accepted into the very famous Juilliard Private Conservatory in New York City. The pressure was mounting though as he entered his late teens, with so many expectations from his Jewish family. The constant questions of what path he would follow. The feeling that he was restricted by a religion that he hadn't chosen for himself. Being the sixties, he was not alone in his feelings, and through his musical connections my father found a new freedom in the young people around him who had stepped out of the shackles society had been placing on them. And so instead of studying, with the help of drugs and free love, he hopped on the hippie bandwagon. His family was devastated. He had so much potential. He was so gifted. So bright.

The drafts for the Vietnam war were becoming more and more of a threat to my father. To him the answer was clear. He had to leave the country. Go somewhere safe. Somewhere he could continue on his new path and, not only be left alone from the government, but also from his family.

The answer was obvious. Denmark! Surely Danny Kaye knew what he was talking about in the song "Wonderful, Wonderful Copenhagen". And confirming how perfect Denmark was as a choice was the never-ending blonde beauties and gourmet cheeses waiting for him on arrival. My dad quickly packed his backpack and his guitar and bought a one-way ticket. He had no plans of returning to the constraints of home. His mother was heartbroken. She adored her son and as far as she was concerned a part of her died that day he waved goodbye.

Alas, Copenhagen was not quite the haven my father had dreamt of. The drug scene was ruthless. The women were harsh. His fairy tale quickly vanished and my dad needed to get out quick. At the time, the cheapest place to go from Copenhagen was Sweden a few miles across the water. He arrived in Lund with no money, no plans, and his guitar strapped to his back.

Was it destiny? Was it chance? Who knows. As far as my Swedish grandparents were concerned it was a disaster.

My parents met in a university loft and instantly fell in love. My gorgeous mother with long, blonde hair and the face of an angel and my foreign dad with a mysterious presence. They were both smitten. My dad's philosophies and mystical dimensions drew my mother in, and she knew in her heart that a law degree could never provide the life she now realised she craved.

What followed next were a couple of years my parents refer to as 'The Search'. They sought the Truth. They tried a little bit of every religion, cult and faith they stumbled across. Drugs helped them in their search. They found different ways to pay for their needs, making little wallets out of leather, working in 'herb gardens' (or so we were told as kids) and busking with my father's guitar.

My father was a complex man. So many unexplored dimensions. Such a desire for truth yet a feeling he was trapped in the mundane. When my mother announced she was pregnant my father felt that this was a good time for him to explore his Jewish roots and hitch hike to the Holy Land. A baby wasn't going to hinder his search. He ended things with my pregnant mother and left her in Sweden to fend for herself.

After weeks of hitch hiking across Europe he arrived in the land of his forefathers. My dad had been hoping to finally experience the

Truth he had been seeking. It was exactly the opposite! My father instantly hated the place. He hated the religious oppression that simply reminded him of his childhood. He hated the aggressiveness of the people. The final straw came the day he nearly got stabbed while walking on the beach in Tel Aviv. He had to get out. And get out quick!

After a few weeks of hitch hiking he arrived at his Danish friend's home. He knocked on the door, and lo and behold, who came to open the door? My now very pregnant mother! Out of desperation, and not knowing where to go, my mother had sought refuge with my father's friend in Denmark. My parents were reunited and decided they would raise their baby together.

They took the ferry across to Sweden to see if any friends there might be willing to let them stay with them. They had no other options.

While living in a friend's apartment in Stockholm, their bed under the kitchen table, my sister Susanna was born. My father started making and selling knick knacks in order to support his family. He made little wooden boxes with tiny segments in them. He filled each segment with a different grain or legume, then covered it in glass for people to hang on their walls. Not surprisingly the money wasn't exactly rolling in.

It was during this time in Stockholm that my father had a bit of an epiphany. If marriage was as meaningless as he thought it was, then why not get married? It meant nothing, so why not go ahead and do it? Once this new truth had settled in his mind the next step was to provide his bride with a ring. With his grain and legume display case sales he couldn't really afford anything remotely metallic as a ring for my mother. Instead he put his coins together and in the middle of a very cold February in Stockholm 1972, my dad went and bought a very expensive juicy peach that had been imported from a faraway land. The perfect gift for the mother of his child.

After my mother ate the luxurious fruit my father kept the peach pit and allowed it to dry for a few days. Then he got busy. He started smoothing the pit on both sides until he eventually reached the bitter almond in the middle. He popped out the almond, got my mother's hand and tried the 'ring' on for size, and with a bit of sandpaper my father was able to create a beautifully unique ring for his bride. Off they went to the Stockholm registry and made their 'meaningless vows' while wearing t-shirts and jeans, with Susanna as a two year old flower girl.

Not long after this my mother noticed those distinctive signs. She was pregnant again. They would soon be a family of four. The pressure on my father was tremendous. How was he meant to provide for his wife and two children? After a few months of trying to become more financially stable in Stockholm my parents finally surrendered. They swallowed their pride and returned to southern Sweden to see if my grandparents would let them stay there. They would at least have a roof over their heads and regular meals.

It lasted three days. Morfar, my grandfather, kicked my father out. He couldn't handle seeing his precious daughter with her drug-addicted loser of a husband. Surely she would see the light and let her man move on? She was still young. She could complete her studies, find a sensible Swedish man with a career, and all this could be put behind them.

Instead my mother took my sister by the hand and followed the man she loved. Again my parents were on the streets. They reconnected with some friends in Lund who allowed them in to their apartment. Instantly my parents knew that they couldn't stay. This drug den was not a place for a pregnant mother and a little girl. They found themselves walking the streets of Lund trying to find something or someone that would provide shelter for the night. It was getting late. They were all hungry and exhausted from their search. Earlier in the day they had walked past a white cottage with a tiny note glued to the corner of the window. *The Truth will set you Free* it said in someone's handwriting. My mother reminded my dad of the note and suggested that if the family who lived in the house were Christian they might be good enough to allow them to sleep there for the night. After all, Christians are meant to look after the needy.

It was worth a try. My parents walked back and found the cottage. They knocked a few times until the door was finally opened by a young woman similar age to them. They explained their predicament. She wanted to know if they were Christians. They tried to say yes they were kind of Christians because they were seeking the Truth, and if she could see it from their perspective they could in fact be considered Christians, if Christ is the Truth, and surely we are all children of God, and so on. I doubt she got the answer she was looking for but she could sense their desperation and she let them in. The cottage itself was actually the front part of a small courtyard that was edged with other homes. They had in fact landed in a hippie commune called the 'Jesus House'. Leah explained that she was the only one there and the rest of the community had gone away for the weekend to a 'Jesus Festival'. When the group of young people returned the next day my parents were blown away by this happy group of people who were 'high on Jesus'. Their joy was infectious. They were hippies just like my parents with the guitars out in force, the long braids, and the lentils soaking for the communal dinner. But there were no drugs. No hopelessness. And they had community. My parents were in awe.

My sister was instantly surrounded by a group of uncles and aunties who adored her. My parents were fed, listened to, and they no longer felt alone. It didn't take long for them to have what they called "a born again experience". For my father, this new birth was cataclysmic. I can still hear him, in his heavy Brooklyn accent, telling anyone he could about what happened as if he was recounting a story that took place a day earlier. His passion for that moment of salvation never dwindled. He was born again! He was a new man! The Truth had set him free!

My brother Raphael was born not long after. They were now a complete family. They had a daughter, a son and a new faith. Life was good. My grandmother offered to pay for the airfares so my parents could move to America and start a new life. My dad cut his long hair, shaved his very big beard, and bought himself a suit. His uncle, who was Vice-President for Warner Brothers, offered him an accountancy job. Things were finally coming together.

They moved to Florida to start their new life with a new found excitement for what God would do in their life. As it turned out, Florida was hell on earth. The extreme humidity. The scorpions. The alligators. It got too much for my mother and for her nerves. She was now pregnant with baby number three, and all she wanted was to be back in the comforts of Sweden. My father was still struggling with the demons of his past. Coming off years of drug use, he was still having hallucinations, disturbing dreams and visions. He felt that he couldn't be the accountant that his family had seen in him. My parents bought one-way tickets to Sweden and returned in August 1974. Two months later I was born.

2

My First Seven Years

My first seven years gave no indication of the way my life was going to unfold. In fact, it's the only time in my life that I lived in one home for more than two years.

My first home was on the fifth floor of a large apartment block. It faced a park and was backed by a garbage tip that had been converted into a grassy hill for us kids to run across in summer and sled down in winter. The apartment was just like any other Swedish apartment at the time, smallish, well heated and very functional. We had a tiny balcony and our basement laundry was shared with the other people in the building. I never felt that we were missing out on anything. And I was blissfully unaware that each month my parents worried about the bills to be paid.

Some of my very earliest memories are more feelings than images in my mind. I remember feeling completely separate from the rest of my family. I didn't have a sense of belonging to them in any way. My sister tried her hardest to pretend that I didn't share an apartment with her, and my brother's role in my life could best be described as the smiling assassin. He would tear around the apartment in full speed and create havoc, at the same time as laughing maniacally. He loved to antagonise, always with a smile on his face.

When I was only 15 months old my younger brother Sam was born. I instantly fell into a carer role and it was the first time I felt a connection with anyone in my family. As we grew I continued to be Sam's little helper. He had a speech impediment and no one could understand him. Except for me. So my first role in life was as an interpreter for my younger brother who would implode if he couldn't be understood. I thrived in my role as his caretaker.

When my mother described what I was like as a child she would always say I was so content. So happy. Not a care in the world. I'm pleased with that description. The thing is, I'm not really sure how accurate it is. I remember feeling very uneasy in my own home. My dad's tension and anger escalated along with the pressures of a growing family and children he felt he couldn't control. Raphael was a force to be reckoned with and my dad was out of his depth. I found the atmosphere too much to deal with. Even at this very young age I started to go elsewhere in my mind to escape the pressure.

This might sound funny, keep in mind though we were on the fifth floor of an apartment block with not many options for entertainment, but escape for me came initially in the form of snails. I would collect these snails after it had rained all night. I would bring them up to our apartment, sit on the couch and let the snails slide across my arms and legs for hours. Pure bliss. Possibly a form of self-hypnosis. Who knows? It worked for me. I could sit there quietly and escape the dynamics of my home while staring at these snails slowly moving across my body.

Another activity that I didn't have available as easily, but it definitely started at this age, was mud walking. After a heavy rain, which thankfully in Sweden is a common occurrence, I would get my gumboots on and find a patch of mud. The deeper the mud the better. With my head down and only focused on the step ahead I would wade through the mud and love the sensation of my boot being suctioned in and having to slowly pull it out. Again, this was a form of escape for me and I always loved hearing the rain pelting down because, not only did it mean more snails for my collection, it also meant there was a chance of a muddy escape.

Although those first few years were quite uneventful, I can so clearly see that the themes that have been carried by me across my four decades had their roots in those early years. Body image is one of the most consuming obstacles in my life and those seeds were sewn when I was a very small girl.

My father had grown up in a very conservative Jewish home. I can only guess that his views on the human body were steeped in a very long history of Jewish hang-ups that were very intertwined with their biblical perception. It's not as if my dad ever actually said that the body is evil, but to me that was very much his message. I remember being only around three years old when I was changing my clothes in the living room. My dad yelled "Get away from the window!". Now, as you might recall, we lived on the fifth floor. There was a park in front of us. The only chance of my body being seen by anyone outside our home would have meant they were in a low flying helicopter. Somehow, without knowing how, I had crossed a line and my dad made it very clear I was never to do that again. Curtains had to be drawn. The body was not to be exposed. A sense of shame started creeping up from the base of my feet.

My grandparents, as well as my uncle who happened to live in the apartment beneath us, were clearly aware of my father's hang-ups. They loved nothing more than making up for my father's reservations about the body by making sure we were exposed to theirs as much as possible. After all, this is Sweden. Sweden is all about nudity and body acceptance. If my uncle and auntie knew that we were coming downstairs for a visit they would make sure to make the most of it. No matter how much we emotionally tried to prepare ourselves it never felt quite right to be greeted by our uncle and auntie with them both sitting on the couch, legs splayed, totally nude.

This happened on numerous occasions, but there is one occasion that stands out from the rest. It was the morning of Santa Lucia, a celebration leading up to Christmas when children dress up as angels and elves in the morning, and while it's still dark, they form a line and in a very quiet and sacred manner start singing Christmas songs special to that day. Each child either holds a candle, a lantern or a tray of traditional saffron buns. The tallest girl with the longest hair gets to be Santa Lucia and leads the parade with a wreath of candle sticks on her head. It's a beautiful tradition. Unless of course you have to do this ceremony in front of your nude uncle and auntie who are doing their best job trying to make you cringe by playing with and poking at their different body parts. There was nowhere to run, nowhere to hide. I simply had to keep my tray of saffron buns steady and wish myself away.

Morfar, my grandfather was also keen to expose us kids to the Swedish values. He had no intention of catering to my father's Jewish hang-ups. He made sure we became very familiar with the male body, his male body to be exact. One way to do this was by greeting us at his kitchen table completely nude, as we ate our muesli. Not only that, he would also make sure he got some morning stretches in while he had an audience. My face would burn as I tried to focus on the muesli bowl in front of me. This was the proof I needed that our relatives were definitely not joining us in Heaven in the afterlife. As my dad would remind us, they would be going straight to Hell. Bodies were sinful. They had nothing to do with the God we served and the less attention they got the better.

Another theme that started during this time was the fact that males were better than females. Again, it was never actually said in those exact words, but the message was loud and clear. Females were weak. More prone to sin. Tarnished somehow. These were messages that came through in my dad's behaviour or as comments to us girls, and we grew up believing it as truth.

The irony is of course that my mother was incredibly strong. A powerhouse. She was raising four young children in a small apartment. She had a tiny budget to work with and yet she never made us feel as if we were going without. She was able to keep us distracted from a man that was still very much battling with his inner demons. Not once in my childhood did I see my mother disheveled or unkempt. She woke early, got herself dressed and presentable, with her long hair up in a bun or a braid. She then had her morning devotions with her Bible in her lap. By the time her four children woke she had already started her day and was busily organising things in the kitchen.

Every night I fell asleep to the sound of her beloved sewing machine. She was constantly sewing clothes for her growing kids, altering clothes that had been donated to us and mending holes. Her days were spent in service to her husband and her children. There was never a moment for her. Never coffee with a friend. No splurging on an item of clothing. No hobbies outside the home. Even with her commitment to her family she still made time to help others.

On Sundays my mother would get her bicycle, put Sam in the seat on the handle bars and me in the seat on the back. Raphael and Susanna would ride along on their own bikes, and off we would go to the hospital. Once there we would go to the ward for the very old and frail patients. We would then put them in wheelchairs and wheel them down the corridors of the hospital basement to the chapel. We then sat through what felt like a very long service only to have the excitement of wheeling them all back again. I have very clear memories of pushing a wheel chair bigger than myself along those dark corridors.

Our life in our fifth floor apartment was interrupted each summer by a magical escape. We would borrow my uncle's car and drive north to Morfar and Mormor's summer shack. Words cannot do justice to this tiny piece of magic on the west coast of Sweden. After a three hour car trip the landscape drastically changes from the flat fields of southern Sweden to forests and huge rock boulders that roll into the sea. Our little shack, and it truly was little with only one tiny living area and a small bedroom attached, was built on the side of a cliff, overlooking the sea with an island directly across. To reach the shack we had to follow a steep path curving around mossy rocks and fallen trees. The smell of the forest was consuming. The wet moss made your senses come alive. In summer we had the thrill of picking wild blueberries and our faces were painted blue as we filled our baskets with these beautiful berries. If we were lucky enough to visit later in the year we would also pick chanterelles. We had no idea how luxurious these mushrooms were, we simply loved bringing them back to the shack for Mormor who would lightly fry them with butter and black pepper.

One of my favourite pastimes was making my way down the steep side of the cliff. Down to our private little jetty. There I would lie, feeling the warmth beneath me, and try to lure crabs out from under their rocks. I would happily do this for hours on end. Our time at the summer shack was sacred to me. It was pure happiness being there. Not only did I get to spend more time with Mormor and Morfar, but I also had nature all around me and the freedom to explore.

As well as spending time with them at their shack, I also spent time with Mormor and Morfar in their home. They only lived about an hour away. As a child, and with no car, that felt very far away. They lived in the most southern tip of Sweden. A tiny little holiday town that is famous for its horse riding, boating, and most importantly the migrating birds that use this spot as a resting place before heading south for winter. I absolutely loved visiting their home. We would go for long bike rides along the coast. We would ride on forest paths. Ride around the harbour. Ride and visit the stables. All the while watching the birds fly above us in V-formation. Again, it gave me that sense of freedom and a connection to nature.

Mormor and Morfar had a steady routine to their day and I soaked up the calm. Breakfast was sacred. A ritual. Nothing was rushed. First the drip coffee was brewed. As the coffee smell filled the kitchen, items from the fridge were put on the table. Sour milk with their own blend of muesli, always served in the same tin. A tin that I now keep in my own kitchen as a reminder. Then the selection of bread was brought out. Crisp bread, sour dough slices, flat bread, it was all there for the choosing. Then came liver paté, Morfar's homemade marmalade and blackberry jam, as well as a selection of cheeses. A daily feast. All this was washed down with cups of tea. Lapsang Souchong or Russian Caravan were the favourites. Oh how I loved breakfast. Besides the initial nude appearance by Morfar, this part of the day was my absolute favourite.

After a day spent riding our bikes or going for a walk, dinner would be made by Mormor. She was known for her roast chicken and meatballs with the most delicious gravy. I make it now for the people I love, and I can hear her telling me to add an extra splash of soy sauce to get that kick.

Mormor was always a bit of an enigma. She had a regal look, as if from a faraway land. It was often a topic of conversation where she might have originated from. There seemed to be a general consensus that she was probably from Gypsy stock. Of course no one really knew but her elegant looks made her a Gypsy Queen of sorts to me. She was elegant, crafty and no one dared oppose her. Her tiny size was no indication of her strength. Her home was her domain and we all feared and loved her at the same time. In her later years she started to paint and I am so grateful for that. It means that no matter where I go in the world to visit family, there is always one of her pieces of art hanging on the wall that reminds me of her. She captured the landscape of my youth. The cliffs of the summer shack. The sand dunes we explored. The streets lined with old houses that we would ride our bicycles down no matter what the weather. Her legacy lives on in her art.

Morfar was so different to Mormor. He was an academic. An imposing man with a booming voice. His two great passions were birds and Latin grammar, and he wanted nothing more than to share those passions with his grandchildren. It never ceased to amaze us how, no matter what we were talking about, Morfar was able to steer the conversation to his favourite topics. My allergy towards learning a new language started around my grandparent's kitchen table. I became an expert at looking interested and making the right noises to appear as if I was listening but all the while my mind was elsewhere. How could there possibly be so much to learn about birds and their migratory patterns? Why is the secret to all knowledge wrapped up in decoding Latin root words? We were a captive audience and Morfar made the most of it.

I am so grateful for those first seven years of my life. I am grateful for the steady presence that my mother created. I'm grateful that I lived close enough to my grandparents so I could feel connected to them despite where life might take me.

3

Coming of Age

A shift happened in our family when I reached the age of seven. My parents were told about a Christian community in Malmö, a city only 25 minutes away. Apparently there was a group of zealous followers of Jesus who felt compelled to spread the Good News to those that needed it most. About twenty families had moved into the poorest part of the city, their goal was to shine the light of Jesus and to make a difference. My parents were intrigued. This was exactly what they had been looking for since those early days in the Jesus House. Being part of a community, living out the Gospel, and shining the light of Jesus into the darkness.

The leaders of the community came to visit us. They were a family with five children. Five powerful children. In fact, the most powerful of them all was the youngest and a seven year old girl. Magdalena. And she happened to be exactly my age. We spent the whole day together as families and two things happened that day. My parents decided that we were going to move to Malmö to be part of this exciting community, the other thing that happened was that I fell under the spell of a new friend. The best way I can describe it is how Annika would have felt the day Pippi Longstocking moved in next door. Absolute awe and wonder. Who was this person? How could I ever match the wild glint in her eyes? Would she ever see me as an equal? As far as I was concerned, the move to Malmö was a mixture of excitement and fear.

Moving a family of six is never an easy task. Moving a family of six with a heavily pregnant mother seems unfathomable. Except in the context of my mother. She packed boxes, cleaned rooms, moved furniture, and didn't stop to even consider letting someone else do the job. It's no surprise that on the actual night of the move my mother went into labour. My dad had to find his way to the hospital in a new city while trying to drive a moving truck. He was so flustered that when he stopped to ask for directions from a passing pedestrian he forgot to put the handbrake on and the truck started to roll back down the hill. Thankfully my mother managed to find the handbrake and stop the truck.

The very next morning we were woken with the news we had another little brother. Ezra arrived six years after Sam was born so he had four older doting siblings. We settled into our new life with our new baby brother.

The neighbourhood we moved into was very different to the town we had moved from. There was a harshness that I wasn't used to, and I knew that it wasn't long before I was going to start school. Thankfully I wasn't starting alone as Magdalena would be in the same class as me, and I knew that with her as my friend no harm would come to me. We quickly became a force to be reckoned with. During the months before I started school our only rule was to be home by dinnertime. We had hours of freedom to explore and find adventures. Our parents had no idea how far we used to go on our bicycles since we never felt restricted to staying within our neighbourhood.

With Magdalena there always had to be an element of risk. A bike race to the city. Weaving between buses and cars. Seeing who could reach the tallest building first. We both knew it would be Magdalena. It always was. But I didn't mind, as I got to be her sidekick and I loved every moment of it.

We searched for brick walls that we could jump off, every time Magdalena would need a higher wall to prove herself on. Sometimes we would join the other kids in the neighbourhood with their games. While marbles were fun to play, there was a more exciting game on offer in the sandpit, pocket knife Russian roulette. We would stand in a circle, feet apart, and take turns flicking our pocket knife as close as we could to someone's foot. The idea of the game was whoever flinched and moved their foot was out. How I came away from my childhood with no foot injuries is beyond me. I look back at me as a seven year old, flicking a pocket knife at someone's foot, and just shake my head.

Once autumn arrived we started school. Having Magdalena by my side made this yet another adventure. I remember our parents telling us that we had to be "a light to the school". I wasn't exactly sure what that meant but I had a feeling that it might be connected to us wearing clothes that stood out from the rest of the other students. We had patches on our knees, and jackets with an extra pocket sewn on. Magdalena even had underwear made from old t-shirts. I was almost jealous. The older our clothes looked, the more we could shine our light for Jesus. By the time winter came around I was practically beaming as me and Magdalena would walk the school grounds showing our love of Jesus by having snow suits covered in patches. We were different to the rest. We were going to Heaven. If only those kids with new clothes could see the truth and start wearing hand me downs.

Our parents struggled with the school system. Not only did it mean that their kids were exposed to children with different values to them, it also meant that we were offered sex education in class. There was no way this was going to happen to me and Magdalena. So now, not only did I have an exemption from eating the blood pudding in the school cafeteria on Wednesdays (supposedly this had something to do with a new word that I heard my parents using with the school principal. Jewish. We were Jewish and could not eat blood. This was news to me. My dad's blood phobia was solved by using the "I'm Jewish" card. I had no idea what it meant but was happy to eat the overcooked carrots and peas instead) but I now got to sit in the library with Magdalena while our class got exposed to the dark side during sex education lessons. I'm fairly sure our library sessions weren't supervised because I have memories of the two of us giggling over diagrams of naked bodies. We obviously didn't quite understand that this was exactly what our parents were trying to keep us away from. Or maybe we did.

My days in school were long and boring. Our teacher was a bitter woman who had no intention of making learning interesting. I would spend the long hours at school drifting away in my mind, looking at the clock, counting the minutes until me and Magdalena could break free.

After a couple years of this our parents decided they had had enough of the public school system. What could secular education offer their daughters? Surely homeschooling was a much better use of our time.

I was thrilled. I now got to spend my whole week at Magdalena's house with her mother Carin as our teacher. I loved Carin and I knew Carin had a special place in her heart for me. Carin was an author who wrote inspiring Christian books for children. Missionary adventures were a favourite topic.

Having us homeschooled was a perfect set up. Carin could write her books, while us girls looked after the house. I'm pretty sure we had at least one work book each. It could possibly have been used once or twice in my year with Carin, although I'm not exactly sure. What I do know is that my formal education stopped abruptly in Grade 3. My days were now spent in more valuable pursuits. And anyway, who needed education? We were pretty sure that Jesus would return at any stage. Probably before Christmas. Why waste our time studying when we would be taken up to Heaven and live in glory? Education was not for us. It was for the masses who were all going to burn in Hell.

Our days were filled with tasks. Hours were spent in the basement laundry where we would wash clothes and sheets and then use the giant rolling machine to flatten the bedding. Magdalena's two story apartment had to be scrubbed from top to bottom. After all, her parents were the pastors of the community and their home was also used for weekly meetings. Their five children all had chores. I shared Magdalena's list, and I had no issues with this at all. It meant more time with her, and the quicker we completed the list the more time we had for our own adventures.

Baking was a daily event. We had complete access to the kitchen pantry and we would spend hours baking up a storm. Broom handles would be balanced across chairs, tables and benches and we would drape biscuits across them. We perfected cinnamon rolls. The trick was to use a whole slab of butter for every batch. We would smear it on, the thicker the better. Our main quest was to find the perfect mud cake recipe. It got to a point where it was no longer about the cake, but all about the batter. We would make a batch of batter and with a spoon each, gobble it down.

We also used our baking as a way to communicate our values. Cakes were baked for families we liked in the community as a means to be able to visit them. The other thing we liked to do with our baking was to teach Magdalena's very proud dad a lesson.

Bjorn was an imposing figure. He took his role as pastor very seriously and he demanded respect. Magdalena and I weren't that convinced. We could see his cracks and we had every intention of bringing them to the attention of everyone else who seemed to think he was a man of honour. One of our favourite things to make was chocolate balls. It was a delicious mix of butter, sugar, oats, coconut, cocoa and coffee. This mix was rolled into balls and covered in shredded coconut. A very Swedish treat. I'm not sure which one of us had the brilliant idea first, but we both worked hard to play a trick on Magdalena's dad. We made one of the balls enormous. So much bigger than the rest. We poked a hole into it and filled it with every spicy item from the pantry: chilli powder, pepper, garlic flakes and Tobasco sauce. We then covered up the hole and rolled the ball in coconut as usual. The balls were plated and brought to the table after family prayer time. Bjorn was always offered the food first in the family, and just as we had predicted, he reached for the largest chocolate ball on the plate. His greed had made him such an easy target. He hadn't even finished his first bite when his face exploded with a colour I have yet to see again.

There was no way the two of us were going to sit around so we ran from the table and jumped on our bikes. I remember pedaling away, looking behind me to see if Magdalena's brother was following us and realising we hadn't thought about this part of the equation. We had been so intent on teaching Bjorn a very important lesson, that we had overlooked the follow up. It took a few days for me to return to their house and I suspect those days were pretty tender for Magdalena's bottom.

Magdalena's family was my escape from home. I tried my very best to graft myself into her family so hopefully they wouldn't notice that I was there. The longer I could stay the better. The longer I could avoid being at home with my family the more peaceful I felt. For most of the year it was possible for me to spend every moment of the day with Magdalena and her family, until it was dinnertime and I had to go home and join my own family. However, summers were different.

Much to my horror, Magdalena's family would spend their summers doing ministry in Romania. They would fill up their caravan with bags of clothes and then, as I stood there fighting back the tears at not being invited to join them, they would wave goodbye as they drove off. I was devastated. Life without Magdalena at the helm was grim. There was no way I could spend my days with my family. I needed something to do. I needed an escape. I knew that as long as I was home by dinnertime no one would ask where I was, so I would pack my bathing suit and towel, and wait for the bus to the city. There was nothing in me that thought it was strange to be travelling on my own to the swimming centre. Once at the pool I would wade into the water and then lay there just floating. Absolute bliss. I was totally at peace. No brothers holding me down trying to tickle me until I farted. No dad raging. No sister stabbing her nails into my scalp. Just me and the ceiling. I would float for hours. My skin shriveled. My mind in another place.

The church that we were going to with this new fellowship group was different to what I had experienced in the hospital chapels. The songs hit a spot in me that was new. They triggered a longing in me. Jesus was referred to as a friend, or at times even as a lover. It was so intimate. When I focused on the word I felt a surge in my chest and a longing for something I had yet to experience. Jesus wanted me, and me alone. He wanted all of my heart. He wanted to search every part of it. He wanted to be with me. He was pursuing me. These concepts were beyond my comprehension but the longing was there. The feelings were there. Now when I was getting lost in my own thoughts as I floated in the pool or as I trawled through deep mud, I would start making up these love stories. Grand love stories that were intoxicating. There were times I was counting the hours until bedtime so I could be alone in my thoughts. I would often work on the same storyline for weeks at a time. Tweaking it each time I replayed it. Adding scenarios. Giving more details. The stories all had very similar themes of longing, separation, transformation, redemption. I loved adding specific scenarios. Rain was always one of them. Lots and lots of rain.

Of course I was the leading lady. I was adventurous and brave living out my life of sacrifice. And while the story spanned the globe and scenarios would change, the man in the story was always the same. He was there to protect me. He was steady. Safe. He was absolutely besotted with me. Just like Jesus wanted to search my heart and know every part of me, so did the man of my dreams. He wouldn't settle at knowing the bare essentials, instead he wanted to know it all. He wanted to know me. All of me. He would patiently wait as I had my adventures. He longed for me and nothing would stop him from pursuing me. I wanted these stories so much. I held them in my heart and never spoke about them.

When I was nine years old my sister Abigail was born. That night my parents left 13 year old Susanna in charge of the rest of us as they went off to the hospital. For the first time in his life, two year old Ezra had a massive meltdown. He screamed all night, as if he was injured. There was nothing we could do to console him. It was so out of character for this happy-go-lucky boy. We were horrified at the level of his distress and wished for our mother to hurry home.

As far as I was concerned, life was good. I spent my days doing chores with my best friend. Our schoolwork was a faded memory now replaced with baking and chores. Our adventures became even more exciting with the addition of a tandem bike. It meant that Magdalena, her two sisters, the neighbour's daughter, and me, could all fit on one bike if we balanced correctly. We could now experience our travels and adventures as one unit. The tandem bike took us down to the cold beach and often to the local water tower that loomed over the horizon like a giant space ship. Our only formal education was spent learning about the Bible and memorising verses, we were quick learners though. I remember Carin even offered us an ice cream cone if we could recite the twelve tribes of Israel by the end of the week. We had them memorised within hours.

One day Magdalena mentioned to me that she was going to be baptised along with her sisters. Why hadn't I thought of that? Being baptised was the ultimate sign that you wholeheartedly believed in the Bible. I didn't want to miss out. I wanted my salvation to be directly linked to Magdalena's salvation. I told my parents that I wanted to be baptised. They were pleased but wanted to know if I fully understood what it meant. Did I love Jesus? Was he in my heart? Had I asked for forgiveness for my sinful life? Was I willing to leave my past behind, pick up my cross and follow Jesus? Oh man! Now they put it that way, I wasn't so sure. I didn't feel like a bad person. I wasn't really sure what exactly I needed to be forgiven for. Did I love Jesus? When I thought about it I really didn't know. I wanted to love him. I wanted to be his friend. But now that I gave it some proper thought I realised that I had no idea who he was. The songs we sang about him made me feel wonderful. I heard that he wanted to be in a relationship with me, but I didn't really know what that meant. All this was too hard to explain to my parents and all I really wanted was to wear that white gown and go into the water.

A few weeks later I had my chance. Magdalena and her sisters went first. One by one they waded into the baptismal pool in the front of the church. The minister held each one in turn and asked them something quietly, and then pulled them back into the water.

It was then my turn. I waded almost knee deep into the water, when I remembered that I was actually very scared of having someone else holding me in water. When I was about three years old a woman that was babysitting us had taken us to the pool and thought it was hilarious dropping me in the deep part of the pool and watching me struggle to keep my head above water. The baptismal pool I was now in was deep. Really deep. In fact, the water had reached all the way up to Magdalena's neck and she was much taller than me! I got down to the last step and had to keep my head back as far as I could as I walked forward, and I still had water going into my mouth. The minister asked me something to do with Jesus and I quickly said yes, not really caring about what it meant anymore. I just wanted to get out. The white gown had ballooned around me. I was too focused on not drowning to remember if I had kept my underwear on when I changed into the gown. The minister tried to pull me back into the water but the gown was in the way. I was spluttering. There was nothing profound about the moment I got baptised. I was just grateful to be alive.

A short time after being baptised a travelling preacher came to visit our community. He held nightly meetings in the basement of one of the apartment blocks and we were invited to come along. After one of the meetings he asked for the children to come forward to be prayed for. We all stood in a line as he lay hands on us. When he came to me he was quiet for a long time. And then instead of praying for me he just started talking. He asked if I knew about Esther in the Bible, the woman who won a beauty competition and saved her nation. Of course I knew the story. It was my favourite. The preacher explained to me in great detail through the interpreter that I was going to be like Esther, I was going to bring salvation. Not just to my nation but to many nations. My beauty would win me favours and I had a very important task waiting for me. Me? This chubby, short girl? What on earth was he talking about? I was pretty stunned by the message, and as I walked back home that evening I asked Magdalena what had happened to her when she got prayed for. Surely if anyone was going to be Esther it was her. She was beautiful.

With long honey-coloured hair, tanned skin, and legs that seemed to never end. No, nothing had been said about Esther. Magdalena had been prayed for and that was it. How bizarre I thought, that the preacher could get it so wrong.

In the summer of 1984 our family had yet another big shift. This came about when my dad attended a Christian conference in Norway. While there, the main speaker, William Gold took my dad aside and explained to him that God had a direct command for the Jewish people and that was to return to the land of their forefathers. My dad was confused. Surely being a Christian meant a completely new life that had nothing to do with his Jewish past? He had found his truth in Jesus Christ. William explained that Christianity without its Jewish roots is an empty religion and that true Christianity embraces Judaism. The two complete each other. Jesus was in fact Yeshua. His mother Miriam. His father Yosef. Yeshua is the long awaited for Jewish Messiah.

William went on to say that as a Jewish man with a Christian faith my dad was in fact a 'complete Jew'. He was no longer waiting for his Messiah. For the first time in his life my dad saw his Jewish roots in a positive light. He saw them in the context of his relationship with Jesus. Being Jewish was no longer something to run away from. No longer something to ignore. It now tied in with his salvation. Dad came back from Norway with (if it was possible) a new found fervor. His daily Bible reading took on a new intensity. He read the Psalms with a new perspective. The Chosen People were meant to return to the Land. The Holy Land. That tiny strip of land in the Middle East where he was nearly stabbed so many years before. That place was in fact his birth right and God commanded him to go. We all knew something was brewing yet we couldn't exactly put our finger on it. The only actual difference was that a badly photocopied paper with the Hebrew alphabet was taped to the toilet wall and we were told to read it as we went ahead with our business.

A few months later, I suspect with the financial support of William Gold, we waved our dad goodbye as he went off to scout the Holy Land. He returned three weeks later, and before even taking his jacket off, he announced we were moving. We were moving to the Holy Land. It was God's command for the Jewish people to return to the Land. Jewish? There it was again. That word! I knew it had something to do with the Bible and me not eating blood pudding at school. Besides that, the word meant nothing to me. And Israel? Where was that? Again, I knew it was a country from the Bible. I knew they wore sandals and robes there. My mind was buzzing. I was moving to Israel? But I was Swedish. I was home. I had Mormor and Morfar. I had Magdalena. Why would I want to move to Israel just because some man called William Gold said we were meant to?

My mother seemed to share my views. For the first time ever I saw a look come across her angelic face. A look of defiance. She was not moving to Israel with her six children. This was lunacy. But according to my dad she had no choice. As my father was the head of the house my mother had to submit. Of course, How could she forget? She was the woman. My mother's response was to pray and fast. With six children aged 13, 11, 9, 8, 3 and 1, my mother stopped eating. She spent her time reading her Bible and praying for an answer. Thankfully within ten days the answer came in a passage from the book of Ruth. "Your people are my people. Your God is my God. Where you go I will follow." The words were burning on the page. And so at the end of February 1985 my mother boarded a plane and spent one week in Jerusalem trying to get her head around the fact that a few months later she would be moving her six children to this totally foreign world.

The date was set. July 10, 1985 was chosen as the day that according to my dad we would leave our meaningless existence behind in Sweden and step into God's will by moving to the Holy Land. There was no preparation for us kids. I do remember my dad telling us that we would eat giant avocados and watermelon and when that wasn't enough of a draw card he explained that once we settled we would go on a camel trek through the desert. That didn't seem too bad I thought. Now that my dad mentioned the desert I remembered the pyramids. And wait, the Israelites they had something to do with Egypt. Oh! We were moving to Israel the land of the pyramids!! I was so excited. Imagine being able to climb the pyramids! Maybe Magdalena could come and visit and we could explore the pyramids together.

My sister Susanna couldn't be swayed by avocados, camels, or the supposed pyramids. She was devastated. I watched her sink deeper and deeper over the next couple of months and I couldn't understand why my parents didn't seem to do anything about it. It was a very scary time.

As the deadline approached our apartment became emptier and emptier. Our apartment block had lots of Gypsy families living there, as was fairly common in southern Sweden. It made life that little bit more interesting. Our apartment was on the ground floor and most mornings, when we stepped outside, we would find a collection of items that had been flung from the above apartments. Forks, pieces of clothing, toys, and the most common of all, chicken carcasses.

I would reach for my bike only to have to remove a chicken bone that had become wedged in the wheel. We were lucky, our next door neighbours had furniture thrown down from the families upstairs. When their toddler daughter nearly got hit by an incoming armchair they ended up building a wire net to catch the missiles. The Gypsies were befriended by my mother and our belongings were being given away to them. I didn't mind so much. I wasn't really attached to any of our things, or so I thought. It turns out that I was. The kitchen table vanishing was really quite shocking to me. There was something so wrong about coming home one day and not having a table. This was real. We were actually leaving. Our lives would never be the same.

I can only remember two goodbyes. Hugging Mormor and Morfar, them cursing my father under their breath, and telling us they would never come and visit.

And saying goodbye to Carin. Oh Carin. I felt her love so much. She told me she had something to tell me as she put me on her lap and held me close. She was so soft. So warm. She knew this was hard for me. She knew that I didn't want to go. She told me that there are things that happen that we don't understand. That she knew amazing things lay ahead of me and I would make book worthy adventures of my own one day. I heard her. This was the first time anyone had acknowledged me, seen my pain in this and spoken about my feelings. I was leaving my country and no one, up until now, seemed to care. In a daze I told her I loved her and that I would come back to her. I was wrong. I never did get to see her again. And I never got to thank her for her steady love during a very difficult time in my life.

A couple of days later we caught the ferry to Copenhagen, checked in our luggage, and stepped onto the plane. The first part of my life was officially over.

4

Jerusalem

As we landed in Tel Aviv the passengers erupted in applause. We had arrived in the Holy Land. My first reaction was to reach for the paper bag in front of me and vomit. I'm not a good traveler and I couldn't wait to get off the plane and get some fresh air. What greeted me was something I could hardly describe, possibly the same feeling I got when opening the door to my grandparent's dishwasher, total heat and humidity at the same time. It caught me off guard. Once inside the building we were greeted by a small delegation. We were returning Jews! After thousands of years in the diaspora we had returned to our homeland. We were handed chocolates and bright red syrup to drink. Our parents were escorted to meet with immigration department officials as well as with the Rabbi. Despite it only being my dad who was Jewish, the Rabbi declared all of us children to be 'kosher' according to biblical law and my papers were stamped 'Jewish', whatever that meant.

It was pitch black by the time we arrived at our new home on the hills north of Jerusalem. It was an absorption centre. A place for returning Jews to get used to their new country, learn Hebrew, absorb the culture, and all at no expense. The absorption centre was almost full. Russia had recently opened up its doors and thousands of Jews were leaving the country for a new homeland. Ethiopian Jews were also leaving persecution and returning to their land. Our new community was practically a flat version of the tower of Babel.

We were viewed with suspicion. Word got out that my mother wasn't Jewish. The Russians and the Ethiopians seemed oblivious to this glaring evil in their midst, but not so the American Jews. They had left the tainted streets of New York behind to soak up the purity of the Holy Land. How dare this defiled woman ruin their experience? My poor mother had to settle six unhappy children into a new country while being snarled at by men in black coats. This is, until they realised she was quite a useful asset in times of need.

One Friday evening we heard a tap on the door. My mother answered and was surprised to find a highly orthodox man outside. He had a black hat, black coat, side curls dangling down his pale face, and a scraggly beard. He kept looking away from my mother while indicating with his head that he wanted her to come with him. Such a bizarre scene to be confronted with, however my mother reluctantly followed this mysterious man through the community we lived in. She followed him down our street, around the corner, along a footpath with the man constantly checking that she was walking far enough behind him but still making sure she wasn't turning back. After a short walk they arrived at the centre's main cluster of buildings. The man motioned with his head for my mother to come into the synagogue. And not just into the synagogue, but into the male section of the synagogue! How could this be? Why on earth would he want her there? They got to the entrance and he kept nodding towards the wall. Over and over he nodded, not saying a word, not looking at her, just nodding. My mother thought the man might have lost his mind when she looked into the room and noticed how dark it was. All the men were ducking up and down with their head in their Bibles as they usually do, but it would have been too dark for them to read the words. My mother had been beckoned to switch the light on!! Someone had forgotten to turn it on before the Sabbath and with no light they were unable to read their scriptures for the evening service. They needed a gentile to flick the switch.

Another event that stands out from our two years at the centre was a few months later. My dad was unable to contain his joy of knowing Jesus was his own personal Lord and Saviour. He had taken the opportunity on the bus back from Jerusalem, with the passenger next to him as a captive audience, to share the Good News of the Gospel. His voice, as it tended to do, got too loud and he was overheard saying the unthinkable. He said that Jesus is the only path to salvation. Our community was in uproar. The religious men who lived in our area gathered together to find a solution. My sister happened to be walking past when she heard them chanting, with their fists in the air, "stone them, stone them!". She rushed home to warn us and was greeted by my dad pacing around the house cursing the demons of death that had apparently arrived in the past few hours. Just as he had taught me to do when having nightmares as a child, my dad was calling out, at the top of his voice, for the blood of Jesus to protect us. This went on for hours. I wasn't sure what was scarier, neighbours who wanted to stone us, or my father screaming at the top of his lungs for the Devil to be rebuked and the blood of Jesus to cover his family.

My dad's moods were becoming increasingly more difficult to live with. He was struggling with the pressures of a new country. He was expected to learn the language and to work in a factory, a job that was provided to him. He also felt he had no control over his children who were struggling with the adjustments as much as he was. All I knew is that I ached for Sweden more than anything else. My mind was imploding with all the new languages I was being exposed to and all of the things I was seeing that didn't make sense. I was expected to go to a school and speak Hebrew and I couldn't even speak English yet. My family was at breaking point. I genuinely thought my fourteen year old sister was going to kill herself. I had no one to talk to. I didn't even have a bike that I could escape with. It was an incredibly difficult time.

I wanted to switch off. I wanted to make it all stop.

Between May and October it doesn't rain in Jerusalem. It just gets drier and drier. I longed for rain. My only mental escape was a two metre metal fence surrounding a local school. I trained myself to balance on the thin beam of metal. Bit by bit, over and over, eventually I would be able to walk around the school, one step at a time. Slowly balancing and letting my thoughts drift away, this is how I processed everything taking place around me. The intensity of our home. The craving for Sweden. My isolation. The longing for rain. Words cannot explain the joy I felt when the first drops of rain fell on the afternoon of my eleventh birthday. Giant drops falling out of the sky and it felt as if they were falling just for me. The air came alive and my lungs filled with the smell of rain. I ran outside, and with my arms stretched open just let the rain drench every part of me. God hadn't forgotten my birthday. He had given me the perfect gift.

It took a while for me to start feeling comfortable trying out my English. I understood bits and pieces by now but I couldn't quite grasp the full concepts.

I heard that someone was going to visit us one day and that it was a bit of an event. My dad was busy stirring soup in the kitchen when someone knocked on the door. I looked up from reading my beloved comics to see two formal looking men enter. They chatted with my dad and a lady followed who smiled at me. Then the house seemed to fill up with a whole bunch of people who all just stood around. The woman asked me to show her my room. I pointed to my bed and tried to explain to her in English why there was a sheet draped in the middle of the room on a string but I didn't quite have the English words to explain that my older sister hated me so much that she needed a bed sheet to separate us. The lady seemed to find it somewhat amusing and had me show her the rest of the miniature house. It didn't take long. Some photos were taken and the crowd left and I went back to my comic book. Later that day I asked my mother what all that was about. Oh, that was the Queen of Denmark. She was in Jerusalem and had heard there was a Swedish family who had immigrated. She had asked to meet us.

We also had an unexpected knock on the door and two elderly couples stood outside with their arms full of baskets of goodies. We had been eating very basic food since we arrived and our eyes lit up at the sight of cakes, chocolate boxes and tropical fruits. With tears in their eyes they explained how they had escaped from Germany forty years earlier and had been given refuge in Sweden. They were thrilled to finally be able to show their gratitude and hugged us as if we had been the ones pulling their small boats to safety. I didn't quite understand why they were so emotional and hugging my mother with such fervor.

My parents had naively assumed that their kids would easily slot into a local school and pick up the language straightaway. Not so. I was not getting anywhere with my Hebrew skills. The problem was not having a common language to begin with. My English was just too basic and I also had no desire to learn Hebrew. I felt no connection to the kids in my class. I missed Magdalena with an ache in my body, I missed our freedom, and I missed the connection we had. Not having a language to express myself with was agony. I would simply sit in silence. Easily a week would go past with me not saying anything to anyone at school. This went on for months.

It was so bizarre to go from being in such a dynamic setting with Magdalena and her family, where I had such a specific role to play, to all of a sudden being invisible. I felt like this for two years. There were so many strange moments during those two years that highlighted how out of touch I was. There was the Day of Independence for example, where the whole school had to dress up in blue and white. The teacher thought she had explained this to me when I showed up in the morning for the ceremony, however I was the only student at the school wearing white pants and a blue top. It was meant to be the other way around. This was such a visual reminder that I had no clue as to what was going on. I had to line up with the rest of the school as they sang the national anthem looking like the odd one out.

And then there was a sports day we had at school. I didn't know it was sports day. I hadn't understood. But I still had to run even though I didn't have the right clothes or shoes. Surprisingly I came first. Then about a month later I was taken to compete in a giant park in the centre of Jerusalem for all the schools in the area. I arrived to my class and got marched to a bus by my teacher. I had no idea where

I was going. Once we arrived I realised there must be a competition. I had no idea I was in it. Again I wasn't wearing the right clothes or shoes. I was handed a number to pin to my shirt and at some point got pulled to the starting line. When the gun went off the other runners began to sprint so I followed. I didn't know where I was going, so I made sure I had other runners in front of me. I still managed to take a wrong turn and run through a deep patch of weeds. With bugs flying into my mouth I kept running while coughing them up. It was a really long race and I figured that as long as I had a few kids in front I would be fine. I finally crossed the finishing line and was still somewhat shell-shocked that I had just been in a race. I could have so easily run faster. Possibly been one of the first. But the main thing was just to make sure I didn't get lost.

Finally, after two very long years of not making one friend, I was given a scholarship to the Anglican International School right in the middle of Jerusalem. I was so relieved. My English had improved enough that I could have a basic conversation and feel somewhat understood and I longed to make friends. I was in the second semester of year six although I had done very little schooling up until now. Thankfully my scholarship wasn't based on my academic performance. I'm pretty sure it was given to us for having the winning combination of being Jewish and Christian. There was only another couple of Jewish families at the school and considering the building had initially been set up as a service to the Jewish people, they probably felt a bit of pressure to balance out the numbers.

Though originally built as a hospital to serve the Jewish people, the school was now a haven for international families seeking English education in a Hebrew and Arabic speaking country. It was a wonderful mix of children of diplomatic families, United Nation workers, missionaries, and wealthy Palestinians and Arabs. I loved it. My classmates were from Ethiopia, Ghana, the Philippines, Greece, Trinidad, Ecuador, Germany, and so on. My teachers on the other hand were an eccentric mix mainly from England as well as other English speaking nations. I had zero interest in learning but I loved being in a dynamic environment once again.

By this stage our family had moved out of the absorption centre and into the middle of Jerusalem. It felt so good to be out of that stifling environment and finally have an apartment in the city. I even had my own room. It was actually a balcony that had been converted into a room, it was freezing in winter, but I was thrilled. I finally had my own space. Somewhere to retreat to. The intensity in the house was beyond breaking point. My father was raging more and more and his temper terrified me. My brother, Ezra, triggered a rage in my father that I had never seen before. He became a wild animal, chasing Ezra around the apartment, moving furniture to reach him. And when he finally got his hands on him, he would beat him. I would lie on my bed and cry as I listened to my dad pounding my brother's body. For my dad it was his godly duty to discipline his children. It went hand in hand with being the head of the house and he saw nothing wrong with his reign of terror over us.

I wanted to connect with my father. Despite the fear, I still wanted him to see me and to see that I was as valuable as my brothers. The only time I felt that my dad connected with me was when we discussed theological truths. My dad would sit on the couch for hours and read his Bible. He would cross his arms and have the Hebrew Bible in one hand, the English Bible in the other, and the dictionary on the arm rest next to him. He would be totally zoned out from what was happening in our home. Sometimes I would go and sit next to him and ask him what he was reading. I would always be able to make a link or a connection to generate a conversation. I knew I was good at it and I knew that my dad knew this. He wasn't teaching me, I was challenging him. Whatever insight he had, I had another take on it. Whatever truth he found, I would have yet another question or angle. I loved proving myself like this. I loved showing my dad I had something to offer. Despite my body rapidly evolving into that of a woman, I was in fact just as powerful as the boys in the family. In fact, I knew that when it came to theology I was the only child that could leave dad in the dust.

My dad seemed to like our theological connection, but not so my changing body. His eyes never went south of my chin. I was only a face to him. I could feel his unease. I could sense how uncomfortable he was but there was never anything said.

It was during this time that I was making friends at school and my two favourite friends were Ali and Amir, two boys in my class. They were best friends and because Ali lived around the corner from me it was a really easy friendship. We would take the bus home from school together and spend a lot of time chatting about friends and life. One day on the way home from school Ali and Amir were saying they were going to have a wrestling match to finally decide which one of them was in fact the stronger out of the two. There was a lot of debate on who owned this title and today was going to be the day we found out the answer. A mattress was placed on the bedroom floor and Ali and Amir started their epic power struggle. After a long battle Ali won. I decided that I wanted to try and see if I could beat the champion. Ali and I stood face to face and, the moment Amir yelled "go", I bent down and grabbed Ali's ankles and pulled them out from underneath him. He toppled. I had beaten the champion! I was elated. I ran home and burst in the door to share the good news that I had beaten a boy in wrestling! I didn't need to match him in physical strength, I just had to be smarter. I was beaming. I looked over at my dad. His nostrils had started to flare. Oh oh. This was a bad sign. My dad's nostrils were a way for us to see where he was at. As soon as the flaring started we knew that something was about to erupt. He took me out on the balcony and, while trying to contain the volcano that was starting in his chest, he said in a voice filled with anger and disgust "Lillian, I never want you to do that again. I do not want a child to come into this world unwanted!". What?? What on earth was he saying?? Surely not. Surely he wasn't suggesting that I was doing something sexual? I was gutted, absolutely gutted. My face was burning. I felt so misunderstood. How could my dad possibly think that of me? ME?? I was the total tomboy. The girl who was more boy than girl, and who hated her girlishness with everything in her. How could he not see that?? I came away from that balcony feeling more shame than I had ever felt before.

Unfortunately there was nothing I could do to stop the changes that were going on in my body. My breasts were growing at an enormous speed. Initially I had tried to ignore them. I tried to not think about the obvious thing that was taking place. But there was no way I could deny that not only was my body changing, it was exploding. Within a very short period of time I had these giant breasts, they were only getting bigger, and there was nothing I could do to stop them. I bought three sweatshirts. Along with some black leggings it was all I wore. It helped me hide. I was comfortable, and it was the best I could do at hiding my breasts. Here I was a blonde, blue-eyed, big breasted, Swedish tomboy. No matter how much I wanted to pretend my breasts away, I couldn't. I was getting yelled at from buses. Men bumped into me on purpose. Soldiers rubbed themselves on me while squeezed onto full buses, and me not being able to move. I had a shop owner chase down the street after me, begging me to come home with him. He would look after me. He would love me.

One day when walking home from the city, absolutely lost in thought, I noticed that someone had been clearing their throat very close to me. It didn't really register until I felt a very weak tap on my shoulder. I turned around and faced a pale yeshiva student. He was wearing a skull cap, he had the locks going down the sides of his white face, small round glasses, and a white shirt with the prayer tassels hanging out. He looked desperate. He pleaded with me. "Please fuck me. I will pay you whatever you want. Just fuck me." I took a deep breath, and in my strongest Israeli accent, I said in Hebrew "I am Jewish!". The look on his face. The sheer terror. He turned around and ran!

5

Teenage Years

My saving grace during this time was the group of friends I made through a local church. Not long before I joined, the church was burnt down by local religious Jews who hated having such an abomination in their neighbourhood. In order for the church to continue, the parking lot was converted into a tent where the meetings were held. The congregation had a core group of people who attended weekly as well as visitors who came and went as they visited Jerusalem. It didn't take long for me to find my place.

As far as I was concerned the cornerstone of this church was a woman called Elinka. Her official role was as the wife of the pastor as well as the piano player. However, Elinka was so much more than that. She was the pulse of the church. The heart. In a congregation full of biblical experts and Dead Sea Scroll researchers, Elinka imparted a sense of love and acceptance and gave the Bible a practical outlet in her humanitarian take on life. Elinka looked like a million dollars. Her body defied age, her makeup was flawless, she wore heels that I had only seen in magazines, and her skirts were shockingly short. She had the glint in her eye of a woman who was soaking up all that life had to offer. I absolutely adored her. Despite being the mother of five children she always had time for me. She invited me into her home and her home became a sanctuary for me.

Elinka and her family had a young man living at their house as well. Jon was originally from Colorado but had lived in Jerusalem for a few years and was studying at the university. He was madly in love with Tali, the oldest daughter, and he became a bit of a handyman for the busy household. Jon and I became friends. If for some reason I couldn't stay in the apartment anymore I would go downstairs and sit with Jon. We would make popcorn and chat about life. Often he would have to study so I would just sit there with him, listening to his music collection, waiting for him to have a break. Jon became the father/uncle/brother that I never had. He was the first male I knew who didn't scare me. The first male who didn't use his gender as a way to intimidate or overpower me. He was kind, considerate and incredibly generous with his time. He was also witty and I loved our conversations. He would tell me about his childhood adventures. He loved the mountains. He loved the desert. His stories told me of a world that was out there ready to be explored. Not once did he make me feel that I was taking up his time or distracting me from his work. He never made me feel that our 14 year age gap meant that we couldn't be friends. He had no agenda. He was just a friend and I had never experienced such kindness before.

As our friendship grew so too did his connection to my brother Sam, and to our group of friends from the church. Our youth group had leaders that the church provided through a volunteer program run by the Southern Baptist Union. They were lovely young people who fulfilled their contracts, but no one compared to Jon. We all adored him. It was impossible to separate Jon from his love of music. It was so much part of him and the more time we spent with Jon the more his love of music rubbed off on us. His guitar playing was contagious. Sam and his friends all started to play an instrument. My friend Jess from youth group was a gifted piano player and a beautiful singer and she would join us when her parents let her have a break from homework. She seemed to be the only one of us who had to focus on her studies. After a while Elinka got us all to lead worship at church on Saturday mornings. Jess would take over from Elinka on the piano. I would sing with whoever else was available that day. Sam would play the bass guitar. Aaron on the drums and Micah on the guitar. Any free time we had we would sit and jam with Jon. Sometimes he would pull out the banjo and take us back to his time around the campfire in Colorado. Those were the happiest times of my life.

Our summers would be spent at camp. Initially as campers, but then as the years passed as camp leaders. And then when that wasn't enough I would do the kitchen duty for the Arabic speaking camps just so I didn't have to leave camp and go back home. I had finally found a place where I belonged. I finally had a group of friends that I connected with. And as the oldest in the group, I had a bit of a mother role and it suited me perfectly.

Jon thrived as our mentor. Tali had yet to see the light about what an incredible man Jon was so he had plenty of time for us. When he was free from his university studies we would all pile into a van and Jon would drive us to the desert to get us away from the pressures of Jerusalem. There he would take us on long hikes during the hot days. I would still be wearing my beloved jumpers despite the temperature being 40°C. At night he would teach us how to make fires and, once we had a proper fire going and the marshmallows were roasting, we would listen to stories and learn new songs.

At other times Jon would tell us to hop in the van and he would drive us north to one of his favourite swimming spots. We would spend the rest of the day in a magical water hole surrounded by high cliffs. Jon would show off his diving skills and the boys would try to copy his crazy moves.

He would also take us to the mountains around the Dead Sea. We would climb through dry river beds and slide down rock formations. We camped on the beach in Gaza. We had night hikes in the Judean Hills. We explored monasteries that were carved out in the mountainside where we had to walk carefully along tiny paths that hugged steep cliffs. Underground tunnels were also a favourite for Jon. We would squeeze through tunnels that eventually led to big caverns and cisterns. He would then pull out candles from his backpack and we would sit around and sing and listen to our voices echo through the many pockets of the tunnel. If there was something to teach us he would. He was learning so much at the university and he wanted to share it with us. Sometimes he would find a piece of pottery on the ground in our travels and explain that this was a piece from the Byzantine period. He made history come alive.

I will never forget one of our desert hikes in the Negev desert. It went on for hours. The sun was beating down on us. We were exhausted. All of us that is except Jon. As usual he was walking with a spring in his step, his face beaming at taking us out of our comfort zones. He never slowed down. Initially we sang to distract ourselves or gave each other riddles to solve. We tried to make the time pass but as the hours went on we were exhausted. Jon just kept saying that it was all worth it. A river would be waiting for us. We were all so excited about being able to swim and cool off. Then to our horror when we got to the 'river' Jon explained, as we looked at the dry patch of sand, that it was in fact an ancient river that had flowed thousands of years earlier. He loved these 'lessons' he had for us. Thankfully he made up for it by taking his backpack off and pulling out a giant watermelon! He had carried this heavy lump for the whole hike knowing full well that we would need a happy ending after such an exhausting hike.

After one of our tunnel adventures, Jon took us to a field that was filled with poppies and beautiful wild flowers. After we had run around and posed for photos he told us how this was the place where David defeated Goliath. Adding his own twist to the story and making us connect with the scriptures in a way that made it all so real.

Jon stretched our knowledge and showed us what living a life of integrity really meant. The boys in our group were challenged to treat women with respect. Us girls were given the gift of seeing what a real man was like. He never demanded our respect but he had all of us wrapped around his finger. All these adventures with Jon were so different to the intensity of the life we had in Jerusalem. The political unrest. The intense personalities of stressed out people.

The trips with Jon gave us a much needed escape, a sense of freedom and adventure.

In the beginning of 1990 Elinka had some very big news for us. She was pregnant. Pregnant with twins. I was elated. My role as their family helper intensified. There was even more I could do. I used to feel that Elinka's house was the centre of the universe. I still do. It's hard to describe their dynamic home. People from all around the world were always coming and going at all hours. Their round, tiny kitchen table that was meant to host four people would often have a swelling crowd of twenty mingled around it. Elinka would always seem to find a way of feeding everyone. And in the most relaxed manner I had ever experienced. Her potato and cauliflower soup could easily feed a room full of people with the addition of water and a few more potatoes. Her spicy green bean and beef stew just needed extra bread if there were more mouths to feed. And no weekend meal was complete without a massive batch of her famous caramel popcorn.

I wanted to be part of the excitement and the pulse that I felt beating through that house. Doing the dishes there was effortless for me. Sorting out cupboards to make space for more food was a joy. I did it all to help Elinka out with something I knew wasn't her strong point. It also meant I didn't have to go home so I often worked long into the evening. I loved every moment I was there, then very late, I would eventually have to go home.

One minor obstacle I had to overcome was that the best bus option for me meant I needed to get to a bus stop on Hebron Road. It wasn't the safest road. It would have been much easier if I could have used the bus that stopped just outside their house on Bethlehem Road. Hebron Road had a different feel. It had a lot more traffic and a lot more workers coming in from neighbouring villages. I was a young, blonde female and a very easy target. I had so many cars either slow down or follow me as I walked to the bus stop, or men coming out to talk to me, that I had to figure something out. My mother told me that I needed to carry pepper in my pocket and throw it at their faces as they approached. I knew that wouldn't work. I would end up throwing it on myself. Coordination had never been my strong point. I found the answer in a very simple way. As soon as I came around the corner from Bethlehem Road and got onto Hebron Road I transformed into a severely disabled old lady. I would hunch over as far as I could go and then, in the most dramatic way, start dragging one of my legs behind me. It meant that the walk to the bus took about four times as long but I didn't mind. I never got honked at or stopped again.

In August 1990 Elinka's twins were born and I had the absolute joy of being there to hold them in hospital. These two little babies all bundled up meant the world to me. Elinka was beaming. There was no evidence that she had just given birth. No sign of exhaustion or being overwhelmed. "Lillian, when it's your turn to have a baby just think of it as a big poo!" I was shocked at her frankness. Talking about a bodily function was total taboo in my world. I didn't respond, but I stored the words away in case I needed them for later.

Not that I thought I would ever need to. I had pretty much decided that being a nun was my destiny. Not a nun in the monastery sense. But it did seem the most obvious path since it meant that my body would never have to be acknowledged or addressed. I could continue having everything from my chin down totally switched off. It made perfect sense to me. My friends started calling me 'the Nun' as well. They started having boyfriends and exploring their sexuality, while I was well and truly not going to get involved with any of that. Jesus was my lover. He completed me. I only desired him. I would often lead Bible studies for the youth group and my messages were heartfelt and true. I really did believe the things I spoke of. I really did have the integrity of someone who wholeheartedly wanted only one thing. And that was to be consumed by Jesus. I knew that I was a bit of an enigma at my school and that I made my classmates feel a bit uncomfortable with my black and white views on the world, unfortunately that was just how things were. Nothing was going to sway me from my path of purity and devotion.

My absolutely favourite teacher, Miss Payne, started a prayer group before school. It gave me yet another outlet to spend time with Jesus, as well as with her. I connected with her. She had also moved around the globe as a child and there was a sadness in her that resonated with me. I doubt many people saw that sadness because she was such a beam of light at our school. Always with a smile, her eyes sparkling with genuine care for the 'third culture kids' in her class. This early-morning prayer group was not as popular to the masses as it was to me, and most mornings it was just me and Naomi sitting there with Miss Payne.

Those prayer sessions were so meaningful to me. I adored Naomi. She was everything I wanted to be. Beautiful, caring, softly spoken, and always ready to say something kind. I felt a connection with her that went beyond the fact that our two older sisters were best friends. In my heart I knew that she was one of the few at school whose devotion to Jesus matched mine. Like me, she was a true believer and follower. It wasn't just something she did to please her parents or to follow some rules. It was real. And in my black and white world that held a lot of weight.

It was during this time that the political unrest in the Middle East was reaching a climax. It had always been strained, especially since the Intifada that began in 1987, but this was different. This was bigger. The rumbles of war brewing were getting louder and louder as we were told that Saddam Hussein was going to blow Israel off the map. Initially these things were just taken as empty threats, but as the months passed it seemed to take on a life of its own. More and more of my friends were being told to leave the country. The missionary kids were pulled out and had to fly back to their countries. The diplomats and United Nation kids followed. We were instructed on how to set up a shelter in our apartments. It had to be sealed so that no toxic poisons would leak through when the missiles hit. Missiles? Poisons? This was new to me. This wasn't a random bomb in the local market. Or a suicide bomb on a specific bus. I was used to preparing myself for that. This was a whole new reality. This was danger on a very large scale.

I tried to ignore thinking about it for as long as I could, but by Christmas 1990 you could almost feel the tension in the air. As my youth group went off to Bethlehem to be part of the Christmas celebrations I was more than happy to stay back and look after the twins that I loved. Elinka had trusted me with the role of babysitter for the event and I wasn't going to let her down. I spent that evening on my own with the twins wondering if it was going to be my last Christmas. I felt sad that I would never experience Christmas with Mormor and Morfar again. I longed for another Christmas in their house, where it got dark by three in the afternoon. I remembered the candles in the windows with the lit star dangling above. The beautiful Christmas tree. The smell of Mormor's meatballs. The table full of her creations. It was a magic that could never be duplicated and I longed to have it again.

But here I was, 16 years old, and possibly facing death if Saddam had his way. By now I didn't go anywhere without a gas mask. We had to carry it in a box with a strap and it had to be with us at all times. I had won the gas mask box decorating competition at school which I assume was one of the teacher's ideas to lift morale. I was quite proud of my box. I had transformed it into a dog. Complete with a head, four legs that made it stand up, as well as a wagging tail. It was quite a work of art and I had many looks as I had this dog strapped to me as I walked around the city. The tail wagging as I walked.

In the middle of January 1991 I woke up to the sound of a siren blaring just outside our apartment window. It was deafening and terrifying. Its sound went up and down, up and down, louder and louder. The message was clear. Get into your shelter NOW. We all jumped out of our beds at lightning speed. Scrambled into our 'safety room' and started to seal the doors with tape and wet towels. The windows had already been sealed in preparation, covered in plastic bags and thick tape. It almost surprised me that my dad had allowed my mother to do this since in my mind God was our protector and there was nothing we could really do. But hey, it was nice to be just like everyone else for the first time as a family and actually follow the rules.

After the initial rush of adrenalin, and after getting the room sealed, there wasn't much left to do. I looked over and could see my mother trying to calm Abigail. She was terrified. She was only seven years old and this was so hard for her. As we waited for the all-clear siren to release us, my mind drifted across Jerusalem. I was thinking about the twins, Abe and Bella. Were they okay? I knew that it would be hard for them. They were too small to have gas masks. Instead they needed to be put into a plastic tank not any bigger than something you would carry a cat to the vet in. How Elinka was going to do that while wearing a gas mask and not totally freak Abe and Bella out I had no idea. I just wished I could be there and comfort them. Thankfully we were eventually allowed back to our beds and I remember thinking that this war had better be over soon because sitting in a tiny room with my family was nerve- racking. It was so rare that we were all together as a family, and the chance of my dad or one of my brothers blowing up seemed more real to me than a scud missile crashing through our apartment.

The next couple of days everyone swapped stories of how they reacted when the sirens started. There were only about twenty students at our school by now so classes were suspended. We had a lot of free time and basically just hung out together. I loved it. Academics were never an interest of mine. I loved learning from life itself by talking to people and hearing their stories. School seemed so pointless.

We had recently started talking about career options in class. We even had someone come into the school to speak to us about which path we wanted to take with our career. Everyone in my class had to say what profession they were hoping to pursue. I had classmates that wanted to be pilots. Quite a few were interested in international law. A couple of psychologists. Doctors. Others were interested in the hotel industry. When it was my turn to answer I said, with a completely serious face, "I want to be a beach bum". My poor teacher was horrified. It was kind of true. It wasn't that I was going to be a beach bum as such, but a beach bum for Jesus. A big difference. I was going to move to the Solomon Islands and spread the Good News to the natives. An Australian missionary had come to our church in Jerusalem. His message struck a chord with me. We had talked for a long time after. He invited me to come to the Solomon Islands with him and his family after I finished school. That sounded so exciting. Up until then I had visions of me being a nun in the deserts of the Middle East, possibly shining my light for Jesus to Bedouins who still hadn't heard the Good News. Being a beach bum for Jesus on a tropical island had a much nicer sound to it.

It was during this very "devoted to Jesus" time in my life that I asked my dad if I could get my ear pierced again. I had had them pierced when I was 14, but I really liked the look of the girls at school who had the second piercing. My dad was horrified. How could I possibly want a second piercing? "Lillian, no daughter of mine is going to have two holes in her ears! What's next? You getting your nose pierced?? And then what? Are you going to start selling your body on the street??" BAM! There it was AGAIN! My dad assuming something about me just because I was female. My sexuality was obviously totally out of control. I was some wild animal who was just busting to throw myself at men for their pleasure. My cheeks burned with anger and I knew that it was pointless trying to explain myself. But it hurt. It really hurt. How could my father know so little about me? How could he not know that my friends called me a nun? That I was known for my purity. That I had no intention of anyone ever, ever seeing my body. I hated my body even more than he did. It was not going to see the light of day. He had absolutely nothing to worry about.

The Gulf War continued over the next few weeks. Eventually it felt like too much effort to go into the shelter. The scuds were mainly hitting Tel Aviv. Elinka and her family seemed to have a pretty relaxed view of the scuds as well after a few weeks of trying to get their twins into their plastic tents. Once we got used to the sirens blaring we would take the video camera and go up on their roof to film. Their roof was flat and we often had parties up there. Now it became the perfect place to catch a glimpse of the incoming scuds, and if we were really lucky we got to see the patriot missiles come shooting up trying to stop the scuds mid air. It was cheap entertainment for us teenagers and something to talk about at school the next day.

The war came to an undramatic end and life resumed its regular routine. The biggest impact that the Gulf War had on me was actually an academic one. With so many students leaving, the school wasn't able to run its usual classes. It meant that I had missed more than half of my school year. But because my classes were missed because of a war I was given full credit for classes that I never took. It just so happened that I had held off taking all the hard classes like chemistry, physics and science for as long as possible. Now I had full credit and I hadn't done any of the work. I also found out that I qualified to do my English O and A level exams as an 'English as a Second Language' student. By now my English was pretty much fluent. There were obvious gaps but not many. And according to the rules I could do the easier versions of the exams, and I passed with top grades.

The principal had a chat with me. If I was to put in some extra effort over the next year and my grades were high, I would not just graduate with top marks, I could actually graduate a year early. This would mean that I could have some time off between high school and my looming army service that was quickly approaching. I was stunned. My schooling had been a mish-mash up until now. My first year of school was fairly straightforward but besides learning to read or write my mind had never been engaged. I then home-schooled with Magdalena which consisted of eating lots of mud cake batter and doing chores. I had the occasional English lesson with my mother which didn't improve my English skills in the slightest. I then went to Hebrew school for two years which meant another couple of years of not learning anything besides how to occupy my mind for hours on end with total silence. Then my first couple of years at the Anglican school was really just about getting used to having English as my main language and getting my head around everything that was happening around me. So yeah, me being studious was a very vague concept. And it wasn't as if being a beach bum really called for high grades. However, here was this other motivation. It could mean an early exit from school. Squeezing twelve years into eleven. Thanks to the Gulf War it meant doing that, minus the subjects that I hated. I had been invited to come and stay with a family in Oregon. They did puppet ministry in Jerusalem every year for the children who attended the Feast of Tabernacles conference, and they were very keen for me to join them and travel through Oregon to different churches and tell kids about Jesus using puppets. How could I resist that offer? School took on a whole new meaning and all of a sudden I was getting top grades in all of my subjects. I had no idea that if I actually wanted to, I could be a good student.

Not long after that I was able to graduate a year early. My report was glowing. I knew I had Saddam to thank. I couldn't have done it without him.

6

God Bless America

It was a huge relief to be out of school. It never sat right with me. My free spirit was never meant to be confined to an institution and I was just grateful to have finished, and somewhat shocked at how well I had done.

My plan was to fly to the States, visit relatives and then do some puppet ministry. Maybe get a job before I flew back to do my military service. I had never been to the States and was somewhat intrigued by what I would find.

I was a wide-eyed 17 year old girl. It was the first time I was free from the shackles of my family and it felt good. I was excited to be given the chance to do puppet ministry. The family who had invited me were incredibly kind and made sure that everyone knew that I was from the Holy Land. I was treated like royalty by the churches we visited. Because of my Israeli status I was the closest thing to Jesus these devoted church goers of Oregon had known. I was asked to say prayers over them in Hebrew, and the pastors often would have me come up and talk about my life in Jerusalem. This wasn't quite what I had expected. Puppet ministry is great because it's exactly that, puppets do the talking and the singing. You get to hide behind a set design and not draw too much attention to yourself. In fact, no attention to yourself. That might have been the case when I did it in Jerusalem. Not so in Oregon. I was a biblical celebrity.

It has to be said that for all their faults, Americans are in fact the most generous people on the planet. Along with their loud voices and big portions comes a very big heart. I have never been as well looked after as I was by the Christians in America. I never went without when I was there. Envelopes with money were shoved in my pockets and I wasn't allowed to argue. After a summer of ministry I was meant to settle down and get a job so I could return to Israel with a bit of money. That was the plan at least. Thing is, the thought of flipping burgers for more than an afternoon filled me with dread. I needed something with meaning. Somewhere I could serve Jesus, not customers.

The answer came in the form of Craig. He had come to our youth group for a few years and spoke at some Easter camps we ran. He was a charismatic man with a passion for young people and for their salvation. When news reached him that I was staying in southern Oregon he called me and told me that he knew exactly what I should do. There was a training centre for young adults in Portland. It would be perfect for me. He knew that I would love it, just as much as the young Australian guy Lee who he had already sent there. It sounded promising. The thought of going somewhere that had Craig's blessing made sense to me. He was good friends with Jon and that instantly made it a perfect fit.

Only a couple of days later I said goodbye to the wonderful family that had been hosting me and got on a bus to Portland. I ended up staying there for the rest of my six month visit.

A lot of things happened in those six months. Probably the most profound thing was that I fell in love and had my first boyfriend. This young Aussie surfer was the first guy to be brave enough to let me know he liked me. This was so new. I had no idea how to respond. Thankfully we had something in common, that being our love and devotion for Jesus. Our time together was spent talking about the Bible and how we wanted to serve Jesus in whichever way he called us. Purity was a must. We both agreed that we would only kiss once we were truly committed to each other. And we could only do that once God told us to. It was a long wait. In the meantime we prayed a lot, talked a lot, and shared Bible verses. I remember feeling so torn. I really wanted to be with Lee. And I really felt that God wanted us together. I just hoped that Lee would be okay with never touching my body once we got married. I didn't mind the thought of us kissing once God gave us the go ahead. But that would be it. My body was totally out of bounds. It was faulty. It was ungodly. And surely our spiritual connection was enough to sustain us.

After a couple of months God finally gave the go ahead, which funnily enough coincided with us staying at this wonderful log cabin in the mountains tucked away in deep snow drifts. We were being hosted by a wonderful woman from the church who adored both me and Lee and she had invited us, along with other young people from our training group, to stay for a weekend. The log cabin was exactly the way a log cabin should be. It oozed romance. It had lofts and wooden beams and a roaring fire day and night. I was pretty thankful that God had finally deemed it kosher for us to have our first kiss.

Lee wanted to show me that he meant business and that he wasn't taking this lightly. He had purchased a gold ring. It was not to be confused with an engagement ring. This was a 'promise' ring. He presented this ring to me with a heartfelt explanation of his desire to follow God's will first and foremost. And that he had every intention of being with me forever but that he couldn't make that promise yet. It's exactly what I needed to hear. As the snow slowly fell outside the log cabin we kissed for the first time. My very first kiss. It was a beautiful moment and I felt like I was the luckiest girl alive. I had crossed over into the world of having a boyfriend and I couldn't think of a better place than being on a mountain, tucked away in deep snow, the stars shining down, Mount Hood watching us, and as far away as I possibly could be from my father and three brothers.

Lee and I were thrilled about our new status. Any free time we had we would borrow a car and drive down to the Oregon coast. There we would walk along the beach and talk about our future. He was heading back to his beloved Australia to study. I had to go back to Israel to do my army service. But we knew that God was bigger than that. If He wanted us to be together then something as insignificant as distance wouldn't be an issue. Our love, and more importantly His love, was big enough to span across the miles.

Despite the good intentions of the people in the church I was feeling more and more uneasy about what I saw going on in there. The American version of Christianity was so different to what I was used to back home. Church was so formal. So much about how we looked. The final straw came one day when, after the morning service, I met a homeless man outside the church. He was a Vietnam veteran, and he was a broken man. I reminded him of his daughter and we talked for hours. I walked across the parking lot to the supermarket and bought him some of his favourite food to eat. He was so grateful and ate every piece in silence. I invited him to come along to the evening service. I had already changed out of my church clothes after the morning service, and because I had been talking to this man for the whole day I hadn't had a chance to get out of my shorts and sweatshirt and back into my dressier clothes. He asked me to sit with him during the service instead of sitting in my regular spot at the front. Once the sermon was over and the pastor asked people to come forward for prayer, the man stood up. He started going to the front of the church and turned to ask if I would come with him. I was happy to sit with him as he got prayed for and I really felt that the church would be able to help him with his broken heart as well as give him some practical assistance. It was such a wonderful feeling to finally have a humanitarian outlet to all the churchy stuff we had been doing. I loved theology and was very good at quoting scripture but it all seemed empty if we didn't do something practical with it. And today I had. I was elated. This was the Gospel. This was exactly what I had wanted my time at the church to be. Once the man was offered a place to stay for the night by a family at the church, I ran up to the pastor to debrief him about what had just happened. Instead of sharing my excitement or rejoicing with me for having saved a lost soul I was told off. I was told off for wearing shorts to a church service. For being a bad example to the young people in the church. For disrespecting the rules. It hurt. It really hurt. This was so completely foreign to me. This would never happen in Jerusalem. Every part of me knew that the pastor was wrong. That he had totally missed the point of what had just happened. I remained silent knowing full well that it was a battle I could never win. This was the American church. So focused on the superficial they had lost sight of the heart of God.

Another thing that was really hard for me during this time was the obsession the church leaders had in making me speak in tongues. In their world you could only be a true Christian if you had the Holy Spirit living inside you. And the only proof of this internal guest was if you spoke in tongues. Now, the problem was that I didn't. Everyone else in the course spoke in tongues except for me. It had never been an issue for me before and no one, as far as I knew, spoke in tongues in my church back home. My parents did but it wasn't something that was really talked about. It was no big deal. No one got extra brownie points for their ability to prove that the Holy Spirit resided in them. Except for here in America Oh how they wanted me to have the full experience. I got prayed over for hours. I had hands laid on me by all the church leaders. Demons got rebuked for blocking the Spirit to descend on me. Every so often in the middle of the prayer I would get a rather big smack on my forehead in the hope that I would fall over and be 'slain in the Spirit'. This was a true sign from God that things were happening. The thing is, nothing happened. I didn't budge. I was given words that I had to repeat over and over again until the tongues would spill out of me. They never did.

Something very strange happened though. The pastor had asked for prayer as he was going through a hard time. We didn't know it at the time, but it turned out that he was having an affair with one of the youth group girls. No wonder he was having a hard time and wanted prayer. We all stood around him and prayed for him. The leaders all had their hands on him and us younger leaders had our hands reached out towards him. After a while I put my hand on him as well and, just as I did, he fell straight back. Completely flat on his back. Everyone was stunned. There was total silence. How had that happened? How had the pastor been slain in the Spirit by a girl who didn't have the Spirit in her? It went against everything they knew to be true.

As my time in the States went on I started feeling quite unwell. I wasn't sick. I just felt off somehow and not myself. There was fogginess in my head that I wasn't used to, a kind of buzzing in my body, a coating in my mouth. My body was tired, I was exhausted by the afternoon. Not once did I connect it to the way I was eating. In Jerusalem I ate salads every day. We had very little money so my mother would stock up on vegetables at the local shouk a few times a week. She would then roll her market trolley home on the bus, up the four flights of stairs. Our dinners would often be lentils with rice, boiled cauliflower with a massive serve of salad. Israeli salads are mainly tiny dices of tomatoes and cucumbers, with a hint of raw onion, a big splash of olive oil and a squeeze of lemon. My mother would always add salad leaves into ours as well. We ate this every day.

I don't think I ate a salad once in my nine months in the States. At the time I thought nothing of it but not one item on my plate could be recognised as a specific food. There was a crumbed piece of unidentified meat, a few pieces of reconstituted deep fried potatoes, a sauce of some variety out of a jar. American food. It was served on a plate with a knife and fork so it must be food.

Breakfasts were donuts that were donated to the church. On the weekends it was pancakes that were made from a mix that only needed water added to it. Served with a syrup that said 'maple' on the bottle but tasted nothing like the maple syrup my mother would buy when we had a bit of extra money. Lunches were sandwiches made with bread that defied gravity. It had no weight in it at all. And it tasted sweet. A cheese slice that was orange. Orange!! How could cheese be orange? And slices of meat that didn't look like anything I had ever seen. Sometimes the meat even had a smiley face on it. It was all new to me. I happily ate it. And I felt exhausted. The solution to this exhaustion, which I had put down to our very early prayer sessions, was coffee. Bitter coffee that was transformed into a heavenly mix by adding a mysterious white mixture they referred to as 'creamer'. It came in every flavour you could possibly imagine and it was so easy to drink. I would drink a few every day when my energy levels dropped.

Now this was strange to me as well. Why did I feel like I had so little energy? In Jerusalem I would spend hours every day walking. I walked to school. Walked to the YMCA. Walked to church. Walked to the Old City and back with my friends. Surely all that walking should have made me tired. We didn't have a car until a couple of months before I had left for the States so my whole life, until then, had meant getting around by foot and bus. Except for in Sweden where I got to ride my bike. Here I was in the States, never having to walk more than a few metres, and yet I was exhausted. It didn't make sense. Soft drinks were everywhere, I figured they must be handed out free at the shops because people drank them like I drank water in Jerusalem. Most of my friends drank Mountain Dew or Diet Coke. I found the flavour so harsh. It hurt my throat but often that was all there was to drink.

Along with the fogginess in my head and the exhaustion, my body started to change. I was so switched off from my body that I only noticed the changes when clothes that I had bought no longer fit me. I just didn't feel like myself anymore in my head or in my body. And not once did I connect it to the stuff I was putting into my mouth that Americans called food. Not once.

It was a very unsettling time for me. I was used to having a sharp mind. Now it felt as if I wasn't quite connecting. I knew that I had to make a decision very soon about my departure. Everyone around me was telling me to stay and that my home was now in the States. They were telling me that I didn't have to do my army service, that I could serve God much better at the church. I had connected really well with the young people in the church and they were begging me to stay. A lot of them came from incredibly abusive homes with stories that were impossible to process. Two sisters being used in masonic rituals with their dad watching as the men took turns raping them. Another girl being forced, by her mother, to sleep with her step-father. Children coming to church and not having eaten for days. Stories that were so far from my reality.

Suicide bombs on buses seemed like nothing compared to this. My only way to respond was to listen to these stories and scramble eggs for the hungry kids. And it made me feel so far away from home. Home that now meant military service. Military service! Me doing military service? The thought seemed so foreign. So bizarre. I had spent most of my life in Jerusalem in a very small bubble. A bubble filled with friends from around the world and local Arabs and Palestinians. I really had no connection to Israelis at all. Most of my interactions consisted of me avoiding comments being yelled at me from guys on buses or from taxi drivers who seemed keen to give me a free ride. I didn't actually have any Israeli friends at all come to think of it. And my Hebrew was basic. Really basic. It was enough to get around with. But to actually have to function? To have a role in the army? It seemed impossible.

Lee seemed very clear about his choice. Nothing was going to keep him from the northern beaches of Sydney that were calling him to return. He was going to be a physical education teacher and he had the next four years of his life mapped out. He was leaving in the middle of January. I decided that the obvious way to get an answer to my questions was to fast. That's what my mother had done all those years before. So I fasted for ten days. My friends were impressed by my will power but convinced me that I would need coffee to keep me going. So I had ten jittery days of fasting. It was far from a spiritual experience. No answer came, but I longed to feel like my old self again. To walk the streets of Jerusalem. To feel the sun. To eat salads. To sit at Elinka's table. I needed to do that. And then I needed to face my fear of joining the masses and becoming a soldier.

Lee and I had a joint farewell party, with both of us beaming at the thought of going back to our real lives. We knew full well that God would reunite us if it was His will. Our friends cried as we said our goodbyes. Their church would never quite be the same without the young Aussie surfer and the girl from the Holy Land.

7

Take My Breath Away

I returned home after nine months away. I had a suitcase full of American clothes that would never be worn again. They didn't belong in my real life. I was back to my leggings and big jumpers. My shiny shoes now replaced with my well-worn Doc Martens.

The mood at home had shifted somewhat while I had been away. Things had intensified. Ezra's rage had escalated. His target was Abigail and she was crumbling under the pressure. I felt a sting of guilt that I had left her to fend for herself, that I hadn't been there to protect her, and that in my absence Ezra's rage had managed to hit new levels. When he was younger it was Ezra that needed the protection. I would shield him from my dad and plead with him to stop hitting my brother or I would try to calm Ezra down before he would explode. I'd try to find a way to connect with him before he went into his blind rage. Now that he was becoming a teenager it was harder to do.

Ezra went from being the victim to being the abuser, and Abigail was on the receiving end. She was trapped. She had to spend long hours alone at home with Ezra. Unfortunately she was an easy target. And Ezra hated her. The rage in his body that had been bashed in by my raging father was now coming out. Abigail lived in absolute terror of her older brother. Her nerves were shattered, her back hunched, and her eyes pleaded to be understood and to be let out of this hell. My parents seemed oblivious, dismissive in fact. I expected that from my dad, but not my mother. How could my mother not see what was happening? See the pain that my sister was in and protect her.

One of the things that my brothers used to love to do was to pin me to the floor and tickle me. Raphael would tackle me from behind without any warning. He loved to shock. Once he had me on the ground my brothers would pile on top of me and they would tickle me while I screamed for mercy. I would be laughing too. Laughing was a natural reflex. I couldn't help it, but it wasn't funny. It was torture. I hated it. I hated having my brothers' hands all over my body. Having them maniacally laughing as tears streamed down my face. I begged for help. Not once did my mother step in. Not once did she tell them it was enough, that they needed to stop and what they were doing was wrong. She would go about her chores as if nothing was happening to her daughter. Being tickled like that was nothing compared to what Abigail was experiencing but it was similar. And the feelings were familiar to me. Being powerless. Living in fear.

I wasn't really able to do anything for Abigail. My life was busy reconnecting with my friends and having lots of interviews for the army. I had already done all of my written exams to see how the army could use me for my upcoming two years. Now that I was back in the country they kept calling me back for more interviews though. Initially the interviews were pretty standard, with them asking me about my background, my family and my weekly activities. As the interviews progressed though, they started changing tone. The men interviewing me no longer had uniforms that could be identified by what part of the army they were from. They wore civilian clothes. They spoke to me in fluent English and they wanted to know everything about me.

As the interview continued they asked me how much I was willing to do. Was I willing to be away from my family for an extended time? Of course. A really extended time? Yes, of course. Would I be willing to be away from Israel for over a year? Possibly longer? Possibly having to extend my army service for more than the regular two years? Yes, yes. I was happy to do it all. I was in. In all the way. And then they asked the biggie. Would I be willing to take a life for my country? Would I be willing to kill? Both indirectly be involved in someone's death, but also directly kill someone. Was I willing to do that? Whoa. Kill. Me kill someone? That was big. It stopped me in my tracks. Where could I find the answer to that? My immediate thought was referring back to the Bible. The Bible was full of killing. God used killing all the time to fulfill a higher purpose. Yes I would kill. I would kill for my country. But more than that I would kill for God. I heard myself say yes. Almost surprised myself at how calm I sounded. The man in front of me seemed pleased. He had his answer.

There were only a few more weeks before I was joining the army and I tried to make up for it by spending as much time as I could with my friends. I had long chats with Jon. Our conversations took on a new dimension. Jon must have known that he was the only person I really listened to at the time because he made a point of showing his concern for me. He talked to me about some of the things that I would face in the next two years and I told him about the interviews. I had been instructed that they were top secret. Only my parents could know. I hadn't told them. I chose to tell Jon instead. I knew he would understand.

The day of my conscription arrived. I had no idea what to expect. Raphael was in his final year of his three year service. He was in the tank unit in northern Israel. I knew that I wasn't really able to ask him about what he experienced. I would see him come home looking exhausted every few weeks, he would stumble through the door, I'd hear him in the shower and then he would disappear to spend 24 short hours with his girlfriend before heading off again for a few weeks. So yes, I really had no idea of what lay ahead of me.

I gave my mother a hug and I could see that she was trying to look neutral. Not once did it cross my mind that this would be hard for her, to see her daughter go off to the army. She never said it was hard and I wasn't able to connect those dots.

I entered the office and some smiling faces handed me a form and I was told to line up and receive my uniform. This was a nice surprise. Israelis are not known for their smiling. I could get used to this. It took a while for them to find a uniform that would fit me. They eventually found one in the men's section. A giant olive green shirt that fit over my chest. I was handed some pants and a belt with a metal clasp. A belt! Not a belt! Did I really have to wear a belt?

I had dreaded this moment for so long. A belt meant there was no chance of hiding my breasts. I went into the change room to put the uniform on. It felt surreal. Olive green pants. An olive green top that had to be tucked into my olive green pants. Then a belt. My breasts covered my entire torso. There was no waist. Just breasts and then legs. I felt so exposed.

I laced up my black leather boots, tucked the black cap into the strap on my shoulder and stepped out of the change room. "Soldier!" "Soldier!" "SOLDIER!!!!!" Someone was screaming. I hadn't registered they were screaming at me! I was now a soldier. And I was being screamed at. And I had been wearing my uniform for all of thirty seconds. I had no idea why they were screaming. What could I have possibly done wrong in my thirty second military career? Could they not wait to call me soldier until I had processed a bit? My cap had been tucked into the wrong strap. It was meant to be on my other shoulder. The screaming continued and I was ordered to get on the bus and to not cause any more problems. My very brief moment of having a smiling face in my army service was well and truly gone.

The bus ride seemed to go on forever. Motion sickness has been a constant travel companion for me since I was a child and today was no different. I held onto the dog tag with my name and I.D. number on it as I looked out the window to try to make sense of my new reality. We were heading deep into the desert and I had lost my sense of direction as soon as we left the hills of Jerusalem. I knew we were heading south and towards Gaza. The desert looked different to the places I had hiked with Jon. Not nearly as beautiful.

We finally arrived at an army base surrounded by dry rocky hills. We were told to line up with our canvas bags on our side and wait for instructions. It was the middle of the afternoon. We hadn't eaten all day. The spring sun was shining down on us. We had to stand for ages and wait for our instructors.

The girl next to me looked pale. I smiled at her. She smiled back and told me her name was Tal. She noticed my accent. She told me that she had just arrived from Australia, that she was Israeli but had spent most of her life in Sydney. Her Hebrew was fluent but so was her English. I was so relieved to have made a friend already. She seemed lovely. She told me that we would talk later and then without any warning she fainted. Just like that. She collapsed by my feet. Instantly medics appeared out of nowhere, put her on a stretcher and carried her away. The only proof I had that I had a new friend was her canvas bag still standing upright in the now empty spot. This was intense. Really intense.

We were put into groups and assigned a tent. Each tent had eight beds. During the day the sides of the tents were rolled up. Grey woollen blankets were perfectly folded on the base of each olive green mattress. We were assigned a bed and told to line up. We were finally going to eat. A couple of girls in my tent were giggling as we lined up, so now we had to be punished. All of us, not just the two rule breakers. Our instructor yelled at us to run to the post a few hundred metres away three times. We would then line up again and see if we were ready for lunch. We started to run and were told to run faster. My breasts were hurting so much. I grabbed my dog tag to make it look as if I was holding onto that while I used my elbows to keep my breasts still as I ran. My back was screaming. And this was all on the first day! How was I going to last the three weeks of Basic Training? We eventually got to march to the cafeteria and my stomach started heaving from the smell. Sewage must have been leaking, and the combination of that, with rubbish bins full of rotting food, was overpowering my senses. As I got into the cafeteria I just hoped that I was going to be able to keep the food down.

We had plenty of food to choose from. Large tubs filled with rice, boiled eggs, overcooked cabbage, oily eggplant, onions, diced tomatoes and cucumbers. It didn't look appealing but it was food.

And there was lots of it. I filled my plate and found a place to sit. This was going to be a long three weeks.

We were shown how to make our beds. How to fold the blankets just so. They had to be perfect. It took a while to get it right. We were shown how to polish our boots and how to fold our uniform at night so that it would look right the next morning. That evening we had a meeting in one of the shipping containers that had been converted into a classroom. With the sun now gone from the horizon the desert was freezing. I was thankful for the thick army-issued jacket but it didn't keep the cold out. I shook as I sat there in the classroom trying to pay attention to the officer who was talking to us. I was finding it really hard to follow. My Hebrew was good enough socially, to get what I wanted at the shops and to answer questions that came up in my day-to-day travels. I could read. I could write. But this was different. The young officer in front of me was talking at a pace I wasn't used to, with words and concepts that were totally foreign to me. I was exhausted. I just wanted to sleep.

Despite going to bed wearing my new army jacket, I was shaking from the cold all night. My body ached from the running we had done earlier in the day. My muscles tensed from the cold. There was no way I could get warm. I felt through my bag and put on every item of clothing I could find. My civilian clothes that I felt like I hadn't worn in a lifetime came back on. So did the extra pair of leggings I had packed. I wore everything in that bag and I was still shivering under my woolen blanket.

We were told to get out of bed at 4:30am and there was no time to ease into the day. After making sure our uniform was on properly and our beds were made to perfection, we had to line up for the day. I was relieved to see Tal again. She was still pale but she smiled at me as we got yelled at for the morning's transgressions. Even the smallest mistake was held against us. Our day was filled with running for punishment. Running for exercise. Eating the exact same food as the day before. More lessons that I didn't understand and more running. My back was raging with pain. I could feel it all the way down to my feet. I had been yelled at for holding my dog tag while running but I kept doing it. It was literally the only way I could run without collapsing. They must have understood because I seemed to get away with it.

After a few days of this we were told to line up and we were issued with an Uzi. This became the focus in between the running sessions and the classes. We were told how to take the Uzi apart, how to clean it, how to carry it in public, and how to store it safely. We were timed when assembling it back together after it being cleaned. We had to be able to do it as a reflex. Super speed. Initially it felt so clumsy but as the days passed we got quicker. We now had to have the Uzi strapped to our back the whole day. This meant that we were now not just running with a water bottle strapped to our belt, we also had the Uzi banging against our back as we ran. I cried from the pain as I lay in my bed at night, still so cold but now sleeping from sheer exhaustion.

We were offered to have showers at night. There was a communal shower about 200 metres from my tent. There was no way that I would even consider going in there. I had a peek as I walked past one day and there were no curtains. No privacy. The thought of having to expose my body to anyone was too much to even consider. No matter how dirty I was. My mother had given me some wet wipes to pack, and at night I used those on my face and neck and hands. I had to use so many to get rid of the sand and even then it seemed to never fully come off. I was filthy and sweaty and my body was literally bruised. I could feel the bruises growing from where the Uzi was banging against my body. We had expected to be let home on the first Friday. It was fairly common for girls to be let home for the Sabbath but we were not so lucky. A couple of the girls in my tent had attitude issues and did not want to conform to the system. The fact that the rest of us got punished for their behaviour didn't seem to bother them in the slightest. Our one compensation was that we were given a phone token and allowed to make one phone call home. I called Jon.

The following week was much of the same. Early mornings. Long days. Freezing nights. A bruised and aching body. Me not understanding the lessons. Bitchy girls. Crying girls. Tal was a breath of fresh air and I was so grateful to have little moments with her when I could.

In the middle of the second week I was called to the officers' quarters. What could I possibly have done wrong? I had tried so hard. I thought I was doing everything right. Was it the fact that I hadn't showered? Did they know? Had something happened at home? I was told to sit down and I was given a cup of sweet tea. They explained to me that a Swedish newspaper had wanted to write a story about women serving in the Israeli Army. When they asked for permission to do the story they had been shocked at finding out that there was a Swedish girl serving there right now. They had asked to meet with me. They wanted to do a story. After some initial security checks they had been given the clearance and I was told that I would meet with them the next day and spend half a day being interviewed. I would have an officer with me the whole time making sure that I only said 'approved' things. I was only allowed to speak in English so that the officer would understand everything that was said between us, and I was to make the Israeli Army look good.

That's not what I had expected. Swedish journalists? Sweden seemed like a very, very distant memory. I still wrote letters to Mormor and Morfar. I still called Magdalena once a year on my birthday. But other than that, Sweden had stopped existing for me. And now there was going to be a story about me in the Swedish paper? How strange! I smiled as I pictured Mormor and Morfar reading about me as they drank their coffee and ate their cheese and bread for breakfast. I knew that there was very little chance that Magdalena would see the article but hoped that somehow someone would show it to her.

The next day was so different from the rest. Once I finished my early-morning chores I was taken to a different part of the base. This was the main part, where both male and female soldiers worked. It was the first time I was in my uniform with men around me. I felt so exposed. With my shirt tucked in and my army-issued jumper stretched to its limits over my chest, my cheeks burned with shame. I just had to switch off and pretend I didn't care. I had so many long looks. So many heads turning. I could hear guys muttering to their friends "Eize Shwedit!". Which translates to "what a Swede" which is another way of calling someone a slut. I had to laugh at the irony that I actually WAS Swedish. But no, I wasn't a slut. I just had massive breasts and trust me, if I could I would happily chop them off right there and then.

The journalists were typical jovial Swedes who seemed rather impressed with their discovery of me. They were so excited to talk to me and asked me all about my new existence. I was hardly an expert on the Israel Defence Force. I had nine days to reflect back on and make profound insights about the army, but they didn't seem to care. I was an 18 year old Swedish girl with an Uzi strapped to her back. This was a good story!

I was taken around the base and asked to pose, pretending to shoot the Uzi. I had to look serious. I had to smile. I had to look as if the future of the Israeli nation depended on me. My main concern was that it wasn't too obvious that I hadn't showered in over a week. It was a fun day for me and it was wonderful to be treated with kindness and interest. I returned to my tent only to be yelled at for taking too long. I was back. Nothing had changed. My fifteen minutes of fame were well and truly over.

On the following Friday we were allowed to go home. A bus took us to Jerusalem and from there we had to make our own way home. I was beyond exhausted. I could hardly think straight. I needed to catch three buses in order to get home from where they had dropped us off. It was Friday afternoon. The busiest time in Jerusalem as everyone frantically gets ready before everything shuts down for the Sabbath. I really didn't know if I would make it to the bus on time before they stopped running. I could hardly stand up. Once I finally got to our apartment I had four flights of stairs to climb and it really felt impossible. I had never felt this level of exhaustion before. I was totally broken. I stumbled through the door and collapsed on the floor. So relieved to be home.

It was late Friday afternoon and I had to return to the base early Sunday morning. Morfar and Mormor had come for a visit and I was desperate to spend time with them but all I could do was sleep. I slept for almost the whole time I was home and nothing felt as good as that first hot shower I had. My body was hurting so much but the hot water felt divine. I tried to look at the bruises on my body and I rubbed some ointment on them hoping it would help them heal faster. It didn't really matter. Never before in my life had I been so happy to be home.

My last week on base felt much easier. I knew what to expect. I had recharged my strength at home. It was only six days that I had to survive. I could do that. Six days. Oh, and then there was the two years after that as well. But six days of Basic Training. I could make it.

On our last day there was a buzz in the air. We were all going to find out where we would end up serving our two years. We had unexpected free time where we just sat around and had nothing to do except wait. So different compared to the past three weeks of non-stop action.

Girls were crying from happiness, crying from disappointment, crying from anticipation, crying from having to say goodbye to new friends. It was a very charged atmosphere. It was finally my turn to be called into the room.

The friendly man in front of me explained that my case was a bit unusual. They had only recently received my file. Up until only a couple of days earlier I was meant to be selected for something very different. My file had ended up with him because my final security clearance hadn't passed. I had too many Arab and Palestinian friends, I was a threat to the State of Israel. Fair enough I thought. With names like Ali and Amir on my long list of friends, as well as sitting next to the nephew of one of the top PLO leaders in school, their judgement was valid. I knew I wasn't a threat, but I could see how they might think so. And now that I had a bit of time to think about it, I couldn't kill anyone. No way. What had I been thinking? A surge of relief went through me and I smiled to think that my friendship with Ali and Amir might have saved me from a very, very dramatic life.

The man in front of me explained that I was chosen to go into the Israeli Air Force instead. He hoped that I wasn't disappointed. Disappointed?? The Air Force was the ultimate! Their blue and beige uniforms were so much nicer. The Air Force soldiers all seemed to have a smugness about themselves that I now got to be part of. Only the best went to the Air Force and I was now one of them!

8

Crossing the Threshold of Life

Israel has too many female soldiers, or at least they did in 1993 when I joined. There were so many of us and we weren't really needed. We were excluded from doing any combat in case we became prisoners of war and got raped. I was thankful for that. I didn't feel the need to prove myself. I just wanted to do my two years and get out. My three weeks in Basic Training had removed any glow I might have had about the army. It was harsh and brutal and brought out the ugly side of humanity. I didn't want to engage with it. I would do my service and then leave.

The base that I was assigned to was the main Air Force medical base. It was very small and quite fancy. I was relieved to be in an aesthetically pleasing place. I knew from my three weeks of the army that I shouldn't take that for granted.

We had the top doctors and surgeons of Israel come and do their month of army service with us. It's compulsory for every man in Israel to keep doing that every year for the rest of his working life. It meant that I got to meet some very interesting people. I didn't have an office since my role was to be the communication point between the US Air Force and the Israeli Air Force. They were working on a project together that had to do with pilots and their health. They had me use the library as my working space and I didn't mind. It meant that I had a constant stream of visitors throughout the day and we would sit and chat about their latest cases or I would help them with their research. This was all done without computers so it was a very slow system and my help was really appreciated. It also meant that in my spare time I could read through medical journals and find out interesting facts, like if you needed to get maggots out of deep wounds the best way is to put a strip of bacon over the opening and the maggots would slither out by themselves. How else would I gather this sort of useful information if it wasn't for my hours of private research in the medical library?

As it turned out the pilot study was running out of funding and my role got suspended as they waited for more money to be donated. I now had more spare time to fill up. I brought my Bible along to the base and would often sit there and read and take notes, of course hiding my Bible as soon as a doctor would come into the library. I really enjoyed my time with the doctors and surgeons and they seemed to enjoy my company as well, often bringing their cup of coffee in during their break to chat with me.

The base was outside Tel Aviv, a couple of hours on three different buses. A long way to commute each morning and evening. Though it did give me four hours a day of thinking time which was great because I was able to perfect the love story that I had been working on as a child. I was able to add so many extra details and tweaks. But the daily commute was exhausting. After about a month on the base I was introduced to the medical commander of the Air Force. He had the most important role on our base and was a very respected man. We hit it off straightaway. He was British and softly spoken, and he was intrigued by the fact that I had gone to a British school in Jerusalem. I asked if he was familiar with it and he was. It turned out that he was a Jerusalemite as well, and after a bit more chatting we realised that we only lived about a five minute walk from each other. Everyone else on the base came from Tel Aviv. He told me that he had a personal driver and if I could be at his house every morning by 6:30am I would be able to go with him in his luxury car. I was having to leave earlier than that to make it to the base by 8:00am, so

I was of course very happy to take him up on his offer. I was already a bit of an enigma at the base with me sitting in the library chatting away to all the doctors and now I was arriving most mornings in a luxury car with the commander of the base. No one seemed to be able to quite understand my status.

It was during this time that I got to know one of the women doctors quite well. She was very kind to me and enjoyed practicing her English with me. She discreetly asked me one day if I had considered having a breast reduction. I tried to remain neutral as I answered, and not show her that talking about my body was beyond shameful to me. I explained to her that I had thought about it but wasn't quite sure how to go about it. I didn't have the money for the surgery and it would be a long waiting list. She explained that she knew all the top surgeons in Israel and that she could write out a referral for me right there and then and have me see someone within the week. She was true to her word and she left me with a letter addressed to her friend. Within a week I was contacted and asked to come in to the main hospital in Israel. I sat in the waiting room and looked around and knew that I had come to the right place. We all had giant bosoms. I was about thirty years younger than everyone else in the room and one of the biggest. When I was called in to see the doctors I didn't even have a chance to take my jacket off before the three doctors in the room all nodded to each other and started writing on their note pads. My surgery was approved. They could tell that I needed the surgery while I was fully dressed. What a relief. The thought of having to undress was really too much to process.

About a month later I was given the date for my surgery. I was to arrive at the hospital the day before and have the preparations performed. I decided that ignorance was bliss and that there was no need for me to know anything about the procedure. I just wanted it done. I wanted the chronic pain in my back to go away. I wanted the sores on my shoulders from the bra straps to heal. I wanted to be able to wear a uniform without the buttons popping open at the most inappropriate times. I wanted my breasts gone.

I met with the surgeon who had to take lots of measurements and draw with a marker on my skin. I tried to force my mind elsewhere as he drew lines on me and thankfully the moment passed without me fainting from the shame. He asked me a few questions. Was I aware that this surgery would mean that I possibly couldn't breastfeed my children? Yes, I knew that. In that moment getting rid of my breasts was a matter of survival. It truly felt that if I didn't have them cut off I might not survive. The pain was so intense by this point that I would often cry myself to sleep. I was becoming more hunched and my shoulders were freezing up from the weight. The hours of travelling I had to do only made things worse. There was never a comfortable position to sit in. I would have to twist my body to such an unnatural angle to accommodate my massive breasts when I sat in a car or bus that my hips were inflamed from the twisting. Breastfeeding to me was not my priority. I had to have these breasts off. If I ever did have babies, which would be a miracle in itself because it would mean conception without being seen or touched by a man, they might just need to get their milk from elsewhere. I was fine with that.

The next morning my mother dropped me off at the hospital very early and I waved goodbye from the parking lot. Not once did I think of asking her to stay with me. I had no fear. No trepidation. I just knew I had to do this in order to be set free. The surgery went ahead as planned and I was wheeled out to the recovery room.

Once that initial adjustment of waking up from surgery took place I was totally fine. Completely hassle free. Despite all the bandages around my torso I felt as if the weight of the world was gone. My shoulders already felt better. My neck felt free, as if a lead jacket had been removed. I had tubes poking out either side of me but I felt fantastic. The lightness in my body was so new. So intoxicating.

My body healed really quickly. Within a couple of days I was back home. I hardly touched the painkillers that I was given. I was so grateful at how well my body was handling the surgery. No one besides my mother, and I assume my father, knew about the surgery. It was a complete secret and I had yet to figure out how to explain to my friends what had happened to my giant breasts.

Besides the constant comments from men on the street nothing was ever said about the size of my boobs. Friends must have known how embarrassed I was by them so it was a taboo topic that never came up.

The Air Force doctor who helped me with getting the surgery so quickly hadn't stopped at that. She continued to be my advocate, and through her connections she made sure that I had over a month at home to heal and rest. She then organised for me to be transferred to another base so that I didn't have to return to where I had been stationed and face the humiliation of everyone's comments and questions. She knew that I drew a lot of attention already and that the men found my body a point of interest. I had told her about my guard duty experience. We only had to do guard duty once a month. This meant that instead of being able to go home for the night we had to stay and do a couple of shifts overnight. A male and female soldier were paired together for safety. We had to change out of our beige uniforms and into the olive green fatigues. With our Uzis strapped to our back we would walk around the fence of the base for two hours. Checking gates and doorways. Checking under cars. Making sure that the base was safe. It was during one of these middle-of-the- night shifts that I was walking along in silence with my male counterpart. I never really felt comfortable talking to the guys on these shifts. I could feel their fascination. Feel their long looks. It was best to just remain as neutral as possible and get the shift done and then lock myself in one of the doctor's rooms and try to get some sleep until the next shift. As we were finishing our two hours of pacing around the base the young man turned to me and asked me where I would be sleeping that night. I tried to ignore his question. He asked me again. He finally turned to me, and in that typical Israeli male stance, where it's really as if they are talking through their pelvis with their hips jutting forward as they speak, he said in his broken English "You know, you would make a very good mattress!". That night I not only slept with the doctor's door locked, but I pushed the metal examination bed that I slept on in front of the door and slept with my Uzi nestled between my legs.

With my new boobs, lighter by 3.3 kilos, I showed up at my new base over a month later. It was a top secret, closed base in the middle of the desert. This would mean that we could only come home every two weeks for one night. I didn't mind. It meant much less travelling back and forth which I was pretty exhausted from. My new role was to be the secretary for the commander of the pilot school. Me. A secretary. That was just hilarious. I couldn't even pronounce the word for secretary in Hebrew - Pkida. The P and the K together made it one of the Hebrew sounds I struggled to pronounce. I dreaded being asked what role I had. How was I going to explain it without being able to pronounce it? I was also possibly the most disorganised person on the planet. I had never had a healthy relationship with paperwork, and to think that I would be entrusted with a whole pilot school was beyond my comprehension. My previous role in the library had been mainly keeping doctors occupied during their coffee breaks and doing the occasional research. This was new territory.

I tried to settle into my new role and not draw any attention to the fact that I was totally out of my depth. Thankfully the girls in the office were incredibly kind to me. Especially Nira. While she had her own tasks to complete she also did mine. She answered my phone calls. Wrote out reports. Filed things away. I in turn decided that the office could do with a makeover and I began drawing cows and sunflowers on every object in the room. Nothing was spared. Thankfully the commander remained quiet about his quirky and useless secretary. He seemed to like the new look and commented on my drawing skills. He was not only the commander of the pilot school, he was also the commander for the aerobatics unit and in charge of the fighter planes doing tricks in the sky for special events. He asked me if I could help him out with the illustrations. He needed drawings that showed when and where the planes needed to turn and twist and at what time. Finally something I could do! I spent hours drawing designs, adding tiny details to the drawings, and really enjoying the challenge of making sure all the times were right. I had no training whatsoever in this role but I was good at it. Word spread and I was given more things to illustrate. Covers for instruction books. Maps. Signs. It was fun and it kept me occupied while Nira did my actual job as a secretary.

The base was far from Jerusalem, there was no direct bus, and it was much quicker to hitchhike. We were encouraged not to because we were so close to Gaza. If I didn't hitchhike though there was a strong chance I would miss the last bus once I got to Jerusalem. It was too risky missing the bus. When hitchhiking I tried to be careful. I wouldn't get into just any car that stopped. I tried to get an idea of who the people in the car were before I hopped in. I still don't know how I managed to stay safe. The pilots on the base heard that I was hitchhiking and would try to give me rides in to Beer Sheva, the closest city, as often as they could. It meant a lot to me that they cared about my safety. My favourite pilot was Isidor. His family had fled Europe in the war and found safety in Sweden. He was raised there and then moved to Israel as a young adult. We would sit and speak in Swedish and he would tell me stories of being a helicopter fighter pilot. He was so sweet, and having him drive me into Beer Sheva in his beat up car with the windows down was something I looked forward to.

Once I got home for the Sabbath I would quickly get changed and rush off to my Friday night job. I really wasn't spending much time at home at all. I knew things were tough. I knew that my parents were struggling. The mood in the home was incredibly intense. Toxic. Ezra was uncontrollable. His rage had surpassed that of my dad. Abigail was a wreck. She was crying when I came back for the weekend, so relieved to have me there. While she never really told me what was going on, I could see on her face that she was suffering.

My parents were suffering too. Their finances were not stretching to meet their basic needs. My father had been managing a book store in the Old City for a few years by now. It attracted thousands of visitors each year. As my dad took over the running of the shop it started to expand. He had a knack for knowing what people wanted to buy. He ordered Christian books and music from around the world. He had handmade jewelry made from olive wood in Bethlehem, and silver from Nazareth. People loved coming into the shop to talk to my dad. He was caring and gentle and would offer to pray with anyone who stepped into his domain. This shop gave my dad the perfect platform to do what he loved doing the most, sharing the Good News of Jesus to strangers. Throughout my whole life I had to put up with my dad asking strangers where they were going to spend eternity. He would use any spare money we had on printing his own tracts about Jesus. He printed small fliers that explained the Gospel in simple terms. He would leave them on buses. Hand them to parking inspectors. His favourite pickle man at the market was given one. No one missed out. My dad was on a mission to get as many people possible into Heaven's gates. It was on the forefront of his mind at all times. Being the manager of the bookstore inside the Old City meant that dad had access to thousands of tourists from all over the world. He took his role very seriously and would often tell us about the encounters he had with people who were seeking the Truth in their travels through Jerusalem.

Unfortunately though the money my dad was earning wasn't covering the cost of a family of eight. There were constant expenses. My dad's monthly earnings didn't even cover the rent for our apartment. We lived by faith. Or at least this is what my parents called it. Each month we trusted that God would bring the money in to cover the rest. It was tense to say the least, with some months better than others, but always tense. Miraculously we never went without. My mother always had food on the table for her six hungry kids. We devoured her food and would come back for seconds. She baked for us and not once did we miss a meal. Things were changing though. I would come back from the base on the Friday and instead of the usual Friday night chicken roasting in the oven, there would be potatoes or plain pasta to eat. Nothing else. No vegetables. No sauce. Just pasta or potatoes or bread. This went on for weeks.

We started to refer to this time as our "Beige Phase". Money was tight. Tighter than ever before. I could hear my parents whispering about it. It was stressful.

Something had to change. And change soon. After about ten weeks of this going on my dad asked all of us kids to be home on a

Saturday afternoon. This was unusual. It was very rare for us to be home at the same time. Our apartment was tiny and us older kids liked to make ourselves scarce. Susanna avoided being home as much as possible. Raphael spent every spare moment from the army with his girlfriend. Me and Sam were with Jon. It was really only Ezra and Abigail who were home. We had no idea why our dad wanted to meet with us. We sat on the couch and waited for him to begin. He explained what we already knew. That our money had run out. We didn't have enough. I'm pretty sure that Raphael said he had some to give to help out but my dad didn't want it. He wanted us to call on God as a family. Pray together. Pray that God would provide for our needs. He explained that after seven years of working in the bookstore he had a sabbatical year coming up, and that he had applied to a Bible school in Dallas, Texas. He wanted to fulfil his long-term dream of studying the Bible for a year. And he wanted to go there with my mother, Ezra and Abigail. This felt a bit strange. I was 19 and my parents wanted to leave home. I felt like it should be me making that announcement, not them. I could tell my dad was serious. His nostrils had already begun to flare, and he hadn't even started praying yet. This was going to be big. It was always awkward when my dad prayed. I hated it. It was so emotive with his chest heaving trying to catch his breath. It reminded me of when he would lose his temper and start raging at us.

He started to pray. I couldn't remember the last time we had prayed as a family. It felt like it was years ago. It probably was. He then went around the room and laid hands on each of us. From the oldest to the youngest, I was wishing it would finish soon.

The next morning I returned to my base. I was hoping that things would change. I really felt bad for Ezra and Abigail having to eat beige food. Both me and Raphael were getting fed at our bases. I had access to Air Force food which was relatively good considering it was army cooks making it. Sam was eating at friends' houses. Susanna was working in a café and had food there. It was really just Ezra and Abigail who were missing out, as well as my parents of course.

Early that afternoon I got a call. It was from my mother. She never called me so I knew something was up. She was excited and wanted to tell me something. Our Aunt, my dad's sister, had called from America. She had transferred some money to us. A few hundred dollars. My mother would be able to go to the market and buy fruit and vegetables. We would have chicken that Friday night. Such great news. I was grateful and said a little prayer of thanks as I hung up the phone. God hadn't forgotten about us. Our beige phase was over.

About half an hour later I got yet another call from my mother. She was breathless. She had just received a phone call from Leah, the lady who opened the door to the Jesus House all those years ago in Lund when my parents needed a place to stay. She didn't go into details but there was a Swiss bank account that had been in her family for a long time. She needed to shut it down for some bizarre reason. I never quite understood but something about Druids tracking her down and she needed to go into hiding. Anyway, the Swiss bank account needed to be emptied. And she decided she wanted our family to have the money in it. A huge sum. Thousands and thousands of dollars. The money would cover all the debt that my parents had accumulated in the past few months. It would also cover the one year tuition for both my parents to study the Bible in Dallas. It would even cover air fares and living costs. Each of us older kids would receive $1,000 to help us now that we would continue living in Jerusalem without our parents. It was a lot to take in. I hung up the phone in a daze. For all his faults my dad did seem to have a certain connection to above. His prayers had been answered. Pretty much within 24 hours.

The move to the States happened without much warning for my parents. They quickly packed the apartment up with all our belongings. They were only going for a year. They would return and have all their things in storage waiting for them. There was no need to be that careful about what was left behind. Little did they know.

Elinka invited me to come and live with her family. They had a one bedroom apartment on their roof and I could live in there. To say I was happy was an understatement. This house was already my emotional home and it felt so right to finally call it my own. As I collected my clothes off my bedroom floor, and moved into my new home on the roof, I was still a bit stunned about how quickly everything had happened.

The other big change that happened during this time was that I had to let my sister help me out with a job that I had on the Sabbath. For the last six months I had become what they refer to as a 'Shabbat goy'. A Sabbath gentile. I worked for one of the richest families in Jerusalem. They were New York Jews in the diamond industry. They had lavish Friday night meals for their family and numerous weekly guests. All their food was prepared by a kosher chef but they needed someone to come in and make their food look beautiful. To present it nicely and create an atmosphere. I can't remember how I heard about this job but I figured that with my blue eyes and blonde hair no one needed to know that I was in fact Jewish myself, and I could pass as a gentile and make some money on the Friday night. I would come home from my base and change out of my uniform into a long skirt and long sleeved top, I would then walk the twenty minutes to their luxury home. Once there I would get to work. I absolutely loved it. I had the most expensive and beautiful types of meat to work with. I spread out thin slices of ox tongue, jellied meats, and patés on platters. Lettuce leaves were used to soften the look. Mormor had taught me from a very young age how to make a rose from a tomato peel. The platters would have roses scattered all around them. Sometimes I would add a lemon rose in the middle of a salad, or sprinkle their cured meats with fresh herbs. I had everything I wanted at my disposal. Edible flowers were ordered in from a delicatessen in New York. No expense was spared. I had hours of playing with food, making the platters look beautiful.

At the end of the night I would wash the dishes. Hours of dishes. From my many hours in Elinka's kitchen I was used to this and I would occupy my time singing my favourite songs. It was a really enjoyable job and I was getting paid huge amounts for my work. When I explained to the family that I had to shift to a new base they were devastated. Their Friday night meals had become the talk of the town. Guests were coming into the kitchen to watch me make these tomato roses that no one seemed to be able to get enough of. I had women taking me aside in the kitchen, offering me more money if I was to come and work for them instead. I had no idea how much the Jewish women valued having the most beautiful Sabbath table. I told the family that I knew someone who was just as good as me with food decoration. They seemed skeptical. I was the ultimate and surely there was no one else? I explained that my older sister knew everything that I did plus so much more. I paled in her shadow. If anyone knew how to make something look beautiful it was Susanna. She would make their Sabbaths shine. And she did! I explained to her that she was not to mention the minor detail of us actually being Jewish. Susanna also knew how to cook, unlike me who had no cooking skills whatsoever. I knew how to bake, but not cook. So now when there were extra guests Susanna could quickly whip up one of her creations and everyone loved it.

The two of us sisters became a bit of a talking point in the very rich circles of the "Diamond Jews" as they were called. Once I moved to my new base I was only available every two weeks. The family didn't mind and often me and Susanna got to work together. It was a lot more fun this way and for the first time in my life I got to see what it was like having my sister as a friend. She treated me with kindness and actually seemed to like me. It was very new and I really loved having an older sister that I could now just chat to and observe the lives of the rich and famous together with.

Eventually I got asked to work on Saturday mornings as well. There was another diamond family and they had watched me interact with their children on a Friday night. They had eleven children. Eleven children who were convinced that they ruled the world. Their three year old was a handful. Every few seconds Rochel, the mother, would call out at the top of her lungs "Menachem... Menachemm ... Menachemmmmmmm COME HERE RIGHT NOW!!!". This went on all night and it made the evening incredibly unpleasant. At one stage when I came in with another platter of fish and ox tongue I walked over to Menachem and whispered something in his ear. He looked up at me and walked over to his mother. She was stunned. Absolutely stunned. How had I done that? What magic powers did I have to be able to get Menachem to listen? My many hours with Abe and Bella had paid off. I had never treated them like babies. They were people with their own personalities. We would chat. I would ask them questions. They would tell me about life from their perspective. All I had done was gone up to Menachem and connected to him by whispering in his ear instead of yelling at him across a giant table full of strangers. Rochel was hooked. She wanted me. Could I please, please come and help her? I saw the desperation in her eyes. She was a powerful business woman, a force to be reckoned with, but she had no control over her children and she wanted my help.

Saturday mornings were my time for church though. From ten o'clock until about twelve-thirty I was at church every Saturday that I was home from the Air Force base. I often led worship with Jess or would do a Bible reading. Bob, Elinka's husband, liked to ask me to do a mini sermon based on a verse that week. I really hated missing church. It was a time for me to recharge my batteries for the week and to reconnect with my community. I would meet visitors from around the world and I was often organising some sort of fundraiser or event. I didn't like the idea of missing out on my Saturday mornings but Rochel was desperate. I eventually told her that I would come on Friday nights when Susanna was working with the other family. And then I would come on Saturday mornings before and after church. She was thrilled. She offered me even more money. I did this for a few months, doing kitchen chores on the Friday night and looking after her kids on the Saturday morning when her husband was at the synagogue. I would stand there in her kitchen listening to the Sabbath rituals going on in the living room. I was so grateful that I wasn't religious. Unlike them I had a personal relationship with Jesus. They were so trapped in their religion. Not me. I had Jesus as my friend. I had Jesus as my lover. Jesus knew me and I knew him. These poor, poor rich people. They had so much money but they had nothing compared to me in what actually mattered. A relationship with my Creator.

Something started to happen though as the weeks passed. A string started to unravel. A string that made me start questioning things that had been so black and white until then. Were these religious families really THAT different to my own weekly church service? They had their prayers. We had ours. They had songs. We had songs. Sure our songs were about Jesus as a friend. Jesus as a lover. Jesus in this intimate relationship with us. But was he really? It's what I wanted. What I desired. What I had craved for since I was seven years old. But was he? Where was the evidence? As I stood there doing the dishes I realised that Jesus was a pretty pathetic lover. A silent type. Distant. He didn't really return my calls. He played hard to get. Whoa. How had I not seen this before? How had I become so caught up in the songs that I hadn't realised that they didn't reflect reality? The songs just expressed the truth that I desired. Now that I thought about it Jesus had never actually stopped and noticed me. He'd never sought me out. My endless requests of him meeting me had gone unanswered. I was just as religious as these people singing their prayers in the room outside the kitchen. I might not be wearing a headscarf, or keep kosher, but I wasn't any different. And my church wasn't any different. We were just as stuck in our routines. Repeating behaviour week after week and thinking that this meant we had a relationship with God. Wow. These thoughts shook me to the core. I tried not to let them unravel too quickly but I could feel them tugging at my heart.

The money that I made from these two jobs was tucked into my bedroom drawer. I never used it. My weeks were spent on the base. All expenses paid there. In the evenings when everyone else would socialise and hang out I would put on my shoes and go running down the long roads heading into the dark desert. The stars would shine in the cloudless sky and I had kilometres of flat roads to run on. Not a car in sight. Not a single person out. I knew that the base was completely tucked away in the desert. I was safe. I could run. No one calling out to me. No one hassling me. It was just me, the road in front of me and the endless starry sky.

Every other weekend I would work and then go to church and hang out with my friends on the Saturday evening, and that never cost much. Maybe a slice of pizza, a burger at McDavid's or a frozen yogurt. My money was starting to pile up.

During this time my brother Sam and I were getting really close. We spent a lot of time together since we shared the same friends from our youth group. We could all sense a change coming, I was that bit older than everyone but they were now all about to graduate from high school and we would go our separate ways. It was almost impossible to comprehend. We were such a tight group. Our friendship that had started many years earlier, and cemented itself with Jon during the Gulf War, was now coming to an end. All those summer camps. Easter camps. Feast of Tabernacles conferences. The adventures in nature with Jon. It was finishing up with the end of school. And Jon was getting married. Finally getting married! Tali had come to her senses about this man who adored her for so long, and who had not given up despite her not showing any interest. Finally after years of waiting, Jon was getting married and it signified an end of an era. Sam had the army looming on the horizon. He didn't want to go. He was scared of what it meant for him. He probably had a combat role ahead of him. It didn't suit his soft heart.

I heard Sam talking to Aaron about wanting to go to the States. He didn't have any money for it but was hoping to go and see our family before his army service. I decided to surprise him. At the time he worked in my father's book store in the Old City. I went to visit him one Friday afternoon. He was happy to see me and even happier when I handed him a massive chocolate bar. We shared a love of chocolate. Something fell out when he opened the wrapper. It was a ticket to America. He was shocked at my generosity. I was thrilled to make him so happy and to give my brother something I knew he so desperately wanted. And it really wasn't a sacrifice for me. I had a whole bunch of money stashed away that needed to be used. The word of my good deed spread among the youth group. There was a buzz about what I had done for Sam. Delilah and Vera came to me a few days later. They were so excited about what I had done for Sam that they wanted to do the same for Aaron. They had a bit of money, but not enough. Would I help out? Would I give some money so we could get Aaron to fly with Sam to the States? This was too exciting. One ticket seemed crazy enough, but to buy two tickets was the best thing ever. Of course I was in. I had never seen money as something you held onto. It was meant to be used. Meant to be shared. Easy come easy go. My money is your money and vice versa. We went and bought the ticket and tried to figure out the best way to give it to Aaron.

That night we waited until about two in the morning. We wrapped ourselves in white sheets, put tinsel in our hair, lit a candle each, and did our best impersonation of an angel. We snuck our way into Elinka's apartment and entered Aaron's room. We changed the lyrics of the song "in the still of the night" to be about us wanting Aaron to join Sam in America. We then handed Aaron his ticket. He looked more stunned than happy. He had no idea what had just happened and fell back asleep. We were on cloud nine though. We felt so good about our gift and quickly started plotting who we could help out next. Generosity is contagious and we had our first taste of what that really meant.

Not long after that Jon and Tali had their wedding and only a few days later it was time to say goodbye. It was the summer of 1994 and it felt like my heart was breaking. The hardest person in the youth group to say goodbye to was Micah. He was the one I figured I would lose contact with first. I knew he wouldn't keep in touch. Our friendship was over and I cried so hard when he sang his goodbye song to the church, "As I cross the threshold of life I have to say goodbye to all of the times we had and we leave these memories behind to face another time, I'll never forget you, my friend". His words resonated in my heart. All the people I had said goodbye to over the years. The friendships that had ended. The missed opportunities to tell people how I felt. The constant knowledge that the friends were only there for a season. My heart was breaking and I really felt as if the only way to survive was to lock my heart and too shut it down. It was either that or feeling the pain that seared through my body. It was the end of a very special era of my life and I would never have that back.

9

The Great Commission

My last few months of army service passed slowly. Weekends felt different. I wasn't really able to recharge my batteries the way I had in the past. I knew that my time in Israel was coming to an end. That I was heading off somewhere. I just wasn't sure where yet.

I had settled into my new base fairly well. One problem that came up was that I hadn't been trained how to use an M-16 which was the weapon that was used for guarding on this base. I was only trained to use an Uzi. It meant that I couldn't do my guard duty, which was part of everyone's role no matter what they did during the day. After a while of being on the base, and not doing a guard shift, I knew that I would eventually be contacted. One day I was told to meet after lunch at the main gate. I had to change into combat fatigues. They were thicker fabric and olive green. When I arrived it was me and about 100 male soldiers. I tried to look as if I was just one of the boys and that this was completely normal. A few trucks came to a stop in front of us and we had to hop in the back. I was helped in and found a spot on the floor. It was a tight squeeze and the ride through the desert was bumpy. We eventually arrived at the shooting range. I was handed an M-16 and told to wait for my turn. I explained to the young soldier in front of me that this was the first time I had touched an M-16. I had no idea how to use it. I had to wait and eventually was taken aside. I had a two minute lesson on how to hold it, and where to place it on my shoulder and aim. I tried to absorb it all. This was very different to Basic Training where we had days of instruction before finally using our machine gun.

I had to have my turn at shooting. The trucks were waiting. The sun was starting to set. I was in the last batch of soldiers lining up to shoot. I laid down in a line of men. There were about eight of us. I had my M-16 stretched out in front of me. It felt clumsy. It was so much bigger than the compact Uzi. I waited for my turn. All eyes were burning into me. I wanted to prove that I could do this. I aimed and starting shooting. It was over almost immediately. I was completely focused and the sound was so loud. I stood up and dusted myself of. I realised that everyone was clapping. All the soldiers were giving me a standing ovation. I had hit all my bullets in the bullseye! It was a fantastic feeling. As we rode back on the bumpy roads through the desert with the sun setting, I felt as if that moment alone made my time in the army all worthwhile. I was good, I was just as good as the boys.

On the Sabbath, when I was home, I would send off lots of letters of interest to colleges around the world. Bible schools in England, Ireland, Canada and even New Zealand. I knew I wanted to study theology. I wanted to understand God. I knew it was the key to unlocking my world. I would come back to my little room on the roof and thick envelopes would be waiting for me. Bible schools seemed thrilled at the idea of having a girl from Jerusalem come and study the Bible with them. Not once did I even look at how much it would cost. If I was meant to go somewhere the money would come. That's just how it worked. The world was my oyster. It was just a matter of finding out which place I was going to. I didn't look into any options in America or Australia. I knew that I couldn't live in America ever again. My nine months there had been hard. It felt as if I had lost part of my soul. The lack of walking, the dead food, the superficial feel of the church. I couldn't shine my light there and I knew it. Australia on the other hand was very attractive to me. Ever since the Australian missionary had come to our church and sung the song "this is the Great South Land of the Holy Spirit, a land of red dust plains and summer rains ...", my heart had surged at the idea of going there. I could see myself in Australia. I could see it so clearly. However, I was so aware that Lee, my first boyfriend, was in Sydney. I knew that people would think I was going to Australia to chase after him and our lost love. Three months after I had returned home after saying good bye to Lee I had found a much longed for letter from him in our post office box late one Friday and then I had run all the way home from the city so I could open it in my bed and really be in the moment. He wrote about his new life. His return to the surf. And there it was, his new girlfriend. He had moved on. Our relationship was officially over. Up until then I had still hoped that God was going to reunite us. That meant that Australia was no longer an option as a destination for the next chapter of my life.

I continued to look into places. New Zealand seemed the most likely. Its list of pros was long. It was English speaking. It seemed exotic. And it was far away from my brothers and my dad. I could face whatever life handed me without them there to interfere.

Being a soldier meant that I had a lot less time to be part of the yearly activities that I loved so much. The Feast of Tabernacles was a fun highlight and I didn't like to miss out. It was a conference once a year that Christians from all over the world would come to. To be honest, it attracted the more unusual variety of Christians from around the globe. The Christians who feel the need to celebrate their love of Jesus with a tambourine or with an interpretive dance. They had a glazed look in their eyes. They had sandals on their feet and wore the Star of David around their neck to show their support of the Jewish people. I personally found them a hard breed to connect with. However, what I did like was that I had a role to play there. Over the years I had become really close with the puppet ministry family. I had unofficially made myself their daughter. I loved seeing them and adored the man who would come with them to teach us about the Bible, Greg. He was old enough to be my dad. But he wasn't my dad. He was a quiet and gentle soul who saw my heart for Jesus and recognized the intensity of my hunger for wisdom and knowledge.

He spent hours with me discussing the Scriptures. Happy to have me debate each point he had and welcoming me to show him a different angle. Unlike my dad, Greg's gentle nature was not coexisting with a raging animal. He only showed me kindness and I adored him for that. There was no way that I was going to miss out on seeing my visiting friends even with me serving on a base far away from Jerusalem.

I had to get permission to leave and ask my commander for a day off. I realised that the timing of wrapping my commander's car in toilet paper in the middle of the night for his birthday, only days earlier, was maybe not the best choice. It had seemed funny at the time but I realised now that it might work against my request. Thankfully he happily gave me the day off and told me to stay out of trouble. I was grateful that, despite him having been assigned the most clueless secretary in the Israeli military, he seemed to like me and put up with my quirks.

I got back to Jerusalem in the evening and went straight to see my American friends at the Feast of Tabernacles. They were thrilled to see me and Greg's face lit up and he gave me one of his giant hugs. They had someone they wanted me to meet. Jeff was the music director for the Feast of Tabernacles. A conductor. He was the principal of a college in Sydney, Australia, and they thought I should meet with him. It was after midnight when he was finally free to talk. The service that night had gone for a long time. I was tired from my long trip. He was tired from his long day, but we hit if off straightaway. His face was alive with kindness. His eyes full of the zest for life. His wife Karen was a steady presence. A wise soul. She let Jeff do the talking but I knew that we would get along. They invited me to come to their college in Sydney and to study there. It meant that I could finally pursue my love of theology. Not just that though, it was a school of the arts as well. I would be able to study photography. My other passion. Wow, the perfect combo, theology and photography. In that moment I knew that I was moving to Australia.

I had to wait a few months though and complete my army service. I still didn't have a discharge date. It kept changing. My month off for the surgery had screwed things up. It seemed as if my details had been lost in the system. Initially I was told November 1994. Then December. Now there was even talk of January 1995. It was nerve-racking. Magdalena was getting married in January. I had to be there. I had held on to our friendship over the years. Sent her letters, postcards and called her from an international phone booth in the city on my birthdays. I got five minutes each birthday. It wasn't much. But I was grateful for the connection. Every minute was expensive so I chose to have a phone call to Sweden instead of presents. I wasn't going to give up my friendship with Magdalena. It mattered too much.

After many requests and letters, and being told to go to different offices, I was finally discharged from the army. I handed my uniform back. Filled out the forms. Was given a letter of recognition for my service to the State of Israel. I was out. I was free. Those last few months had an impact on me though. For years and years later I would dream about the army. Dream about being stuck in the system. Thinking I was going to be let out only to be told I had another two years to go. Or the letter telling me of my dismissal getting lost so I spent the rest of my life waiting to get out. I would have these disturbing dreams a few times a month.

I was thrilled to be out. Thrilled at my new taste of freedom. Thrilled to have gotten out from yet another institution. The world was waiting. I had all the money I needed for tickets thanks to my work as an undercover gentile. I paid for my round-the-world ticket in cash. My first stop was Sweden. I wasn't going to miss my best friend's wedding. As the plane took off, the tears started to roll down my face. I cried and cried. I couldn't even explain it. I was happy to go. Happy to start this new stage of my life yet the tears wouldn't stop. My chest heaving from the pain of yet again saying goodbye and having to start afresh.

I was arriving in Sweden just before Christmas 1994. I was so happy that I was able to spend this special time with Mormor and

Morfar and being back in their home. Hugging Mormor and smelling her familiar leather jacket that reminded me of my childhood. It felt so right to be there and to sit with them around their table and talk. They didn't disappoint. They had all my favourite foods ready for me. Mormor knew how much I loved fish balls. These horribly processed fish balls that you buy in a tin and make a white sauce from the brine. It's the Swedish equivalent of spam. It's poor man's food. I could think of nothing better. Mormor made me a huge amount. With her potatoes gently boiled with dill. She gave me chocolate pudding with cream and meringues. My favourite dessert. Morfar told me about birds and Latin root words. Nothing had changed. It was so good to be home. Despite the cold and the frost we rode through their quaint little town of Falsterbo. Past the harbour. The horses in their stables. The paths through the mossy forests. I was so happy. My face alive with the cold sea air. I had a little over a week of being immersed in memories of my childhood and I loved every moment of it. I then hopped on a train to make sure I didn't miss out on Magdalena's big day.

Seeing Magdalena again made my heart sing. She had met a young Swedish man on a missions trip to Romania. He was lovely. I was thrilled for her. She hadn't married a man like her father. Fredrik was gentle. He was humble. He was in touch with his feminine side. He adored Magdalena. I knew that if there was a plate of chocolate balls in front of him, he would never reach for the biggest one. He passed the test.

The wedding was fantastic. I sat there watching in awe. They had funny skits and songs. Stories were shared. It was a magical evening and I felt a pang of sadness that I had missed out on this tradition. By being plucked out of Sweden I had been missing out on these rituals. These milestones that resonated with me so deeply. I was Swedish but I didn't belong.

My next stop was America. I was dreading it but I knew I had to do it. My parents had decided to extend their one year visit so they could receive a proper certificate from the Bible school they were attending. They wanted me to come to Dallas to see them. The city of endless freeways and Christians with fake smiles. How was I going to survive Dallas? Abigail nearly smothered me when I arrived. She clung to me as if her life depended on it. In hindsight I think it did. She was at breaking point. The tiny student apartment was like a prison cell for Abigail. She was stuck at home for hours at a time with Ezra. Ezra, now in his teens, was getting more and more violent. Abigail felt like a prisoner in her own home. My parents were out doing day and night classes. Abigail and Ezra were forced to go to strict Christian schools that valued obedience and silence. Ezra was restricted more than ever and he took it out on his sister. The mood in the apartment was heavy. I tried to lighten it up but Ezra was very hard to reach and connect with. I knew he loved me but he wasn't able to show it. His rage had consumed him.

During the time I was in Dallas, the woman that my grandfather had married later in life had died. Their house needed to be packed up and sold. I offered to fly to Florida and help my aunt with the work. I had never been to Florida, and even though I dreaded the humidity, it had to be better than being stuck in a student apartment in Dallas.

My aunt was grateful for my help. We drove down from her house in Atlanta and got to work. I had never really connected with my American grandparents. It felt good to be able to do something for them. My dad's mother was called Lillian. I was often compared to her. She had the same laugh as me. My horse smile, as I would call it, came from her. Also my sense of humour. We both loved to shock. Stir the pot as people would say. I didn't know much about her. She was famous for her New York cheesecake and for starting her day standing on her head because it was good for her constitution. I had met her a couple of times when I was young. Without having a shared language it made it hard to connect with her, but I did feel a connection. I just couldn't quite put my finger on it. Grandma Lillian had always been on a quest for health. Sadly it was this quest that eventually killed her. Along with standing on her head each morning, she was also taking a tonic that was meant to strengthen her liver. Instead it poisoned her blood. She had years and years of being unwell. My parents had finally decided to fly to see her in December 1981. After years of saying they couldn't afford it they made the decision to go. Us four older kids got palmed off to various families in the community, and with Ezra in their arms my parents flew to see Lillian. They were greeted at the airport by the whole family. Everyone in their fanciest clothes. Lillian had died while my parents were flying over. Being a Jewish funeral meant that she had to be buried straightaway. My parents were taken straight from the airport to the burial. My father never got a chance to say goodbye to his mother who adored him.

Grandpa Shmuel had remarried. His kids never quite forgave him for how quickly he seemed to forget their beloved mother. He married for comfort. To be looked after. For company. Grandpa came to visit us in Sweden and Israel over the years. His wife Rachel often came with him. I knew Grandpa Shmuel better than I knew grandma but I never really connected with him. He was a kind man with an easy laugh but I also sensed a raging animal within him. I felt an anger that was just below the surface. I never got to see it. But I knew it was there. It was in my father. I kept my distance.

Now he was gone and I was there to clean up his house. It meant three days with my aunt. She had always been a distant figure to me. I had never had a chance to get to know her in the same way my siblings had with their more frequent visits to the States. She was kind and reserved. I wanted to know about my grandparents. I wanted to understand. I wanted to know why my father was the way he was. I wanted to understand the anger. The wild animal that I grew up with. I wanted to hear about the war. What had happened to my grandfather. Was there a connection? Surely there was. Surely my grandfather's pain came out in his rage. Surely my dad had been on the receiving end of that. And in turn showed the same rage to his sons. Who in turn let it out on their sisters. I could see the connection so clearly. I wanted to make sense of it. My aunt was much younger than her brother Alan and her older sister. She might not have seen the rage like they did. She might have had a different experience.

Either way, I came away from my time in Florida not knowing any more about my history than when I arrived.

I returned to Dallas and tried to be the sister that Abigail needed me to be. She soaked up every moment she could with me and cried when I told her that I couldn't stay and that I had to go. Australia was waiting. I had received my student visa. I only had medical checks to finish up and I could do that elsewhere. I had a few more stops before leaving the States and I needed to go. It wasn't easy saying goodbye to her. Knowing the terror she was in. Knowing that she feared for her life. It was hard saying goodbye to Ezra as well. He had always had a special spot in my heart. I could see that his rage stemmed from pain. That he wanted to be understood. That he wanted to be held and loved. I knew that. He just wasn't in a place to be able to communicate that.

Sometimes I would accompany my parents to one of the many meetings that the Bible school had. I dreaded these meetings. Loud music. Barbie dolls in trench coats worshiping Jesus with their hair spray making me want to sneeze. Smoke machines to create a mood. Emotive language that made me want to stand up and scream that this was so wrong. This was not the Gospel. This was a circus. Wake up people! You are being lied to! I remained silent and managed to sit through the meeting without gagging. But only just. American Christianity was getting harder and harder to swallow.

It was during one of these times that I saw a little notice up on the wall. A badly photocopied piece of paper saying that there was a speaker coming to a local church. A missions speaker. Everyone was invited. I looked closer and couldn't believe my eyes. Bruce Olsson was coming to speak!! Bruce Olsson!!! This was the man who Carin had written about! The man that she told stories on tape about. The man that had been a missionary to the Indians in South America. My absolute idol. My guru. My very own Indiana Jones. It was too exciting for words. I had heard his stories over and over again. Carin's voice on the tapes that came with me to Israel. I would listen to her tell the stories. Falling asleep to her telling me about Bruce nearly dying from the poison of the arrows. This was him! He was coming later that day. I had to go! I begged Raphael to take me. My parents were busy but Raphael had a free evening. He was living in Dallas with my parents and he had a motorbike. I pleaded for him to take me there. Nothing was going to stop me from seeing my idol. If I had a choice of seeing Bruce or Jesus I would have chosen Bruce. Bruce was adventurous. He was brave. I knew his life story so well and I had just assumed he was dead. But he was alive! He was alive and in Dallas. And I was going to meet him. I just hoped that I would be able to get through the crowds of people and see his face. I would ask Raphael to take me early so I could at least get into the building. Even if it meant me standing out the back I wanted to be in the same building.

Raphael was happy to drive me there. His need for speed along with having his sister join him was a thrill he didn't want to miss out on. We got to the church in record time. I had expected a mega church. One of those churches that Dallas is famous for. Instead we entered a tiny building. It was more like a room. It was in one of the poorest parts of Dallas. A few chairs were in a circle. An old lady smiled at me. Was I here to see someone? I explained to her that I was here to see Bruce Olsson. The Bruce Olsson. Was I in the right place? I was, I was just a bit early. I would have to wait. Over the next little while the chairs around me filled up with other elderly people. There were about eight of us in total.

Eventually Bruce walked into the room. He reminded me of Bob, Elinka's husband. Gentle, wise, with a kind face. He oozed humility and showed no signs of wanting to be worshiped. I quickly realised that falling on the floor and bowing in his presence might make him feel somewhat uncomfortable, so I restrained myself. Bruce Olsson was in front of me! He smiled at me. He then asked me my story. He wanted to know my story! Wanting to know why I was there. I told him everything. Told him about Carin. Told him how she had filled my childhood with stories of his life. He was amazed at how much I knew. Told him how I had moved to Israel but brought the tapes of his stories with me. How that only a couple of years later Carin had died from cancer. Bjorn insisted that God would heal her. Carin didn't need medical intervention. She needed a miracle from God. I told Bruce how everyone in our community had prayed and fasted. Magdalena and her siblings were told that God was using Carin to show His glory. She would be healed. More people would come to know Jesus through her healing. They were not allowed to be sad. They had to have faith. The cancer would be gone in the name of Jesus. Sadly Carin died. She died with no medical intervention at all. For three days they kept her body in bed. The community in shock but still praying for a miracle. Bjorn still believing that his wife would rise up. God made Lazarus rise from the dead. Surely Carin would rise too. After three days of not being allowed to grieve for their mother, Magdalena and her siblings watched as the authorities came and took their mother's body away. They never saw her again. God didn't bring her back.

I told Bruce all of this. I needed him to know. He listened to everything I said and asked me more about Carin. I felt as if I was honouring Carin's memory by sharing her story with a man who she admired from afar.

Bruce went on to ask me about my time in Jerusalem. Why I was moving to Australia. He wanted to know it all. He was so interested. He was so intrigued. The old ladies and men seemed happy to just sit there and listen. They let us speak. Bruce Olsson made that whole evening just about me. He only spoke about his own story for a few minutes and didn't feel the need to share any more about himself. Thankfully no one seemed to mind hearing about my life in Israel. He hugged me goodbye. Thanked me for my stories. Told me that God had big plans for me. That he wanted to read about my adventures one day and that he was sure my stories would be much better than his. I floated out of that room. I couldn't be happier. Bruce Olsson had validated my existence and I had a chance to tell him about Carin. It was a perfect night.

My parents took me to an Australian restaurant as a farewell. We hardly ever went out to eat. In fact, it would have only been a handful of times since I was born, and it was only when my grandfather would come and visit from Florida, and he would pay. Going out to eat was a very rare treat. Reading menus to me was so foreign. Having a choice of what to eat was confusing. It felt so bizarre to be eating something different than the person sitting next to me. As we sat down at the 'Outback' restaurant I looked around. Kangaroos and koalas were the only thing I recognised. Nothing else connected with me. I knew absolutely nothing about Australia. Well, not exactly nothing. I knew about Crocodile Dundee. I knew about Nicole Kidman. Lee had shown me a picture of the Opera House. That was the full extent of my Aussie knowledge. It hit me pretty hard that I was stepping into the unknown. My thoughts were interrupted by Ezra's loud voice. He was furious. His steak had been served with some lettuce and a slice of tomato. He had told the waitress he wanted no vegetables. NO VEGETABLES! How dare they get it wrong? How could they put vegetables on his plate? My mother tried to take them off but he flipped out and exploded with rage as he stormed out. We quickly ate our meals in silence and rushed out to the parking lot. It wasn't exactly the farewell meal my mother had in mind.

I was so relieved to say goodbye to my family. They were too intense for me. My nerves couldn't handle it. I just wanted peace. Peace and harmony. I longed for silence. Quiet voices. Meals enjoyed without tension. Cuddles on the couch. I would often look at Bob, Elinka's husband, giving his daughters long hugs. Sometimes his arms would just be around their waist and he would have his chin leaning on their shoulder. I wanted that intimacy and tenderness. A soft glance as I walked past. I had seen it with other families. Watched in awe as they seemed to be able to co-exist without drama. Without friction. Sure there were arguments and fights. I knew that. I had seen that too but it was never the overriding feeling. The undercurrent was love and safety and I had never felt that in my own home. I was always on edge with my family. Always ready for someone to blow up. I had to keep a low profile. Not draw attention. If I did I would be mocked. Raphael would find something to tease me about. Get his brothers to join in. I didn't want it in my life. I didn't want the pressure. I just wanted calm. I wanted to float in the pool and stare up at the ceiling. I wanted to surround myself with people who desired peace.

My first stop was Portland. I felt that I should return to the friends that I had made a couple of years earlier. They had been so kind to me. They deserved a visit. I wanted them to see me as myself. Not the girl they knew that wore makeup and wore uncomfortable shoes to show her devotion to the American God. I wanted to go there wearing my Doc Martens and be myself. I would complete my medical tests there so that I had all the right paperwork for my move to Australia.

I was welcomed back with open arms. I stayed with a couple with two young kids. They were so lovely and we had lots of laughs about my previous time with them. They wanted to hear about my army service. Asked about my family. They were so excited to have me there. They were hoping I would stay. Hoping I would change my mind about Australia. I explained to them that I knew that I needed to go there. They had a few whispers between them and then left the room and came back a couple of minutes later. I was handed a massive camera. They wanted me to have it. They knew that I would need it for my studies. I was so touched. I had been praying for a camera. Well, not praying as such. I never prayed for things. I hated that. But I did have many moments of hoping that God would provide me with a camera. I wouldn't be able to study photography without one. And my money couldn't stretch that far. I still had to buy my ticket for Australia and it was going to cost more than I thought. I was so grateful for their generosity. Again struck by how these Christian Americans had so many things warped when it came to God, but when it came to being generous they were way ahead of the world. They truly understood that we are meant to help each other out. I loved that about my American friends. A young couple with not much money and still handing me an expensive camera as their gift.

With my medical tests completed I was now going to my last stop. All the flights to Australia flew out of California. It meant that I could go and visit my friend who lived in Los Angeles. Sivan had moved there after she graduated from high school. She was busting to get out of Israel. She had taken on her American lifestyle and was keen to show me the sights. She drove me to Hollywood and pointed out all the famous places. The movies that had been filmed in different spots. I had no idea what she was talking about. Popular culture was a very distant reality for me. I had no idea about famous people or movies. I knew who she meant when she mentioned 'Pretty Woman', and I was happy to realise that I could point out who Marilyn Monroe was when we saw her statue, but that was about it. The sights of Hollywood fell flat for me. I had no interest. Instead I was shocked to see all the homeless people there. The heavily coated men and women pushing their trolleys full of their only belongings. The dead look in their eyes. The hopelessness. How could this be? How could they co-exist with the Hollywood stars? How could people be lining up to see the sights of Hollywood and not notice that there were hungry people pushing trolleys around them? How could I be on the receiving end of so much generosity every time I came across an American? Being handed envelopes with dollars stuffed into it and now even a camera. And here were people who needed it so much more than me and they seemed invisible to the masses. It shook me to the core and I sat at the airport trying to process my time spent in America. So many contradictions. So many good-hearted people. So much wealth. So much poverty. So much religion and so little understanding of the heart of God. I felt very loved here but totally didn't belong. I was happy to get out.

I hadn't realised but the cheapest ticket to Australia had a few stops along the way. One of the stops was in New Zealand and my mind had settled on that. I was happy to have a chance to not only see this country that I had wanted to go to, but also meet with my parents friends who lived there. What I hadn't paid attention to was that the plane was also going to stop in a few tropical islands along the way. A minor detail. My main concern was just fitting my clothes into my suitcase. I decided to wear all my heavy clothes to make more space. After all, it was April, it wasn't such a hot time of the year. I had totally overlooked the fact that these tropical island we were stopping at to drop off passengers, were just that, tropical. I had a grand tour of the Cook Islands, Tonga, Samoa, and who knows where else we landed, with very thick pants and a few layers of woollen jumpers. I was so clueless.

I finally landed in New Zealand with my now damp clothes. I had to catch another small plane to get to Palmerston North where I was meeting my parents' friend. I flew over New Zealand and was surprised to see rolling paddocks and sheep. In my mind I had expected rain forests and magical lakes. This was very different. Nice. But different. Something in me told me that I should have maybe done a bit more research before embarking on my trip. I was asked if I would be willing to preach at the local university. There was a meeting there once a week and it would mean so much if I could lead the service and share the Gospel from my experience. Despite a bad case of jet lag I did just that. Shared from the Bible with this group of university students. They in turn were amazed that I had never heard of fish & chips and promptly went and bought some for me, along with a packet of Tim Tams which they told me I had to know about before I got to Australia.

It was a whirlwind trip. Only three days in New Zealand. Two of those were spent travelling. It seemed a bit strange that I had even gone to New Zealand, but I was grateful I had. The friends I had stayed with were so lovely. As I sat down on my seat and felt the plane rise I had a bizarre thought. I had just completed the Great Commission! Jesus' command to his disciples was to go out from Jerusalem to Judea, Samaria and to the ends of the earth and spread the Good News. I had just done that! I had preached in Jerusalem. I had preached in Judea and Samaria through various camps and youth related activities. And now I had been to the ends of the earth, and shared the Gospel in New Zealand! I had done it. I couldn't think of anyone else that I knew that had done this. Especially in that order. Especially a woman! Could I possibly be the first female to complete the Great Commission? Surely not? Either way, I was here. I was on a plane to Australia. I had no idea what waited for me but it felt right. I was on my path.

10

For Those Who've Come Across the Seas

As I landed in Sydney, April 26, 1995, I was thankful that Jeff, the principal had told me he would collect me from the airport. I realised that I didn't even have enough money to pay for a bus.

I was greeted with a giant smile and a big hug. Jeff was so happy to see me, but he was in a rush. He was running late and would I mind waiting a couple of hours while he finished a meeting? I didn't mind at all. He drove us to the city and parked the car. We walked down to the wharf and he asked me to wait there. There I was, sitting by Sydney Harbour, no idea what that giant bridge above me was called. I looked at it for quite a while. Looked at the old buildings. They reminded me of England. How bizarre, I thought, I'm in Australia but I feel as if I'm on the set for a Dickens movie.

Jeff eventually came out from his meeting. Had I enjoyed my time? Was I impressed with the Sydney Harbour Bridge? Oh, so that's what it was called. The Sydney Harbour Bridge. I smiled politely. It was a nice looking bridge. But I wouldn't say I was impressed. Seeing the sun set behind the Old City, the Golden Gate reflecting the sun as I headed down the hill from visiting my friend on the Mount of Olives, that was impressive. The Sydney Harbour

Bridge held no meaning to me. It was big. I was happy it was there. But no, I wasn't impressed.

Jeff drove me to his house in Five Dock and introduced me to his bubbly daughter.

After dinner, over a massive bowl of honey popcorn, they told me that I could sleep downstairs in the apartment that a few of the students shared. There was a spare bed. I wouldn't need to pay for the first few days but if I wanted to stay there I would need to contribute to the rent. Of course! Rent. I had never had to pay for that before. Elinka had let me live in the apartment on their roof for free. I suspect my many hours in their house cleaning and cooking was my payment. It had never been discussed. In my travels people had always opened their homes to me. This was new. Weekly rent. I had better find a job. And find one soon.

I was introduced to the students downstairs. They all studied at Mission College where Jeff was the principal and Karen was in charge of the theology department. I was surprised. These students who were all going to a Christian college, they seemed so, how could I put it ... NOT Christian. They swore. I could see empty bottles of alcohol around. They had a blank look in their eyes that I connected with the 'unsaved'.

I asked them how I would get to the city from there. I needed to find a job. They thought that was hilarious. I had just landed. Not even unpacked my bag. And I wanted to find a job. Most of them were unemployed and told me how they had tried finding work for weeks when they had arrived in Sydney. It's too hard. There are no jobs. They would lend me some money for the ferry into the city but I shouldn't expect to find anything. I decided to wait until the next day. It was already getting late and I was tired. There was so much to process.

The next morning I woke with a start. Something terrible was going on. There was a loud noise that I couldn't quite place. I lay there in bed trying to make sense of it. Something was screeching. Actually, not something, lots of things were screeching. The sound was so intense. Constant. After lying in bed trying to comprehend where it might be coming from I finally stepped outside and realised it was coming from above. The prehistoric noises were in fact birds. Just birds. Birds starting their day. I had never heard anything like it. Maybe at the zoo. But hearing one caged bird making an occasional sound was nothing compared to this. This was a chorus of prehistoric birds announcing to the world that another morning had started. It hit me that I was in fact on the other side of the world.

After a cup of Milo I was able to borrow some money from one of the students and I caught the ferry into the city. I loved being back on a ferry. It reminded me of Sweden. The salty air on my face. The seagulls flying above. I breathed in deeply. I smiled as I thought of Barbra Streisand in the movie Yentl. When she eventually got on a ferry and got closer to New York. Finally free. Finally able to study the Torah despite being a woman. Something in me connected with her. I restrained myself and didn't break into one of her songs. I tried my best to look as numb to the world as my fellow ferry passengers.

Sydney was already bustling. Business men and women power walking to their offices. Tourists milling about. Delivery boys trying to beat the morning rush. I loved it. It was thrilling. Old buildings. Tall buildings. Cafés. I could feel the pulse of the city. I loved that there were so many people around. I followed the throngs of people leaving Circular Quay. I didn't have a plan of where I would go. I just wanted to get a feel for my new city. I found myself on Pitt street. Walking along. Smiling at the people. So happy to be here. It crossed my mind that I should have possibly borrowed a bit more money. I only had the exact amount to catch the ferry in and out. Not even enough to buy myself a bottle of water.

I kept walking and realised that one of the buildings that I had passed was called Mission. It took me a while to connect. Wait, that was also the name of my college. Mission Institute for Ministry and the Arts. I wondered if there was a connection. Funny how two things would share a name like that. I retraced my steps and walked into a fancy foyer. There was a bookstore right inside the entrance. And a bit further down there was a cafeteria-style restaurant. It seemed nice and relaxed. I asked one of the waiters if there was a manager I could talk to. Michael was busy but if I could wait he would chat to me later. Eventually I met with him. He wasn't much older than me and very friendly. I told him that I was looking for a job. He explained that there really wasn't anything available.

What about in the bookshop? My dad owned a bookstore in Jerusalem and I had some experience with that.

Was I from Jerusalem? Michael assumed from my accent that I was from the States.

Yes, I'm from Jerusalem. How long had I been here?

Oh, I arrived yesterday and would really like a job because I'm going to be studying at Mission Institute.

Michael looked somewhat surprised and smiled. He told me he would put my name on the books. He would find me some shifts. If I could buy myself a white shirt, black pants and some black shoes, he would provide an apron. I was in. He then offered me to stay for a free lunch.

That night when I had dinner with Jeff and Karen they just laughed when I told them my story. They knew things were going to work out for me, they just hadn't realised how quickly. Now that I already had a job sorted I might as well come into the college and look around. I wasn't going to start until the second semester in July. But they wanted me to meet the lecturers and get a feel for the place.

The next day we drove to the college. It was such a short drive. Why would we not walk? It would have only taken 25 minutes or so. When we got there Jeff took me around and introduced me. He seemed very proud to have a real Israeli joining his beloved group of students. He made sure to tell everyone that I came from Jerusalem. That I had been in the Air Force. I could tell that everyone adored Jeff. He genuinely seemed to care about all the students and he would ask about their families and follow up on concerns that they may have had.

I stayed with him throughout the morning. His secretary was a bit concerned that nothing had been done about an upcoming fundraiser they wanted to have. An autumn bush dance that wouldn't be able to go ahead. My ears pricked up. Did they want me to organise the bush dance? I had plenty of time. I could easily do it between my shifts at work. I was happy to take it on. They were thrilled. Was I sure? It was a big job. It involved a barbecue. Would I really be able to do that? I had just arrived two days earlier. Sure I said. I've got no problem with that at all. Just one thing. What exactly is a bush dance? I had never heard of it before and I needed them to explain it to me. Jeff just laughed and shook his head. Who was this girl from Jerusalem? I asked if I could have access to a phone. And if there was a spare phone book.

A couple of days later I presented Jeff with the details. I had called around a few places. I hadn't realised how far away they were. But when they had heard that I didn't have a car they were happy to deliver most of the things. I had a butcher donating sausages. A bakery that would donate two crates of bread. Schweppes were more than happy to give us drinks for the occasion. It wouldn't cost the college a cent to feed everyone. Not just that. I had asked the students that I was living with if they could help out. Most of them were studying music at the college and they were happy to organise the play list for the night and make sure that the sound system worked. They even organised someone who could call out the dances. Whatever that meant.

Jeff and Karen took me under their wing. I really loved being grafted into their family. The rent downstairs was too expensive for me. I knew I needed to set money aside to pay for my school fees that were looming. A couple at the church that Jeff and Karen went to at night had asked if they knew someone who was good with kids. Someone who could give them a hand, and live at their house and do some chores in exchange for a bed. It sounded perfect. They lived right across the harbour so I would be able to take a ferry across to the city for my shifts at Mission. I said yes before I even met them.

As it turned out, they still wanted me to pay for my bed. Quite a lot. It was so new to me. Australians view of money. Christian Australians view of money to be precise. They didn't seem to see their money in a communal way. That it was there to be shared. Here were these two lawyers, living in one of the most expensive spots in

Sydney and they wanted me to pay a lot of money so I could sleep at their house and look after their kids. Thankfully I was getting more shifts at Mission, and I also liked the mother. She had a sadness in her eyes. She seemed to be drowning in her role as a mum and a lawyer. A balancing act that never quite worked. Either her clients missed out, or her kids. She couldn't do both. We spent a lot of time talking. Her sharing from her heart. I was out of my depth but I knew that she valued our chats.

After a couple of months of this I was finally ready to move into a student house that belonged to the school. My studies were about to begin and I needed to be closer to the college in Five Dock. Jeff took me around to the different houses to see if there was a spot for me. I was introduced to a few of the girls that lived in one of the houses. Jeff was disappointed. The girl that he had really wanted me to meet wasn't there. She was off having surgery. Jeff let out a big sigh. He obviously had a very soft spot for Alice. I knew he had a soft spot for all his students, but I could tell this one was extra special. He explained to me, while standing in the doorway to her empty room, that Alice had come from Adelaide to study music at the college. She had the voice of an angel. In fact, she was an angel. He knew we would get along. She just had to come back from surgery and heal up.

I was told that there was no spare room at the house. Jeff had misunderstood, so he took me to another house in Five Dock where I ended up renting with six other students. They all seemed pretty bizarre to me. Except for one. Hayley. Hayley had only a few months earlier arrived from Tasmania. Despite being only 18 she fit into the category of 'salt of the earth'. Her integrity shone through her massive smile and bright eyes. I was thrilled to hear that we would be studying theology together. Hayley became my trusted friend. She helped me ground myself those first few weeks. I knew that I was so different to anyone she had ever met before. I knew that she was intimidated by my story. She felt as if her life in quiet Tasmania could never measure up to my stories from Jerusalem. I felt safe in her presence and looked forward to our early-morning walks to the college.

I loved studying theology. It was the perfect fit for me. I had so many questions. So many things that didn't make sense. Thankfully my lecturer, Dr. Raymond, didn't mind my constant comments and interruptions. He didn't mind being challenged. He took me aside one day and said he had never quite had a student like me. He felt that when he stepped into our class it would transform into a Yeshiva. He became the Rabbi and I was the student who would argue back and forth. He loved it. He delighted in my questions. Thankfully the rest of the classmates didn't seem to mind and I had hours and hours to try to get my head around concepts that I just couldn't seem to grasp. Most of my classmates were guys. Guys who looked like they were suffering a slow death having to be there. I never quite understood why they were there. One classmate who stood out though, and who I quickly aligned myself with, was Fiona. Fiona was larger than life. Her laugh filled the room. She came from the western suburbs of Sydney and had the sharpest mind I had ever come across. She knew everything. Every little piece of trivia she knew it. And she loved to pass that knowledge on. She was hilarious.

With Hayley on one side and Fiona on the other I couldn't be happier. I had Dr. Raymond to harass about my deep questions about God. Why was God referred to in the plural in Hebrew? He explained that it symbolised that God was in fact three. Father, Son and Holy Spirit. No I thought. That's not it. It's deeper than that. It didn't sit right with me. My dad had never been able to answer me either. Now Dr. Raymond was disappointing me as well. The answer remained elusive.

One of the great things about Fiona was that she had answers for everything. Well, maybe not the answers to the theological questions I had. But she knew everything else. She taught me about Australian pop culture. Australian authors. TV shows that I just had to know about. Fiona was also married. Unlike me and Hayley who were possibly the two most sexually ignorant females in Sydney. Or at least that's how it felt. Fiona was more than happy to share her experiences. Every so often she would arrive in class and say something about not having slept that night because of all the wild sex. Hayley and I were both stunned. Shocked that she was so open. That she had no shame. No shame at all. It was so new to me but also so refreshing. It was always followed by a giant laugh.

After a couple of months of this I finally mustered up the courage to ask her something that had been laying heavy on my heart. I was about to turn 21. My birthday was just around the corner. I really needed a question answered and Fiona was the person who would be able to explain it to me. What exactly was sex? How did it work? Could she, step by step, explain the process to me? We were sitting outside the college building eating lunch. Fiona's eyes popped open. How could I not know? I was twenty and didn't know about sex? Hayley was sitting there next to us nodding. I was pretty sure she didn't know anything either. Fiona was ready to fill us in. Happy to pollute our minds with her sordid stories. What did I want to know?

Okay, here was the thing. No matter how much I thought about it I just couldn't understand how a husband and wife could be lying in their bed dressed in their pyjamas one minute, and then the next they would be naked and the man inside the woman. I didn't get it. I couldn't see what took place in those moments before it happened. How did you go from fully dressed to having sex? What was said? How did things fit? What exactly was put where? Could Fiona please, bit by bit, explain it all to me. She did. Over the next hour she sat there and graphically told us every little detail. I got her to go over bits again. But wait, the penis actually gets hard? Like hard, hard? How can it go in then? Wouldn't it break? Oh it bends. Right. It bends. It's hard. But it bends. Things were becoming clearer. I was still struggling with the concept of those pyjamas being taken off, but in my mind's eye the room was dark and all the clothes would be safely back on by the time the sun rose. I was so grateful. Fiona had done what no one had been able to do before. She had explained to me the mechanics of sex without me dying of embarrassment. Her relaxed take on life, and her desire to pass on knowledge, was the perfect combination for me. I finally knew what having sex was. What a relief. I seriously doubted I would ever experience it for myself because, after all, it did involve my body, but at least I would have a better understanding what more and more of my friends were up to.

My 21st birthday happened to fall right in the middle of my exam timetable. It felt wrong to get my new friends to come along to a celebration. I didn't really like birthday parties anyway. They always felt so clumsy. I wanted to do something though. It was a Sunday and it felt as if the milestone needed to be acknowledged. I didn't have much money to spare. I counted out what was in my wallet. There was enough for something special. I headed to the shops. I bought a baguette, because my parents always shared a baguette on special occasions. A can of salmon, because it was cheaper than the smoked salmon that reminded me of New Year's Eve with Mormor and Morfar. An avocado, to remind me of Israel. And a pineapple, to highlight that I was in Australia. It was the perfect combination. I was so pleased my money had stretched so far. But where should I eat it? I had to be in the city for the night service at the Mission.. Of course! I would take the ferry in and go and sit on the steps of the Opera House. And that's exactly what I did.

My 21st birthday was celebrated with a solo picnic on the steps of the Opera House with tourists giving me weird looks as I happily ate my baguette and cut up my pineapple. It felt good. It felt right. I was acknowledging parts of me that made me who I am. Sure it would have been nice to spend the day with friends but there were so many important people in my life that wouldn't be able to be there so in a way it was just easier to do it on my own. I packed up my things and headed off to the church service.

Dr. Miller, who at the time was the head of the Mission, always liked to come and say hello to me. Jeff had warned him that I had a tendency to say things that were quite shocking and Dr. Miller seemed to enjoy my frankness. I didn't disappoint. I always had a story for him. Something that had happened in my travels. Tonight he came up to me as usual and asked me how I was. I told him that I had just celebrated my 21st birthday. He congratulated me and asked me what I had done for the big day. I told him about my perfect moment on the steps of the Opera House. How nice it was to sit in the sun and eat my food. I had a big smile on my face that wasn't matching the face in front of me. Dr. Miller eyes were starting to well up with tears. Had I really just spent my 21st birthday alone? Had I really no one to celebrate with? I tried to explain to him that I didn't need more than that. The day had been acknowledged. Not according to Dr. Miller. He was wiping tears from his face and told me that no one should ever celebrate their birthday alone, especially not a 21st.

The service was about to start. It was broadcast on radio so he had to rush off. I was touched by Dr. Miller concern for me. It felt nice to have someone care so much. Once the service had started and the singing had stopped Dr. Miller explained that he had a special visitor tonight. He wanted everyone to meet someone very precious. It took me a little while to realise that the person he was talking about in front of the church, as well as on the radio, was in fact me. He wanted me to come up to the microphone and share about my life a bit. And then he got everyone to sing Happy Birthday to me. It was a very sweet moment and he was right, birthdays are not meant to be spent on your own.

After the service a little man approached me. He had a certain look about him. He reminded me of Mr Bean. He wanted to congratulate me on the big occasion and wish me a good year. He had always wanted to travel to the Holy Land but any spare time he had he would fly to Sri Lanka. Sri Lanka? Why did he fly there? He explained that he had become involved in an orphanage and tried to help them whenever he could. Did he go alone? Or in a group? He travelled alone. Just something he liked to do to add some meaning to his very mundane life as a business owner. Would he like someone to go with him next time? I had lots of experience with kids. I had done puppet ministry. I had worked at summer camps. Knew lots of fun songs. Knew games that kids loved. Could I come with him? Would he mind if I tagged along? I would find the money somehow. I always did. Mr Bean wasn't too sure. He explained that Sri Lanka was in the middle of a civil war. That it was very dangerous for him to go there. The part of the country that the orphanage was in was in the Tamil region. Had I heard of the Tamil Tigers? A terrorist group? No, I hadn't. Never heard of the Tamil Tigers. But I had lots of friends in the PLO. They were really friendly. Terrorists had a friendly side. They didn't scare me. Could I please come along. Mr Bean needed to think about it. He would get back to me.

A couple of weeks later he approached me after church. He really couldn't see me coming along. He had spoken to some people and it just wasn't safe. Wasn't safe for anyone. Especially a young woman. And the roads were now closed. There were checkpoints along the whole way. Only church workers were allowed through. What if I dressed up as a nun? Would he be okay with that? I could easily find some clothes that would pass as a nun. I already had a big olive wood cross from my dad's bookstore. I could find the rest. Please, I would really like to go. And if I could survive Jerusalem I could survive Sri Lanka. Mr Bean smiled. I think he realised he had no say in this. I was going to join him and he might as well just accept it. He wanted to know about my parents. How would they feel? My parents? How would they feel about what? Of course they would be fine with it. I had already gone to Australia. You couldn't get any further than that. My parents would be fine. I would let them know in my next fax that I was going to Sri Lanka.

The summer holidays were coming up and I managed to score another job. The busiest Christian bookstore in Sydney was happy for me to work in their café. Koorong was one of those bookstores that when you step inside you are convinced that you have landed in America. The scented candles. The endless self-help books. The cheesy wall hangings. It made Christians feel good to go there. Gave them an oasis from the secular world. It made them feel closer to God. Not me. I hated it. It gave me a rash. I was pretty sure I was allergic to all things Christian paraphernalia. It was so distant to the God I knew from Jerusalem.

It was a job though. And I needed the money. I was a waitress and I was good at what I did. Except for one minor issue. My accent. My annoying accent. It was always there. Always present. Even if I said tomato sauce instead of ketchup the accent was there to trigger a response. I could see the look in the customers' eyes. I knew the question was coming. I started handing out the menus without saying anything so at least the barrage of questions could come after they had decided on what they were eating. But then it would come. The dreaded question.

Are you American? No.

Oh sorry. Canadian! Of course. How rude of me.

No, I'm not American. And no, I'm not Canadian. I was born in Sweden. But I grew up in Israel.

Israel?? Really? I have always wanted to go to Israel. Or, my uncle went to Israel last year. He loved it. He sent me a post card from the Dead Sea.

And on and on they would go. Chatting to me like I was there to hear everything and anything to do with the Holy Land. They could sit in their holy café, in their holy bookstore and talk to a waitress from the Holy Land. The full experience. I was giving them a moment of glory.

My manager didn't seem to share these warm fuzzy feelings. I was taking too long at each table. My orders weren't coming in quickly enough. Customers were staying too long. Taking up too many tables that could be used for new orders. I had to stop. I couldn't talk to my customers about my private life. It was impossible. There was no way I could stop the barrage of questions without making the bookshop look bad by saying that I was banned from answering. What was I going to do? I needed this job. I needed the money. I had school fees to pay off. I had rent coming up. A trip to Sri Lanka.

The answer came in the form of a business card. I had them printed out at a local shop.

I'M NOT AMERICAN
I was born in Sweden but grew up in Jerusalem
(Please don't ask me more during work hours)

I handed these out just as I saw their eyes registering that I sounded funny. Just before that first question came out, the business card was handed to the customer and I was able to get back to my job. My manager wasn't quite sure what to make of it but was happy to have a fast flow of customers again.

The new school year was starting and I was able to move into the college dorm that was right behind the post office in Leichhardt. Jeff offered me the first choice of room. I was happy to have the last room down the corridor. The one right above where the mail was delivered to the post office each morning. I loved mail. Loved getting letters. Being able to look out my window and see all the bags of mail made me happy. I didn't mind the noise.

I was pleased to see that Alice, the singer that Jeff had wanted me to meet was going to have one of the rooms in my dorm as well. I had seen her around the campus. We hadn't really spent much time together. I had heard her sing. I knew she had a giant Fijian boyfriend. But that was pretty much it. Her friend Victoria was also moving in. Victoria was also studying music alongside Alice. Victoria was Italian and I knew instantly that we would get along.

The mood in the house was good. I was really happy about the different people sharing my space. It was an eclectic group, and being the first one to move in put me in the role of mother of the house. A role I always seemed to find for myself.

Alice was hard to get to know. She seemed to be quite unwell. Alice also had migraines. I wanted to help out but wasn't quite sure how. I decided to go and sit with her on her bed. Find out if there was something I could do. She seemed happy to have me there. She started talking about her life. Growing up in Adelaide. Very much part of the church. When she finished school she had gone to Romania. She had wanted to help out with orphans. The stories were still haunting her. She told me about her Fijian boyfriend. How she had always thought she would marry a black man. As I listened to her I felt as if I already knew her. She seemed so familiar. Her story resonated with me. I felt a connection. We spoke a similar language. She also saw symbols in life. Drew meaning from them. She also desired to know the truth. She could see people's hearts. Go beyond their words. I sat there on her bed. Watching her pale face. I knew that I had a new friend. More than a friend. Despite her weak body I could see a similar glint in her eyes that reminded me of Magdalena. Her devotion triggered memories of Jess in Jerusalem. I knew that she was going to be my friend for life. Whether she wanted to be or not.

I returned to my room knowing that I had to do something to help Alice. I had a bit of money saved and knew exactly what I needed to do. Leichhardt was an Italian suburb. The streets were lined with shops displaying the most beautiful food. There was a small butcher not far from our dorm. I often walked past it. Looking through the window at the meat. Pork legs hanging down. Wooden blocks displaying marbled cuts. Not once had I been inside. It was way out of my budget. It felt good to finally walk through the doors. To smell the salty meats. To be greeted by the friendly Italian man. I told him I wanted a steak. Just one? Yes, just one steak. One big steak. The best one he had. It had to be big. He cut one especially for me. Making sure I was happy with his craftsmanship. I wasn't able to tell if the steak was good or not but judging by the smile on the man in front of me, and the price tag, I knew it was perfect.

I hurried back to our dorm. Up to the small kitchen above our rooms. I realised that I had no idea how to cook a steak. This would be my first. We didn't eat much meat in our family. A roast chicken on Friday nights and a mince casserole mid-week. This was new for me. I stood there in the kitchen. Watching this slab of meat sizzle in front of me. I wanted it to be just right. I wanted Alice to devour it. I wanted her pale face to absorb the goodness from the meat. I wanted her to be my friend.

My studies and my work took up most of my time. I tried to find as much time as possible to hang out with my dorm mates but I also wanted good grades. I really enjoyed my new friendships and I was starting to accept how different my Aussie friends were from those I had left behind in Jerusalem. Dr. Raymond's class was still enjoyable. So was Karen's class. She wasn't really teaching me anything new but I enjoyed her style. I liked how she presented the Bible to my classmates who seemed to know so little about the Bible despite calling themselves Christian.

One day Karen said something that shook me to the core. She hadn't intended to. She was just trying to explain the song about the river of Babylon. How the Jews sat down and wept. They were held captive. They couldn't be in Zion where they belonged. She explained how it was more than that though. The Jews really felt like they could only serve their God within the boundaries of their country. Now that they were captive in Babylon they didn't have access to Him anymore. They needed to return to the Land in order to worship their God again. To be in union with him. She explained how wrong they were. We can have access to God anywhere. We are not bound by countries or location. God is everywhere. We have access to him no matter where we call Him from. The tears started to roll down my cheeks. I tried to wipe them away. I didn't want to cause a scene, but I knew that she was wrong. I knew that the Jews in Babylon were right. They were weeping into the river because they knew, just like I knew, that God remained in Jerusalem. I had lost contact with Him. The God I served was only accessible through my community back there. The American God and now the Australian God held no meaning to me. I had been running on near empty since leaving Jerusalem. I'd been running on fuel that had been stored up from my years of devotion with my youth group. It was running out. My tank was nearly empty. I was surviving on fumes. What would be left once it was empty? Who would I be without my connection to God?

It was just about this time that Paul Meier came to speak at our college. He is the author of the popular book 'The Five Love Languages'. He had been invited to speak to the counselling students at the school but us theologians were invited as well. It was a three day course. As I sat there listening to him I knew what I wanted to do. I wanted to study counselling. All this theology was driving me crazy. It was an inward spiral that led nowhere. I needed a practical outlet. I needed to find a way for me to use my knowledge in a way that could help people in a practical way. I stayed behind after the sessions. It turned out that he knew quite a few people from Israel. He had met with them hoping to start up a clinic in Israel. Listening to him I knew I wanted to be part of that. He knew Naomi's parents who had a counselling centre. It felt good to have that connection. I imagined being able to return to Israel with a degree in counselling and be part of the solution over there. I wanted to be part of the reconciliation between Jews and Arabs. I wanted to facilitate dialogue. I wanted to meet with families who were suffering in silence like my family had been.

As the months passed I felt more and more uncomfortable at the college. I had always struggled with institutions and I was now not just studying in one, I was also living in one at the dorm. Having to follow the rhythm of the day that someone else decided for me, it was getting too much. My head felt like it was going to implode. The communal meals were starting to resemble a mental institution. How were we any different? One evening it all got too much. As I sat there eating my meal I slowly started smearing the food on my face. Spoonful after spoonful. The noisy room became silent as everyone sat and stared at me. Initially people had laughed. But as I continued it started to freak them out. I had lost the plot. Their happy mother, who was always looking after them, had lost her mind. She was smearing herself with her food without any expression on her face. It was a weird moment. A very weird moment. It was exactly how I felt though. I was losing my mind being stuck there and I wasn't exactly sure how to break out.

A few days later the feeling came over me again. This time when I was at the college. I was sitting outside with some friends. To me their conversations sounded so inane. So repetitive. So mindless. I craved my friends from home. I missed the intensity of our dialogue. This Aussie way of talking was so empty. So shallow. I just lay down on the asphalt. I lay there for ages. Perfectly still. I looked like a corpse. As if I was the centre of a crime scene. Someone grabbed a piece of chalk and drew an outline around my body. It was official. I was dead. I had nothing more in me. I knew my time was up.

My trip to Sri Lanka was around the corner. Mr Bean had just organised the tickets for us and we were going to leave in a couple of weeks. I had faxed Jess about the trip. Telling her that I was going to an orphanage. Her army service was finished. Jess had been chosen as best soldier in Israel. She had given it her all. She needed something totally different to do. Could she come with me? I was overjoyed! Jess! My closest friend from Jerusalem who I adored. She was similar to me in that she loved knowledge. And just like me she was a tomboy. Other than that we differed. Jess was gorgeous. Good at everything she did. An incredible piano player. Her voice could make her famous if she chose. She had the world at her fingertips. And she had chosen to go to Sri Lanka with me. I knew we would make great nuns together. I was counting the days for the departure.

During this time I had become closer to Alice and her boyfriend. He in turn had introduced me to his friend Joeli. According to Alice, Joeli was interested in me. I was shocked. A guy interested in me? Joeli would come over when Alice was seeing her boyfriend and we would all hang out in Alice's room together. Joeli was also Fijian. He was very shy and incredibly kind. The fact that he liked me was intriguing. The thought of having a boyfriend was exciting. I had only ever had Lee the surfer. It had been so intense with him. So profound and meaningful. I wasn't sure if I could do that again. Something light-hearted and fun though, that seemed doable. I had Alice tell Joeli that I was keen.

I explained to Joeli that I was happy to be his girlfriend. However, and it was a big however, my relationship with God came first. If I ever, ever, ever felt that him being my boyfriend would possibly distract me from God then I would end things straightaway. Joeli thought that was fair enough and agreed to this very serious arrangement. We only had a few weeks together before I was flying to Sri Lanka. One night we were kissing and Joeli made the critical mistake of placing his hand on my stomach. My stomach! My stomach was totally out of bounds. I gently removed his hand from my stomach and continued to kiss. Something bothered me though. I had enjoyed the feel of his hand. It had made my body respond in a way that I wasn't used to. Oh no!! It hit me like a lightning bolt. This is how girls get pregnant. It starts with enjoying a hand on a stomach. Next thing we would be having sex. I sat straight up and told Joeli that I wanted to go home. He lived in Bondi so it was a long taxi ride back to Leichhardt. He looked pretty confused the whole ride back. What had he done? Why did I want to leave so soon?

I got home and had a shower. As soon as I knew the taxi would have dropped him back home again I went out to the pay phone on the street. It was the middle of the night. I called him up. I then very calmly explained to him that he was a lovely man. I really liked him. He had been so kind and generous. But, he had come between me and God. He was a distraction. I could no longer be his girlfriend. It was over. I didn't even give him a chance to respond. I just hung up the phone and went to my room hoping to get a couple of hours of sleep before classes began.

Alice's mother was coming to stay for a few days. She was a lecturer in Adelaide but was spending some time in Sydney. Despite her incredibly sharp mind she was very easy to talk to. I shared with her that I was struggling with the lack of an outlet with my theology. That I really felt as if counselling would be better suited. Her face lit up. If I wanted to study counselling she knew just the place. The college that she worked for in Adelaide was offering a fantastic program. The best in the country. I should go there. I could transfer my credits from the theology course and go straight into a counselling degree. It sounded good. Sounded like the perfect fit. But just one thing, could she show me on the map where Adelaide was. I had no idea.

I told Anna that I was off to Sri Lanka but I would look into tickets to Adelaide before my departure. I went out that day and spoke with a travel agent. She told me that they had a special to Adelaide. It wouldn't cost that much. But I would have to book that day. The ticket was refundable so I might as well buy it. I could always get my money back if I changed my mind.

I packed my bag for Sri Lanka. Thankfully I wouldn't need to dress in a habit in order to pass as a nun. I just needed a long black skirt, a long sleeved white shirt, a black cardigan and the giant wooden cross. My hairstyle already resembled a nun so I didn't have to make any changes there. I took the bus to the airport and met Mr Bean. Ready for my next adventure.

11

What if the Hokey Pokey is What It's All About?

I had no expectations of my trip to Sri Lanka except for us having one stop over in Bangkok. Wherever that was. I knew so little about the region. It was a complete mystery to me. I knew the name of every country in Africa, thanks to my teacher in Jerusalem who hammered it into us. Mr Talbot would also pin every TIME magazine cover of a world leader to the classroom wall and forced us to learn all the necessary details so we could connect with the story. At the time I resented him for it. But even in the short time since I had left school I had been able to make sense of news stories because of Mr Talbot's forceful teaching style. He wanted us to know about the world. Not just from our international friends but from a political understanding. So I could point to every country in Africa as well as the Middle East and name it. The same with Europe. But Asia. That was something different. I had no idea. Besides the obvious ones like China and India I was clueless.

I realised how little I knew once we landed in Bangkok and walked the streets trying to find our hostel. We had stopped at a little café and Mr Bean ordered food for us. I had never in my life tasted anything like it. I sat there and marvelled at the flavours exploding in my mouth. It was spicy. Yet sweet. Creamy yet bits of crunch. My mind was trying to make sense of the flavours. It was years later that I realised that one of the flavours that I had first encountered that night in the bustling metropolis of Bangkok was lemongrass.

I hadn't even considered sleeping arrangements for the trip. I had such a relaxed attitude when it came to guys. Not only did I have three brothers, but I hung out with the guys in my youth group as if they were brothers too. I had spent plenty of nights on floors shared with them as we camped or wanted to stay up for an occasion. It was never an issue. In fact, I really got along better with guys than with girls. I felt it was easier to relate to them. Less drama. As long as they weren't violent I felt much better in their company than with a pack of girls. So having to share a small hostel room with Mr Bean was not even worth a mention. It was only when I caught a whiff of his nerves just before bed that it hit me that this might be awkward for him. Travelling alone with a girl half his age. There was really no need for him to be concerned though, he was practically sharing a room with a nun. After a night in Bangkok we flew to Sri Lanka.

Colombo greeted us in its full glory. We arrived early morning and the city was already bustling with life. I couldn't believe the intensity of the heat and the humidity. I felt as if my lungs had filled with hot water and it was hard to catch a breath. I had always struggled with humidity. Seemed as if I was more suited to the cold climate of Sweden where I was born than the humidity of Florida where I was conceived. I quickly realised that the clothes I had brought were not going to be appropriate. I was dripping with sweat and we had only just left the airport. We had to spend a couple of days in Colombo waiting for Jess to arrive from Jerusalem. I just couldn't get over the swarms of people. How was it possible to squeeze that many people into one space? And how could they all be so tiny? I felt like a giant. We caught a train from an old, beautiful train station and travelled down the coast. We spent the day in the Port of Galle. A beautiful seaside town. Gorgeous old buildings. We had lunch at an old hotel that made me feel as if I was on a movie set. It was very sweet of Mr Bean to take me here and show me a bit of the sights. I had expected to be doing ministry straightaway and hadn't even considered being able to feel like a tourist for a couple of days.

Jess arrived and it felt so good to be reunited with my friend. Our connection was still there. After a year in Australia, where conversations were so different to what I was used to, it was incredible to finally have my friend that I could speak to in a way that resonated with my mind. Our conversations stretched me. They challenged me. We both desired to learn more. To see more. To be more. Jess tapped into a part of me that not many of my new friends knew about. That part of me had been starving for a year. Hungry for substance. Even in a Christian setting my conversations in Australia never seemed to go into the areas that interested me. Puddle conversations I called them. To have access to Jess was a breath of fresh air for my mind as well as my soul. We grinned at each other. Here we were, in Sri Lanka, dressed as nuns. Ready to drive up the east coast to spend a month at an orphanage. Isn't this exactly what we had been dreaming about in Jerusalem as teenagers?

The drive took longer than expected. There were so many roadblocks and checkpoints to go through. Each time the car had to be searched for explosives and weapons. We did our best to look like stoic nuns. It wasn't hard. Neither Jess nor I were scared. This was easy. Jess had just spent two years being in the Israeli Military Police. She had searched plenty of cars herself. She knew what was involved. If anyone looked nervous it was Mr Bean.

We finally arrived at the orphanage. The sun was setting and the water in front of the white building was reflecting the orange and the purple from the sky above. It was beautiful. The children who greeted us were also beautiful. The boys had already gone to their building for the night so we only had girls to greet us. Gorgeous girls. All wearing bright white shirts and blue skirts. Their identical black oiled hair parted in the middle into two braids. Their faces shone. Giant smiles greeting us. We were surrounded by girls that wanted to hug us. Who wanted to be the first to hold our hands. To tell us their names and ages in their sing song English. Mr Bean was clearly loved as well. I had never seen him so happy. So full of expression. This awkward little businessman from Sydney seemed to take on a new persona in the context of the orphanage. For starters he wasn't short anymore. Compared to the locals he actually seemed quite tall. And here he mattered. He had status. He was important. They treated him like royalty. I could see why he loved coming here so much. Maybe this wasn't so much about him helping the orphans. Maybe they were helping him. Making him feel important. Making him feel powerful. I was getting pulled into a dorm and lost sight of Mr Bean.

The girls wanted us to see where they slept. They wanted us to see their belongings. Two or three items each. A comb. An old box or trinket. A faded photo of a loved parent now gone because of a civil war that no one seemed to be able to explain to me. Jess and I were going from bed to bed. Each girl so excited to have us there. Wanting us to know about them. Being validated. It was evening and we needed to eat before heading to the guest house where we were staying. We were shown our seats in the eating area. Flowers petals had been placed around our table showing our status as esteemed guests. I noticed that we had knives and forks. No one else did. Just the three visitors. I looked over at Jess. She had moved hers out of the way. Just like I had. If everyone else was eating their dahl and rice with their hands so were we. The girls thought it was hilarious. They had never had visitors before that ate like them. They tried to show us how to grab the rice and dip it in the dahl and place it in our mouths without making a mess. We must have looked so funny. The girls were all giggling at us and beaming with their giant smiles. Even though they had made a special pot of dahl just for us that wasn't spicy, our mouths were burning. I loved the taste of curry powder but this was something different. This made my eyes water. I gulped down the sweet milky tea and tried to focus on the rice.

We were made to feel so welcome. The girls adored having us there. Not only was this an orphanage for children whose parents had died from the civil war, landmines, shootings, or even from malnutrition, this was also a training centre to give these orphans a chance for employment once they finished school. I respected the man who was in charge of the orphanage so much. He had not only seen a need to house and feed these abandoned children, but as they grew he had come up with a way to look after their long-term needs. The boys were taught mechanics. The girls sewing. Up until recently this hadn't been available and so many of these young girls were being sent off to rich families in the Middle East as maids. They were called maids but it really was a form of modern day slavery. Many of them were never seen again. Small amounts of money were sent back each month as the girls worked long hours, often in cruel homes. I met one of these young women. A single mum. She was only about 18. She was very lucky to have come back. She thought she was going to die in Lebanon. The family she was with would beat her daily. All she wanted was to be back in Sri Lanka with her little boy. She worked at the orphanage as a helper and was so grateful that she got to see her little boy every evening.

Jess and I weren't exactly sure what we were going to do at the orphanage. We figured that we would be told what was expected of us. No one seemed to know. The girls tried to teach us their songs as they brushed our hair for hours at a time. Tamil words made my tongue twist inside out. How was I supposed to make those sounds? Jess seemed to find it much easier and was singing along with the girls within a couple of days. We taught them how to make friendship bracelets. We had found a little shop selling string in the nearby town and the girls loved to choose colours and come up with new designs. Jess and I had spent hours doing this back in our days as summer camp leaders and it was just as much fun over here in Sri Lanka. We taught the girls some songs as well. We had so many to choose from. But there was one that was the favourite. The Hokey Pokey. No matter how much we tried to sing our much more refined options, it was the Hokey Pokey that won. The girls couldn't get enough of their now favorite song. They thought the actions were hilarious and would collapse laughing after each round. How could we deny them such joy? We sang it over and over again. Their joy was infectious.

We spent a bit of time with the boys as well. They liked to play volley ball with us on one of the patches of grass. A net had been stretched out between two trees, and despite the heat Jess and I would play a game or two in the afternoon once school classes were finished. We did this a few times until one unfortunate day when my foot got caught in a hole hidden in the tall grass. I tripped over and managed to twist my ankle in the process. My foot turning all shades of blue and purple was completely fascinating these inquisitive children. After a few moments of staring in wonder I had some of them come up and poke and prod my foot. So fascinated that a body could create those colours all on its own. I was surrounded by a sea of faces and I was in so much pain. Jess was trying not to laugh. I was lying on the ground in agony with a circle of kids all around me in awe of my now very purple foot. I was helped to a clinic in town and had to risk my life hopping across a very busy road in order to get there. The whole time having Jess trying to hold me up while laughing until she cried. Because of my white skin I was seen straightaway. I felt so guilty being led straight in to the doctor while mothers with lifeless babies were still waiting in long queues outside. No one said anything. No one complained. Of course having white skin means you get superior treatment.

My one footed status didn't really make a big difference to my day. I could still have my hair brushed. I could still make friendship bracelets. I wasn't able to participate in the ongoing Hokey Pokey love fest but I could watch. The other thing I could do was take photos. I realised very quickly that none of these kids had photos of themselves. I told Jess that I needed her help. I wanted to give the children a gift before we left. I explained to them that they were each able to have two photos. One of themselves and one with either their siblings or friends. They were so excited. I wasn't exactly sure how I would pay for having the photos developed. It was going to be a lot of money on my very restricted budget. But I knew I had to do it. These children needed to be validated by having a photo of themselves. I knew how much my photos meant to me. It was something I really wanted to do. It took a couple of days but we managed to photograph all of the kids. A portrait each and then a more relaxed photo with a sibling or friend. The girls took this very seriously and spent a long time brushing their already perfect hair to look their best for the big moment.

We had been invited to go out into the countryside to visit some of the poorer families. The man who ran the orphanage would often go out there and pray with the families and sometimes deliver some donated goods. Jess and I were happy to come along. We got to visit quite a few families. Each living in the tiniest huts you could possibly imagine a family living in. The floor was sand. Perfectly swept sand. Some had even made designs in the sand with their homemade broomstick made from dried out twigs. Their homes were empty. An old pot. A few rolled up mats to sleep on. What struck me was how neat they were. Spotless. So much care had gone into their home. Even in their absolute poverty there was a beauty. So different to the poverty that I had seen in America. The children that came to our church were the poorest of the poor. The few times I had to go to their homes I would have to try my hardest not to gag from the smells that greeted me at the door. Broken toys scattered around. Walls smeared with foul smelling mud or worse. I didn't want to know. Broken windows. Broken doors. Broken mothers greeting us at the door. The poverty here was different. Each family member perfectly clean. Hair combed back. They were proud of their homes. Inviting us in. We had been cooked for. Cooked for!!! These families with absolutely nothing were wanting us to eat their food.

We were served curries made from crabs they had caught that morning, cooked in coconut milk from the coconuts that kept falling around us. Our mouths burning hot as we ate these lovingly made meals. I knew Jess was feeling the same way. How could we possibly sit here and eat while these families just watched us? Surely they needed it themselves. But no, they wanted us to eat and were grinning as we used our hands to eat their offerings. I will never forget their generosity. Their happiness at seeing us in their homes. Most of the families we met had no fathers. The men had been killed in the war. Leaving behind the mothers to fend for themselves. No aid from the government. No safety net. They had to survive. I felt so useless and wished I had something practical to offer.

We were told that the leader of the Tamil Tigers had heard that we were visiting and he wanted to meet us. Mr Bean explained that this was really a great honour and we shouldn't feel afraid. Afraid? Why would we be afraid? If he was inviting us over then there was nothing to be afraid of. Jess was similar to me. Status never intimidated or impressed us. People were just that, people. So what if this dude was the head of a terrorist organisation? Surely he was just like the rest of them. And he was. Just like we thought. He offered us very sweet milky tea and biscuits. He introduced us to his monkey that lived on his shoulder. He asked us about Israel. He was impressed that both of us knew how to shoot Uzis and M-16s. Just a lovely afternoon tea under the Sri Lankan sun. I pulled my camera out to take photos of his beloved monkey. Two guards who had been very quiet jumped up. "No photos. No photos!" I hadn't realised the security factor around our visit, what a big deal it was to have this man meeting two westerners. In the end he agreed to let me photograph him and his cheeky friend as long as I promised to not get the photos developed in Sri Lanka. I had to get them developed back in Australia. I agreed but was slightly frustrated. I knew that it was cheaper to get photos developed in Sri Lanka and I had so many photos to get done for the orphans. Now it was going to cost even more.

Our time in Sri Lanka was coming to an end. There was only one more event that needed to happen before our departure. The orphanage had been working hard on setting up a garden. It was a beautiful space with little paths and miniature hills. Gorgeous tropical flowers had been planted. It was a magic spot and there was going to be a ceremony to celebrate the occasion. It had taken quite a while to get this dream to fruition and everyone was very excited about the big day. A few days earlier the head of the orphanage had told us that he wanted me and Jess to name the garden. It was a very big honour. We were really touched by his request and we wanted to come up with the perfect name. In the end we settled on a Hebrew word Tikvah. It's the name of the Israeli National Anthem and it means 'Hope'. That was our message to this beautiful group of children that we had fallen in love with. Even though they loved to sneak up behind us and put lice in our hair, lice that they had found in their daily grooming sessions, we had fallen in love with them. We had nothing to offer them. Well, besides lots of friendships bracelets and a new dance that was sure to bring them hours of joy. Hope was the best we could do. I spent a couple of days painting a sign. They wanted it in both Hebrew and English. It was ready just in the time for the big day. After much pleading and begging Jess and I had promised that we would wear saris for the special occasion. No one dared to believe that it was true. Two white girls wearing their beloved saris. This was the hot topic. The boys kept asking us "Miss, will it really happen? Will you really wear a sari?" We agreed that if we could find a sari that fit us we would each be wearing one. Much to my surprise they had giant sized saris on offer and there was no escaping it. Both me and Jess appeared on the morning of the celebrations wearing saris. We hadn't realised how much this actually meant to the kids but we could see it on their faces as we arrived. Me still hobbling on my foot. We were two goddesses that had just arrived in their garden. The excitement levels reached new highs.

Even though we had arrived early the orphanage had already been transformed. Flower garlands were draped everywhere. Mandalas, made from grated coconut and rice coloured with flower petals and spices, were carefully being finished off on the ground. Surrounded by more flowers. As we entered the garden kids ran up to us to drape flower garlands around our necks. Strand after strand was placed over our head as each beaming child lined up with their lovingly made garland. It was getting heavy. I was an easier target being quite a bit shorter than Jess but I could see that she was struggling under the weight of the flowers as well. This was going to be a long day. I hadn't realised that a lot of people were driving up from Colombo for the day. Sponsors of the orphanage. Church leaders. The Bishop. They were all arriving. All wanting to meet us. The sun was getting higher in the sky and the flowers were getting heavier. Eventually the ceremony officially started. The children sang. I'm pretty sure that me and Jess sang as well. It's hard to remember. We were pretty delirious by this stage. I was again reminded of how well behaved these children were compared to other kids I had come across in my travels. Not once did they have to be told to be quiet. They sat completely still during a very long and hot ceremony. Not shifting from their spot on the floor. Faces glowing with excitement, happy to be part of such a momentous occasion.

Eventually me and Jess were asked to cut the flower garland that had been placed across the entrance to the garden and my sign was revealed from beneath the cloth. Our month had come to an end. Our work at the orphanage was done. I wasn't exactly sure what work had actually been accomplished. I felt that I had been given much more than I had offered. I knew the photos would be a hit. I knew that we had made lots of kids very happy. But no, the month there had only highlighted to me that if I really wanted to give something it needed to be long-term. Popping in for a month is almost cruel. All these kids getting so attached to you, and then you just head back to the comforts of your own home. It didn't feel right.

Our month together was over. Jess and I needed to part ways. She was moving to Amman in Jordan. She wanted to learn Arabic. Her Hebrew was flawless. Twelve years at an Israeli school followed by two years in the army meant that she was one of the locals despite not actually having a citizenship. Her parents insistence that she went to a Hebrew school had paid off. She was now moving to Jordan. She was already involved in a fantastic organisation that did reconciliation work between Arabs and Jews. A couple of years of intensive Arabic study would mean that she could be fluent in both languages. If it was possible my admiration for this incredible woman went up another level. She had the world at her fingertips. We smiled as we said goodbye. Promised that we would keep having these adventures. It hurt to say goodbye but I was so grateful that she had joined me for that month.

I was also heading back. I wasn't exactly sure if I was staying in Sydney or moving to this city called Adelaide, a city that I still hadn't quite worked out exactly where it was. But before that I had one stop to make. Alice's boyfriend had a cousin in Kandy. A beautiful mountain city in the cool hills of central Sri Lanka. It was famous for its tea plantations and I had promised I would visit. Once I said goodbye to Mr Bean I caught a train by myself to Kandy. I was left breathless at the beauty of the train ride up the hills. Rain forests on both sides of my train carriage. Birds that I had never seen before. Morfar would have been beside himself. There was no way I could capture any of it with my camera so I just stared out the window in wonder of what I saw.

As the train approached the station I realised that I had no idea who I was actually meeting. I had a moment of hoping that the guy had more information about me than I had about him. Alice's boyfriend was never that into details. As it turns out I didn't have to worry. This giant Fijian man was standing on the platform. A sea of people around him. They parted when I stepped off the train and we were ushered out to the car. It took me a while to register what was going on. On the way to his house we stopped at a temple to see a giant Buddha. We had only stepped out of the car when I realised that we were getting more attention than the Buddha himself. As it turned out, this giant I was visiting was in fact a bit of a celebrity. He was a rugby player that everyone seemed to know about. We got stopped for autographs. Cameras were pulled out. I had 24 hours of feeling incredibly famous. I was happy to hop back on the train and catch my plane back to Sydney.

As soon as I returned I went back to the travel agent to see if I could change my Adelaide flight. I needed a bit more thinking time.

Change your ticket? No, sorry, but your ticket is non-refundable. You can't change it.

There it was. I was moving to Adelaide. I made a point of looking on the giant map in the travel agent's office to locate this new home of mine. Adelaide. The city that I thought was Adelaide was in fact Melbourne. The city I thought was Melbourne was Canberra. Adelaide was actually a bit further west. In the middle of nowhere it seemed. Tucked into the bottom of this giant country. Wow I thought. That is far away from pretty much everything.

I only had one last thing to do. I needed to develop those photos. When Dr. Miller heard about my trip on my last Sunday night in Sydney he told me that he would pay for all the photos to be developed. I was so relieved. I was able to hand them over to Mr Bean who promised he would take them on his next trip over.

I had completed my task. Adelaide was waiting.

12

Taking the Plunge

I was grateful that Anna, Alice's mum had said that she would meet me at the airport. My luggage had grown in the one year I had lived in Australia. My belongings now fit into my suitcase as well as a cardboard box. It wasn't easy lugging it around.

Anna greeted me warmly and I was happy to be reunited with her. I liked her. She was a lovely combination of an academic and a gardener. Her love of research and the dirt was a new mix to me in a female. The only other person I knew like that was Jon, and he seemed a million miles away from Adelaide.

As she drove me to her house from the airport she explained to me that if I ever got lost in Adelaide all I had to do was look for the hills. If I could see them I would know that I was facing east. I was grateful for that piece of information. Directions had never been my strong point and it seemed pretty easy. Hills east. Beach west. Even I could manage that.

We had to stop and wait for a train to pass. The red lights were flashing for what seemed like ages and the warning bells were letting us know that a train was approaching. We waited and waited. Anna explained that we were on Cross Road. A main artery that cuts through the centre of Adelaide. Finally the train came. I was surprised to see that after all that drama of the lights and the bell there was only one carriage. ONE! It sped past in a couple of seconds. Hilarious! I didn't even know trains could travel as solo carriages. It looked so funny. It was tiny. Like a toy train whizzing past. I felt as if I had arrived in a miniature train model set. Or possibly Legoland. Everything was so small. As if it had shrunk. I realised that the sign that had greeted me at the airport might have been stretching the truth somewhat. 'Welcome to the City of Adelaide.' City seemed like a big word for this place. It didn't feel like a city. I couldn't sense a pulse or a rhythm.

As we pulled into Anna's driveway she asked me "so which way are we facing Lillian?". Let me think. The hills are east. I looked up. Looked around me. As far as my eyes could see the hills were right there. From left to right. A long line of hills. I had no idea. South I said. We must be facing south. Anna's eyes said it all. This girl she had just picked up from the airport was so lost.

Anna explained that her and her husband James were happy to host me until I found somewhere to live. What a relief. Yet another family I could graft myself into. Alice was living in Sydney but her three brothers still lived at home as well as her gorgeous five year old sister. For the next couple of days I just tagged along to wherever Anna went. Anna worked long hours at the college. I had been told it was the best place in Australia to study counselling. In my mind that meant that the building would somehow reflect that. I was wrong. The college was sharing a building with a Christian high school. A very drab looking building and I really hoped that the teaching style was going to be more inspiring than the building itself. Anna explained that she would be able to spend more time with me that weekend since there was so much work to do at her office during the week. I kept myself busy while she worked. Introducing myself to the different staff members. The librarian seemed very nice. Nice enough that I felt comfortable asking if there was a chance she might have some work for me. "I used to work in the library in the Israeli Air Force." She seemed intrigued. She did have work for me but couldn't pay. She could organise for my work to go towards my fees instead. Would that suit me? What a relief! My second day in Adelaide and

I had managed to find a way of paying for my school fees. Things were looking good.

Because I was still getting a ride in with Anna every morning and riding back with her late at night I had all day to spend at the college even if I didn't have classes all day. It meant that I spent a lot of time sitting in the communal dining area. This was a chance to chat with the students coming through. It was a great way to make friends and I enjoyed the different conversations I was having. I also got a chance to see what people were bringing in for lunch and dinners. I was still struggling with what Australians considered edible. They were not nearly as extreme as my American friends but not far off. For lunch students would eat these long buns with a huge amount of icing on top followed by a carton of ice coffee. How could that possibly be lunch? Dinners were often a pizza or a pie. Not as a treat but as a regular thing to eat. No one seemed to think about making up a salad at home and bringing it in. Even a sandwich seemed like too much effort.

I got to know some of the students a bit better since we shared the same schedule. They reminded me a bit of Fiona in Sydney. Loud, crass and had big laughs that filled the room. I found them easy to talk to. One of them befriended me. She told me a bit about her life. She had been married a while back. Married? Surely she wasn't divorced? I hardly knew any young people who were married, let alone divorced. It seemed so foreign. She explained that her marriage was annulled. It had never been consummated. It was hard to follow her story as my mind tried to make sense of what she said. She told me that her mother was Aboriginal. Had become pregnant as a teenager. She was forced to have a late-term abortion. When her grandfather came to collect his daughter later that day he had heard a noise from the bin in the clinic. He had searched around. And there in the middle of tissues and bloody rags he had found his granddaughter. Still alive. Crying quietly and kicking her legs in protest. His only response was to take her home and raise her as his own. I was pretty shocked by the story. I knew nothing about Australian history. I knew nothing about anything really. All these things seemed so out of my reality. She explained that her ex-husband actually went to the college as well. He was a student here and she would introduce me.

A couple of days later she did just that. Paul had come into the dining area with his briefcase strapped to his shoulder. He was taking out his Greek workbook ready to do some revision. We were introduced. He seemed nice. Serious but nice. His face lit up when he heard I came from Israel. We talked a bit about that. He explained how he worked at the local Christian radio station. He had a youth program one night a week. That sounded interesting. I told him I would love to come along sometime. Paul told me he had some Greek homework to complete but we could talk another time.

Over the next week we would have a chat when we saw each other around the college. I found out that he was a really good student. He was getting top marks in all his classes. He was studying theology and we had a lot to talk about. I enjoyed his take on things. It was such a relief for me to have someone to talk to that wasn't doing the typical bland conversations that I was still struggling so much with. Paul was intelligent. Really intelligent. I liked that. I liked that we could talk about theological concepts. He seemed to like that I knew what I was talking about. He invited me to come to the radio station with him. I spent the evening there. Impressed with his ease in front of the microphone. He was so animated on air and teenagers would call in from around Adelaide to chat and to request songs. He played songs from edgy Christian bands and I could tell that he was very comfortable in his role. He explained that he was also a chaplain and often spoke at high schools about Jesus. Would I be interested in coming along sometime? Of course I would.

That night when he dropped me back at Anna's house we decided to go for a walk. It was a lovely evening. The light rain meant that it wasn't that cold despite it being in the middle of winter. And the rain was making the Jasmine bushes smell intensely. We walked around the quiet streets enjoying the scents and watching people sitting inside their living rooms watching TV and commented on how they were missing out on real life.

I found Paul really easy to hang out with. He had a gentle nature and our conversations were always interesting. After a week of us spending more time together Paul invited me along to one of his high school lunchtime programs. He did these with another guy who was in charge of the music. Paul would do the preaching. And this young guy, with a great voice and a giant afro, would do the singing. His name was Guy Sebastian.

By now I was sensing that Paul was quite interested in me. More than a friend. Initially I hadn't even considered it being possible because for one, I had never really attracted guys before and secondly he was quite a lot older. I was 21. He was thirty years old. Thirty seemed really old.

Paul started opening up more about his life. He had had a fairly normal upbringing. His parents were not Christian but he had started going to a Salvation Army church as a teenager because of his girlfriend and he had come to love Jesus through them. He joined the navy after school and spent six years as a submariner. That was pretty impressive. A submariner. I had never met one of those before. He was medically discharged from the navy because of a bout of mental illness. He had then started going to a Bible College and miraculously God had healed him. Healed him completely. There was no sign of the mental illness whatsoever. He was now a top student so it was obvious that his brain was fully functioning. Wasn't it amazing that God had healed him? It was. Really amazing. It was a great story. God was obviously very much part of his life.

Paul and I spent more time together outside of college. I would spend time at his house while he studied. He seemed to get quite lost in his love of study so I would occupy myself with my own homework or look through his book collection.

One Sunday afternoon Paul suggested we have a picnic and he brought along his guitar. We ate a nice lunch that I had put together. Baguette, because to me every special moment needed baguette. I had suggested canned salmon as well but Paul convinced me that brie and salami were a better option. I was happy with his choice. It was nice to have Paul show interest. After we ate Paul played the guitar for me and then leaned down and kissed me. It seemed so romantic. My guitar playing theologian kissing me after a picnic in the hills. This was love. Such pure love. I couldn't exactly pinpoint how I felt about Paul. He was a bit elusive. But I loved our conversations. Found his mind fascinating. And he obviously loved God a lot. What else could a girl from Jerusalem ever want?

Paul and I spent more and more time together. I was hanging out at his house a lot. Anna tried to suggest to me that maybe it wasn't such a good idea that I spend so much time there. Temptation would be hard to resist. I knew she was right. Things had already progressed pretty far. I was surprised at how physical our relationship was becoming. I thought back to my boyfriend in Sydney. I had ended things with him because he had placed his hand on my stomach. And here I was doing things with Paul that technically belonged in the marriage bed. Well maybe not exactly in the marriage bed but they were heading in that direction pretty quickly. I wasn't completely comfortable with it. Paul seemed a bit distant. Our conversations were still great but he was a bit hard to connect with emotionally. I put it down to stress. He was putting a lot of energy into his studies. He was giving a lot with his radio and chaplaincy. Maybe if I just gave him a bit more love he would be able to connect a bit more.

I was starting to question if this relationship was really a good thing or not. I was getting quite a few comments at college about being careful with Paul. Don't rush anything. No one said anything specifically but I got the feeling that people were concerned. They obviously couldn't see what I could see. See Paul's amazing mind. Hear the great conversations we were having. Paul had told me that he wanted to show me the different places of his childhood. The schools he went to. The house his grandmother had lived in before she took off and left his 13 year old mother to look after her four younger siblings. The places had meaning to Paul and one evening he drove me around to each place telling me the story. It was a windy night and his stories seemed tinged with sadness. We ended up at the beach. Paul told me that it was Henley Beach. Would I like to walk out on the jetty with him? I thought that sounded great.

By the time we got out of the car we realised that the wind had really picked up. Paul wanted to know if I was sure that I still wanted to walk out on the jetty? To me it was exciting. I didn't mind that the sand was already starting to whip into my face as we stood at the base of the jetty. I was wearing my hiking boots and I was ready for an adventure. As we walked out on the jetty the wind only got stronger. By now the waves were crashing up on either side of us. The wind howling. The spray of the waves hitting our faces. Paul yelled out to me and asked if I wanted to go back to the car. No way. I was going to get to the end of the jetty.

As we kept walking it got harder to move forward. It felt as if we might get swept off. We were holding onto each other. Our faces turned downwards to protect ourselves from the harshness of the wind. As we neared the end of the jetty it felt as if we were being pounded by a massive force that was coming in from the ocean. As if the powers at be didn't want us to be out there. Forcing us to return. It made me want to go further. To push myself all the way to the end of the jetty. The noise was deafening. Neither of us tried to say anything. Even if we had screamed at the top of our lungs nothing would be heard. Only the sound of the ocean roaring along with the wind.

I stood there. This force raging into my body. I wasn't afraid. I wanted to feel it. I wanted it to know that I could match its strength. My face was wet from the waves crashing around me. My hair was whipping around. I felt as if the wind blew right through me. Emptying my lungs of air. My whole body consumed by the combined forces of the sky and the ocean. They were in me.

Paul started to shift. He wanted us to go back. We walked back to the car. Neither of us spoke. Something had happened out there. I couldn't say exactly what. I just knew that something had happened.

We went back to Paul's place. As his housemate finished up a Bible study with some worship songs, Paul and I had sex for the first time. My virginity gone. Something that I had been told was so sacred. So special. So holy. It was lost to the sounds of Geoff Bullock's song "Lord I give you my heart I give you my soul, I live for you alone". I could hear the group in the living room singing each word. I lay there, my silk pyjama shorts still on. The ones that Fiona and Hayley had bought me for my 21st birthday. They had remained on the whole time. Fiona was wrong. You didn't need to get undressed to have sex. You could keep your pants on. What a relief!

I was now no longer a virgin. I hadn't waited for my wedding night as I had always said I would. I had given it away before a ring was on my finger. I had broken the golden rule: "if it's not on, it's not in!". With no ring on my finger I had still let Paul in. Strangely enough I didn't mind. It wasn't actually such a big deal. And sex, well, it wasn't exactly the amazing act that I had expected it to be. What was the big fuss? A bit of grunting and groaning from a silent man, me more a spectator than anything else. I didn't quite get it.

It took me a couple of months to actually catch on that this might be something that I could enjoy too. If I switched my mind off somewhat. Surrendered a bit. Tried to connect with my body to a certain extent. Then yes, I could join in on the grunting and groaning. Who knew? Sex was fun! I could see in Paul's eyes that he needed it. It made him look alive. For once. There was no way I could tell from anything else that this was special to him. There was no dialogue. No feedback. No quiet whispers or calling out. Absolute silence. If it wasn't for that very brief moment when he came inside of me I wouldn't actually know that he had even enjoyed it.

One thing I did know was that this meant that we were going to get married. I was only ever going to have sex with one man. So Paul must be the one. It was as simple as that. The hesitations I had started feeling about his emotional absence, his silence and his constant headaches that meant he didn't want to participate in the many suggestions I had of things we could do together. All those voices from a deep place in me had to be set aside. Paul was now my husband. It was just a matter of me getting a ring on my finger to show the world that we were legally married. As far as I was concerned our marriage had already been consummated that night at the end of the jetty. Even though the experience on the jetty didn't actually feel like it involved Paul as such, but because of what followed in his bedroom later on, I just linked the two together. Paul and I were married in the eyes of God. We just needed a ring and a signed document for friends and the government to seal the deal.

Paul liked the fact that I wasn't into jewellery. I never understood the concept of a diamond ring. Why on earth would I want to wear that? If I had that sort of money, which I knew that we didn't, I would want to spend it on an experience. A trip somewhere. A tropical island. Tell the natives the Good News. Diamonds meant nothing to me. Paul wanted me to have a ring though. He wanted men to know that I belonged to someone. That I was no longer available. I tried to explain to him that he didn't need to worry. Men never looked at me in that way. He insisted.

Not long after we were in Glenelg. We walked past a jewellery store. The items in the window reminded me of home. Jewellery from Israel. Each item was handcrafted. Each piece unique. Silver and gold were fused together. I knew that my ring would come from this little shop. We stepped inside and were greeted by a bearded man. He had a thick German accent. He was working away on his next creation but looked up and spoke to us. Asked us if we had something in mind. We explained that we were looking for a band. Something simple. Nothing fancy. We were getting married and wanted a ring for the occasion. He smiled and explained that this was a very good place to buy a ring from. He and his wife, who I now noticed as well, had been working together for thirty years. They had never been apart. They spent each day together and the ring we would choose was beautiful because of the love that they shared. Perfect I thought. A ring with a story. A German love story. I just had to pick out the one I wanted. I eventually found it. It was a silver band. My new German friend explained that he never used white gold. It looked too manufactured. Too shiny. As if it came from a factory. He liked silver much more. It had a depth to it. The band was uneven. You could tell that it had been handled. If you looked closely you could see a streak of gold. Not much. But gold had been smudged into the silver band. It was beautiful. So perfect in its imperfection. I knew that no one else would have a ring like that. I tried it on. It fit perfectly. Paul chose one for himself. Similar but even chunkier and no gold in it. We asked our new friend if he could set them aside. We needed to wait until we had a bit more money. The rings weren't expensive but with both of us students, and Paul's only income being a pension from his time in the navy, we just didn't have the cash. We were farewelled by two smiling Germans with their arms around each other.

Paul's parents were thrilled about our news. They told me I was very different from the previous girls that Paul had introduced them to. Despite us having nothing in common they still seemed relieved. They laughed as they recounted the story of how Paul had returned from one of his submarine trips in Malaysia with a girlfriend Rosa. Rosa was a prostitute that Paul had befriended. They had fallen in love and Paul had brought her to Australia for a new life. It hadn't lasted long. Rosa was very different to the sweet girl that Paul had first been introduced to in Malaysia. Once her tourist visa expired Paul's parents were so relieved that she had to fly back home.

I tried to look neutral. My mind was whirring. Rosa the prostitute. Prostitute!! What? Somehow this little detail had been excluded from Paul's navy days. Paul's parents had continued talking. Oblivious to what was going on in my head. To them having their son with a prostitute was no big deal. Harmless fun. Their house had a calendar with naked women on it. All a bit of a joke. I got it. It was part of their culture. It didn't mean anything. No one minded. Except I did! A prostitute. Yikes. This was a bit harder to ignore than Paul's growing silence. But I did. I had to ignore the growing feeling of unease. I didn't say a thing. Our wedding was still a few months away but in God's eyes we were married. There was no room for doubts.

Paul's mother was the queen of organisation. She never let a dirty plate sit for more than two seconds before it got whisked away to the sink and washed, dried and put away. She was a woman of action. She wanted to know about this upcoming wedding. What did we have in mind? What were the details? She was happy to put some money towards it but she would need to know what was happening. We hadn't really thought it through but we knew that there was only one place to have the ceremony and that was at Henley Jetty. Henley

Jetty at sunrise. To symbolise a new start. Poor Margaret. I'm pretty sure that it was in this very moment that she realised that the game had changed. She was totally out of her comfort zone. A wedding on a jetty. At sunrise? We explained that it was important to us. No one else needed to come along. As long as we could get someone to actually legally marry us we were happy to just have it be us.

What about a dress? Wouldn't that be cold outdoors? I explained that I wasn't planning on wearing a dress. It wasn't part of our tradition as a family. We wore jeans. Marg was horrified. Jeans! Could I please, please wear a dress? It didn't have to be a wedding dress. But a dress. I said I would think about it. But if I wore a dress she would have to be okay with me wearing my hiking boots with it. Hiking boots?? Yes, my hiking boots were symbolic to me. They had taken me through many desert hikes with Jon. They were going on many more adventures. And I was going to wear them on my wedding day to symbolise a life of adventure with my man. Marriage wasn't going to stop me from the Great Adventure. Marg just gave me a look. Would I wear these hiking boots to the reception as well? What reception? We didn't need a reception. Marg tried her hardest to explain that it was really important to them as a family to have a reception. Somewhere everyone could go and celebrate together. She had friends and workmates that were special to her that would want to be part of it. Alright. We could have a reception. No, she didn't need to organise it. I would do it. Yes, I'd let her know if I needed money but I probably wouldn't. Receptions shouldn't need to cost a lot of money. There it was again. That look.

It turned out to be quite fun planning a wedding. A pastor that studied with me offered his church as a free place to have the reception. The church was in Brighton Beach. I liked that the ocean theme continued. I contacted Farmer's Union. Paul loved their iced coffee. He drank it every day. They seemed surprised at my request but yes they were happy to donate iced coffee for the big day. Food was a bit trickier. The wedding ceremony was at sunrise. At 6:47am to be precise. I doubted many would come for that. But I knew we had friends who would want to be at the reception. I decided to ask about 15 women from the college who I knew were coming. Instead of a wedding gift could they please bring a cake? Turns out that every single one of them said they weren't very good at baking but would buy something from the cheesecake shop. Simple. I had my reception planned.

When I told Marg a couple of days later I could tell she was holding back her real thoughts. She wanted to know about decorations. What decorations had I organised? Oh man. Not decorations as well? This was seriously getting too much. I had agreed to a dress of some sort. I had even agreed to wearing shoes with heels for the reception. I had drinks sorted as well as a huge amount of cheesecakes. That wasn't enough? Apparently not. Marg wanted it to look 'nice'. Fine, I would organise something. Leave it to me. I called a party shop. How much would it cost for thirty balloons? I figured I could get Marg to pay for this. Up until now it hadn't cost a cent. Colours? Oh man. Colours. No, I didn't want white or pink like the lady assumed. I wanted it to be happy. A celebration. Red, blue and yellow. Make it ten of each. There. Done. I had my reception organised. Everyone could be happy.

The big day approached. April 19, 1997. Charles Smith, Paul's favourite lecturer, had agreed to marry us. I really liked him. He genuinely seemed to care about us both. He had a twinkle in his eye and spoke from his heart. There was only one problem. He came from England. Apparently the same part of England that the priest from the movie 'The Princess Bride' came from. It was hard not to laugh every time he opened his mouth. And he was going to marry us! There was a very high chance that somewhere in the ceremony he would need to say the word 'marriage'. I really hoped that I would have enough will power to suppress my laughter if he started the ceremony with "Mawage. Mawage is wot bwings us togeder tooday. Mawage, that bwessed awangment, that dweam wifin a dweam ...".

I figured that not many people would be there anyway. As it turned out I was wrong. Paul's parents said they didn't want to miss it. So did his brother, uncles and aunties. Our friends from college. Even Fiona was going to fly down from Sydney to be there. She was eight months pregnant but didn't want to miss out on her favourite Jew taking the plunge at the end of a jetty at sunrise. I had no idea so many people would want to come. Marg said she had known all along. She also said that people would be hungry. They wouldn't have time to eat breakfast because of our crazy starting time. Yes, I would let her organise to have a lady make pancakes after the ceremony. She would just need to check with the council first.

Everything was in place. The big day was just around the corner. Paul and I decided to drive down to the jetty to have a look. Take it all in. The last time we had been there it had been so intense. It would be nice to see it in daylight and picture us walking out on the jetty. When we got to the jetty I could see that Paul was confused. Something was wrong. I looked around. There was the jetty. But there were all these cafés and shops. I didn't recall them from our evening a few months back. It was the wrong jetty! Paul thought it was called Henley Beach when in fact we were at Grange Beach. God had met me at the end of Grange Jetty. Not Henley Jetty! I could see Paul panicking. It was too late to change anything. There wasn't enough time to get council approval. Henley Jetty would have to do. We could stand on the end and look out across the ocean and see Grange Jetty in the distance. We would make sure to ask someone to get a photo of us with the real jetty in the background. Sorted! The big day could start.

Alice flew in from Sydney a couple of days before the wedding. She said that she wanted to make my hair nice for the day. She often curled my hair and put makeup on me in Sydney as a fun activity. It was the only time I ever did that. I agreed that she could. We would need an early start. If we had to meet at the jetty at 6:30am for a 6:47 start the hair and makeup would need to begin at 5:00. That seemed very early and we would need an early bedtime the night before. Except I couldn't find the shoes that I had agreed to wear for the reception. I had promised Marg that I would wear them and now they were missing. Alice and I spent the whole night driving from house to house trying to find these shoes. These shoes that I didn't even want to wear. They were in a rubbish bag in the car the whole time. We got 45 minutes sleep that night.

When we forced ourselves to get up in the dark we got dressed quickly. A friend of Paul's had made me a simple dress. I was happy with it. It cost $70 for the fabric and the sewing. Marg covered that cost as well. As I was lacing up my hiking boots I looked over at Alice. She was getting dressed in white. She very much resembled a bridesmaid. Something I had told her I wasn't interested in having for the day. I had never quite seen the point of bridesmaids. Surely they were a distraction to the real event. But here she was. Doing a very good impersonation of one, even her white shawl wrapped around her shoulders couldn't take away from the fact that she had a very special status that morning. I had to laugh. She was such a romantic. Fine. She could pretend to be my bridesmaid. I'd give her that.

Alice completed my hair and makeup. She knew the rules. No colour. Nothing flashy. It had to look natural. It had to look as if I wasn't wearing makeup. She'd done a good job. We were ready to step out of our motel room and walk down to the jetty to meet the gathering crowd of people. There were so many. Who knew that we had that many people who cared about us? As I looked around at the smiling faces I felt something get forced into my hands. It was a bunch of white flowers. Anna was wrapping my hands around them. She had spent the night arranging them for me. When I tried to protest she told me you can't have a bride without flowers. Fine, I'll hold the flowers. Jeez. It really wasn't easy trying to just get married. There were all these extra things that I had never even considered to be important. Obviously they were. Just not to me.

Charles came up to me and said it was time to walk down the jetty. Paul joined us. As we walked down I looked behind me. There were so many people following us. Some fishermen were standing on the jetty. Enjoying their early-morning ritual. "Mamma Mia!!" The small Italian man grinned. He gave me a kiss on my cheek and wished me a life of happiness. We continued down the jetty. All our friends gathering around us. The ocean was perfectly calm. The sky was clear. All of a sudden a dolphin jumped out from the water.

It was the perfect morning. And just as the sun rose the ceremony started. Thankfully I managed to keep myself from laughing at Charles. It was a beautiful ceremony. We had written our own vows. We exchanged our handcrafted rings. All the time Alice standing as close as she possibly could, looking very much like a bridesmaid.

The ceremony was just what we had wanted. Everyone came up after and let us know how meaningful it had been. How profound. So intimate. See? It's fine to do things as you want. Not follow the script. We don't all need to have cookie cutter weddings. Who says they need to follow a formula? The pancakes were a hit. Marg had been right. Our friends were hungry. I noticed that there was a guy there who I didn't recognise with a fairly impressive camera. He came up to me with a massive grin on his face. He was from the Advertiser, the local newspaper. News had reached him that a couple were getting married at sunrise on a jetty. He didn't want to miss the story. This was big. Not much happens in Adelaide besides footy injuries, the occasional beached whale and creepy murders. This was something out of the box and it needed to be reported. We agreed to posing for photos and in return we had quite a few professional photos of our wedding at no cost at all.

Paul and I had been given a night in a fancy hotel looking over the ocean by a friend. They had felt sorry for us spending our wedding night at home. It was a very fancy room. Perfect for Paul to do his Greek revision in. I spent my much anticipated wedding night sitting on my bed watching my new husband go over his Greek verbs. The next morning the paper was delivered to our door. There we were. An article about us and some photos of us grinning about our future together.

13

Earth Mamma

Paul and I started our new life together in a house not far from the college. We couldn't believe our luck. The house had a sauna! I was really looking forward to a winter with a sauna but it was not to be. Within three months of getting married I was pregnant. Less than a year after arriving in Adelaide. Paul was thrilled. He beamed as he repeated out loud. "I'm fertile! I'm fertile!" Our first child together was conceived right after our daily ritual of watching M.A.S.H together. Paul loved watching TV. It had never really been my thing. We had one off and on during my childhood. Mainly off. To my dad it was a tool of the devil. So were movies. They were to be avoided. At all cost. I remember my mother convincing my dad to come along to see a movie with us. Possibly the only movie I ever saw with him. He walked out half way. "I don't want to have my emotions controlled by a screen." He said as he left the theatre. I could see tears on his face. Clearly Anne of Green Gables was too much for my dad to handle.

For Paul though, TV was an escape. And if I wanted to spend time with my new husband I might as well get used to watching TV. A lot of TV. The news. Sixty Minutes. The Simpsons. Cheesy American sitcoms from the eighties. He loved it all. I had a crash course in popular culture the first few months of our marriage. It made me twitchy. I needed action. Sitting watching TV made me restless. I needed something to happen. It was a similar feeling to when I was a child. All the girls around me were into horses. It was just what you did as a preteen girl in southern Sweden. I convinced my mother to pay for classes. The stables were not far from our apartment. I could cycle there on the weekend.

There were so many girls wanting to learn how to ride a horse. I was put into a group and week after week we were instructed about the care of horses. How to brush them. How to feed them. How to clean out their stables. There was so much that needed to be explained. They sure stretched those classes out. I was so incredibly bored. I just wanted to ride a horse. I had visions of being given a helmet, a saddle and being able to ride around the flat fields surrounding our neighbourhood. Maybe even riding out to the water tower by myself. Galloping away from my family. Not cleaning out a stable.

Learning to ride a horse was a slow, slow process. Eventually we were taught how to put the saddle on. And then how to climb on. Each step involved a separate class. I was going crazy. I just wanted to ride a horse! We were then allowed to be slowly walked around the inside of the stable. A teenage instructor taking her role very seriously. This was killing me. Week after week. Finally we were told the good news. We had passed the initial training. We would finally be allowed out on the street. We would be able to ride our horses around the block. I was thrilled. All week I thought about it. The excitement building. Me on a horse. On the street. Such freedom!! I could feel the wind in my hair. The horse beneath me. Such power!

As usual the process was painfully slow. Lining up for the helmet. Lining up for the saddle. Brushing the horse. It felt like hours before we were allowed to lead our beasts out into the street. After a lot of waiting we were given the go ahead to mount our horse. I wasn't sure how many girls were there. The line ahead of me seemed to reach all the way up the street. An incredible long line of horses with girls on top. Instructors alongside. All the classes had been combined for the big event. It took a lot of organising and it had to be done just so. The twitching in my body was becoming unbearable. I was so incredibly restless. Why oh why couldn't they just let us ride? I knew I could do it. Knew I would be fine. I was being forced into submission when freedom was so close. The giant horse below me. The fields calling our names. I just wanted to go. I wanted something to happen. The twitching intensified.

I started to nudge my horse a bit. Just a bit. But still, it was a nudge. I waited. This was a well-trained horse. I nudged some more. A bit stronger this time. Still nothing. This horse was so Swedish. Totally following protocol. I couldn't contain myself anymore. I looked at the long line of horses ahead of me. Looked back at the long line of horses behind me. And with the strongest force I could muster, without drawing too much attention from the instructors who were waiting beside us, I kicked my horse as hard as I could. His front legs came up in an instant. Kicking the horse in front of us in the process. The horse behind me neighed as my horse sped off and left me behind. It was pandemonium.

I was on the ground. My horse charging down the street. Horses running everywhere. Teenage instructors calling out. Trying to calm everyone down. The moment was gone. The outing cancelled. We were all led back to the stables. My cheeks were burning. I knew I was guilty. I hoped that no one else knew that. I hoped they assumed that my horse had just tapped into a wild side. I rode my bike home. Announcing that I was back for dinner. No one needed to know. I was just happy that my helmet had protected my fall.

That's how I felt about TV. I just needed real action. Sitting there waiting for Paul to engage with me. Wanting to do something. Go somewhere. Talk. Anything. It's probably why I got pregnant. I just needed something to happen instead of watching yet another episode of the Simpsons.

Financially things were pretty tight. I didn't need to worry though. Paul was in charge of the money. He did it all. Paid the rent. Paid the bills. Gave me my allowed amount for the fortnightly shopping. We would go together. I didn't have a driver's licence so it meant something we would do together. I really looked forward to these outings. It meant spending time with Paul who otherwise was busy studying or practicing his guitar. I had no idea what items to buy from the shop. Domestics were a complete mystery to me. I knew I had big shoes to fill. Margaret was the ultimate. Paul would tell me about her beef Stroganoff as he slowly ate my burnt offerings. I was good at baking. But Paul didn't like baked goods. Didn't like sweets. He liked savoury. He liked his mum's cooking. I was trying. I was really trying. I started buying the same little sachets from the shops. Surely it couldn't be that hard. I just needed to fry the meat and add water to these little magic mixes. My efforts were appreciated but I could tell that Paul would much rather just order his favourite takeaway instead of eating my creations. Chicken and chips were his staple. He would eat that and have a couple of bottles of beer. Sometimes followed by red wine. I did find it interesting that he always seemed to have enough money for alcohol. Even when there wasn't enough money for fruit. I'm not sure why but I never questioned it. I just accepted it as how things were. Sometimes he would say that his parents had given him a slab of beer. It seemed fair enough. His parents had a never-ending supply of alcohol in the house. Why wouldn't they be giving that to their hard working son who was doing so well at his studies? I didn't complain. Paul would often buy me a family block of Cadbury chocolate at the same time as stocking up on his ever diminishing beer supplies. The perfect distractions from the mind numbing TV shows I was watching night after night.

My belly was growing. I was pregnant. It was hard to gauge how much of the growth was baby related and how much of it was thanks to my Cadbury consumption. I was just grateful to have a husband that was so generous. We didn't have much money but he still made sure I had chocolate. I would sit there and eat row after row. The top of my mouth feeling gluggy from the overly sweet squares while Paul enjoyed his variety of drinks. During the day we were both at school. By now I had been elected as President of the Student Council. It meant more time commitments. I often led worship sessions in the morning. I would look after new students. Organise fundraisers. I really enjoyed it. It was a good distraction from my classes. I was really struggling with those.

It felt as if everyone who was going through the same counselling degree as me was overly bitter at what life had handed them. Classes became a place to vent. Who knew there were so many men who hated women? Who knew there were so many women who hated men? Everyone seemed to have their own list of grievances. My classmate Laura and I started keeping a tally. Each complaint got a tick next to a name. It kept us occupied. It kept us sane. We were by far the youngest in the class. Most of our classmates were in their thirties and forties. We really felt as if doing this degree was a cheap way for them to have therapy. It was very hard to be interested in the topic when it was continually interrupted by someone who had an example from their life of the pain inflicted upon them. Mainly from a spouse. Or a parent. Usually from the opposite gender. I made sure my assignments got done. Did my readings for the tutorials. But I wasn't engaging in the lessons. I didn't want to become part of the masses. Didn't want to be a man hater. Or blame my parents for my faults. It was such an ugly trait and I wouldn't join in.

Laura and I got along really well. I enjoyed her company. Her uncle was the school principal. She had gone to a very Christian high school. But she was spunky. She had an edge. She invited me to come to her parent's farm for her birthday weekend. I was thrilled to be able to go. Paul didn't mind me going. Said he would be able to get some more schoolwork done. It was the first time we would be apart since we married. I spent one night away. Helping Laura with the work needed to pull off a 21st birthday party. I finally understood why my picnic on the Opera House steps wasn't deemed worthy. Australians took their 21st birthdays very seriously. Photos from their childhood. Embarrassing stories in the speeches. I hadn't realised that turning 21 was such a significant milestone. In Israel the milestone is at age 12 for girls and 13 for boys. And of course I had missed out on mine since we didn't really have any of those traditions. I realised that I had pretty much missed out on every milestone so far. Never really belonging to the country I was in. Or having parents who were bucking the system. Either way it meant that I didn't have those events that map out our lives.

A couple of weeks later I got home early from college. I was tired. My bump was getting heavier. The house was empty. Paul was still at the college. Some bills were in the mail. I figured I might as well have a look and then pass them on to Paul to pay. I was shocked to see our phone bill. It was a huge amount. Bigger than our weekly rent. Surely there was a mistake. The phone company must have added something extra on. I looked through the numbers. There was a phone call from two weeks earlier. The date rang a bell. It was Laura's 21st. I didn't recognise the number. I decided to dial it. See who would answer. My face started to burn as I heard a very seductive voice giving me my different options. Did I want an Asian lady to speak to? I slammed the phone down. Shocked at what I had heard. I sat there holding the letter. My mind racing. Trying to make sense of it. Paul got home a while later. He hadn't even put his briefcase down when I told him that our phone bill had arrived. His face was pale but very quickly cleared up as he started to explain.

The night that I had gone to Laura's house he had been reading the passage in the Bible where Jesus asks the men who were going to stone the prostitute who there was without sin? It made him think about these poor prostitutes. How difficult it must be for them. How they must struggle so much. He wanted to know what would bring them to such a low point. To a point of giving their body to a stranger. He wanted to do some research. He found this number in the paper and called. The lady he spoke with was lovely. So grateful that it wasn't a man who was desperate for sexual contact. It was someone who cared. Someone who wanted to hear her story. They talked for ages. She felt heard. He listened to her pain. He was able to minister to her. It was unfortunate that the bill was so high. He would need to ask his parents to borrow some money. But he was grateful for the opportunity to help someone. He understood her pain. Understood that passage in the Scriptures better.

I hadn't expected that answer. I didn't know what I was expecting. But not that. It was fair enough. Prostitutes obviously needed to be heard. It was very considerate of Paul to facilitate that. I felt bad that his parents would have to pay so much money. I knew they would though. They were very generous when asked. I kind of wished we could have used that money for us though. We had a lot of expenses coming up and this would mean that we couldn't ask them for help for a while. I went on with my evening. Trying to ignore the unease that was brewing inside me.

Paul was gaining popularity at the college. The staff were paying attention to his work. He was getting top marks in everything and was now asked to not only lead tutorials but also to fill in when lecturers were away. I was thrilled at his success. One of his tutorial students asked if Paul would be able to give her extra theology lessons. She was a lovely lady. In her late forties. Very wealthy. Very, very wealthy. She would come to our house once a week for these extra tutorials. Paul loved having all of this acknowledgement. Denise was not just impressed by Paul's insights. She also loved his class presentations and the sermons he would give from time to time. She explained to us during one of her visits that she was involved with an organisation that looked for young leaders in Australia. It was nationwide. Those that got selected were sent to Canberra for a training course in leadership. Would Paul consider participating?

This was a fabulous offer. A huge boost. The break through that Paul had been waiting for. There was only one catch. The long weekend in Canberra coincided with the birth of our baby. In fact, it was a week after my due date. Surely I wouldn't be fine with him going? I knew Paul had to go. This was too good to miss. Even with our baby arriving. I explained very carefully to Paul that he needed to go to Canberra. I wholeheartedly knew that he was meant to go. It was risky because there was a huge chance our baby would come at the same time. But if that did happen, I had already made peace about Paul missing the birth.

Denise was impressed with my dedication to the cause. She looked me up and down. How would I like to go shopping with her? Go and get myself some new clothes? We could have a day together in the city. Have a shopping spree. I was taken aback. A shopping spree? Didn't that just happen in the movies or the cheesy sitcoms that Paul liked to watch. Why on earth would I like a shopping spree? No thanks. I tried in the nicest way possible to tell her I couldn't think of anything worse. But I did tuck her offer away. Feeling like I might have a chance to redeem it down the track for something a bit more up my alley.

The college had moved location by now. It was now in a beautiful building. An old English structure. Built to be an orphanage. It was a very nice change from the high school that it used to be in. The college had to expand. It was now offering an education stream as well. Training young people to become Christian teachers. I decided to double my workload. I would do both. Continue with my counselling studies as well as do the teaching degree. It seemed very doable. I didn't have much to complete with my first degree and I would complete the teaching degree while my baby slept next to me in class. Easy!

On the first day of the education degree we were introduced to our lecturers. Anna, now the head of the department, asked everyone to come up and give a two minute presentation about themselves. It was an icebreaker. A way to show who we were. We could tell a bit about our story. Share some photos on an overhead projector. Read a favourite passage from a book. It was an opportunity to connect with our new classmates. I was one of the last to share. I hadn't prepared anything. I was so busy with activities for the student council. Busy watching crap TV with my new husband. Busy growing a baby inside me. I stepped up to the podium and started to tell my story. All of it. Only thing was, I was speaking in Hebrew. First people looked bewildered. Then amused. Then just plain weirded out. I could see Anna motion with her hand that I should wrap it up. Move on to English.

After the activity had finished up I tried to avoid Anna. I figured she would have something to say to me. I felt for her. I knew she wanted me to follow the rules but I just couldn't. Someone tapped me on the shoulder and was wanting to talk to me. This tall man with a giant smile. He introduced himself. Said his name was Jason. He had moved across from Melbourne with his wife Jo, two young daughters and baby boy. He was in the same course as me. He thought my presentation was wild. How crazy that I hadn't explained my story in English afterwards. He really wanted to know more about me. He was sure that I would get along with his wife. He would love for us to be friends. I liked Jason straightaway. His energy was infectious.

A few days later Jo came along to the college with her kids in tow. A keen mind. She might be a housewife with three kids but she was something else. I felt a connection. I was really happy to hear that they didn't live far from the college. Walking distance. It meant that I would be able to meet with them outside of college. I still hadn't got my licence. I was either needing to catch public transport, which was hard to do unless all you wanted to do was to go into the city. It was that or get Paul to drive me which was hard with his college commitments. While Jo and I talked I got to hold her baby boy. He was absolutely gorgeous. Chocolate eyes. Totally bald. Long limbs. And a gorgeous grin. The perfect six month old baby. I wanted the baby in my belly to be just like him. He curled up in my arms like a little monkey. If my baby was anything like Jack I would be overjoyed.

A few days later I was invited back to Jason and Jo's home. It felt so warm. There was such a generous energy there. I felt very welcome. I really liked this family. We didn't have anything in common. Their lives were so different to mine. Jason and Jo had both grown up outside Melbourne. Lived there their whole lives. Only now moving across to Adelaide to study but would return to Victoria later since that's where their families were. I could tell they were all about family. Their eyes lit up as they spoke of their brothers and sisters. Funny stories about their parents. Nieces and nephews. Jo's family had the same configuration as mine. Three boys, three girls. It was almost impossible for me to imagine having all my family live within a couple of hours or each other.

At this stage I had my parents in Virginia Beach, choosing to stay a bit longer in the States so my mother could transfer her credits and do a Masters in Counselling. Susanna was in Kurdistan. Raphael was still living in Dallas. Sam was in Jerusalem. Ezra was living in Virginia Beach but was about to join the U.S. Air Force and be stationed in Italy. Abigail was living with my parents as well. So yes, our families might have sounded similar in numbers and genders but that's where it ended.

I really liked how in the midst of making a soup or changing a nappy Jo was still able to have an in depth conversation. Still able to take a point I made and go further with it while putting a bandaid on her daughter's knee. It was so refreshing. So great to connect with a woman like this. In those hours in her home I added her to my basket of strong, wild women who looked at life from a deeper perspective. Magdalena, Jess, Alice and now Jo. She fit right in.

As my due date approached and I knew that I needed to have a back-up plan for the birth in case Paul was in Canberra, Jo was the obvious choice. I asked her if she would be okay to be my birth support if Paul didn't have a chance to catch a plane back in time.

I had been really fortunate to be part of a pilot program at a public hospital. They were trialing having a midwifery service that involved each woman being assigned the same midwife the whole pregnancy, birth and post birth care. I had heard about the program through a weekend workshop that Paul and I took to prepare us for the birth. It was meant to be an eight week yoga course that culminated in a two day workshop. There was no way I would go along to a yoga class. Knowing full well that it would open me up to all sorts of evil forces.

However, I liked the idea of the birth workshop. It was run by a woman who was born in England but grew up in Israel, who had been in the Air Force and, bizarrely enough, who also had a breast reduction. How could I say no to a birth workshop with her?

It was during this weekend that I kept hearing the name Aurianne. Everyone spoke of Aurianne. She was the ultimate if you wanted a natural birth. Natural birth. I wasn't exactly sure what that meant but it had a nice ring to it. I made sure to get her details and made an appointment at the hospital. I was so grateful to get a spot in the program. Aurianne was just as lovely as I had been told. A humble woman. A very still presence. A calm soul. She almost whispered when she spoke. She welcomed us both with open arms. Wanted to know our stories. Me being pregnant seemed almost like a side issue. Aurianne wanted to get to know us. Not just my bump. It felt right. I knew I was in safe hands. Each visit to the hospital we would chat about our lives. My belly getting measured discreetly as we spoke. Everything was going ahead beautifully. The only issue really was the fact that Paul was about to fly to Canberra. Part of being in this program meant that I had access to the birthing centre. A double bed in the room. Mood lighting. All hospital equipment hidden behind regular household items like paintings and shelves. It looked like a home. It would be lovely to birth my baby in this safe space. Possibly a bit of worship music playing in the background. My loving husband massaging my feet as I nibbled on a block of Cadbury chocolate.

As the day approached my belly was getting bigger. Much bigger. No matter how relaxed Aurianne was, she still needed to report back to the hospital about her findings. On one of my visits she had a sad look in her eyes as she explained that my growing bump was becoming a concern for the hospital. As much as they wanted to support me having a natural birth this was going to be a giant baby. It would need to come out soon. Not just that but I would need to have a doctor come and check me out. Aurianne had tears in her eyes. She obviously knew more about the implications than I realised. Not long after a doctor stepped into the tiny room that Aurianne used. The mood shifted straightaway. Up until then I had only had Aurianne as a contact point. The doctor was abrupt. Listing off all the dangers I was putting myself into. Convinced that I was risking myself and the baby. This could potentially be an emergency situation. Involving an innocent life. Was I aware of that? Did I really understand the seriousness of the situation? Clearly I didn't. I was too busy growing a baby that I hadn't realised I was hosting a time bomb. Each second bringing me closer to certain death and destruction. The doctor spent a lot of time measuring my bump. Feeling for the baby's arms and legs. It hurt. He was rough. My pelvis ached. How could Aurianne get the same answers but not inflict any pain in the process? How could these doctor's hands be so harsh? So mechanical.

Didn't he realise there was a woman attached to the bump he was manhandling? "4.6 kilos. At least!" According to the doctor that's how much this baby weighed already. And I had a couple of days until my due date. This was a monster. This baby inside of me was giant. The doctor suggested I deliver the baby straightaway. The whole time Aurianne just held my hand. Looked me in the eyes. I could tell that she didn't believe anything this doctor was saying. His words filling up the tiny room. The doctor left the room in a huff but not before telling me that I knew what I needed to do. He was right. I did. I knew that I had to dismiss everything he had just said and just let this baby do what it needed to do. I didn't have a giant growing inside of me. I just had a short torso. Just like Mormor did. Like my mother. Like my sisters. A short torso that doesn't allow much space for a baby to grow. Alice had moved to Adelaide after unexpectedly becoming pregnant despite being told that she was infertile from the surgery she had just before I met her at Mission College. Her dancer's body, with its long torso almost hid the fact that she was pregnant at all. Her baby could stretch out completely. Align itself with Alice's long spine and stay hidden. My baby on the other hand was poking right out. Scaring doctors. Or at least this doctor. I was relieved to see him go.

Aurianne reminded me that the doctor just had to follow protocol. We didn't actually have to do what he had suggested. We just needed to listen. Hear what he said and then choose for ourselves. We chose to let the baby stay in. Paul was flying out a few days later. It seemed inevitable that he would miss the birth but we had both made peace about that. Paul was thrilled to fly to Canberra with Denise and her husband. It was a huge privilege and it really felt like the start of something new for Paul. Who knew where this opportunity could lead?

Thankfully the baby was very happy to remain inside me. However, on the day before Paul was returning from Canberra the doctor decided that enough was enough. He wouldn't play my game anymore. I needed to come into the hospital and get some gel inserted that would trigger the labour. I called Jo. She was happy to drive me there. She came and collected me straightaway. Aurianne had come in especially to be there for me and to explain the procedure. She also had to break the news that the doctor had decided that I couldn't birth in the birthing centre. I was too overdue to be considered safe. This meek and mild angel of a midwife was holding back. I could tell that she wanted to swear. Curse this doctor who was using his power for evil instead of good.

The gel kicked in straightaway. I could feel my body responding. A pulse had started deep down in my being. It was starting to send out a message. My life was about to change. I was on a path that I couldn't step off from. The birthing process had begun. We were told to return once the contractions were stronger. Jo got me back to her house just in time for Paul to step through the doors. It was just after midnight. He had made it back from Canberra! He wouldn't miss out on the birth of his baby. I was thrilled. My husband had been able to participate in a life changing leadership course and now he would also be at the birth with me. I had taken a risk, trusted my gut and won. I hugged Paul and asked him to take me home. My body was starting to hurt.

That pain continued through the night and by early morning Paul drove me back to hospital. I hadn't slept at all. I figured that the baby must be coming soon. When I got to the hospital the doctor was there waiting for me. He asked for more gel to be inserted. Aurianne left her sleeping kids at home to make sure that she was the one who did it and not the doctor. I was grateful not to have his hands inside me. The gel hit me like a train. This time I got slammed. The pain I had been in now a distant memory. My body was now consumed by aliens or demons. I wasn't sure which. But it hurt like hell. My body was no longer mine. It was getting thrown around by a force much greater than me. I had absolutely no control. I was trying to ease the pain with hot water from the shower. It helped a bit but as the pain intensified I tried to get away from it.

I threw myself around the bathroom. My legs banging against the tub. I was howling. Screaming from the pain. What was happening to me? Why had no one told me that birth was a death? That I was about to die. I could see the balcony through the window. We were on the fifth floor. If I could only climb over the fence and jump off! Instant death was the answer. Why go through this only to die in agony? I wanted it to stop. I pleaded, I begged. Give me something! Give me something please!! God!! God!! I was calling out to God for help. He had always been a silent force in my life. But He had never been as silent as he was while I was in the process of birthing my baby. I called out again and again for God to help me. Nothing. Nothing at all. At one point my voice broke. I pleaded with Aurianne. Please. Give me something. I need something. Did I want some pain relief? Did I want to scrap my plan of having a natural birth?

No! It wasn't pain relief that I wanted. I wanted a bullet. I wanted Aurianne to fetch my Uzi and shoot me on the spot. How could she not know that? I looked over at Paul. He looked concerned. His Greek work books in front of him. I tried to comfort him with a look but instead I just screamed out in pain as yet another pack of demons began tearing my body apart. There was a towel rack on the wall in the bathroom. I grabbed on to it. Pulling my body up as I screamed. Amazed at the force I could feel in my body. The sound coming out of me was so foreign. It belonged to an animal. A wounded animal. That was it. I was no longer a woman. I was a wild animal. Who was about to die. I let out a scream that didn't just fill that bathroom. It filled the whole hospital, it reached from the hills to the ocean. And in one giant push that had nothing to do with me. A baby slid out of me. Just like that.

In an instant there was calm. The water from the shower still pouring over me. Washing away the blood. I was holding a baby. I was holding my baby. These massive eyes were looking at me. Taking me in. Asking me if I was the mother. I held the body against mine. This was my baby. I was a mother. The smell was intoxicating. I couldn't stop inhaling. Those eyes looked around the room. Looked at Paul. Looked at Aurianne. Taking it all in. How did we go from a room filled with such noise to absolute stillness? This baby had created peace. Everything was all right in the world. Something shifted inside me. A vault that I never knew existed moved in my chest. Just where I thought my heart was. A giant weight moved. A stone rolled away and this river of utter and complete love gushed out of me. I was in total awe. This flood that came from the centre of the universe was now flowing out of me. Consuming me. I was a mother.

In that moment I felt united with all the other mothers who were at that very exact time sitting in that sacred space of holding their baby for the first time. In that moment I went from aligning myself with men. Thinking that I could match them in their power. I could be one of them. To sitting down with my sisters around the globe. Our breasts bare. Holding our babies close. Inhaling their scent. Exhaling our love. I was smitten. This baby in my arms had triggered a love that needed a language of its own. For the first time in my life I was speechless. I sat there in awe. Smiling at this baby. Slowly starting to take in the rest of the shape. The eyes. The face. The perfect lips. The nose that seemed so familiar. The forehead. The perfect body. I had a son. It had taken ages to even register. The love that I had for this person in my arms had flooded in before I even knew if I had a son or a daughter. But now I knew I had a son. I looked at his face. His wise face. I knew he was Asher. I was the mother of Asher. I finally belonged.

14

Red Rose of Cairo

The incredible thing that happened after Asher was born was that my brother Sam contacted me. Out of the blue I got an email from him. I never heard from him, and here he was emailing me.

> *Lill, I'm coming to Adelaide! Long story but I got a gig with the team from Feast of Tabernacles. Will explain later. I'll see you in three weeks!*
>
> *Love, Sam*

I was shocked. My brother Sam coming to see me? This would be the first time I had a family member come and visit me in Australia. And it was Sam! My brother that I shared so much with. We had all our friends together. All our memories of trips and playing music with Jon. All those hours of walking our friends home after a night in Jerusalem. He would be here. With me. He would meet Asher. He would be an uncle to my son. It was hard to imagine. And what was that about the Feast of Tabernacles? Really? Sam had become a Feastie Beastie as we used to call them? Those extra-terrestrial beings that seemed to have that Shekinah glow around them. The glossed over eyes. Saying Yeshua instead of Jesus. Often a tambourine tucked into their embroidered bag from the Old City. The men with beards. The women with long braids rolled into a bun. I avoided them at all cost.

Now my brother Sam had become one of them. It was hard to believe. Sam the charmer. Sam who made women swoon. Even men were charmed by Sam. His eyelashes so long that they faded and got split ends in them. His eyes twinkling. When Jeff from Mission Institute met him on one of his trips to Jerusalem he returned with the news. "Your brother is identical to you! Just more hairy!" It was the nicest thing anyone had ever said to me. Sam has a certain dynamic about him that makes you feel as if you are with a celebrity.

Paul was excited as well. Paul really liked Sam. They had met six months earlier in Israel. Around the time of my wedding, Susanna had announced that she was getting married as well. It was incredible. My sister Susanna was getting married, and only six months after me. I couldn't miss it. I had to be there. The wedding would be in Cairo. Susanna had the brilliant insight to invite her family to her wedding. Unlike her younger sister who just assumed no one could come so why not save some money on postage? The invite arrived the same day as Paul's tax return. We would be able to go to my sister's wedding. Paul would meet my family! I was only four months pregnant so travelling was not an issue. Marg wanted to know what I would wear. Wear? I would wear something comfortable. Maybe something light since Cairo is hot. No, I wasn't going to buy something just because it was a wedding. Margaret tried to explain that it's nice to wear something special for special occasions. In the end I looked through her wardrobe and picked something out. It was comfortable and light. Perfect.

Raphael and Sam met us at the airport in Tel Aviv. I was beaming. I was back. Back in my country. I had my husband by my side. My baby inside me. It was so good to be home. Raphael was overjoyed at having something to tease me about. I was pregnant. That didn't just happen. Lilli-Fox, as he liked to call me because of my connection with big breasted Samantha Fox, had been bonking. I now became Bonki-Fox. Oh the pleasure it gave him. I had been at Elinka's house for about an hour when I got grabbed from behind. "Bonki-Fox!! It's soooo good to see youuuu!"

Ugh. It had started. Raphael and his incessant tickling. It was so wrong. Had always felt so wrong. Now being pregnant, my body belonging to Paul, my brother's hands were more profane than ever before. I looked him straight in the eyes.

Raphael, don't ever tickle me again. Ever. If you even attempt to tickle me I'm telling you right now that I will touch your balls. I will actually reach over and touch your balls. I'm letting you know now that if you don't want your balls touched by your sister, don't ever tickle me again!

He could tell I was serious but decided to totally ignore what I said. Ezra had overheard the exchange. He was fuming. How dare I talk to my brother like that? Did I not realise what I was saying? You can't touch a man's balls. They are special. They are out of bounds.

You need to apologise Lill, tell Raphael that you didn't mean it. Raphael seemed to be gaining strength from hearing Ezra talk.

Yeah, Bonki-Fox, relax already, don't be so serious! His hand coming in to tickle my ribs.

In a flash I went to grab his balls. It was just a touch on his jeans but Ezra exploded and flew out of his chair. I stood up and told him that it was the last time he would ever try to tickle me. And it was. He never tickled Bonki-Fox again. I walked away, glancing over at Paul who had been there the whole time and not said a word. Not once coming in to defend me and to tell my brothers that they needed to lay off, that they needed to respect their sister. Nothing.

We travelled down to Cairo the next day. It would be my first time in Egypt, unless you counted a very brief snorkelling session in the Red Sea on a school trip. Cairo felt like the Old City of Jerusalem on steroids. Total mayhem. Crazy traffic. Testosterone pulsing through the market. Men calling out. I was very happy to just be there for the wedding and head home as soon as we could. I didn't like it at all. Susanna's soon-to-be husband, Youssef, wanted to take us to the pyramids. I had never been a tourist in my life. The pyramids seemed a good place to start. I tried to look interested. The heat was overwhelming. The men seemed to think my body was a billboard. Staring at every part of it. Trying to see what was on offer. I lasted for less than an hour. A couple of photos of me pretending to kiss the Sphinx, one of me hugging a pyramid, and I was ready to call it a day.

Susanna had all of us with her as she got ready for her wedding. Raphael was having a great time showing Susanna some moves for her wedding night. It was hilarious. The same old family dynamics, but now with all of us as adults. The wedding ceremony itself was very traditional. Everything exactly how it should be. There were no dolphins jumping in the background. No Italian fishermen. Our weddings could not have been any more different.

If you get married in Cairo there is only one place to have the reception. On the Nile. On a boat on the Nile to be exact. I would like to say that I spent the evening dancing on the Nile overjoyed by my sister's new marital status. But no. I was so exhausted from being pregnant. I had to lie down. I tried to stay awake but I couldn't. The last thing I saw before nodding off was Raphael dragging Elinka onto the dance floor. She was wearing her tightest red dress. She looked hot. She wasn't going to miss the chance to bust some moves while floating along the longest river in the world. No way! She was the lady in red. The rose of Cairo. The woman of the night. Little did she know that the next time she would find herself in Cairo it would be for a very different purpose. Arriving in disguise. To rescue the bride who was now sitting next to her groom.

My brothers had organised to fly back to Israel but Paul and I couldn't afford it so we took the bus with Elinka. We figured it was pretty straightforward. We were wrong. So wrong. Elinka had found some fresh basil growing on the side of the road. She loved fresh basil. She picked handful after handful. By the time our taxi had arrived and had taken us to the bus stop something was seriously wrong. Elinka was pale. Cold sweat on her face. She was starting to pass out. I got Paul to run over and buy bottles of water. I washed her face. I then poured water down her head and her back. Nothing helped. She was burning up. I tried to call Bob in Jerusalem. Was there anything we could do? She needed help. Bob said we just needed to get her on the bus. Get her home as soon as we could. It was the bus trip from hell. Every moment of it. Elinka violently vomiting and in total agony. I can't travel at the best of times. I was pregnant. And on a bus. With a vomiting woman. Riding through the bumpy desert roads. It wasn't long before I was vomiting as well.

That bus trip with Elinka became my symbol of hell on earth. I actually used it as a marker for how horrible my birth with Asher was. At one stage while trying to figure out how to jump over the rail of the fifth floor balcony in the birthing room I remember yelling out to Paul "now it's even worse than the bus trip from Cairo!!!".

So yes, Sam was coming to visit me, and both me and Paul were thrilled. We had three short days. Thanks to those endless hours practising guitar with Jon, Sam was now part of the travelling Feastie Beasties. I tried not to laugh. When he wasn't needed for his Shekinah duties we were able to take him around Adelaide and show him the sights. We took him to the Central Markets. Down to Henley Jetty. Ice cream at Glenelg. It was just such a treat to have Sam there. He asked if he could give Asher a bath. I loved that. He really seemed to enjoy being an uncle. Asher was the first baby any of us siblings had so it was pretty amazing to share the experience. Sam had tried to be macho over the years but it just didn't work. He's really happiest with an apron around his waist and baking in the kitchen. If you picture Robert Downey Jr and Nigella Lawson merged into one, you have my brother Sam.

I told him how hungry I had been those past three weeks. How we hadn't really had any food. Our money had gone into baby expenses and the money from the government hadn't arrived yet. I had never felt so hungry in my life. It got to a point where I was looking around the house wondering what household items might be edible. The cushion next to me on the couch? Could I eat that? What about the potted plant in the kitchen window? I was beyond hungry and Paul didn't really seem to understand that. We had some crackers and soup mixes in the pantry but they were running out. We had been given some Easter chocolates from Marg. Some chocolate eggs each and

Marg had bought me an Easter Bilby. An Australian native. A bit like a bunny but a longer nose. It reminded me of Asher. It's dark eyes and long nose had such a strong resemblance to my baby boy. It stayed on top of our fridge for two weeks until I finally succumbed. My hunger won. Sam heard this and kicked into gear. He walked to the shops and came back with bags of goodies. Fruit, yogurt and snacks. He then got busy. He cooked up a big batch of pasta bows. Poured in a meat sauce he had whipped up with lots of garlic and tomatoes. He then added a big tub of cottage cheese into the mix. He divided it up into single portions and put them in the freezer for later. For the next couple of weeks I lived off Sam's kindness. I was so grateful. It was completely new to be on the receiving end of nurturing and kindness. My academic husband had his focus elsewhere. If it wasn't his beloved Greek it was his music. And every spare moment was now consumed with him becoming famous through this God-given gift.

My friend Victoria, who had lived with me and Alice in Sydney, had moved to Adelaide as well. She was also studying at the college hoping to become a teacher. Her voice was incredible. A powerful yet very feminine sound. Paul was very pleased when she agreed to do vocals for him. This was it. He was finally going to become famous. My husband who had no time to hang out with me, all of a sudden had all this spare time to record music. It was amazing. He tapped into this stream of energy where headaches no longer had power over him. He gave his music his all. By now Paul had graduated top of his class and was lecturing at the college as well as setting up a chaplaincy course. He was also being asked to preach at more and more churches. Most Sunday mornings we were at a different church. Often travelling to a country town for the opportunity. Paul was a gifted speaker. I loved hearing him preach. People responded to him as well. He was a very clever combination of passionate yet academic. He brought new light into the Scriptures. I loved watching how animated he was when he spoke in front of people. His face alive. His eyes making contact with the congregation. I tried to ignore the feelings that were coming up inside. Tried to dismiss them, but it was pretty clear that Paul was so absent in our home. So emotionally absent. Yet as soon as he had a microphone in front of him he was alive. I told him that the best thing he could buy me for our anniversary would be a microphone that he could use at home. To have a husband that gave me eye contact, spoke to me with an animated voice and used facial expressions was beyond exciting to me and I craved it from the depths of my being.

One afternoon when I was sitting in an armchair after having fed Asher, I was all of a sudden overcome with emotions. As if a giant pillow of heavy sadness had landed on my chest. I began to cry and cry. In that moment I knew that Paul would not live a full life and die too soon. I couldn't stop crying.

I knew it was something to do with alcohol. My mind was racing. I knew there was alcoholism in his family. But there was in mine as well. It couldn't be that. It must be something else. Maybe a drunk driver. That must be it. Paul would get hit by a drunk driver and die. I got nothing else. I just knew that it was an early death and something to do with alcohol. I cried for hours. Sitting there holding Asher. Despite all the tears and actual howling I had this overwhelming peace around me. I would be okay. The favour that I had always felt would continue. I was safe. Asher was safe. Everything would be okay. It took me months to tell Paul about what had happened. He dismissed it. I'm not sure he even heard me.

As time went on Paul decided that he would add movie script writing to his repertoire as well. His creative juices were flowing madly. He needed to get them out. There was no time for me or Asher. I knew that he loved us, he just wasn't able to show it. Around this time my sister Abigail contacted me. She was struggling so much. She was desperate to get away. Could she come and visit me for a month? Of course she could. I would love for her to come and hang out with me and Asher. I hadn't been able to be a sister for a long time. It would be so wonderful to have that opportunity. I knew that she would love Asher as well. As it turned out Abigail arrived and was a complete nervous wreck. All the lights had to be on in the house in order for her to sleep. She would jump if I reached for something next to her. Her body on high alert at all times. It was heart breaking to watch this 14 year old girl so terrified. When our month together was coming to an end Abigail begged to stay. She couldn't imagine going back home. Thankfully my parents understood that she needed her sister. They were okay with her living with me. Centrelink also approved and Abigail was able to enrol in a local Christian school and be seen as my own daughter.

We had been invited to go up to the Adelaide Hills to have afternoon tea with a lady from the radio station. I was really excited. I had only been in the hills once and it felt magical to me. The closest I had come to feeling like I was in Sweden during my time in Australia. The air was cleaner. I felt as if there was more oxygen to breathe. The house we were going to was in Bridgewater. Even the name sounded gorgeous. We had a lovely afternoon. This lady had German heritage and kept offering Paul different alcoholic drinks that he was happy to try. I didn't even consider the fact that he was driving.

On the way home Paul said he wanted to show Abigail a place where we could look out over Adelaide and see the view, by now it was dusk and the roads were so different to the straight roads of the city. I was keen to go home because I hadn't brought enough formula for Asher to stay out long and I knew that I wouldn't have enough breast milk for him. Once we got to this lookout point Paul said he wanted to have a beer. I was a bit surprised because our money was tight, even a bit of a struggle with the petrol to drive up to the hills. As we headed out the restaurant door to finally leave I saw this contraption on the wall. I looked closer. It said it could measure your alcohol levels to see if you were fit to drive. How cool! I had no idea these existed. I wanted Paul to give it a go. Just for a bit of fun. He seemed reluctant. I insisted. It would be fun and didn't cost much. We could teach Abigail about alcohol consumption. Paul blew into the tube. Even in my ignorant state it was so clear. Paul was totally over the limit. He was not safe to drive. In fact, he wouldn't be safe for a few hours. I was shocked. He was about to get in a car in the dark! On winding roads that he wasn't familiar with. Get his son, wife and sister-in-law to join him while completely over the limit. I couldn't even say a word. They froze in my throat.

I tried to distract Abigail so she wouldn't realise the seriousness of the situation. Asher was hungry. He hardly ever cried but he started to complain. We ended up using our last bit of money that was meant for groceries to buy dinner. The cheapest things on the menu were still expensive. I was so upset. Not angry. Just shocked. I realised that I had seen Paul drink much more than this and get into our car. Because he was so switched off it was impossible to tell if he was under the influence or not. His eyes were often blood red but he said that was from the headaches. My mind was pounding trying to make sense of this man I was married to. He was becoming more and more of a stranger to me.

Sam announced a bit later in the year that he was getting married to the love of his life. Every single family member was going to be there. So many of our friends from Jerusalem. Relatives that I had heard of my whole life. Even Mormor and Morfar were making the trip to Wisconsin for the big event. I wanted to go. I had to go. This was Sam. I couldn't miss his wedding. Our bank account was empty though. We were struggling to make things last to the next fortnightly pension payment from the navy. Asher's nappies were expensive. So was his formula. But the thing was, I had to go to this wedding.

I decided to use an offer that I had tucked away from months earlier. I had been offered a shopping spree by the lady who was getting private lessons with Paul. I never took her up on the offer. I decided to call Denise. Explain to her that I had to be at this wedding. Was there any chance that she could lend us the money? We could pay it back over time. She seemed a bit surprised but after talking to her husband they agreed that they would pay for our tickets. I was thrilled. We were going to Sam's wedding. Abigail would use her return ticket and then stay on in the States and finish high school there.

We arrived in Wisconsin right before Christmas. Sam was getting married in a Wisconsin forest. It would have to be a quick ceremony. I looked around. The forest beautiful in the snow. Lanterns everywhere. Sam's bride an ice queen coming through the trees with her white cape. The faces of so many people I loved. Even Jess was there with her new husband. Carla, Sam's bride, was the 15th child in a family of 16. When I asked her if she had any relatives that might be able to lend us a snow suit for Asher she laughed and said she was sure she could find one among her 52 cousins.

My dad was the minister in charge. I saw him handing out sheets of paper to the guests. I assumed it was an order of service. I was wrong. It was a list he had made up of how to live a healthy vegan life. My dad's first love was Jesus. His second love was health. He had had a heart attack not that long before. He woke after being in a coma in the hospital. There was a tray in front of him with a hamburger and a brownie. In that moment he decided that he needed to go back to his hippie roots of being a vegan. It was a rebirth. Similar to being born again with Jesus. Everyone needed to hear the good news. No one was going to hell with their diet of unhealthy food on his watch. So just like he had done with the tracts about Jesus, my dad started printing out his health commandments and handing them out at opportune moments, like his son's wedding.

Those few days in Wisconsin were incredible. It was a reunion of so many people that I loved. We sang together. Went for walks together. Ate together. Our spouses got to know each other. The love was still very much there from our youth, only that we had all grown up that little bit. Crossed the threshold of life somewhat. All of us pretty happy where life had taken us, confident in our choices and blissfully unaware that most of us were about to get bitten in the ass by reality pretty soon. Our carefree days well and truly over.

Sam's wedding was the last time my family all got to be together. That was 1998. We never managed to pull it off again. We wanted to, but it never happened. Susanna in Egypt. Raphael still in Dallas. Me in Adelaide. Sam living in Jerusalem. Ezra joined the U.S. Air force and was stationed in Italy and Iraq, and Abigail moved with my parents to Springfield, Missouri, so that my dad could study for his Masters of Divinity.

It was time for us to head back to Australia. We had an amazing visit in the States but on my last day there both me and Asher got really sick. A vicious tummy bug. I was finding it hard to even stand up without having to run to the toilet. I couldn't imagine sitting on the plane. After the trip that we had for my sister's wedding I never travelled again without travel insurance. I was told that we were able to stay a few days longer in Wisconsin at no extra cost. Our tickets could be changed. I was so relieved. Even three days would help. When I told Paul the good news he immediately said he wanted to get back to Adelaide. He had more recording to do. He didn't want to wait another few days. I was shocked. Here I was, unable to even stand up to change a nappy and Paul didn't want to look after me. He was so focused on his projects that he couldn't see my predicament. He ended up flying back on his own and me and Asher followed a few days later. I felt neglected and uncared for. It really stung but I tried to dismiss the feelings as much as I could. It was getting much harder to ignore the signs.

15

Hope

Not long after we returned from our trip to my brother's wedding I realised I was pregnant. I wasn't exactly surprised. I was totally out of tune with my cycle. Not knowing at all when I was fertile. It was something I hadn't even considered looking at. There was very little sex going on anyway. Paul seemed to only want to when there was an element of risk to our love making. He was keen if we were staying at someone's house or possibly had the chance of being caught. The more mundane, risk free intimacy that I craved held no appeal to him.

It came as no surprise to me that Paul started to show signs of interest when we stayed in my parent's house in Virginia Beach. In fact, we stayed in my parent's bed. They had set up camp in the freezing garage right next to the washing machine so that Paul and I could have some privacy with Asher. My parents were always like that. So considerate and generous. After Paul came inside of me he collapsed and said he had seen a rainbow. He couldn't get over how beautiful this rainbow was. He talked about it for ages. And he knew that it meant that I was pregnant. I tried to brush it aside. Me being pregnant was sweet but possibly not the best timing. Paul's drinking was increasing. He was mentioning financial pressures more and more. The other thing that I tried not to look at, but I knew it was very real, was the fact that Paul was incredibly jealous of my attention to Asher. Even though Paul adored his son and absolutely loved him, he really struggled with my attention being on our gorgeous little boy with the curious face.

Most nights I would lie in bed, hot tears streaming down my face. I had never felt this alone. Ever. And I was lying next to my husband. How could that be? How could I feel so terribly lonely and yet be next to someone? It didn't make sense. My head was pounding. My chest was pounding. All I wanted was for my husband to reach out and touch me. Any indication that he cared. That he valued me. That he wanted me. Nothing. It was as if I had this black hole living in my home. Sucking out all my emotions. All my energy. I wanted him so much. I wanted to understand him but he just sucked me dry. I was desperate for connection. Desperate to explore my newfound sexuality.

I was also desperate for friends. I decided to invite a couple over from the college. They were older than us but I really liked them. Richard seemed familiar to me. He had that carefree spirit about him that reminded me of my friends back home. He was musical and playful and didn't equate being a Christian to not having a sense of humour. Richard and his wife Sonja came over and I tried to make one of Elinka's Arabic dishes. A combination of eggplant, cauliflower, diced lamb in layers, and then the rest of the pot is filled with rice. You cook it together and then flip it over on a plate and serve. It looked so easy when Elinka made it. I flipped it over, and it flopped. Totally flopped. The lamb was tough and under cooked. The eggplant soggy. The cauliflower hard. Total disaster. However, the conversation was good. Richard told us about the church that they went to. He suggested Paul and I come along. There were some young couples there that were great. We would get along. I was so excited. A group of young people at a church. This was exactly what I needed.

I told Paul later that night in bed that I wanted to go to the church. Paul wasn't so keen. He liked the freedom of visiting different churches where he could preach then leave. He didn't feel the need to belong to something. I did. I needed to belong. I tried to explain that I needed friends. Paul told me that I already had friends. Alice and Victoria. I hardly ever saw Alice. She was living with her parents, raising her little daughter who was only four weeks younger than Asher. Even though we had babies the same age our paths hardly ever crossed. I only saw Victoria when I bumped into her at the college or when she came over to record music with Paul. I needed more. Paul said I had lots of friends at the college. I did. I knew everyone. I was friendly with everyone. But that was very different to belonging to a group of friends. I really needed him to understand my loneliness. He tried to convince me that I was happy. I looked happy. I sounded happy. I was happy. He needed me to be happy. I realised as we spoke that there was no way Paul could face my sadness. My happiness was critical to his sense of self. The heaviness in my heart all of a sudden felt much heavier. I needed this church. I needed to connect with like-minded people. I told Paul that I had to go there.

It took a few weeks but we finally made it. It was Valentine's Day 1999. I sat down in my seat and exhaled. I could see Richard at the front being part of the worship team. I looked around me. Lots of young people. Lots of old people. Kids running around. This felt very familiar. During the service Asher was on my lap but he kept looking over across the aisle. A little girl was sitting with her parents. Similar age to Asher but with big blue eyes and wispy blond hair. They kept looking at each other and eventually both managed to untangle themselves from their parents' arms and crawl out to each other. They met in the centre of the aisle. A beam of light was shining through the ceiling window. It was picture perfect. So sweet. I looked across at the girl's mother and smiled. She smiled back. Thanks to Asher I had my first friend and was thrilled that we would have someone to invite to his upcoming birthday.

My father had sent me a letter that just so happened to arrive the day after Asher's first birthday. A day where I spent most of my time trying to focus on not throwing up. We had gone to the zoo to celebrate Asher turning one and I had bought a sausage to eat. That sausage did not want to stay down. It didn't feel pregnancy related. I never really had morning sickness as such. This just felt like a dodgy sausage that my body was rejecting. So when I opened the letter from my dad the groundwork had already been done by a $2.50 snack at the zoo.

I pulled out a photocopied piece of paper. My dad had scribbled something next to the heading. THE VEGAN GOSPEL. It didn't exactly say that. But it might as well have. I'm not sure how many photocopied sheets he sent out but I assume it was as many as he could afford.

My dad had his first convert! I only skimmed through the article. I had already decided. I had converted to veganism. So there I was, a few months into my second pregnancy, still not fully recuperated from my first one, starting a new eating plan with absolutely no concept of what healthy food was. I just figured I needed to avoid anything that came from an animal. Easy! Unfortunately my midwife made a comment about how babies will get the goodness they need from the mother no matter what she ate, and in my naive mind I didn't fully grasp that Aurianne didn't mean that I could survive on sandwiches and Skittles alone. That was pretty much what I lived on while being pregnant with my second baby. Paul was still wanting his meat so often he would order a piece of roast chicken and some chips if I was too tired to cook him a proper meal. Any energy I had was going to my husband and Asher. Eating a sandwich was much more convenient and the Skittles helped when my energy levels got low.

As my belly got bigger Paul was spending more and more time at work. He loved what he was doing at the college. Loved teaching. Loved writing curriculums about chaplaincy. Loved mixing with the lecturers. I was thrilled for him but also wished we could have more time together. We had moved to a more central location so I spent a lot of time going for walks with Asher in his Emmaljunga pram. One day while we were out I saw Paul drive past. Once I got home I said that we had seen him on the road. I asked if he had noticed the sexy woman with the pram. "Sexy? There is nothing sexy about a mother." I had been trying to be funny. Just something light-hearted to make conversation. I hadn't expected such a full-on response. Nothing sexy? Wow. I swallowed hard. That was not easy to hear. His words stung. Did he not realise I was now a mother for the rest of my life? Motherhood would never stop for me. If he didn't find me attractive now as a mother he never would.

I had never felt sexy. Paul's words only really confirmed what I already felt. It just hurt to hear it. I was getting a lot of compliments though. My vegan lifestyle, and the sandwich and Skittle diet, were working wonders. Weight was dropping off. Each prenatal check-up proved that I was in fact losing weight despite my pregnant belly growing bigger. I only noticed because the numbers had to be written down in a little book. I was so out of touch with my body that besides those numbers I really didn't know what was happening to me. Except for one thing. I was starting to get severe throbbing in my legs. Varicose veins were appearing. Not just my legs. As I got close to the end of my pregnancy I was horrified to realise that varicose veins could exist in my groin as well. The pain was intense and it made standing for long periods of time almost impossible. Things like doing dishes made me shift from foot to foot hoping that would ease the pain somewhat. I told my midwife about it and she explained it was common. It didn't feel common. It felt like a fist was pounding me between my legs.

The pain from the varicose veins coupled with the pain from my lower back, that was still recuperating from Asher's birth, was enough incentive for me to go along to a chiropractic appointment that one of the couples at church had mentioned to me. I had never heard the word before but the couple seemed so sweet and had offered to help me when they realised that we were on a very small income. Ken and Briony had a chiropractic clinic in a beautiful old house. I felt safe with Ken who was very gentle with my back and explained each manoeuvre.

My biggest concern about the upcoming birth was not about the pain. I still had flash backs to Asher's birth on a regular basis, normally as I was drifting off to sleep or when getting tired in the afternoon. No, my main concern was what would happen to Asher when I was away in hospital giving birth. He had hardly spent any time away from me in his now 18 months of life. He was so attached to me. He fell asleep holding on to my hair and the thought of him being left with someone else was very hard to fathom. The only person I could think of asking was Alice. Her voice was soothing. She had such a gentle nature with children and I knew that she adored Asher. Despite how little we saw of each other I knew that she would be the easiest replacement for me.

I was so grateful when she agreed, especially when I realised that she was going to leave her own daughter at home so she could fully focus on Asher. Once my due date was well and truly gone Aurianne gave me the words I had been dreading, the hospital couldn't wait any longer. I would need to be induced again. I had wanted to avoid this so much. I was given a date. I was not allowed to remain pregnant past October 10. I liked that number. Ten out of ten. Perfection. As it turned out, there was no sign of my baby wanting to come out. Ken had explained to me that I had a tilted pelvis which meant that my babies never quite engaged. There wasn't enough pressure on my cervix. The hospital got their way and booked me in for an induction.

Paul dropped me off at the hospital early in the morning and drove back to our house to be with Asher. We didn't want to keep Alice away from her daughter for any longer than was needed. Gel was inserted and the wait began. Nothing happened so later in the afternoon a second amount was inserted. This time I got a reaction. Instant pain in my legs. Both legs hurt but the pain in my right leg was so much worse. I tried to move around to try to ease the pain. As I sat on an exercise ball in the shower I tried to use the force of the water on my leg. Nothing helped. It felt as if a boa constrictor had slid into the room and wrapped itself around my right leg and was squeezing its prey to death.

Paul arrived at four in the afternoon with his Hebrew grammar books. Now that he had been to Israel to visit he was hoping to return there to study. Hebrew had replaced his Greek. As far as I was concerned it was exactly the same. As I howled in the shower from the pain in my leg I could see Paul through the doorway reading his books. Murmuring to himself. Not one offer of help. I knew he didn't like to give massages but it would have really helped. Even if it wasn't a good one. Just having someone there. Touch. To know I wasn't alone. But I was. I was so alone. Tears rolling down my cheeks. Wondering if I had made the wrong choice. Maybe I should have asked Paul to stay with Asher, and asked Alice to stay with me instead. She would have been the perfect partner. Heat packs. Cold face washers. Sips of water. Sitting with me in silence or telling me to breathe out the pain.

By now it felt as if I was going to burst. When Aurianne came to check on me I told her I was scared I would burst a vein in my groin. She told me not to worry that it was very common but she would have a look. Her face said it all. The pain was so intense. My leg. My groin. They hurt more than the contractions themselves. The tears streaming down my face though were not from the physical pain. They were from realising that my husband was now watching 60 Minutes on TV. The news had finished and he was now moving on to another show. By now I was calling out and moaning from deep within me, and Aurianne asked me to get on all fours out of reach of the shower. This time I had to push. A new sensation for me. Aurianne called for Paul to join us.

Already? That was quick!

Quick? Four hours might be quick when you are studying Hebrew and watching TV. Four hours of having a boa constrictor squeezing your leg full force and having your groin about to explode is a very long time. Especially when totally alone. I started to grunt. That ring of fire I had heard about was now making itself known. I pushed three times and my second baby slipped out of me and was handed to me between my legs.

I held my baby close. So relieved it was all over. The baby was crying. Not so much crying but making sure I knew he wasn't happy about being forced out into the cold room. I looked down at him. I looked again. It wasn't a boy. I had a girl! I couldn't believe it. I had a girl. A girl. How could I possibly have a girl? I had always seen myself as someone with sons. I was so used to male energy. Something in me must have assumed that I wasn't able to create a girl because I was shocked at this little girl in my arms. I was in total awe that I could create a female. A girl. A girl! I have a girl. I kept saying it over and over again. I kept saying it as my body started to shake and my teeth rattle. Heated blankets were being wrapped around me to stop the shaking as I kept repeating my new mantra. I have a girl. I have a girl. She was beautiful. So beautiful.

I recognised her straightaway. Her little face was etched by the same artist who made Mormor and Susanna. The same mouth. So familiar. Paul said her name first. Tikvah. Hope. A hebrew word that we had made into a name. Paul really liked it. I wasn't so sure but figured we were having a boy so agreed to it. Looking at her in my arms though the name really suited her.

As we left the hospital the next morning, with Paul and Asher coming to collect us, one of the nurses exclaimed,

You got your pigeon pair!

I had never heard the term before. Pigeon pair?

A boy and a girl. Your family is complete. No more babies for you.

16

Dead Man Walking

Those first few days of toddler and baby were hard. Oh how I longed to have family close by to help me. Thankfully I had a phone call out of the blue from Briony, my chiropractor's wife.

Would I like some meals organised?

Meals? Yes!! Yes I would.

Briony sounded thrilled at my quick response. A couple of days later Briony and Sonja burst through my door. In a flash they were filling my freezer with lasagnas and chicken pies. My vegan days were thankfully over. I had become so depleted towards the end of my pregnancy that I was feeling light headed and iron supplements didn't work. There was only one thing that I could think of. Steak. A massive steak. My vegan chapter only lasted six months and that was a good thing because I had never tasted anything as delicious as those lasagnas and pies in my freezer. Not only did Briony and Sonja make sure I was fed, they also started cleaning up my house.

Briony spent the whole time cleaning my laundry room. I thought it was so bizarre. My laundry. Why would she do that when there were so many other areas that needed it? Over the next few weeks I understood. There was something so amazing about being able to walk into my laundry with its shiny sink and do all the loads of washing without having to navigate through mess. My one haven in a messy house. I was so grateful for what they had done. The food and the cleaning was so practical, but it was more than that. Their act of love had shown me that I was now part of a community that cared. I didn't have to start my first few weeks with a new baby being so hungry that I could eat the furniture. I was being nurtured and looked after.

Tikvah was only a couple of weeks old when I got some terrible news from Jerusalem. Naomi, the girl I used to sit and pray with before school, had tried to end her life. I was shocked. Completely shocked. Naomi! Beautiful, beautiful Naomi. Our two year age gap meant that we never hung out as friends. She was more of a mentor to me. She probably didn't even realise that. But her kindness and sweet nature and her integrity inspired me. If there was one person at school I wanted to be like it was her. We had a connection because of our similar heritage. Her mother Nordic and her father American. In a school full of different cultures Naomi and I slot into the same box, but more importantly, she shared my faith. There were other Christians in my school but as far as I was concerned Naomi, and her best friend Sharona, were the only other 'real' believers. Sitting together in prayer so many mornings had given us a connection and to know she had tried to take her life was too much for me to comprehend. As I lay there at night feeding my baby girl hot tears flowed down my face. Picturing Naomi's parents. Her sisters and her brother. Feeling their pain. Knowing my community was rallying around them in Jerusalem. A constant vigil around Naomi's hospital bed. A steady stream of friends showering her with love as she lay in a coma. I wanted to be there. I wanted to go home.

Paul was making arrangements for that to happen. He wanted to study in Jerusalem. On Mount Zion in fact. For him it was a dream come true. As a theologian nothing would be better. Our intention was to move to Israel as soon as we could afford it. Paul had decided before Asher was born that he wanted to be referred to as Abba by our children. The Hebrew word for dad. I thought it was a bit cheesy but figured he could choose for himself. I wasn't going to do the same since I had no connection with the word Imma for mother. I was Mamma. I knew it irked Paul's family that he was called Abba and that we kept mentioning a move to Jerusalem. It did seem pretty unrealistic though since our financial situation was pretty grim but Paul kept telling me it would happen.

My main concern at the time was Paul's health. His eyes were red most of the time. Glassy. I was learning more about health in my own pursuit of feeling more energetic. I was gleaning more information about food as medicine as I was searching for answers for Asher's terrible eczema. I had never even considered reading labels before. Just trusting that if something was for sale it would be safe to consume. Surely the government wouldn't allow food to be sold that could be dangerous for us? As Asher's eczema worsened I started to borrow books from the library. Paul's red eyes really worried me. I started paying more attention to them. Noticing that they would flare up after he drank alcohol. That kind of made sense to me. But it didn't make sense that they were often red when he came home from work. Surely he wasn't drinking at work? It was all so confusing and in the midst of a toddler and a baby there wasn't a lot of room for talking about it with Paul. He reassured me that his eyes were fine and he never drank more than he should.

When Tikvah was about four months old Paul got home one evening and I could smell him before I saw him. His eyes were glassy and red. I asked him if he was all right. He seemed distant but explained that he was fine. He had met with his co-worker for lunch and they had talked about a youth program they wanted to run at the college. As I continued with making dinner Paul went and sat down in the living room. I was happy for him to be home and giving the kids some attention while I tried to get everything ready for our meal. All of a sudden Asher ran into the kitchen.

Abba sleeping!! Abba sleeping!!

He was pulling at me to come. Dragging at my shirt to follow him. As I got into the living room I could see Paul collapsed in the armchair. Asher was pushing at him for a response. I called out to Paul. Felt his face. I had no idea what to do. This would be my first time to call an ambulance. The operator told me to ease him to the floor and try to get a response. He was so heavy. He had a pulse but there was no sign of life.

An ambulance was on its way. The paramedics worked on him for a bit while I distracted Asher and held Tikvah. The paramedics were taking him to the hospital. We wouldn't be able to come in the ambulance. I didn't have anyone to ask for help so I called a taxi and asked the driver to stop at an ATM so I could take out some money. I had never used our bank card before but I was so happy I had remembered to take it out of Paul's wallet before he was whisked away.

When we got to the hospital they took us to a private room. There was no bed in there. It almost felt more like a safety room. Paul was sitting up in an armchair. He hardly reacted when we walked in. I was carrying both kids because the pram wouldn't fit in the taxi. The doctor was asking questions so I just stood back listening while keeping an eye on Asher. Words like medication, mental history and psychosis were being used. I could feel something very cold growing inside me. He was healed. Paul was healed from schizophrenia. There was no need to have this discussion.

I explained about his red eyes. Said maybe his liver wasn't working properly. They wanted to keep him in the hospital for observation. They wanted to give him medication. I explained that he would be fine. He just needed some rest. He just needed to get home. I could see the nurse looking at the doctor. Nothing was said. Papers were signed and Paul was free to go home. He still hadn't said anything to me. It was almost midnight by the time the taxi brought us home. Paul fell asleep immediately and not long after both the kids were asleep too. I lay in my bed with my eyes wide open.

Something terrifying had happened but I couldn't dare admit it. It was too scary to even begin making sense of. I lay there for hours just praying for my husband. Praying for my children's dad. Pleading with God to heal Paul. Heal him from what exactly I didn't know. I just knew he needed healing. In the morning I looked over at Paul and I wasn't sure if he was still alive. He was so perfectly still. He always looked like Jesus in the tomb when he slept but this was a lot more intense. I felt for a pulse. He was alive.

Later in the morning I checked on him again. His eyes were open but he wasn't really there. Didn't want to talk to me. Totally expressionless. It was hard to inhale. The coldness in the centre of my body pounding. I had no idea what to do. I needed more than prayer. I wanted to connect with my husband so desperately. I said a few things to Paul to show him I was there for him. Whatever he needed. His eyes were open but he wasn't looking at me. I went back to the living room and got our little TV out. We usually kept it in the study. I found the kids programs. I knew they existed but had never actually seen them. Asher and even Tikvah were hooked straightaway. Perfectly distracted. I went back to my husband. I needed him to respond. I needed him to return. To show me a sign of life. I knelt next to him. Our mattress on the floor. I gave him a kiss. It felt clumsy. Like kissing a corpse. I lent down again. Kissed his face. Still nothing. I moved his blanket aside. I had never done anything like this before. It was so foreign. So distant from my experience. It was the only thing I could come up with that might get a reaction from my husband. I would get him to return to life by having him in my mouth. I looked up at his face. He still looked like Jesus. He didn't rise from the dead. But one part of him did. A few minutes later I walked out of our bedroom in a daze. What had I just done? Who was that man in our bed? I had nothing left up my sleeve. I had tried everything. I went and sat with my kids and watched TV. Realising for the first time that the songs we sang at our weekly playgroup circle came from a show on TV called Play School. Who knew??

Later on that afternoon Paul was up getting himself some toast. A mental health team had booked in to visit him and by the time they arrived Paul was chatting to them as if nothing had happened. Next morning he got dressed as normal and headed off for another day of teaching his students about the Bible. Nothing was said. No acknowledgment of what had happened. I watched him speed out of our driveway wondering who this man was that I was married to.

A couple of weeks later Paul's eyes were redder than normal yet again and this time I convinced him to have a blood test done for his liver. Thankfully he agreed and a little while later announced that the results had come back just fine. I was relieved and surprised. I took the opportunity to ask Paul to not drink more than two drinks at a time. I told him I thought that maybe him passing out after his work lunch was connected to the alcohol he drank that day and Paul agreed he would stick to two drinks.

Life went back to its steady hum of church on Sundays, playgroup on Wednesdays and Paul teaching or recording music and doing his weekly radio program. I told myself that everything was fine. And it was. Except for when that cold feeling reared its ugly head. But mainly it was fine. I was staying busy and Paul seemed to be all right, despite his eyes telling a different story.

I never quite understood how, but at the end of 2000 we were able to book tickets to finally move back to Jerusalem. Instead of going directly there we would stop over and visit my family who were still in the U.S. after all these years. My mother had finished her Masters in Counselling in Virginia Beach and they had now moved to the buckle of the Bible belt, Springfield Missouri. My father was doing a Masters of Divinity there. I planned the route so that we could catch up with some friends along the way. It really didn't add that much to the cost of the tickets to break up the long trip. We would then fly to Sweden as well before we landed in Tel Aviv. I was so excited that I would be able to visit Mormor and Morfar again and introduce my little family to the magic there. Magdalena was also happy to meet up which would mean us seeing each other for the first time as mothers.

We left at the end of summer, in February. I still couldn't believe it was happening even as we had a garage sale to get rid of all of our things. It seemed so unreal. I was finally going home. We were waved off at the airport by Paul's family. Me thinking back to us leaving Sweden as a family in 1985. How angry Mormor and Morfar were. I knew Paul's parents were upset but they did their best to remain neutral. As the plane lifted over Adelaide I looked down and thought to myself that I had missed my chance of getting to know it. I had been so busy with motherhood that I hadn't really seen much of it. I could see the desert stretching out beneath us. Remembering how I thought I was coming to Australia to spend time with the indigenous people. Instead I was heading to Israel to hopefully work as a counsellor.

Our first stop was Sydney. Thankfully Paul had an auntie there that we could stay with while waiting for our connecting flight. She asked if we needed to use her computer. Paul disappeared in the study as I stood on the balcony feeding wild parrots with Asher and Tikvah. After a while I could see Paul walking towards me. His face pale. He had just received an email from Jon. The college on Mt Zion where Paul was going to do his Master Degree had just closed down. That day. The parrots were screeching for more seeds. Their rainbow wings no longer captivating me. Closed down? How? Paul didn't have many details. Jon was very apologetic. Was hoping we hadn't left Adelaide yet. Paul and I looked at each other. What should we do? We were at a total loss. This was the whole reason we were moving back. There was no plan B. After a few moments of silence Paul asked if I still wanted to go. I did. So did he. We would just go. See what happened. Surely something would come up.

We flew to Portland. My main reason for going there was to show Paul the log cabin I had fallen in love with. I'd fallen in love with it, and in it. It was such a special place and it meant a lot to me that I could return there with my husband and kids. Mt Hood was just as beautiful as I remembered her. The log cabin smelling of the wood fire. The feather doonas still as cosy and with the snow lightly falling around us it was just as magical as I remembered it. Surely Paul would find this place romantic. As far as I was concerned this was the most romantic place in the world. I had always wanted to spend time in a log cabin with my husband and here was our chance. I wanted to make new memories here. My first kiss a distant memory. Paul knew this. I kept waiting for him to acknowledge how special this was for me. To show he cared. It never happened. When I tried to draw close to him he pulled away. It took me a long time to fall asleep in the most romantic place on earth. The feather doona not protecting me from the heavy weight that had landed on my chest and making it hard to breathe. Why didn't my husband want me?

Our next stop after Portland was Madison, Wisconsin. Sam was living there with his wife Carla. It was exciting because I had been told so many times that I would love Madison. That it was so different to other American cities. Being a university town it attracted interesting people from around the world. We were going to spend a week in Sam's tiny unit but I figured that would be all right since we could spend most of our time ice skating or playing in the snow and only coming back to their home for meals. As it turned out, I started to cough just after getting off the plane. By the next morning I had a fever. The pressure in my chest building. I had never been this sick before.

Carla kept disinfecting the floors and door knobs hoping to keep everyone else from getting sick. Paul didn't quite understand the seriousness of how sick I was and spent a lot of the time visiting Barnes & Noble while Sam and Carla were at work. I was left with Asher and Tikvah in a tiny home with no TV. How could he not see I needed his help? I eventually begged to go to a doctor who prescribed me antibiotics so that I could get on the plane to Springfield. This trip was not turning out as I had hoped. Surely things would get better.

It was great to see my parents who very quickly stepped into the role of grandparents. My dad reading books to the kids. Going for little walks to see squirrels on the power lines. My mom helping with baths and suggesting outings on the weekend when she didn't have to go to work. Abigail was living in Springfield as well and working at a coffee place called the Mud House. It was the coolest café I had ever been to and when I was able to have a little bit of time to myself I would go there and order a frappe and pretend that everything was okay. I knew it wasn't.

I just couldn't be honest with myself at how bad things had become. Paul was away most of the day. Book shops he told me. Still working on his Hebrew. I had really been looking forward to this part of the trip. Where maybe Paul and I could have some time to ourselves while my parents were around to help out. I tried to suggest it but Paul said he was happy to find his own things to do. He told me that he spent most of his time at Barnes & Noble but his breath said something different. I overheard him asking someone about different breweries in town. Really? He was visiting breweries? Where was he getting money for this? I knew that asking him was futile. He always had some story and because I wanted to believe him I did. The alternative was too scary. I turned a blind eye for as long as I could.

I spent my time looking after the kids and getting my driver's licence. I didn't really see why it was so important but my mother kept telling me that I should. Over and over she would remind me that this was a perfect chance. That she could take me out driving while Paul looked after the kids. She had a point. After passing my theory test my mum took me driving through a cemetery a couple of times. It seemed easy enough. I decided to go for my test as soon as possible. I passed by one point. I was so not ready to drive. Still not used to being on the right side of the road. Not quite understanding the importance of indicating before merging. But I had a licence! Some level of freedom.

I had been locked in the house for so many weeks with the kids. My dad attending lectures. My mother working. Paul supposedly studying Hebrew at Barnes & Noble. The only excitement was every so often we would have a tornado warning and have to run down to the basement and wait as a tornado went by. I had passed my driving test on a Friday morning. The same Friday my parents were leaving town for a conference and the same Friday Paul had decided to drive to Nashville to see if he could find a producer for his music. He was convinced that he was going to be famous for his music and Nashville was the obvious place to go. We waved them all goodbye and it hit me that I had a rainy weekend with the kids on my own. I had to do something!

I booked a taxi to take us to a car hire company. Thankfully they didn't ask how long I had been driving or notice that my license had been issued earlier that day. I got the kids in the car and drove off. Total freedom! The rain was pouring down and it took me a while to figure out the windshield wipers. But I did. And I was free. I was driving my kids to the science museum with the biggest smile on my face. Cars honking all around me. Cars swerving as I merged into lanes without warning. At one point going through a red light. I was so not ready to drive but at that very moment I didn't care. I just needed to get out of the house and choose to do something for myself and my kids.

Paul came back from Nashville without a record deal. He didn't say much but I knew he was disappointed. He had spent a lot of time recording his songs and getting Victoria and Alice to do vocals for him. He had really believed he would become famous through his music. Recently he had been working on a movie as well. So he began to pour himself into that now, along with his Hebrew. His desire to be famous was stronger than ever now that we were in the Land of Opportunity.

Staying with my parents for such an extended time was not easy on any of us. When I had booked the tickets I thought it would be great to have a proper amount of time with my parents so they could really get to know Asher and Tikvah. To maybe make some memories that would stretch out until we all saw each other again when they joined us by moving back to Jerusalem. That was always the plan. My parents had never intended to be in the States for such a long time. But their eyes were always on Jerusalem even though all our belongings that we had stored with friends had been unpacked and given away.

I felt desperate about Paul but I had no one to tell. His behaviour was bothering me on such a deep level but I was too afraid to even admit it to myself. Things were not right but I couldn't really explain how exactly. The thought that we were moving to Israel with Paul like this was starting to keep me awake at night. Jerusalem is hard enough to live in for anyone. The tension there can be too much even for the healthiest person. It's like living in a pressure cooker. Everyone finds their own way to deal with it, or they end up in a special ward in the hospital. The 'Jerusalem Syndrome' ward. That's where all the visitors to Israel who think they are Jesus or Elijah or the Virgin Mary end up. So common that there is a whole ward set aside for them. Now here I was starting to think that maybe my own husband would become one of them. It was a truth I didn't want to look at but his fixation on becoming famous, his withdrawal from the people who loved him the most, and his obsession with the Bible was really scaring me.

I started to look at a plan B. Maybe Israel wasn't such a good idea? Maybe life in Australia was best after all? Maybe we could just do what everyone else did? Buy a house. Settle somewhere. Paul could continue with his lecturing and preaching. I could finish my studies and become a counsellor in Adelaide. Maybe try to tap into the Jewish community there instead and be part of some reconciliation between Jews and Arabs. Jess was doing something similar in Israel. Maybe I could do the same in Australia? I started to look at house packages in the Adelaide Hills. Could we afford to build one of those ugly package homes? Maybe Paul's parents could lend us some money? Real Estate advertisements became my late night escape once the kids were asleep. The peace and quiet of Adelaide might be exactly what we needed as a family. Bringing Paul to Jerusalem might actually be a disaster.

I was sitting at the kitchen table scrolling through land packages online when Paul came home. He'd been out late again. I looked up at him. His eyes burning red. Glossed over. Instead of his usual silence with me he started to speak. His speech slurred. I couldn't believe it. He was drunk. Totally and utterly drunk. I had never seen him drunk before. My mom turned from the kitchen bench and I couldn't bear the thought of her realising that her daughter's husband was drunk. I had never told anyone about him passing out when Tikvah was a baby and ending up in hospital. He hadn't even been drunk before that happened. My heart was pounding as I pulled him into the bathroom.

If he passed out here there was nothing we could do. There was no way our travel insurance would pay for a drunk, self-inflicted hospital visit. Why would he drink himself into a stupor when he knew that this triggered his mental stuff? There, I said it. His mental stuff. I couldn't deny it any longer. He had mental problems and alcohol triggered them. I knew that. He knew that. And here he was drinking our money away and risking his mental health. It broke me. Totally broke me. I tried to talk to him. Beg him to see how important it was he didn't drink too much. We couldn't risk him passing out again. Having another episode. What if he didn't snap back like he did last time? Paul was staring at me. Not saying a word. Not responding in any way. Words were wasted on him. I pulled off my wedding ring. I could feel its weight in my hand. I told Paul that I couldn't wear it anymore. I couldn't wear it when I had a husband who wouldn't talk to me. That he only spoke to people who he valued and I obviously wasn't one of them. I wanted him so much. I wanted my husband. But he needed to start behaving like one. And start behaving like a dad. I handed him the ring and said he had six months.

Do whatever you can in six months to get help. Talk to someone. Get counselling. I don't know. Just be proactive and do something. It can't come from me. There is nothing I can do to help you. I'm not going to ask you again. I don't want to be a nag. You have six months of me not bringing this up again. I won't ask you about your drinking. I won't ask you if you are getting help. I'm trusting you that you will do something to change what's going on. And if you still want to be my husband in six months time then please give the ring back to me with new promises. New vows. Show me that I'm worth something to you. Show me that your kids are worth something to you.

Not a word back. I told him that I would ask him in the morning about this to make sure he had heard it and then nothing more would be said for six months. I closed the door behind me so he could have a shower and hopefully wash off the past three years of our marriage.

The next day I checked with him. Had he heard me the night before? Yes he had. Did he understand that he had six months to save his marriage? Yes he did. I exhaled. He had heard me. I just needed to wait a bit longer and I would finally have a husband!

My dad spent a lot of his time upstairs studying in his room. We didn't see him during the day at all but he would always make sure he sat down with everyone at dinnertime. Eating his giant salad along with his beloved beans and brown rice. Every meal was the same for him and he loved it just as much each time he devoured it. Sometimes he would tweak the beans by adding kale into it. I had never heard of the stuff but he seemed happy enough. I would often join him. Beans and brown rice was my favourite food as well and it was so handy having a dad who would soak the beans and cook industrial size portions every few days.

Theological conversations and beans with brown rice. That's where me and my dad connected. It wasn't much but it was enough. I had really hoped that this visit with my parents would give me a chance to connect with my dad somewhat. We hadn't really had a chance to make new memories since they moved away from home when I was 19. I would often get a letter, then a fax, and now emails from my dad where he told me about his latest revelation about God or food. According to him, he was a new man.

He was a new man with his health gospel. I wasn't too sure about the rest. Time would tell if the monster I knew from my childhood was still lurking in the background. We had already been there over a month when I got my answer. Asher and Tikvah spent most of their days watching TV which was so different from our Aussie way of life. My dad got stressed if the house got messy so the regular crafts we used to do at home was not really an option. Asher and Tikvah would normally spend hours cutting and gluing and making things from cardboard. Play dough was a favourite as well. All messy activities.

In the end the TV became the friendliest option to keep everyone happy. I knew it was making my kids restless though and they were starting to ask about going to the playground. I explained that we would try to do it later when Abba got back. Asher asked again and before I could fully understand what was happening I heard this loud noise coming from the top of the stairs. My dad was yelling something as he bounded down the steps. In an instant he was rushing at Asher. I had left a broom leaning against the wall and he grabbed that as he charged at Asher. I swooped Asher up as I screamed "Nooooooo!" to my dad. I was in total shock. I grabbed Tikvah from the floor and ran out the house.

My heart was pounding. I was in total disbelief at what I had just seen. My dad rushing towards my son with a broomstick. His face full of rage. His voice filling the house. Asher's eyes wide in terror. Having never witnessed any form of violence and here was his grandfather coming to attack him. How could I have allowed this to happen? Why had I risked visiting? The monster of my childhood still alive and well had now leapt into the storyline of my own children.

I stayed outside until Paul got back. I asked him to take the kids to the park. I explained what had happened and I needed to have some space for myself to process. I sat at the Mud House and wrote a letter to my dad. I told him how we had come to stay with him hoping to build a relationship. How much I wanted my children to have a grandfather. That as a child I tried as much as I could to protect my siblings from his rage but there wasn't much I could do being so little. As a mother though I would never ever allow my children to be exposed to that again. It's my role to protect them no matter who the perpetrator is. I had tried so hard to keep my children away from violence and fear. He needed to know that one generation of Goods had been so screwed up by his rage and that he had a responsibility to make sure that this next generation would not have to go through the same trauma.

It was hard to write. My attempts in the past to have my dad see the consequences of his actions had fallen on deaf ears. A total inability to take responsibility. My dad's regular answer was to say he had forgotten most of our childhood. I finished my letter with saying that I needed him to remember this event. To remember so he wouldn't forget and then repeat it with any future grandkids. Do whatever he could to not forget this. There really wasn't much more that I could do. Our visit was coming to an end and a few days later we said our goodbyes. As usual nothing resolved but my mother apologising for my dad and saying she was so sorry it had happened.

We were flying out of New York and got handed a silver dollar coin in mint condition as we boarded the plane. We were on the inaugural SAS flight to Copenhagen. Lots of celebrations were going on. They suited my mood. I was so grateful to be getting out of America. It had been such a hard trip. I tried to think back to a moment where anything had made sense. Just one moment that made the trip worth it. The only thing that stood out was a day we spent as a family in a Japanese garden. My brothers had come over for a weekend to visit. We had spent a few hours walking through miniature gardens and ponds. Over bridges and beside decorative statues. Such unfamiliar territory for our family. I caught a glimpse of my parents holding hands. For anyone seeing us in that garden we would have looked like a normal family. That was my one happy memory from over two months in America.

Sweden was a breath of fresh air. I could feel myself breathing deeper. The salty ocean air in Falsterbo was exactly what I needed. Mormor and Morfar's house still smelling exactly how I remembered it. My kids running over the tiny hill next to their house and spending hours at the playground less than a minute away. This is what they needed. Space and fresh air. My body felt happy. Happier than it had felt in a long time.

I went for a bike ride with Morfar. Down the small streets with the storybook houses. Through the forest on the mossy paths. Down to the harbour hearing the ropes smacking against the masts on the boats lined up. One of my favourite sounds. The seagulls screeching. Down my favourite path along the ocean. The reeds and the sand dunes feeling so familiar. My heart bursting as my senses were coming alive with so much beauty. The beauty of feeling connected to a place. The migrating birds flying in formation above me.

I knew I didn't belong here but I felt so free. So at peace. I followed Morfar with his perfect posture. Him sticking his arms out completely straight to give warning to passing motorists of us turning. Exactly as he had done when I was a child following behind him. Nothing had changed. My life in Falsterbo was my one constant. The only part of my childhood that still remained. I inhaled the sea as much as I could. Recharging those parts of me that need to be connected to the ocean. I didn't want this bike ride to finish.

I got to have one day with Magdalena. One crazy day of her helping me buy a second hand Emmaljunga pram so I would have something in Jerusalem. She found one in Lund, the town I was born in, so we caught the train and rushed through the maze of cobbled streets trying to find this elusive pram. Both of us laughing at us being mothers now, swapping our childhood adventures to running through streets searching for prams. It didn't matter that we hardly ever saw each other anymore. Hardly any contact. The instant we were together it was as if nothing had changed. Our connection just as strong.

We had only spent a few days in Sweden but it was so worth it. My time with Mormor and Morfar so precious. I had tried as much as possible to soak up my time with them, knowing full well that this opportunity was quickly slipping away as I could see the years take their toll. Mormor still painting despite her eyesight diminishing and Morfar now needing to help her more and more in the kitchen. I hugged them tightly as we said our good byes, trying to inhale their smell deep into my being.

Israel was next. Sweden had been exactly what I needed. A balm. Everything would be okay. I was going home and we could make it work. The hills of Jerusalem were waiting for me. Hummus with warm pita. Watermelon with feta. Cardamom coffee in the old city. I was going home.

Jon had helped arrange for us to use an apartment that was empty after an American family went back home earlier than expected. He warned us that it was unfurnished and small but I was just happy that we would have our own space and not feel as if we were intruding. When you live in Jerusalem it's so common to have people come to stay and there is always room for another mattress on the floor. I knew that Elinka would offer but I felt with there being four of us, it might not be such a good idea. Especially with one of us being in a pretty unfriendly headspace.

I shouldn't have worried. Paul was thrilled to be back in Jerusalem. His gloominess left behind on the plane as we landed in Tel Aviv. He had a spring in his step. His energy levels were high. Out and about meeting with his friends. Well, my friends who were now his friends. It was so great to see him happy. I watched him with Jon and the other guys and was reminded of the man I married. Of course once we returned to our apartment he was back to his regular self but at least socially he was interactive and having fun and it gave me some sense of hope that things were improving. I knew that he would go to bars and drink but I stuck to my promise of not saying anything about it for six months, and I trusted that he was sticking to the two drinks.

The pram that Magdalena and I had hunted down in Lund was perfect on the hilly streets of Jerusalem. I was able to take Asher and Tikvah anywhere I wanted to go. Our tiny little apartment was in the German Colony so it meant that I could walk into the city centre feeling the hustle and bustle that I was so familiar with. I could walk to Elinka's house and sit at her round kitchen table as the kids played on the roof. I had made a new friend called Martha. She lived on Mt Zion at the college that had now shut down. I would push the pram to go and visit her while our kids played in their wading pool overlooking Jerusalem. We would drink cups of tea at her red kitchen table. Her husband Greg often popping in to say hello. He was the caretaker of the property and despite all the things he was called on to do he always seemed to find time to come home for a few moments. I saw how he looked at his wife with such tenderness. How he adored her so openly.

I asked Martha about it later. Was he always like that? It really seemed as if he worshiped the ground she walked on. Martha laughed. Yes he did. He really did. Every night he would massage her and tell her how much he loved her. Massage her every night?? Really? I didn't believe it. Really, every night? "Yes, every night." Sometimes just a foot massage. Sometimes her neck and shoulders. Other times her whole body. But yes, every day ended with a massage. I sat in awe. I couldn't remember the last time Paul had agreed to give me a massage. Come to think of it, I couldn't remember the last time he had touched me. I looked at Martha. Possibly the most beautiful woman I had ever met. A picture of calm. Her children absolutely wild but she didn't even seem to notice. Her presence completely different from the usual highly strung Jerusalemites.

No matter how much I walked I still needed to return home to an expressionless husband each day. I would ask him about his day. Ask him if he had heard about any jobs. Our friends were suggesting things but none of them were what Paul wanted. They were below him. I knew there was no point in trying to explain that everyone has to start somewhere. My dad had worked in a factory when we first came to Israel and then become the manager of a bookstore in the Old City. Jerusalem was like that. You just take what you can and then opportunities open. No, Paul wanted his dream job. He wanted to lecture or to preach. He wanted to rub shoulders with the top Biblical scholars. Men who had studied the Dead Sea scrolls for years. Experts in the field. Paul had a degree from a college in Adelaide and studied Hebrew in his spare time. My Biblical Hebrew was still way better than his, and mine was pathetic to say the least. How could he be so out of touch?

I offered to look for work myself. I could probably find something. No, he didn't want that. I should be with the kids. I had to agree. Jerusalem is a hard place to look after kids. None of the kid friendly spaces like Australia or Sweden. There were playgrounds to visit but my kids were so put off by the stench of cat urine. I was put off by the broken glass in the sand. My kids missed the freedom of Falsterbo. There was no way Paul was going to be able to look after the kids for a day when I was at work. He could hardly cope with 15 minutes while I was in the bathroom.

Elinka offered to take Asher and Tikvah to the zoo. Something fun to do. It meant a day for me and Paul to be alone. I told him that we needed to make some decisions. We couldn't be in this limbo land much longer. I loved being home. But I couldn't stay in Jerusalem with Paul not wanting to accept the job offers that were coming in. His dream job might be around the corner. I didn't know, but I knew we needed money. And I knew that we couldn't keep doing this anymore. I couldn't live in Jerusalem with a man who was totally alive outside the home and then Dead Man Walking as soon as he walked back through the door.

Not long after that we got on the plane and returned to Adelaide. Total relief swept over me. Lillian belonged in Jerusalem. Lillian the wife and mother didn't. I needed to get back to the City of Churches. I had to set aside my longing to be home and look at what was best for my marriage and my kids. Sadly that meant back to the quiet streets of Adelaide.

Alice and her husband were caretakers of a giant old mansion in the Adelaide Hills at the time. It was rundown and waiting to be sold. We would be able to stay there until we found somewhere to live. The house was freezing in the middle of winter but it was so good to be back. Alice was able to look after the kids while Paul and I searched for rentals. We found two. One by the beach and one in the hills. We just couldn't decide where we wanted to be. The ocean had always called to me but being surrounded by trees and nature was so appealing. In the end we decided to let fate decide. Whoever would choose to accept our application would make our decision for us. Both did. At the exact time. We were back to making a choice. I knew there was a church in the Adelaide Hills that was meant to have a very close-knit community. In that very moment that is what I craved more than anything else. The hills won.

A couple of weeks later we moved into a tiny place that looked like a ginger bread house. Two bedrooms, a small living room with a fireplace, a tiny kitchen with ferns outside the window. It was perfect. The kids loved running around the backyard full of citrus trees. It was cosy and it was our home. Things were going to be okay.

We started going to the local church that I had heard about. There were lots of young families and it wasn't long before Paul was asked to preach. I joined the local playgroup and started to make some friends. Paul got his job back at college and started working at the radio station. Our life had a bit of a rhythm to it again. I had stuck to my promise of not mentioning anything to Paul about his drinking, trusting that he was getting help. It was now five months since I handed him my wedding ring and not a day went by when I didn't think about how much I wanted our marriage to start afresh. How much I needed Paul to make some new promises to me. How much I craved for us to be united.

I started to wonder how Paul might go about it. What was he planning? Would it just be a casual conversation one night once the kids had gone to bed? Or would he put some effort into it and make it something a bit more special? Five months in limbo land had felt like forever and I was so keen for a fresh start. Excited to hear from Paul about how he had gone about the transformation. I hadn't seen any signs of improvement but was still hoping that the work was being done on an internal level.

The six month milestone went by without Paul mentioning anything. I decided to give him the benefit of the doubt and stayed silent. It was now seven months since I gave him my ring and Paul came home with blood shot eyes. He often did, but this time I couldn't stay silent anymore. The six month milestone was fading quickly in the distance and my 27th birthday was around the corner. I couldn't bear the thought of dragging the heaviness into yet another year of my life. Paul started to say something critical about me. His way of distracting us from the topic of his drinking. Instead of remaining silent or entering into the dialogue I just looked at him straight in the eyes and asked him where my ring was.

What ring??

My ring Paul. My wedding ring. Where is it? It's more than six months and you haven't given it back to me.

His face was blank. The room was silent. I kept looking at him.

I lost the ring.

You lost it?

I couldn't believe what I was hearing. You lost my wedding ring?

Yeah, I lost it.

Where did you lose my wedding ring? Again the room was silent.

I lost it at the Discovery Centre.

Paul had taken Asher to the Discovery Centre a few days earlier. Nothing added up. I took a deep breath.

Paul, you know this is not about the ring. I actually don't care about the ring. Tell me what you have done in the past six months to get help. Who have you spoken to? What has changed?

The silence was squeezing my chest. I had been waiting for this moment for so long. When Paul finally spoke his words cut so deep.

I haven't spoken to anyone. I don't know why this is so important to you Lillian. I'm fine.

I lay in bed that night with tears streaming down my face. Most nights I fell asleep crying but tonight was different. The tears were burning me. How could I be so worthless to this man? How could he not see how much I desired to be connected to him? How much I craved to be seen by him. How much I wanted us to be together. To be a family. For him to be a husband. For him to be a dad to his children. I had so much love to give him but he was refusing to receive it. He didn't want it. He wanted to be left alone. Left alone on his quest for fame.

The next few months were the hardest I had ever gone through. I felt as if I was in a constant state of choking. I was making new friends at church and in my community but I was running on empty. My body started to protest. I had constant diarrhoea. I got shingles. I was watching my husband get more and more preaching opportunities, more subjects to teach at the college, and even win an SBS TV script writing course. Yet at home he was completely and utterly void. Dead Man Walking. No eye contact. Hardly a word being said to me and the kids. Meals eaten in silence. His mind elsewhere. Again I joked that I would buy him a microphone to use at home. I wasn't really joking. Paul came alive in front of a microphone. He was a dynamic speaker. Engaging and funny. Thought provoking and inspiring. I longed for a tiny bit of that at home. Any sign of life. There was none.

Four months later Paul finally agreed to go to counselling with me. He reluctantly went. Alice watched the kids for us. It was an hour and a half session with Relationships Australia. The counsellor tried to get both of us to share our story. Paul didn't say much. He was there because I wanted him there. According to him I was making a big deal out of nothing. As we were coming to a close the counsellor said to Paul that he needed to really start looking at some of his choices very seriously. He needed to decide what he actually wanted. Did he want this marriage to work or was he willing to accept it ending with divorce?

Divorce? Paul almost laughed.

Lillian wouldn't divorce me. She doesn't believe in divorce.

Paul was right. I didn't. The counsellor made a time to see us again four weeks later. In the meantime he asked Paul to not have more than two drinks at a time. Paul needed to show me that he was wanting this marriage to work. Alcohol was too much of a trigger for the mental health issues from his past and any more than two drinks was too much of a risk right now.

A week later Paul was reversing out of our garage. I ran back inside to grab a bag I had forgotten so I waited until Paul was out and helped him shut the garage door. As I waited I looked into our yard. I had never stood in this spot before and there was an opening in the fence. Not very wide but wide enough for me to see a giant pile of cans and bottles. Over a metre wide and piled up to my waist. As I sat down in the car I told Paul. Could he believe that our landlords had left that behind when they rented the house out to us? I knew they were young and obviously had a bit of a wild side. But still, seemed so crazy to leave that behind when everything else was left in such pristine condition. Paul agreed. He really agreed. In fact, he was actually engaging in conversation with me. Something started niggling inside me. Paul chatting to me was so unusual. What was going on? A little voice inside me was saying something. I didn't want to listen.

By the time we reached the freeway I couldn't ignore it anymore. Those cans were not just any cans. Those were VB cans. Paul's favourite beer. And those bottles were long neck bottles. It hit me like a bolt. That pile wasn't left over from our landlords. They all belonged to Paul! In the few short months that we had lived there Paul had been able to create a giant pile of empty cans and bottles. He came home almost every night with two long necks to drink and they went into the recycling. So these were on top of that. The voice was so loud I had to ask.

Paul, are those your bottles and cans? He denied it. I asked again.

Paul, tell me if they are.

Total denial and this time anger. I asked him again, but this time I asked him to swear on the Bible. He was silent. I had my answer. I had already known. I had known from the moment Paul started chatting to me. His eagerness to speak showing me that something was up. If he had remained his normal silent self I would have let the moment slide.

I reminded Paul that his drinking would split our family apart. Begging him to take me seriously. To take the counsellor seriously. To open his eyes and see what he would lose. That I couldn't live with a man that lied about his drinking and was willing to risk his mental health on an alcohol addiction. I couldn't do it. I would leave him. I really would. He reminded me that I don't believe in divorce. I didn't, but the Mother Bear in me did. The Mother Bear that was birthed in the agonising hours of my first labour. She believed in divorce. She believed in children having a father that was safe. That Mother Bear that Paul was unwilling to acknowledge was alive and well.

Only a few days later, when we were away for Easter with Paul's family, I reached for one of his cans of Coke for a sip and realised it had whisky in it. I then looked at the Coke cans scattered around him that all ended up having whisky in them. The Mother Bear had enough. While Paul was asleep on the couch, his beloved Simpsons not enough to keep him awake, I went into our room in the holiday shack and collected our belongings. I then told the kids we were going home. Once Paul woke up from his long afternoon nap I asked him to drive us back to Bridgewater. I was leaving him. I couldn't wait for him to take his mental health seriously anymore. I had given him the ring a year ago now. Almost to the day. Nothing had changed. He was only drinking more and more. Lying more and more. If we were worth something to him he would have gotten help by now.

We drove back in silence. Paul not showing any signs of being upset about losing his family.

I called Alice. Can I come and stay? I need somewhere to stay with the kids. No questions asked.

Of course.

She would have the mattresses ready for us. Paul offered to drive. He almost seemed amused. Was this funny to him? He helped me with our bags. Unloading them for me. He was never this helpful. He didn't even say goodbye as he hopped back in the car. That was it. I had left my husband and as far as I could see he didn't even seem to care.

The kids were thrilled to be back with their best friends and spent their days making cubby houses and fairy lands in the rose garden surrounding the mansion. As the day got darker I would count the moments left until I could clock off from motherhood and just cry and cry. I had walked down to the closest town and bought myself a packet of cigarettes. Each night as the kids were finally tucked into bed I would stand outside under the huge starry sky and smoke one cigarette. Just one slow cigarette. I didn't even know why I did it. Alice would stand next to me and we hardly spoke. We didn't need to. My marriage had gone up in smoke and there was nothing to really say.

After seven days and seven cigarettes I called Paul to say that I was going to contact Centrelink and tell them I was now a single mother. This would be his last chance to tell me he wanted our marriage to be saved. He told me to go ahead. I did. I threw out the rest of the cigarettes and I called them up. I was standing in this giant walk in pantry with mice darting past me telling Centrelink that I was now on my own. The tears making it hard to speak. Lillian Good a single mother. My mind could hardly grasp it.

Two weeks later I still hadn't heard anything from Paul. He was about to come and collect the kids to go buy some fancy clothes for his brother's wedding. His mother had organised it with him. All I knew was that Paul was arriving at 11:00am. I was happy that he would see his children. They hadn't asked about him but I thought it would be good for them to see him and spend some time with their dad. By 11:30 he still hadn't shown up. He was never late. By noon

I knew something was wrong. He wasn't answering his mobile. Our home phone was ringing out. I needed to go there and see for myself. Alice's husband said he would look after the kids so that Alice could drive me to my little gingerbread house in Bridgewater. It was only a ten minute drive and my heart was pounding the whole way.

We could see his car parked outside the house. We walked up to the house and couldn't see Paul in the living room. He wasn't in our bedroom, or the kids room or in the kitchen. The only other place to look was in the garage. I couldn't do it. I had this feeling of dread come over me and asked Alice to do it for me. Could she please check the garage for me? She could see in my eyes that I was desperate. He wasn't there. Alice had checked everywhere. I exhaled. In my mind he was hanging in the garage, thankfully he wasn't.

We walked back to the living room and I saw the Yellow Pages lying there. I looked closer. There was blood on the couch. I flipped through the Yellow Pages until I came to a page with drops of blood all over it. Sure enough. There it was. The mental health crisis line. I started calling the hospitals. He wasn't at Flinders Hospital where we had gone when Tikvah was a little baby. He was at the Royal Adelaide Hospital. They asked if I was his wife. I said yes. They forwarded my call to someone who could tell me more. The evening before Paul had called for an ambulance but said that he couldn't afford one. He told them that he had left his car outside with the keys in the ignition. Could they please have one of the paramedics drive him to the hospital in our car so he didn't have to pay for the ambulance? They said no. They couldn't do that. He had passed out while still being on the phone so they came anyway. Found him collapsed on the couch and took him straight to the hospital in Adelaide. He was in the Psychiatry Unit if I wanted to come and visit him. I thanked them and hung up.

I told Alice that I would drive our car to her place. Since arriving back in Australia I had a couple of driving lessons to get used to being on the left side of the road. I was still very uneasy about driving but knew I just needed to do it. She said I could follow her. We drove along the freeway below the speed limit. Me clinging onto the steering wheel. Me knowing my life would never be the same.

Once we got back to the mansion Alice offered to drive me to the hospital in the city. I knew I had to see Paul. I was dropped off outside his ward and made my way in. I felt as if I was in a movie. A terrifying movie. A woman standing in the hallway banging her head on the wall. A man screaming from his room. Doctors walking past not seeming to notice anything amiss. I could smell urine. Or was it bleach? It was hard to tell.

The place gave me goose bumps. And there was my husband's room. In the very back. I stood in the doorway. My Dead Man Walking now wrapped up like an Egyptian mummy. Bandages from his neck all the way to his toes. He turned to look at me. The doctor was in the room. He explained that Paul had cut himself all over his body. Sliced his arms. His stomach. His legs. His feet. Deep cuts. Even his toes. I didn't say anything at all. The doctor left. Paul's eyes were wide.

Are you not going to talk to the doctor? Are you not going to get me out of here?

I shook my head. Paul couldn't believe it.

They want to give me medication. They are telling me I need medication.

I told him it had nothing to do with me. If he didn't want it he could tell them himself. Or he could take the medication like they suggested. It really wasn't for me to say any more. Paul was shocked. I went over to his bedside table and got his wallet out. Took his bank card and left. I spent about 45 minutes in the city shopping. A couple of tracksuits that would be comfortable for him in hospital and a new shirt and jeans for him to wear when he got out. A shirt and jeans that had no bloodstains on them. Also some new undies and socks. It felt good. I could hand over Paul's card and know that his money wasn't going to be pissed away. His money. I now had my own card with money of my own coming in from Centrelink.

Once I returned to the hospital I asked for help to get Paul into a wheelchair and rolled him through the corridors to the main entry.

Again I handed his bank card over to the hairdresser and Paul had his hair cut and his face shaved. I then rolled him back to his room. Once he was back in his bed and his bank card back in his wallet I said good bye and left him there.

Alice drove me back up the hill in silence. I got into the shower and let the hot water burn my skin. Hotter and hotter. The water searing me. Tears pouring out as the profanities started. Fuck you Paul. Fuck you. Fuck you, you mother fucker. Shitting fuck fuck. Shit fuck, fucking shit. You fucking fuck fuck. I couldn't stop. You mother fucking fuck! Fucking hell fuck you mother fucker. My body burning. The swearing getting louder and louder. How had he allowed this to happen? How had he not gotten help? How could we be worth so little to him? The mother fucker! He really had fucked with the wrong mother. It was over. My marriage really was over. I turned the shower off and collapsed into bed. I curled into a ball and pulled the doona over me. I wanted to sleep and never wake up.

17

Happy Single Mum

The exhaustion was overwhelming. Months, if not years, of trying to connect with my husband had taken its toll. I had poured myself into him and all my energy had been sucked into a black hole. I wanted to sleep. Stay away from all the comments and questions that I knew were just around the corner. I couldn't face them. Sleep was the only solution. Alice understood and distracted the kids as I tried to sleep my pain away.

Once Paul announced that he was coming out of hospital I asked him to take anything that he wanted from the house and find somewhere else to live. I needed to return home and start again. He took the computer, the microwave, the TV, and said he would be back for his car when he was allowed to drive again. All the items that had any monetary value were gone. I was so relieved. Each of those things were so strongly connected to Paul and the house felt lighter once they were out.

The computer was the only concern because I knew that I would need to start up my studies again and finally finish off my counselling degree so I could get some work. The computer also meant contact with my friends and family around the globe. I didn't have to worry. My neighbour across the street was happy to sell me a computer. He knew I didn't have any money. My computer cost me a dozen freshly baked rock buns. Rod's favourite treat. His wife Jeanette asked me if I wanted to do some cleaning a couple of hours a week for some extra cash. I was being looked after. We would be all right.

I was relieved to be back in our gingerbread home. The bloodstains on the couch and the missing knife from my wooden block in the kitchen the only signs that anything had happened. The kids didn't even ask where Abba was. As my first Friday back home approached I knew exactly what I wanted to do. I no longer had to ask Paul to drive us, and have him say that he didn't want to. I could do it myself. I just had to face my fear of city traffic. I told the kids we were going to China Town for dinner. They were thrilled. It was hard to get there on the bus from the hills with a pram. Now that I could drive, Friday nights at the Central Markets and China Town for dinner became our new little family's weekly ritual. I loved chatting to the different stallholders. Most of them remembered me from when I would come in with Asher on the train as a baby and just walk around and chat. This quickly became our favourite part of the week and often we would leave early afternoon and stay till bedtime.

Having the car meant a whole new world opening up for us. Requests started coming in from different friends. Naomi, one of the mothers at church, asked me if I would join her at the market every month in Stirling, a gorgeous little town in the Adelaide Hills. Her dad had come up with a way for Pacific Islanders to make their own coconut oil in order to generate their own income. It was a huge opportunity for them to become self-sufficient. Only thing was, they needed sales. The general public still believed that coconut oil was unhealthy. Naomi explained to me the science behind why coconut oil was in fact the healthiest option. I couldn't really grasp it but I loved the texture of it and I knew that if Naomi deemed something kosher it was. Thankfully she would be with me at the market and be able to explain the science to potential customers. I was there for support and to give customers free hand massages. Easy. And so much fun. It gave me an opportunity to do what I love the most, chatting to strangers. Naomi's dad was very grateful for our small but heartfelt contribution. Every sale made a difference at this point as coconut oil was received with such scepticism.

Another friend Becky also wanted me to help her out with an idea she had. Adelaide was starting to receive more and more asylum seekers. Would I be interested in coming along for a weekly catch up in the city to help Irani and Iraqi mothers learn English? Of course! The word spread and it wasn't long before we had about twelve mothers and their children meeting in a conference room at the Immigration Office in the city. Asher and Tikvah would join me to hang out "with the ladies who don't speak English" and play with the other children under the tables as the mothers would drink cups of tea and try to learn all the new concepts of life in Adelaide.

I really felt for them. I knew how hard and isolating it was to be in a new place even with already knowing the language. It felt so good to be able to support someone else in the same process. As it turned out, our little group grew very quickly and it wasn't long before we were offered a space in a council building in the northern suburbs. We could become a proper playgroup where we had activities for the children and toys to play with. A much friendlier environment for all of us. Despite the language barrier our friendships deepened and we started getting more offers of having meals at different homes. Asher and Tikvah got used to us driving to new parts of Adelaide and being welcomed into homes where the evening meal wasn't served until very late at night, way past their bedtime, and we would sit on carpets while served huge amounts of fragrant rice and perfectly cooked spicy meats.

The generosity of these families was so overwhelming because I knew from helping them with their banking how little they were surviving on each week, yet they were so much wanting to shower us with their hospitality.

Not long after I became a single mother I heard there was a new sourdough bakery not far from us. Hahndorf was a German tourist town and they now had a bakery run by an Israeli. I was intrigued. I got to know the owner and his partner and it wasn't long before I started to sell bread for them. I would do taste testings in shops that catered for health conscious people. The Organic Market in Stirling, a gourmet shop in Burnside, as well as a couple of stalls at the Central Markets. It was lots of fun and I loved getting paid for talking and feeding bread to strangers. What could be better?

It was during one of these mornings selling bread at the Central Markets, when a lady came up to me to taste the bread. Everything about her reminded me of my mother. I had to ask her. Was she Swedish? She was! She was thrilled to hear that I was as well and laughed when I told her that I was also from Israel. She insisted that I come over to her house and meet her daughter was an artist. Aaron, her boyfriend, an author and their quirky friends. After five years in Adelaide I felt as if I had finally met some like-minded people. Eccentric and whimsical and, most importantly, ridiculously silly. I didn't get to see them very often but when I did it recharged my batteries. Thankfully they invited me to spend Christmas with them. I had already booked in to do dishes for a church lunch for the homeless in the city while Asher and Tikvah went to their grandparents house with Paul. Spending Christmas Eve with this eclectic Swedish group was the closest I could come to being "home" for Christmas and I was so grateful for the invite.

I was struggling more and more with the people at church. Or maybe they were struggling with me. Not much was said about my new status of being a single woman but I could feel their disapproval. Quite a lot of people stopped talking to me all together. Others clumsily tried to tell me that they were praying for me. I had one well-meaning woman at church take my hands and stare into my eyes and tell me that I had made a very bad decision marrying Paul. A very, very bad decision. Really? I had made a bad decision? What about the decisions Paul had made? It was so frustrating. I didn't want to go into it. People would see what they wanted to see. I didn't feel the need to tell people what had happened in our marriage. It was too complex. And with Paul still teaching at the college and working at the radio station, I didn't think everyone needed to know the sordid details. It was quite strange though. I had gone from being a preacher's wife to a single mother. In Christian circles, I had gone from the top of the ladder to the bottom very quickly. I had lost my status that I never realized I had until it was gone. Strangely it felt so much better on the bottom.

Only weeks before our marriage ended Paul and I had organised a Passover meal at our church. Over fifty people came. We ate roast lamb and Middle Eastern food and Paul spoke about the symbolism of the Passover meal. Explaining how the Lord's Supper, or Communion as many call it, and drinking the wine and eating the bread that represents the blood and flesh of Jesus, actually stems from the Passover meal. How Jesus was celebrating this annual ritual with his closest friends. Holding up the cup of wine that represented the Salvation of the Israelites out of Egypt, and having the audacity to say that this cup was actually his blood. That HIS blood was the Salvation of Israel. Then taking the bread that was a symbol of God's redemption of the Israelites, the bread that showed God's provision, Jesus now saying that this unleavened bread was HIS body. The whole of the Passover Seder points to Jesus as the Messiah and Paul explained the symbols throughout the meal. It shed new light on the communion that so many Christians partake of without knowing the Jewish roots behind it. Not realising that it's woven into the Hebrew ritual of the Passover meal. It was a huge eye opener for the people in our church and we had so many of them come to us and ask for more information. Explaining that they had never looked at the New Testament in the context of Judaism before. Some even said they had never even thought about Jesus being Jewish or that there was any connection between the two.

My marriage had ended months earlier when I still had people coming up to me asking when Paul and I would have another Jewish event at the church. Refusing to believe that we were actually no longer together. Others making comments about how happy I seemed. I got the feeling it bothered them.

I tried to keep going to church despite it feeling more and more awkward. It was still the only community I had and the closest thing I had to family in Australia. I struggled with so many aspects of church. I tried to ignore them and put my energies into the things I valued and not focus on the requests for money to be given to their building fund. One of the men at church who I really respected for his social justice outlook, asked if there were people who were interested in joining him on Saturdays to teach English to Afghani asylum seekers who were working in an abattoir. A local church had offered a space to be used so that the men didn't have to try to find transport for the 45 minute drive to the city.

I was keen to help. I knew what a difference it had made for the women I was helping out to have English speakers spend time with them so I quickly said I would be happy to come along, as long as they were okay for me to bring my children. As it turned out having Asher and Tikvah there was perfect. These men, many of them dads, had fled their country for safety. Leaving their wives and children in order to save their lives. They were Hazara. A persecuted minority from the mountains of Afghanistan. They told me, in their very broken English, how their fathers or brothers were murdered and they were next. Many of them had escaped with only hours to plan. A lot of these men came from villages. Rural villages without running water or electricity. No concept of the world around them. They had never even been to a city before, let alone left their country. As they arrived at their next destination they were only given instructions on where to go next and many didn't even realise they were in Australia until they were told upon arrival.

My heart went out to these men who were now thrilled to have some kids to play with. Carrying Asher and Tikvah on their shoulders and chasing them around the room. Quite a few people from the church had come along to help out so we were split into groups. I was partnered with a man who introduced himself as Leonard. A local minister. We spent the afternoon teaching English and both of us realising very quickly that the workbooks were useless and it was much better to just make conversation. These men needed more than grammar and spelling. They needed to connect and be heard. We quickly became a very animated table and tried our hardest to not draw too much attention to our group. Leonard and I would grin at each other across the table. We were having so much fun.

Over the next few days I kept thinking back to Leonard. There was something really special about him. For a minister he was very relaxed and informal. He was witty and very kind. None of the usual ego I would associate ministers to have. He had mentioned to me that he was single. Had he purposely done that or was it an innocent piece of information? I had to acknowledge that I was really attracted to him.

It didn't take long before Leonard and I would meet together without our Afghan friends. Leonard was beautiful. Twenty-four years older than me and absolutely beautiful. He adored me. Really adored me. I had never had attention like this before from a man. He was kind and attentive and made me feel desired. He knew that I couldn't sleep with him. That was a boundary I still couldn't cross with my marriage still not legally over. I needed the divorce to come through before I could even consider being intimate with a man. Leonard didn't mind. He showered me with the love that I was so starved of. He would cook for me, or hug me while I would cook a meal for us in his kitchen. Then dance me across the room to music from the fifties. He brought me flowers just because. Told me I looked like a movie starlet. He was exactly what my raw wound needed. Years of neglect were being wiped away by a sweet minister who seemed to understand my heartache and pain. He took me to his little hobby farm and as we drove around in his ute, delivering straw to his cattle, he would tell me about his trips around the world and how much he longed to return. We sat by his dam and discussed theology and the loneliness of marriage.

We invited our Afghan friends to spend an evening with us on the farm. They all jumped into the back of the ute and laughed as Leonard drove them up and down the hilly paddocks looking for logs for our fire. They wanted to know everything. Pointing to trees and wanting to know the proper name. What was the word for the car we were in? The Aussie word ute totally new for them.

As we got into one of the paddocks, Mohammed stepped into a fresh cow patty. Everyone roared with laughter. What is this name?? What you call this? Leonard started to say "cow dung" but

I interjected with a more appropriate word. Shit. This is shit. They looked at each other. Shit! They knew this word. They had heard it at the abattoir. Ghulam looked across to the neighbouring paddock and pointed to the bull. A light went on in his eyes. Bull ... shit. Bullshit. Bullshit!!! He finally understood! He was jubilant. So were the rest of the guys. The English language had just come alive for them. They all started chanting "Bullshit Bullshit Bullshit". Asher and Tikvah joining in. This mystery word finally had meaning! We had a wonderful evening around the fire. Cooking meat and singing songs but nothing quite beat that moment in the paddock when a group of lonely Hazara men finally understood the true meaning of bullshit.

When Paul told me he was taking our car I didn't need to worry. Leonard had one that I was able to buy off him very cheaply. It felt so good to be looked after and be on the receiving end of someone who genuinely cared for me in such practical ways. This was completely new for me. Leonard was the best thing that could have happened to my heart those first few months after my marriage ended. I hadn't been looking for a relationship at all. Still in shock at finding myself single. Divorce was only something that happened to other people. It was never going to happen to me. Ever.

As much as I wanted to focus on my unexpected romance I had some serious decisions to make. I had to complete my studies so I was able to get a proper job. The only way I could study was to put Tikvah into child care. As a stay at home mother the idea of child care was completely out of my reality. It felt wrong on so many levels. I also needed to get some money. Even a little bit of money would help. I was trying to encourage Paul to have the kids for a few hours each week. He wasn't really interested. Told me it was too hard to have both of them. I said that they would feel distressed being split up. They were always together. He finally agreed to have them for a few hours every Sunday. I approached the Organic Market in Stirling and asked them if I could get a waitressing job there. They had gotten to know me from my bread tastings I had done. They gave me a Sunday shift. I was so grateful. It wasn't much but it was enough to help me pay for my extra expenses.

I have never been an academic person but I now had a huge incentive. I needed to get a proper job. I needed to start my career. My mind boggled at the thought of me, Lillian Good, being a single mother with two children and a career woman! That was so far from the image my heart was set on, being a wife and hopefully mother of four. My new life was so busy, but in my quiet moments I was still grieving the loss of not being the mother of a large family. Not being a wife. I had to accept my new status and move on.

Paul seemed to be keen for me to move on as well. One Sunday when I dropped off the kids he asked me if I had made any long-term plans. Plans? I told him about my studies and how I was hoping to maybe open up a counselling centre in Adelaide with some classmates. Paul asked if I had considered moving to Sweden. Sweden? No I hadn't. Paul said I really should. That way I could be close to my parents again. Get the support I needed. Sweden would be better financially for me and it would mean having my parents there to help me out. They had recently moved there after their very long stay in the US. It had come unexpectedly.

A few months earlier my dad had been out for his regular, early-morning 'prayer walk' as he called it. He would get up at 4:00am and walk for a couple of hours. For him a perfect opportunity to get fresh air as well as pray. He loved his daily ritual and enjoyed the empty streets. One morning though he didn't return. He had been found on the side of the road by a passing jogger in a pool of blood. He was rushed to hospital and the doctors weren't sure if he would survive or not. Two drunk teenagers had been looking for something fun to do after a late night party. They had a metal baseball bat with them. As my father walked past them deep in prayer they whacked him as hard as they could in the back of his head. He crumpled to the ground and the two teenagers took off thinking they had just killed a man.

The small city of Springfield was shocked as the news spread. How could something like this happen? Word got out that the man was a Jew from Jerusalem. A Jew studying at one of their Christian seminaries. It was almost as if Jesus himself had been attacked on their streets. Money started pouring in as my dad lay in a hospital bed in a coma. Strangers wanting to help. My dad's story triggering an outpouring of love from the local community. The money covered the outrageous hospital expenses. That in itself was a modern day miracle. Not just that. There was enough money for my parents to finally leave America. My mother had been wanting to spend some more time with her parents as they were ageing quickly. Once my dad was strong enough to travel they packed up their belongings yet again and moved to Sweden. Three months later Mormor died.

Now Paul was suggesting that I move there as well. To Sweden. It seemed ludicrous. I had been hoping that Paul would be trying to spend more time with his children. Encouraging him to have them overnight. Try to build a relationship with them. It had taken them over a year to even ask where he was. His absence not noticed for such a long time. I wanted my kids to have a relationship with their dad and here he was telling me I should move to Sweden with them. I told him I wouldn't. That we were staying in Adelaide. That our kids needed a dad. Paul seemed disappointed with my response. A couple of weeks later his request made more sense. He let it slip that he had reconnected with an old girlfriend who lived in Sydney and was hoping to move there and start a new life. It was hard enough to understand his lack of interest in me as his wife, but to realise he was so flippant about his own kids really hurt. I knew he loved them. He really did. Adored them in fact. His face would light up when he saw them. He just couldn't care for them. He was so wrapped up in his own pursuits that being a father felt like too much effort. I ached for my children. I wanted them to have a dad so badly.

My life was so incredibly busy. I was juggling my studies, waitressing, teaching English to the Hazara men, helping with the playgroup for the asylum seeking mothers, doing the occasional taste testing for the bakery, running fun events for the church and helping Alice out as much as I could with her huge work commitments. She now had four young kids and was still working as a voice instructor. I had ended things with Leonard because I just couldn't give any proper time to our relationship. It was during this incredibly hectic time that my mom was able to come and visit me for the first time.

She loved the Australian scenery and marvelled at our exotic birds. Life had not been easy for her the past few years and her trip to Australia was a breath of fresh air.

My dad decided that he wanted to come and visit me as well. I was surprised because he hadn't showed much interest in my life. He was still very upset with me for leaving Paul and most of our contact since my divorce was very brief. My dad had really connected with Paul and respected his preaching and Biblical teachings. He still couldn't fully comprehend why I had left my husband. Constantly reminding me that divorce was in direct opposition to God's commands and his covenant. Now he was saying that he was coming to visit me. The day before he was meant to fly out I got a call from my mother. My dad had suffered yet another heart attack. He was in a coma. His trip cancelled. My poor dad. He had only recently recovered from the baseball bat bashing. Still not being able to taste or smell from the head injury. Now he was in hospital again.

Once he was well enough to talk he asked that I fly to Sweden instead with the kids. He would pay. He was now a pastor for a small international church. A tiny income. Yet he wanted to pay for us to fly over. So generous. He always had been, but it still really touched me that he was able to give so freely.

The timing was perfect with the visit. My brother Sam was visiting with his wife Carla and their two kids. We had a great time in Falsterbo together. Taking bike rides to the beach and having our kids play together. I finally had a taste of what it would be like for my children to have cousins. Ezra decided to come and visit dad as well and brought his girlfriend Lydia with him. The kids adored her gentle and sweet nature. Incredibly Susanna was able to fly over from Egypt as well with her son so before we knew it we had a proper family reunion going on. My dad loved having his kids come in to the hospital to visit and having some time with each grandchild.

Unfortunately Abigail was unable to join us because she had made plans to visit me in Australia before dad had the heart attack. When she realised she couldn't change her tickets she decided to fly to Cairns and wait there until I flew back to Adelaide with the kids.

While I was away I organised with the church to move into the manse next door. It was available for new tenants and thankfully they agreed to let me rent it. Their only concern was that I might not pay the rent on time like previous tenants had and made it very clear to me that this was not a private arrangement through the church. It was a completely separate contract with the real estate agent. I was more than happy to agree to that and make sure that any issues went through the agent and keep the church out of the equation. It seemed fair enough. I could understand their concern.

Once we had returned from Sweden, and gotten over our jet lag, we moved into our new home. The church manse. It was a great house with a huge backyard. We were thrilled. Only a few days later Abigail flew from Cairns to join us. Life seemed to be on track. I was less than two months away from turning thirty. My bachelor's degree was only a few assignments away from being finished. Some of my classmates were already looking around for a place we could rent together for a counselling space.

After a couple months of dabbling in the murky waters of the online dating scene I had decided that I needed to set aside any hopes of repartnering and accept the fact that I was going to be a single career woman with two children. I had spent about six months feeling like a dark cloud was over me but I was finally starting to make peace with my new reality. I decided that on my thirtieth birthday I would declare my new decade my 'Abstinence Decade.' I had two kids and a career to focus on. No time for romance.

18

Romanse

Twelve days before I turned thirty I still hadn't figured out what I would do to celebrate the occasion. In many ways I was busting to get out of my twenties. They had been so full-on and I was so keen to start a much quieter decade. Six months of grieving the loss of my dreams to have a large family had made way for some positive anticipation for this next chapter in my life. What would life look like for Lillian the career woman? It felt so foreign yet I knew that I had something to offer as a counsellor and I was excited about being able to contribute on a bigger scale and to more than just my home and friends.

It was October 17, 2004. A Sunday evening and I was feeling restless. I realised that I didn't have to stay home as I normally did. I could pop out and Abigail could look after Asher and Tikvah for a while. This was new to me. I was so used to doing everything with them. I told them that I needed some space and without really having a plan I just walked down our driveway to the church on the same property. I didn't normally go to the evening service, in fact even the morning service was becoming more and more rare with me finding it so hard to ignore the inconsistencies in the church.

I sat down in the closest empty seat and tried to focus on the sermon. A young guy was preaching and he was very earnest. I thought back to a time in my life when it could have been me up there. My world so black and white. I had all the answers. It was hard to pinpoint when exactly things had started to unravel for me. Obviously living with a preacher who was so gifted when it came to speaking about the Bible, but then a complete asshole at home, was an easy place to start but I knew it went further than that. Studying theology in Sydney and realising that I had more questions than answers hadn't helped. That so much of the Bible is really just man-made. Someone's interpretation.

The unravelling went further back though. For me it had begun when I worked for those wealthy Jewish families in Jerusalem. Listening to them sing the Sabbath prayers and realising that I wasn't any different to them. I was just as religious. This intimate relationship I claimed to have with Jesus was just wishful thinking. That I had brainwashed myself to believe it by singing these songs about this supposed relationship that I was meant to be having, while in reality it was just a relationship I craved and longed for, but there was actually nothing there. Like the man I ended up marrying. Jesus, who was meant to be my Lover, was actually just a typical male giving me the silent treatment.

As the sermon came to a close I noticed that a guy I had spoken to a couple of times was sitting just a few seats away from me. I was pretty sure his name was Andrew. A new friend of mine had a bit of a crush on him and had told me that he had moved across from Melbourne and his mum was dying from cancer. He was into social justice, especially after a trip to India with one of the guys from our church. He came to talk to me as people started getting up from their seats and asked me if I felt uplifted from the sermon. I knew he was being sarcastic. Without missing a beat I went into great details of how inspiring the sermon was and that it's really made me see the error of my ways.

The two of us were obviously on the same page when it came to the church. He went on to ask me how my kids were doing. I was impressed he remembered from our very brief encounter months earlier. I tried to think back how long it was since I had chatted to him and realised it was back in May. Just about the time I had decided that my thirties would not have any boyfriends in it so there was no point pursuing a guy who seemed somewhat intriguing. I told him that things were great with the kids. We were having a wonderful time. My sister was now living with us and life was busy but fun.

Aren't you supposed to be bitter and angry? That's how single mothers are meant to be, no?

I laughed.

No, not me. I'm a happy single mum.

He went on to say that he was so jealous of me. He would love to be a dad. He had only recently convinced his boss to let him work part-time so he could have more time doing fun stuff. I obviously didn't give him the reaction that he wanted because he went on to explain that engineers never work part-time. They squeeze in as many work hours as they can each week. It was so rare to have the freedom to not work full-time.

I told him he might be exactly what I had been searching for. He looked surprised and waited for me to continue. I explained that I needed a male in my life. A token male. Someone who would come and hang out with my kids. Do fun stuff. Take them on nature walks. Bike riding. Things that challenged them somewhat. There was way too much estrogen in the house with it just being me and my sister as adults. I needed some testosterone for my kids. His eyes lit up. Told me he would love to do that. Would love the opportunity to hang out with my kids. His friends were leaving church so we quickly exchanged numbers. Instead of my name I wrote 'Happy Single Mum' next to my number. We organised for him to come over on the following Thursday. I told him we live in the manse next door. Turned out he lived in a manse as well. The one down the road.

The next day I was lying on our trampoline as I often did when I needed time to think. Looking up at the giant trees, I realised that I really didn't know much about Andrew at all and here I was asking him to hang out with my kids. From our little encounter the night before I realised that we would have lots to chat about and I didn't really want Thursday to be just the two of us offloading on each other about the state of the church. He was meant to be hanging out with the kids. I should meet with him first. As soon as I thought that I quickly dismissed the idea. He would think I was interested in him. He would get the wrong idea. Normally I would have left it at that.

However, the past couple of days Abigail and I had been talking about our internal voices. Those little voices that don't actually belong to us but they sit in our mind and shoot down the ideas that we have. They are constantly sabotaging our true intentions. This was a perfect example of that. I had made a decision to be more aware of my internal dialogue and here was my first opportunity to act on it. I thought through it all again. Andrew is coming to hang out with my kids. I hardly know him. It would be good to meet with him first. I should organise to do that. Nothing else. No other intentions. No hidden agenda. That was that. Instead of letting those internal voices dictate what I did, I sent him a text and asked if he wanted to meet for a drink to chat before Thursday. I wasn't a drinker but couldn't think of any other place that would be open at night.

Andrew was happy to catch up at the Aldgate Pub and we chatted for hours. The conversation was so easy. Andrew had so many things to say. So many things he believed in. Social justice was obviously a big topic for him which I liked. Sadly there were now so many beige people in my life. He was far from beige and he really was a breath of fresh air.

It felt wrong to end the evening so I explained that he was welcome to come over if he wanted to. I reminded him that my sister was there, just to clarify that I wasn't suggesting anything else besides a friendly cup of tea. The three of us ended up talking till four in the morning. The conversation flowed really easily and at one point I thought that maybe Abigail and Andrew could end up being a couple. They would look cute together. Andrew with his long hair and beard and Abigail with her knitted beanie.

A few days later Andrew showed up on his bike for our nature walk. I had promised the kids that I would come along until they got to know Andrew for themselves. We walked down to the Bridgewater playground. It's a beautiful space full of trees with a creek running through a tunnel that the kids loved to explore. I sat down at a picnic table and watched my kids play. Andrew was hopping across the creek with them. Using different rocks to stand on so they wouldn't get wet. Each jump further than the last. The sun was shining through the tree tops reflecting on the water bubbling around them. That very moment I had a very clear yet very bizarre moment of knowing that this was now our new family. Just like that. I hadn't heard a voice as such. Just this very clear and still knowing. This was us now. We are a family.

I tried to shake the feeling off. Dismissing it for my overactive imagination. But it remained. This is us. This is our family. I tried not to stare at Andrew as we started walking back to the house. It was an incredibly strange feeling, so different from when we had walked this same path only a short time ago. I turned around and noticed a dog walking behind us. He followed us the whole way home. He seemed to think we were a family as well. Hoping he could be adopted in too.

I tried to rationalise things over the next few days. Telling myself that Andrew was just there for the kids. But no matter how much I tried I knew it was more than that. He was now part of my family. I didn't even feel as if I had a choice in the matter. I just had to accept it. I received a text from Andrew asking me what I was up to. I told him I was just waiting for the kids to fall asleep and then I was going to have some thinking time on my beloved trampoline. He could join me if he wanted. Only a few minutes later I got a text from him. He was waiting for me on the trampoline. In that moment I knew that he was not just interested in the kids. He was interested in me. I walked to the trampoline in the dark knowing that my life was just about to change.

We lay there under the stars talking. I was trying my hardest to not roll into him but two bodies on a trampoline tend to roll into each other. A lot of effort went into staying as neutral looking as possible. We had a lot to talk about. Where did we begin? I suggested we begin with A and work our way through the alphabet. Asking each other questions starting with each letter. When we got to C, Andrew asked, "Children, do you want more of them?". Yes, yes I did. I explained how I had spent half a year coming to terms with the fact that I wouldn't have more. But yes, in my heart I wanted more kids. I knew it deep within me. We stayed out there for hours talking. We stayed until the birds started singing and I quickly jumped up and explained that I had to go. Like Cinderella hearing the midnight bells ring, I was gone in a flash. I needed to be a mum. I needed to be inside when my kids woke up.

A week later I turned thirty. Instead of the 'Decade of Abstinence' ceremony I had planned, we went camping in amongst sand dunes on the Yorke Peninsula. Me, the kids, Abigail, and of course Andrew. When I was thirty years and a day old Andrew kissed me for the first time, in a tent with the ocean roaring in the distance. I marvelled at how we now had this new person in our family and I couldn't really even say that I had wanted it. I just needed to accept it.

Andrew poured himself into his new role as dad. He spent every free moment at our place. Teaching the kids how to ride bikes. Telling them about space. His travels through India. Tikvah started to call him Dad straightaway. She loved having a dad that so clearly adored her. All this time that Andrew was with my kids meant that I had time to get my assignments done for college. Andrew could hang out and create adventures while I could lock myself in front of the computer and study.

It wasn't long before Andrew didn't even bother going home at night. The kids were asking him to read bedtime stories and asking for him at breakfast. It seemed crazy for him to be anywhere else.

We started telling friends that we were a couple. I liked to add, "I live in the Baptist Manse and he lives in the Anglican Manse, and now we have a roMANSE". I thought it was so funny. I couldn't say it for very long because Andrew officially moved in with us. There was no need for us to have two houses anymore. I notified the real estate agent about an extra tenant so it could be on the records. They didn't mind.

However, the church did. Initially they tried to make it out that they were just concerned about my general welfare. I had a visit from the pastor and one of the elders. They told me that they were visiting me because of concerns for my wellbeing and for the children. I thanked them and told them not to worry. We were fine. Was this about the house? No of course not. This was not about the house. I explained that I had an arrangement through the real estate and I had notified them about an extra tenant. No. No. This wasn't about the house at all. Just about my wellbeing. I thanked them. I week later I got called into a meeting at the church with all the elders present. They all knew me. I knew all of them. I knew that every single one of them in that room had skeletons in their closet. I knew which of them had children out of wedlock. Or whose kids were sleeping around with who. Not one person in that room had a 'clear' record. Yet not one of them spoke up when I was told that I was living in sin.

I reminded them that they might not agree with my choices but I had an agreement through the real estate agency and I had been told that the church was not to get involved. I knew that was to protect them from me not paying rent, what I didn't know was that it meant that the church would completely disregard that if it suited them. A few days later I got a letter in the mail from the real estate agent saying I needed to be out of the house in ninety days. No explanation given.

We had already decided to drive to Melbourne over Christmas so that Andrew could introduce us to his family. House hunting would have to wait. It's an eight hour drive between Adelaide and Melbourne if you don't stop too often. Thankfully Andrew was happy to do all the driving. His family made us feel very welcome. They lived in a huge house so we had two bedrooms to ourselves. It was really special to get some time with Louise, Andrew's mum. I knew that she had battled cancer for a while and that anything social was an effort for her. She did her best to spend time with us in the living room though and only retreated to her bed as the exhaustion became too much. Often she would just sit on the couch with blankets over her legs watching the rest of us having fun. We didn't get much of a chance to talk but she made sure to let me know how special it was for her to see her son so happy. She had been praying for her son to have a wife and kids and didn't think she would live to see the day. Her prayers had been answered through this instant family and nothing could make her happier. I smiled. It felt good to give this woman such a precious gift. Andrew was a natural dad and I loved that his mum was able to see that for herself.

It felt clumsy to celebrate Christmas when it really felt as if Louise wasn't going to live much longer. Since leaving Sweden as a child I had never really done much for Christmas but I always made sure I did something to mark the event. I loved to create some sort of cosy feel for the occasion. When I realised that Andrew's family were going to eat their Christmas meal under bright florescent lights and it was going to look like just any other dinner I popped out to the shops to buy a couple of candles. A tea-towel became a mini tablecloth. With the gingerbread kits I brought along for Asher and Tikvah, I was able to create a bit of a Christmas feel.

It was so little but Andrew's dad was impressed by what a difference a candle could make.

Our conversation turned more intimate and we started talking about fears that we had. I explained that I had always had nightmares about empty swimming pools and giant waves slowly creeping in from the horizon and engulfing the ground I was standing on. In fact, I had a dream about it the night before. Standing on a cliff and realising that the wave in the distance was getting bigger and bigger and that the cliff wasn't going to be high enough. We started talking about tsunamis and what they actually are. None of us exactly sure. Andrew's dad went and got the encyclopaedia from the other room and read out what tsunamis are. The next day the book was still out next to the burnt out candles. The tsunami page still open when the news started to come in. The Boxing Day tsunami had killed so many people. The numbers climbed by the hour.

All I could think about were the kids in the orphanage in Sri Lanka. Were they safe? I hadn't kept in touch with them once I left. I hadn't needed to. Jess had returned to Jerusalem and our church was so taken in by the plight of these poor kids. Donations were made and after that a group of young people flew over to Sri Lanka on a regular basis with school supplies and other items that were needed.

I spent the next week glued to the newspaper reading as much as I could. Eventually the news came in. The whole town we were in on the east coast of Sri Lanka had been wiped out by the tsunami. Thousands still missing.

Andrew struggled with my need to read the paper. He didn't understand why I was spending so much time 'leeching off' other people's pain. We had gone camping with some of the friends he had grown up with and he was frustrated at me reading the newspaper. I tried to explain to him that it was something that I did. When things happened around the world I usually had a friend who either lived there or was from there and it made it a lot more real. I liked to read about it. It seemed to bother Andrew. Actually lots of things seemed to bother Andrew. Now that we were hanging out with his friends I noticed how many things Andrew seemed to have an opinion about. A strong opinion about. It was getting somewhat tedious to hear his constant negativity. He seemed to be angry at so many things. I had already noticed how he didn't like being corrected either. Especially by women. There were so many great things about him but it was getting harder to ignore the bristles.

A few weeks after we returned from our trip to Melbourne I went for a walk with Abigail. She was really struggling with having Andrew in the house and I thought it would be good to go for a walk once the kids were asleep. I didn't get a chance to spend much time with her alone so a walk would be perfect. After we had been walking for a while Abigail said she wanted to talk to me about something. She didn't want to upset me. I braced myself. I knew what was coming. She told me that she didn't feel right about Andrew. That there was something about him. I remained silent. There was a darkness about him that made her feel uneasy. I knew exactly what she was talking about. I felt it too. I just couldn't admit it to myself. It was too scary to admit.

It was too scary because I had just found out I was pregnant. I knew Abigail was right. I had aligned myself yet again with a man who had a dark side that still had power over him. I couldn't exactly put my finger on it but I knew it. I knew it deep down inside. This man who was so wonderful to my kids, who had vowed to look after me and my two children. Who was now paying the rent and paying for our food to show how committed he was to be a dad and partner. This troubled, yet generous man who had now fathered a child who was growing inside me. I kept my pregnancy quiet for as long as possible. I just didn't want to have to deal with people's comments until I was fully showing.

We eventually found a house to move to and Abigail decided she wanted to go back to the States. She couldn't share a house with Andrew anymore. I was sad to see her go but also relieved. In many ways having Abigail there triggered the stuff in Andrew that I struggled with. He so clearly didn't like her. Without her on the scene there was one less thing to provoke him. I needed as much harmony around me as possible. This pregnancy had completely drained me of my energy.

My first two pregnancies made me really tired but this was something else. I was totally and utterly exhausted. It was hard to keep my eyes open after 7:00pm. All I wanted to do was crawl into a hole and hide away. I knew my kids would be okay. Andrew was there to look after them. For the first time as a mother I could switch off and someone would be there to take over. I had never experienced that with Paul. Andrew was the complete opposite. He was constantly proving himself to be an incredible dad despite his short time in his new role. Not only was he constantly coming up with new ideas for the kids to do, he was also spending more time in the kitchen wanting to cook.

His thirtieth birthday was approaching and we had organised an Indian themed birthday party for him. Because I was planning a homebirth we hired a small local hall to celebrate in so that we could keep the pool set up in the kitchen if needed. Andrew's birthday was only two days after mine and our baby was due the day in between.

I assumed the baby would arrive late like my first two so I figured we could risk having a party on my due date. Andrew's parents and sister were going to drive over for the party and hopefully be around to see their first official grandchild.

The party was a great success but there was only one thing on Andrew's mind. Our baby. He was desperate for the baby to be born. He had already arranged to take a few weeks off from work once the baby arrived but the agony of waiting was getting too much for him and he decided to stop work in anticipation. I was grateful because I was so large by now. Absolutely giant. This baby was huge and my body was bigger than ever. I knew that if I was having the birth in a hospital they would be telling me that I needed to be induced.

We had decided on a homebirth so that the hospital couldn't dictate what would happen. I was convinced that the reason my births had been so painful was because I hadn't gone into labour naturally. Being induced meant that my body didn't have that slow build-up that it needed to prepare for the birth. Instead it got hit by contractions out of nowhere and went into shock. This time it would be different. The only problem was that the baby was showing no signs of wanting to come out. Neither of us were too concerned. We felt this baby would come when it was ready. Others didn't share those feelings. Andrew's parents were concerned because they had had a niece who was stillborn. I had friends calling me telling me that I was putting my baby in danger. My midwife came over daily and checked on the baby. Listened to the heartbeat. Made sure my blood pressure was all right. There was no need to panic.

When it was 21 days after my due date we went into hospital to have an ultrasound to check that everything was all right. The doctors were horrified at how overdue I was. Told me that this baby had to be born. Yes, everything was technically fine, but the amniotic fluid was low and the baby couldn't stay in any longer. If this baby wasn't born within 24 hours I had to return for an induction.

They did a quick measure and told me the baby was too big. Especially the baby's belly. I wasn't sure if I should believe them. The doctors had said the same thing about Asher. Telling me he was giant and he was only 3.6 kilos. They had been saying he was at least 4.5 kilos. Either way, I decided to try anything I could to help this baby out. I tried three lots of castor oil. Andrew cooked me the spiciest curry he could come up with. We had sex more times in 24 hours than I thought was possible. Nothing helped.

Eventually my midwife suggested that she rupture the membrane. The water breaking would activate the birth. I reluctantly agreed. I had hoped to avoid intervention but it was better than going into hospital. Anything was better than going into hospital. Once the membranes ruptured I started to walk up and down the steep streets around our house. When I came in for a rest I had three midwives massaging me hoping to trigger reflexology points. Incense was burnt that was meant to stimulate the birthing process. I was in awe of the care and nurturing that these devoted midwives were giving me.

Finally, after 24 hours of getting the labour started, I could feel cramping deep down inside me. Over the next few hours the cramping increased and I eventually asked Andrew and the midwives to fill up the birthing pool in our kitchen. The water felt so good. I stayed in as long as I could. Moaning in pain. The pain unbearable but I was so grateful to at least be at home in pain instead of in a sterile hospital with strangers.

I had gotten to know my two midwives really well. Tania was the support midwife and she was spending just as much time helping us as our main midwife. A third midwife had been asked to come as well. I knew Lisa from a monthly homebirth group that I had started going to. She was Welsh so I really didn't understand much of what she said but I really liked her. Could tell that she had lots of experience. She was working at the fanciest private hospital in Adelaide but was hoping to start working independently as soon as she could afford it. She was so horrified at what she saw happen in the hospital. Women having C-sections for no reason all the time. Doctors making women feel as if their labours were taking too long only so they could clock off at a decent time. Women being bullied out of natural births for the convenience of the medical staff. She was so fed up with being part of the system and longed to get out. I was so happy to have her with us. Even though she was only there for support because of how overdue I was, I knew that I was in safe hands.

The birth was taking a long time and I was screaming out in pain. I could hear my midwife tell Andrew that I was in transition. He would soon be holding his baby. I kept screaming. My eyes rolling back in my head. Expecting to feel the baby between my legs any moment. I finally put my hand down there to feel for the scalp only to realise that I wasn't even open. Five hours I screamed so my lungs emptied. This was torture. Absolute torture. After all those hours I got pulled out of the pool because I needed some gravity to help this baby descend. Somehow I managed to get to my bed. Our mattress thankfully on the floor.

The screaming was so loud that I knew that all our neighbours would be hearing me as they tried to sleep. There was nothing I could do to control it. The pain was worse than anything I had ever experienced before. Just when I thought that it couldn't get any worse it did.

Eventually the pushing stage started. Nothing I had heard prepared me for this. A force surging through my body yet the baby not moving. When it did move down a tiny bit it would slide up again. My three midwives directing me in what to do. Push, breathe, pant, pant, pant, PUSH ... I tried to follow what they said but the baby was stuck. Really stuck. The damn doctors were right. This was a huge baby. And the angle of my pelvis was making it pretty much impossible for this baby to come out. My midwife was out of her depth and thankfully Lisa was there to take over. She knew exactly what to do. Two sets of hands were inside me and the baby's shoulder was hooked out.

The pain was excruciating but I could feel progress being made. The baby was slowly coming out. Andrew kept calling out what he could see. I felt as if I was going to split in half when the baby's tummy was passing through. Finally the baby was out. Total silence in the room. The midwives were rubbing the baby's chest. I started blowing on the face. Willing this baby to land. To take the first breath. It felt like such a long time. Thankfully there was no panic. After a bit of a splutter the baby started to cry. This giant bruised baby had finally arrived. We had a girl!

I collapsed on the bed. Letting the after pains shoot through me. Relief that it was over but in total disbelief that I had survived the pain. Andrew held his long awaited baby girl. He was totally smitten. His face melted as he looked at the bundle in his arms. We had already decided on a name. Andrew's mum Louise had kept saying she just wanted to live long enough to meet her grandchild, it would mean one more summer before the cancer won. We were now able to give Louise her much loved granddaughter and we named her Summer.

The next few days Andrew floated around. He was in total awe of his baby girl. As the swelling subsided we realised that Summer had the most giant blue eyes. Beautiful blue eyes that looked even bigger each day. She had been so bruised when coming out that it was only a couple of weeks later that we could really see what she looked like. I had my own healing to do as well. The birth in itself had been so excruciating but now I had haemorrhoids to deal with. It felt as if shards of glass was poking into my bottom. Nothing helped. I tried everything. Ointments, pain killers, rubber gloves filled with water and then frozen and stuck into my bottom. Anything for relief. Nothing worked. Those first couple of weeks were so painful. Summer weighed 4.6 kilos and it was obviously too much for my body to handle.

Amazingly, Andrew's family drove across again to meet with their granddaughter. Louise wanting so much to hold Summer. Two long trips in a month was a big sacrifice for Louise. We spent most of their visit just enjoying each other's company. Louise too exhausted to give Summer a bath but happy to watch. It was only a brief visit but Louise asked if she could take me out for lunch one day. She wanted some time alone with me.

I was touched at her gesture and I drove us to Hahndorf and asked Louise to choose a place to eat. As we shared a salad Louise told me how grateful she was for me. She wanted me to know that she admired my mothering and my patience with my children. She repeated what she had told me a year earlier about how she had almost given up hope that she would ever see Andrew have a family. He had caused them so much hardship when he was younger. Mistreating his sister for so many years. Louise had tried to imagine what sort of woman he would end up with and had prayed that he could find someone strong enough to handle him. I tried to smile. Tried to show her that her prayers had been answered. She was dying of cancer. She needed to know her son was all right.

I wanted to cry though. I wanted to tell her the truth. I wasn't strong. Well, I wasn't strong enough. I had survived a lot in life but Andrew was wearing me down. His negativity and constant criticism was too much for me to handle. I couldn't tell her that even though I looked strong I was really weak. I smiled and said that Andrew was a good dad. That was the truth. She went on to say that seeing Andrew be a good husband was so important to her. She knew we weren't married but she wanted me to know that she saw us as married. I wasn't sure why she started talking about a family friend. Her husband's friend. How he had cheated on his wife. Louise told me how disgusted she was and that she didn't like her husband spending time with that friend. It still made her feel uncomfortable years later. She went on to say that she knew that Andrew was difficult to live with but at least he was faithful. I agreed. I knew he was. We had to return back to the house. I could see that Louise was fading. For a quiet woman she had done a lot of talking. It was obvious that she had wanted me to know these things that were close to her heart.

Only a few months later Louise passed away. Andrew had arrived in Melbourne a week earlier to help out. I drove across with the kids and got there just in time. She died the morning after we arrived. I had spent the evening massaging her hands and feet. Telling her that she was loved. I had brought a candle to light but was surprised to see that Andrew's dad had already lit one in the room. Louise had been battling cancer for such a long time but it was still a shock that she was gone. Andrew loved his mum and grieved deeply. Thankfully he had two kids who adored him and a gorgeous baby girl who loved being with her dad. As well as another baby on the way. Before his mother had died Andrew was able to tell her that he was going to be a dad again. A father of four.

Our friends did their best to hide their shock at another pregnancy so soon. They shouldn't have been surprised. Nothing about us was really conventional. We had already pulled Asher and Tikvah out of school. Tikvah was struggling so much with feeling restricted in her creativity. She had daily tummy aches and was having more and more tantrums. Pleading not to go to school. Academically she was soaring ahead in class. Her work perfect. Her spelling and reading ahead of her years. She just couldn't cope with being stuck in an institution. I pulled her out for a term but very quickly realised that she was so much happier outside of school. Asher soon followed. Paul was seeing the kids more often now and even he agreed that the kids seemed happier and more at ease. It was nice that he noticed.

There was a lot of friction between me and Andrew. I couldn't even pinpoint exactly what it was about. It just seemed like we both misunderstood each other all the time. Something that I said neutrally was taken as an attack. I was told that I was screaming at Andrew even when I hadn't raised my voice. I felt that Andrew was becoming more and more critical with the kids. Especially Asher. He seemed to take out his frustrations on me by giving Asher a hard time. The one moment in our week that we all seemed to set our differences aside was our Friday nights at the Central Markets and China Town. I was thrilled when I realised that Andrew had the same ritual as us. We had never seen him there since he usually arrived after we had headed back up the hills for the night. But now as a family we could go together. Andrew's friends from church would often go as well so it was a great way to end the week. We would arrive early and just enjoy bumping into different people. Often we would grab a table and sit for hours as the kids played on the rails outside the public toilets.

Things were not improving with me and Andrew but there wasn't really much I could do. I wanted things to work out between us, I really did. I knew he wanted the same. We just didn't seem to be able to find any common ground. I was wanting us to talk about our marriage. Andrew seemed to want to talk about politics. He had recently started reading political books and was becoming more and more passionate about things going on in Israel and Palestine. He seemed offended at me not wanting to get into it. Me saying that things were so complex and that it was impossible for him to have a valid opinion until he had spent some time there. I really didn't want to get into it. The Middle East conflict was the last thing our marriage needed right now.

The birth of my fourth baby was around the corner and I felt the best thing I could do to prepare was to make sure I didn't gain too much weight. According to my midwife the reason my last birth was so hard was because Summer was such a big baby. If I could try to keep my weight lower there was more of a chance to have a smaller baby.

We had decided to ask Lisa to be our midwife. She had stood out during Summer's birth as the obvious choice. In many ways I felt that Summer was only alive, or at least not brain damaged, because of Lisa's incredible skill during a very difficult birth. She was thrilled to be asked. I still struggled to understand her Welsh accent but I loved her wonderful mix of warmth and expertise.

I knew that my babies didn't want to come out no matter how long I waited. This time I would help things along on the due date so as to not risk a Christmas baby. Thankfully it didn't take nearly as long to get things going. I tried to go for a walk, like I had twelve months earlier in anticipation for Summer's birth, but my legs wouldn't hold me up. Once again this birth was very different to my previous ones and I tried to just go with the waves of pain that were starting to roll in. Lisa was at another birth so she had asked her friend who was a midwife to sit with me until she could join us. I was in awe at how committed Lisa was to her birthing women. I knew how much she gave each birth so to come straight to me after being at a birth was a beautiful gift. I knew she could have easily told me that she needed some time to rest in between but instead she came straight over to replace the stand-in midwife.

The moment Lisa arrived my contractions started to kick in properly. Almost as if my body had waited for her to arrive. This birth was incredibly hard and difficult as well but not nearly as traumatic as the one twelve months earlier. I could feel the baby making progress and after a lot of pushing, and me hanging on to Andrew, I pushed another little girl out.

She was adorable. She had this tiny little nose that pointed up. Just like a little forest creature had crawled into my arms. Her eyes dark brown like her older brother. I knew she would be my last child and I took the opportunity to cut the umbilical cord. I was so thrilled to have this gorgeous little being join our family. I held her close and inhaled her, totally smitten.

Andrew cradled her as I showered and just as I was about to hold her again I started to get the shakes. Just like I had with each of my girls. This time the shaking wouldn't stop though even as warm blankets were placed around me. My teeth chattering. Nothing could warm me up. I eventually vomited and fell forwards on my bed. Once I came to Lisa and Andrew asked if I was alright and told me I had been asleep for about ten minutes.

Asleep? Why would I have been asleep? Andrew asked me if I wanted to hold the baby. Baby? What baby?

Andrew looked at me strangely. Our baby. Do you want to hold her?

A baby? I've had a baby? What baby? I had a baby?

My mind was trying to make sense of what I was hearing. I could remember giving birth. I could remember cutting the cord. But a baby? My mind was spinning. I didn't have a baby. How could he be saying that? I wanted to scream. I felt as if I was trapped in a nightmare. I tried to reach for some water but my hand wouldn't move. I was watching it lie still as I tried to make it obey my command. I went to say something to Lisa but other words were coming out of my mouth. I could hear myself saying things that didn't match with the words I was forming in my head. It was getting harder to breathe. My lungs hurting for air. I asked for oxygen. I couldn't form a proper sentence so I just said "oxygen, I…need…oxygen".

Lisa had been checking me over to see if there was anything wrong. No haemorrhaging. My pulse was fine. Nothing seemed out of sorts except my very bizarre behaviour. I could feel something pulling me away. As if I was starting to leave my body. I realised I was dying. It hit me that this is how mothers die in childbirth. It didn't have to be during the screaming and agony of the actual birth. They die after as well from complications. I was going to be one of those unfortunate women. I tried to pull myself back into my body. Asking again for oxygen. I was going to die. My children would no longer have a mother. I knew my girls would be okay. But what about Asher? He was so attached to me. What would happen to him? I had to live. I had to stay.

I could see Lisa and Andrew giving each other looks. They didn't seem that concerned. There was nothing dramatic going on as such. Just me behaving strangely and trying not to use up my last bit of strength in saying words that didn't quite come out right. Eventually Lisa handed the oxygen to me. There was no mask for my face so it was just a tube. I tried to put it into my nose but my hand still wasn't cooperating. I was moving the tube in slow motion over my face. Andrew smiling at how silly I looked. After a while they decided that it was best if an ambulance was called. I was still acting so strangely. My eyes rolling around. Once the paramedics arrived I was strapped into a stretcher and wheeled out of our house. I looked up at the ceiling and it felt as if the walls and corners were dancing for me. Moving in and out to a silent song. The trees outside our house bowing down as I was rolled into the ambulance. An oxygen mask was placed over my face and I could finally inhale properly. My lungs opening up. My mind started to clear. We were only partially down the freeway when I could speak properly again. I let the paramedic sitting next to me know that I was all right.

Once I arrived at the hospital I was treated so gently by the nurses. I thought they might all be upset with me for having a homebirth. If they were they didn't show it. Each one of them asked me if I was okay. If I needed anything. Did I want to hold my baby? That's right! I had a baby! A little girl. I remembered her tiny little nose. Like a little squirrel. When Andrew walked in the room I reached out to hold my little girl. She was even cuter than I remembered her. Sage Louise, I had my fourth baby. I could finally stop and let my body heal.

19

Not Without My Sister

I had four children. Two and two. The image I had always had in my mind. Paul and I used to talk about having four kids. Two and then wait a few years and then another two. Now I had them. Just not with him. It wasn't how I expected it, but it felt complete. Four. A good number. The trauma of what happened after Sage's birth still lingered though. I needed to talk about it. Have someone acknowledge how scary it was. I had really felt as if I was dying. Feeling myself drifting away to another place. Being pulled away by a force. Watching as my body remained but me slipping away. It had rattled me on such a deep level. Not the dying so much but the fact that it wasn't being acknowledged.

I tried to talk to Andrew about it but could tell that he just wasn't able to engage with me. He said I looked cute. That I had a bit of a smile of my face and looked really peaceful. The fact that I was waving the oxygen tube across my face showed that I obviously didn't need it. Using it more as a fan. I tried to explain that my hand wasn't cooperating. That the smile on my face wasn't in any way an indication of what was going on internally. Like most things that we tried to talk about, it very quickly headed into argument territory and it just wasn't worth it. I had my four kids. I was a very fortunate woman. I needed to focus on that. Lots of births are traumatic. It was obvious that I needed to move on, or that was at least the message I was getting.

When Sage was only a few months old I had a friend contact me and ask me if she was able to come over and talk to me about something. She was someone very special to me but we didn't get much time together and she never initiated meeting up, so I knew that this was something out of the ordinary. I offered her a cup of tea as she sat down at my kitchen table. Asher and Tikvah were building a fort in the backyard. Summer was playing with my pots and pans on the floor and Sage was wrapped around my chest in a sling. I looked at my friend's face and wished that I had been able to have some kid free space so we could properly talk.

She told me that she had a really hard request. That I should in no way feel obligated but that this was her last chance. I sat down in front of my friend and asked her to continue. She went on to explain that she had never really thought about becoming a mother during her twenties and thirties. Now in her forties she wanted a baby and no matter how much her and her partner had tried, she wasn't able to become pregnant. They needed someone to donate eggs. Would I consider donating to them?

This was a big request. Donating my eggs. I looked at my friend. I could see myself sitting there. Having to ask someone for their eggs. What an incredibly hard thing to do. I was so touched by this agonising request. My heart ached for her. She went on to say that she knew I needed to talk to Andrew about this, and that if he agreed it would still need to involve counselling from the IVF centre. She explained that the procedure itself was quite invasive and would mean a few months of hormone treatments for me and so on. I looked down on Sage sleeping on my chest. Summer now on my lap. I could hear Asher and Tikvah laughing outside, giving each other instructions on how to make the fort stronger. I had my answer. I thanked my friend for asking me. Told her I would talk to Andrew and let her know as soon as I could. We finished our cups of tea and hugged.

When Andrew came home later that night I told him that we needed to talk about something big. Once the kids were asleep I explained what had happened a few hours earlier in my kitchen. Seeing my friend in such a hard place. Knowing that if it was me in the same situation I would be wanting to throw myself at the mother in front of me, pleading for her eggs, but of course needing to sit back and be as neutral as possible. I had never experienced anything like it. The closest I had come was the few months between a miscarriage and Asher being conceived. I could think of nothing else but getting pregnant. I was consumed by it. I had this pulse that wouldn't rest until I had a baby growing inside me. All of a sudden it seemed like everyone around me was either pregnant or pushing a pram. Nothing else would satisfy me until I could call myself a mother. That craving had only lasted four months. A tiny chapter.

Here was a beautiful friend of mine who had been trying for much longer and had now been told that she was unable to produce the eggs needed. Andrew listened. I could tell this was hard for him. He had lots of questions. I knew I had to let this take as long as it needed to. I wouldn't be able to rush him. This was incredibly complex for him. He was attached to my eggs. Said that it would be like us giving away one of our children. How would I be able to see this child of mine being raised by someone else? Wouldn't I feel guilty if something happened to the child? What if our friends split up and this kid no longer had two parents? How would I feel then? He reminded me that this baby would be just as related to him as Asher and Tikvah. It would have a different dad but the same mother. He loved Asher and Tikvah so much and couldn't imagine not being part of their life and now I was suggesting we give a baby away? How would I feel if someone asked him for sperm? Would I feel comfortable about him donating that to our friends?

They were good questions. They needed to be asked. We talked for hours that night and the following three weeks. I kept coming back to the same answer. My friend has just as much of a right to become a mother as I did. I was just very fortunate that I didn't have any problems conceiving. Of course I had to donate my eggs. Yes we could talk about all the 'what ifs' but who was I to judge who was deemed a worthy parent? I reminded Andrew that we can't control what happens. Here I was a divorced woman with four kids to two different dads. If anyone couldn't judge it was me. Andrew seemed to struggle so much about our friends not really being a 'traditional' couple, somehow not meeting his standards. It felt so hypocritical to me. Surely we couldn't play God like that? We had been asked, the only right thing was to do what we could to help someone else share in the joy of becoming parents.

I was surprised at how long it took Andrew to decide. He loved being a dad more than anything else. He spent any time he could with his kids. Never seeing them as a hindrance or interference. He wanted to be part of every dimension of parenthood. Never making it out that caring for a child was a mother's role. He was totally and utterly consumed with being a parent, and yet he was struggling so much to have me donate my eggs to someone else. Thankfully we were able to continue the discussion without it ever getting too heated and it felt really good when we finally had our joint decision. Andrew had taken the scenic route to get to where I had been from the very first moment I was asked. We had very different ways of arriving at our answer but after three weeks it really was both of us who wanted to give this couple a chance of becoming parents.

My friend was right, the process was quite involved. We needed to have counselling sessions as a couple as well as the four of us. It wasn't just the obvious questions being asked. Like the clinic wanting to make sure that me and Andrew didn't feel like we had any say over what happened to the baby once it was born. It was more complex than that. How did we feel about the embryos? What if not all the embryos were needed? Would we be okay with them being discarded? What about them being donated for research? These questions were much harder for me than the decision to help my friend have a baby. No matter how much my beliefs and values had changed over the years I still couldn't get past the truth that life begins at conception. No matter what size or shape, once that life has begun I could not in any way see myself choosing to end it. Inside or outside of a body.

When I was in the army every female soldier was offered three free abortions. I had friends who had abortions. I could understand where they were coming from and why for them they felt as if it was the only solution. I just knew for me that I couldn't do it. When I became pregnant the first time, a couple of months before I got married to Paul, the doctor had asked me if I wanted to abort. She knew that Paul worked at a Christian radio station and that I was studying at a Christian college and was the President of the Student Council. It would not have been a good time to become pregnant. An abortion would have been justified in a lot of ways. I walked out of the doctor's office hoping the child growing inside me hadn't heard the doctor. There was no way I would kill my baby. As it turned out, two weeks later I miscarried. No one needed to know what had happened.

And here I was, less than ten years later, telling a fertility counsellor that once the eggs left my body I would completely surrender them. They were no longer mine. My friends could choose for themselves how they wanted to proceed. I really meant it. I was giving eggs. Embryo, baby and child were totally out of my domain. The counsellor deemed us ready for the procedure. First we needed blood tests. Even Andrew needed blood tests. Once that was done we were told that the treatment could begin. I would be given drugs that pretty much made my body go into menopause. The medication would make me tired and grumpy. Or in my case, more tired and more grumpy. I wasn't quite sure how I would go with four kids at home and feeling even more exhausted than usual. I asked Andrew to be extra patient with me and told him I would need to switch off the moment he came home from work. It would only be for a few weeks. I would then be given injections that would stimulate my ovaries to produce eggs. Lots of eggs. It would be PMS times ten. Hormones raging through my body so that I could make as many eggs as possible for harvesting. Once the eggs were ready they would be removed through my vaginal wall during a minor surgical procedure.

It was hard to get an exact timeline for how long things would take. There were a lot of factors and variables to consider. Andrew and I had been talking about legally getting married for a while and were trying to set a date. Now we had to make sure that the egg donation would be well and truly over by the time we had our ceremony. It seemed a bit ridiculous getting married when we were already a family. Surely a piece of paper wasn't needed to make us official? For me the deciding factor was the clumsiness of what to call Andrew. It felt silly calling him boyfriend. Partner was way too clinical. De facto was awful. The convenience of being able to call him 'Hubby' was enough for me. I knew I was totally committed to him.

Things were pretty unpleasant between us, but unlike with Paul there were no addictions or dangers to deal with. It was really a personality clash and that faded in the light of us having four children together and us wanting to raise them in a family. In many ways Andrew and I were great together. I really wanted him. I wanted us. Unfortunately that didn't seem to be enough for Andrew. He wanted me to need him. It came up again and again. "I want you to need me Lillian" I didn't. I really didn't need him. I thought that was clear from the beginning. When we first met I was a happy single mum. I had a full life. After having put my studies on hold I was just about to complete my degree. I was about to embark on a career. I had two incredible kids. I was involved in lots of meaningful activities. I didn't need Andrew. I wanted Andrew.

I still really wanted Andrew. I wanted an intimate and loving relationship with him. But no, I didn't need him. It caused Andrew a lot of grief. It came up in so many conversations. Conversations totally unrelated to the topic. Somehow Andrew was a victim in our relationship. He felt rejected. For me it couldn't have been further from the truth. I wanted a connection with him so badly. I craved it. The intimacy I never got to experience with Paul I wanted so much with Andrew. Yet there was a barrier. I couldn't understand it. I knew Andrew wanted to feel loved by me. I knew that he didn't.

And here we were planning a wedding in the midst of that. As much as I knew that I was aligning myself officially with a man who I didn't really feel right about, I knew that he was a good father and that the things that bothered me about us could be worked on. Life with Andrew would probably never be easy as such but that was a small price to pay for us to be a family together. I loved who we were as a unit. As a family. I loved that my two older kids had a dad.

We set the date for the wedding for early December. It would mean that my mother could fly out to celebrate with us. She had come to help after my two last births and it would be great for her to come out for something a bit more relaxed. We wanted something very informal so we decided to do the official papers beforehand. We would have a civil ceremony so that we didn't need a person officiating at our actual wedding with our friends. It would make it a lot more intimate and personal. Andrew and I were great at organising events together. That was one area in our life that we seemed to agree on quite easily. Neither of us wanted anything fancy. We wanted it to be meaningful and authentic to us. It was all about celebrating who we were as a family and making sure as many friends as possible could be there, and not having to spend much money. The obvious choice was a picnic in a beautiful garden in the Adelaide Hills. The kids would love running around while the adults could sit on rugs and eat. Our neighbour agreed to make fruit and cheese platters. It was all too easy. The wedding itself was still a few months away and we already had everything sorted.

In the midst of four kids and now the fertility treatment starting for the donation process I wanted to make sure that there wouldn't be much else on my plate leading up to the wedding. Thankfully the medication wasn't as difficult as I had been told and I was able to continue doing what was needed at home. On the evenings I did have to fall into bed early Andrew was happy to take over. Even the hormones that were needed to stimulate the eggs weren't that bad. I was feeling achy and tender but still very manageable. It was bizarre to think that, unlike a regular cycle where I would normally produce one egg, my body was now busy making ten times as many, if not more. The nurse that was overseeing my treatment was happy with how I was progressing. She couldn't really tell how many eggs I had brewing but told me it wouldn't be long before they would be ready to harvest. It was a relief because the swelling was getting intense and at times it felt as if things couldn't stretch any further. I was looking forward to having the procedure done with.

I was waiting to hear from the nurse about my blood test results when I got an email from Raphael. My dad was in hospital again. He'd had a massive heart attack. My dad was now living in Jerusalem. My mother had told him that their marriage was over a couple of years earlier and he was now living there, happy to be back in Jerusalem, away from the long dark winters of Sweden but very upset about his marriage being over. And now another heart attack. I really felt as if I had to fly over. I had always had a difficult relationship with my dad. I struggled with so many things about him, and vice versa. Me 'living in sin' with Andrew and now having two "bastard" children hadn't helped things in the slightest. I didn't want my dad to die with so many things undealt with between us.

I told Andrew that I needed to fly home. He understood. With his own mother having passed not long before he knew how important it was to be there. Thankfully Andrew was more than capable of looking after the kids. Four kids with two of them under two and Sage only nine months old. Andrew didn't for a moment say that it was too much for him to be left with. I had friends who couldn't leave for a weekend without needing to make meals for the husband to reheat. I felt very grateful to be partnered with a man who was so capable in the home.

The only concerns were that I still had eggs growing inside of me to donate, as well as a civil ceremony arranged for my marriage. I called up the Registry Office and they were able to change the date to only a few days later. The ceremony was booked for mid-morning.

I had my final internal ultrasound that morning. The doctor saying the eggs were ready to harvest a couple of days later. I practically jumped off the table saying I had to get to my wedding on time. The nurse trying her hardest not to look shocked. I ran out the building and drove off to get married with lubricant still between my legs. When I arrived at the registry office Andrew and the kids were already there waiting. The ceremony was more formal than I had expected but over very quickly. We decided to have an early lunch in China Town to celebrate. It was a beautiful October day, a perfect day for being told I had lots of eggs to donate and to get legally married. Andrew and I spent that night sleeping in the back of our car on a property in the Adelaide Hills. It was an impromptu wedding night. It wasn't the most comfortable night with me feeling as if I was about to burst from all the eggs inside me but it was a luxury to have a night away with my new husband.

The next day I went to the clinic for the surgery. It was a very straightforward procedure and after only a couple of hours I was able to go home. Over thirty eggs had been harvested. No wonder I felt like I was going to burst.

Only a few days later I waved goodbye to my family and flew off to be with my dad in Jerusalem. So much had been happening recently that I needed to just sit and process it all. I would have a few hours in Hong Kong and I was exhausted. I decided to pay a bit extra so I could use the airport lounge. My body was still achy from all the medical procedures and I needed to get some sleep. The lounge was fantastic. Not only did I get to sleep and have a shower, I was also able to use their computers while waiting for my flight. My friend had been telling me for a while about this thing called Facebook. It sounded similar to MySpace. Something which I hadn't really been able to get my head around. She kept insisting that I would love Facebook and that it would be a great way for me to stay in touch with my friends around the world. I wasn't so sure. I hadn't had a chance to check it out with so many things going on, but now with a few hours left before my flight, and with no kids that needed to be fed or have their nappy changed, I figured I might as well try to set up an account. It couldn't hurt. I probably wouldn't use it much but at least my friend would stop bugging me about it.

I was flying to Tel Aviv with EL AL. I was wondering if everyone would start clapping when we landed and sure enough they did. Every time I had landed in Israel since we first arrived in 1985 the plane had erupted with applause. Back then, as we stepped off the plane onto the tarmac, people had knelt down on the ground and kissed the burning hot asphalt. So happy to be in the Holy Land.

This time there was no need to walk on the tarmac with the airport all renovated. I looked around in awe. Such an incredibly beautiful airport.

My brother Raphael had only flown out a few hours earlier, I was sad to miss him since we hadn't seen each other since a weekend together in Springfield seven years earlier. Ezra was there to collect me though and it felt so good to be back with him again. I knew he was going through a hard time since he and his girlfriend Lydia had split up. We didn't stay in touch much but I knew through my mother that Ezra was struggling. He had finished his time with the U.S. Air Force and was now living back in Jerusalem. Thankfully he was so that someone could be close to our dad.

Ezra drove me straight to the hospital where dad had just woken up from surgery. He looked weak but was very happy to see me by his bed. He now had a defibrillator next to his heart. It looked like a packet of cigarettes under his skin. The doctor explained that it would kick his heart back into life if he had another heart attack. My poor dad, these constant things happening to his body. I really felt for him.

There wasn't much I could do, but having me there meant that I could help out with making vegan meals for him, and more than anything just support Ezra who seemed to be struggling with the burden of looking after our dad. One major concern was trying to find a place for dad to live. He had so little money and really needed somewhere that had a space for cooking since his diet was so rigid.

Ezra and I went to look at places for him to move into. There was a tiny place in the Old City that would be great but it was too expensive. Another at a guesthouse but no cooking facilities. Finally we found a room in a monastery. We had been calling our dad a hermit for years and to have him live in a monastery overlooking the Old City was the perfect fit. It also meant he wouldn't be alone which really appealed to me. Kind-hearted nuns would be close by in case he needed anything.

Ezra and I were grateful to finally find something and decided to go for a walk on the Promenade just down the road. It's a beautiful walk overlooking the Old City and the Judean Desert. It's one of my favourite places and having Ezra there made it even more special. As we stood there looking at the Temple Mount, the sun starting to set so the walls of the Old City were lit up in gold, Ezra told me he had a question for me.

Somehow I already knew what he was going to ask but waited until he spoke. He explained that he had no memories of his childhood at all. That it was totally blank. He only had one faint picture but he wasn't sure if it had happened or if it was a dream or maybe even a movie he had seen. The only image he had was me holding him and these dark beings with chains pulling at his body.

My heart ached for him. That this was the only memory he had was so incredibly sad. I confirmed it had happened and asked him if he wanted the details. He did. I told him which house we were living in. How dad had yet again chased him around the house and beaten him. How afterwards Ezra had grabbed a kitchen knife. How he screamed and raged in his room for ages until the screams became shrieks for help. How I had run into his room and seen him on the floor. How it looked like his limbs were being pulled in every direction. How I held him as he screamed that he was being chained and dragged away. Me pleading for the blood of Jesus to cover him since that's what I had been instructed to do since I was a little girl and I felt completely terrified at the forces pulling at my brother.

Ezra was silent. Just staring at me as I gave him details of one of the scariest moments of my life. When he finally spoke he said that while I was telling him what happened he was starting to see more things from his childhood. Seeing himself hiding under furniture. My dad trying to reach him. My dad screaming that he'd had enough. Tables being turned over. Bunk beds being moved so my dad could get to him. Had that really happened? Ezra wanted to know. Yes Ezra. It had. So many times.

Tears were rolling down my face. How had he forgotten? The images were locked into my mind forever yet for Ezra he had completely forgotten. Forgotten that we lived with a raging animal. Now it was starting to come back. I told Ezra that I had tried to protect him. Pleaded with my dad to stop. Other times I would hold him after the bashings had stopped. Wishing my dad had hit me instead of my little brother.

I told Ezra it had gone on for years. And that over time Ezra had started to do the same to Abigail. Ezra remembered that. He knew he had tortured Abigail for years but had forgotten that he had been tortured first. I could see things making sense for him. He had heard so many times that he was a troublemaker. That he was such a terror as a child. He hadn't realised why.

I told Ezra he needed to get some help. To seek out someone who he could talk to. That these things don't just go away. That he owed it to his future wife and children to get help. I explained that our dad had been beaten too by his own dad. Grandpa had come back from the war and his son triggered a rage that belonged in the battlefield, not in the home. He hadn't gotten help. Neither had our dad. Now Ezra needed to end this cycle. Get the help he needed before he married someone. I told him he just doesn't know what's around the corner. I knew he felt like he would never find anyone again after things ended with Lydia but this was really his opportunity to get help.

I was so grateful to have this moment with him. I could see that he heard me. I could see the shift happening inside him. I knew that he finally understood why I had struggled so much with my dad over the years. Struggled with the hypocrisy of his religion while not owning up to the abuse in our home. Ezra finally realised that I hadn't been making up stories about my dad as I had been accused of by my brothers. He had blocked it all out. Ezra thanked me and told me he was so happy I had come. So was I. My trip to Jerusalem had been to spend time with my dad but all of a sudden it made much more sense. I was coming to be a sister more than I was coming to be a daughter.

Abigail had flown in to be with dad as well. As soon as she had heard about the heart attack she had booked a flight and the two of us were taking food into the hospital so our dad didn't have to eat the hospital 'garbage' as he called it. Cooking for my dad wasn't an easy task and we spent a lot of time trying to get it just right. On one of our visits to dad the nurse asked if we could take him for a walk around the hospital to get him used to walking again. Dad was so weak after the heart attack and surgery and he had lost so much weight on his already slender body. The hospital gown was enormous on him as we slowly walked down to a nicer part of the building.

Abigail and I were on either side of him to make sure he wouldn't collapse. Dad holding on to the IV pole for support. He looked so frail but managed to walk for about ten minutes before asking to sit down. After he caught his breath for a bit he asked if I had heard from my kids. He wanted to know if everything was all right at home. I explained that Andrew had driven over to Melbourne for a few days with the kids and how much fun they were having. That he was doing such a good job on his own.

I knew this was a hard topic for my dad because he was so uncomfortable about us not being married. I felt that focusing on how wonderful Andrew was as a dad would hopefully distract him from the life of sin we were living in. I told him how the wedding was happening only a couple of weeks after I would get back from my trip and how we were able to have our legal ceremony before I flew over. My dad said that we would need to be married in front of God for the wedding to be validated. Was I raising my children in the Christian faith? I told my dad that I wasn't exactly sure what that meant anymore and that I was raising my kids with the message of Jesus. Loving those around us. Helping the lonely. Feeding the hungry. Right now it was more about the practical side of the Gospel as I worked through what I actually believed.

Abigail had been silent the whole time but started to say something about love, it was a gentle comment and was meant to be supportive. For some reason it triggered something in my dad. In a split second he went from the frail old man in a giant hospital gown to the dad of our childhood. He roared at Abigail to shut her mouth. His nostrils flaring, his body arching over her. We both jumped back in shock. The lion had returned. Nothing had changed. We both stared at him. His chest heaving. His face still red.

None of us spoke. I took the IV pole and we all slowly walked back in silence to his room. There was nothing to say. He was so pathetic. His two daughters having flown around the world to be with him. Going to the markets and cooking for him. Bringing him food to eat. Putting our lives on hold to spend time with him and he still couldn't contain his rage, even in his weak physical state. I almost felt sorry for him.

The next day I came in again with some food. Nothing was said about what had happened. Instead my dad told me he wanted to pay for me and Abigail to fly to Cairo to see our sister Susanna. He knew that I had been trying to find some flights for us since it would be crazy not to see her as she was so close. Susanna had recently given birth to a little girl who still hadn't gotten a passport so she wasn't able to travel. There were no tickets left in economy and of course first class was out of the question. Now my dad was telling me that he wanted to pay for us to go. I tried to remind my dad that he didn't have much money and he needed all of it for rent. He insisted. He wanted me and Abigail to see Susanna. It was important for him that his daughters got to see each other.

He was such a contradiction. So generous. So kind-hearted. Always putting others first. Yet he had just raged at us like an animal less than 24 hours earlier. I went back to Elinka's house where we were staying and told Abigail that we were flying to Cairo. Dad was paying. We would have three days with our older sister and her family.

A couple of days later we were at the airport checking in at the first class desk. We had to laugh that our one time to fly first class it would only be a one hour flight. What a waste! As we stretched out in our seats two men sat across from us. They introduced themselves and said they had been told two Swedish sisters were joining them. They were brothers, one of them worked at the Israeli Embassy in Cairo. It was just the four of us flying first class. The guy working in the embassy gave us his number and said if we had any issues we could contact him. Travelling with a beautiful sister had its perks.

We were thrilled to be reunited with Susanna. It was so rare for us to spend any time together. Last time the three of us had been in the same place was in Virginia Beach after Sam's wedding. That was the beginning of 1999. It was now the end of 2009. Ten years! We had three days to catch up on ten years apart. Three days to be aunties to our five and two year old nephews and three month old niece. We would have to soak up every moment. Make the most of it. Take lots of photos and create memories that would last us till the next time.

Susanna is an incredible cook and had made a Lebanese cinnamon chicken dish for our arrival. As much as the food was delicious it was hard to ignore the mood in the home. Youssef was obviously trying to be hospitable with us there but he was yelling at his son for even the tiniest thing. While Susanna went to bring the dessert out I could hear him yelling at her in the kitchen. Abigail tried to distract our nephew as his dad roared and I sang a little song for my niece in my arms. Our three days had felt very short when planning the trip but if things continued like this it would be very hard to enjoy the visit. I was hoping that things would settle down and maybe we had just caught Youssef in a bad mood. My mother had hinted that things weren't that good for Susanna and Youssef, mentioning his temper but never going into details. I was hoping that we had seen the worst of it. Unfortunately that wasn't the case.

The next morning Susanna had made us a beautiful Egyptian breakfast with plates full of labneh, olives, baba ghanoush and foul beans. Warm pita bread being used to scoop each mouthful up. Everything washed down with mint tea. Youssef was loving it. He was a huge man with a massive appetite. Susanna went back in the kitchen to get more of the beans when Youssef flew up from the table. I hadn't even noticed what my nephew had done. Maybe reached for something on his dad's plate. It all happened so quickly. Youssef dragged his son into the bedroom and was screaming. We could hear him beating our nephew. Our nephew calling out in pain. I looked over at Abigail who was frozen in terror. Tears streaming down her face as she held her little niece. I then looked at Susanna. She stood in the kitchen doorway. Mouthing to us that she was sorry. Sorry that we had to be part of this.

Abigail started pleading that I do something. There was nothing that could be done though. Youssef was in a white rage. He was still roaring in the room. Our nephews still screaming as he was being pounded. I couldn't just walk in the room and force him to stop. Youssef was way too volatile. So we just sat there. Sat in silence as the screaming settled down. As the sobs from our nephews started up.

Eventually Youssef walked back to the table and started eating his beloved food as if nothing had happened. Mouthful after mouthful. I watched him gorge. This man was so dangerous. Like Paul he was a minister who showed one face in front of the church and one at home. I had been lucky though, Paul had never been violent to us. The man sitting in front of me was a dangerous man. Ruthless. He had just beaten his little boy and here he was telling me that we better hurry up so we could get to the pyramids before it got too hot.

We spent a couple of hours there. Susanna at home with her baby girl. Me doing my best to be a tourist while my gut was churning at what I had witnessed that morning. I had no interest in the pyramids. Not when I was there for Susanna's wedding and even less now. My mind was racing. Something had to be done. My sister and her kids were trapped with a monster. I had to do something. I couldn't just pretend that this was acceptable and go back home.

We hadn't had any time with Susanna alone since arriving the day before. Youssef was with us the whole time. That evening we were all going out to a party at Youssef's cousin's house. I would try to talk to Susanna then. Thankfully the beautiful house was full of people. Youssef had a larger than life personality and his laugh was filling the room. As he helped himself to the tables full of food I pulled Susanna away into a quieter part of the house. I told her I needed to be really blunt with her. That I couldn't remain silent. I said I could see what was happening in her home. I could see that her kids weren't safe. I needed her to know that if she wanted to get away I would help her. I would do whatever I could to help them escape. I just needed her to tell me if that's what she wanted.

I knew this was incredibly hard for her. It might be the first time she ever talked to anyone about it. She didn't go into detail but said yes, she needed help. She knew her kids were in danger. What I had seen wasn't the worst of it. If she wasn't a mother she would have stayed and put up with abuse but she had to make sure her three children were safe.

It was all I needed to hear. I thanked her for letting me help and told her I would come up with something. She just needed to trust me. We slipped back into the crowded room and didn't speak again the rest of the evening. In my head I was frantically trying to figure out my next step. I had just promised my sister I would help her escape out of Egypt. How the hell was I going to do that? I needed to do this right. It was way too risky if anything went wrong.

I emailed Andrew later that night. I didn't go into details. I just explained that Susanna and her kids were in danger. They needed to escape. Would he support me? His response was immediate. Of course. Whatever it takes. Don't think about the money and just do what you need to do. It was the perfect response. I just needed to know that Andrew was on my side with this. The details could be figured out later. As I lay in bed I whispered to Abigail what I had talked to Susanna about. Explained that I had no idea how it would happen but that we needed to get Susanna and her kids out. Abigail said she would do whatever she could to help. I knew she meant it.

The next day we had planned to go shopping. Youssef was going to a church meeting and we had some time with Susanna to buy souvenirs. Instead we scrambled through all her documents and paperwork and ran through the streets of Cairo to get everything photocopied. I had my little niece strapped to my chest in a sling as we went from place to place. We didn't know how the escape would happen so I wanted to make sure Susanna had cash in case she needed it. It was easier said than done and we didn't have much time.

At one point as we were running across the street dodging cars I yelled out to Susanna. "Who do you want to play you in the movie?" We burst out laughing. It was just so crazy. We decided that Kate Winslet would play Susanna. Drew Barrymore Abigail.

We couldn't figure out who would play me but it was just what we needed, something to laugh about. This was terrifying stuff, as a woman Susanna had no rights in Egypt. Trying to get away from her husband with her children could put her in jail for life.

Our bags were filled with copies of important documents and photos that Susanna didn't want to risk losing. We bought a few souvenirs as well to make sure we had something to show Youssef if he asked why the bags were so heavy. As I hugged Susanna goodbye I knew that everything else in my life had just faded away and I would only be able to return to it once Susanna and her three kids were safe. I had never before in my life felt such clarity. I just had no idea where to start.

I remembered one of the brothers we had met on the plane. He worked for the Israeli Embassy. Surely he would know how to get someone out of Cairo. He didn't. He said it was too hard. Egypt is so strict. Women can't travel without their husband's approval. Damn.

Somehow we had to get her out with Youssef's approval. How could we do that? I was flying back to Australia only a couple of days later. I couldn't leave until I had a some sort of a plan. I had to think fast. It had to work. We knew it was critical to keep this as quiet as possible. We would only tell the people who absolutely had to know.

Elinka was the first. We knew she would do anything to help Susanna. We asked her to write an email from her husband who was a pastor. Saying that as a church they wanted to pay for Susanna to come with her children to see her father who was dying. Yes he had improved a bit but things had gotten worse. He wanted to see his grandchildren. We knew that Youssef would like an email from a pastor in Jerusalem. It would feed his ego.

Youssef agreed to Susanna coming for ten days. What he didn't know was that they would only stay for three days. They would then fly to Sweden. Susanna wasn't given any details at all. She just knew that she was coming to Jerusalem and that the rest would be organised for her. The less she knew the better. It was too easy for her to say something if the stress got to her. I was worried about her traveling alone from Cairo. It's not easy to travel with young children at the best of times. To do it while escaping from an abusive husband would be too much for anyone's nerves.

I asked Elinka if she would help out. She was thrilled to. I had to fly back to Australia but I felt as if enough of the plan was in place and I could do the rest from there.

It was great to see Andrew and the kids again but my focus was elsewhere. I spent all my time on the computer trying to work out the plan. I met with lawyers in Adelaide. Would my sister be seen as breaking the law by removing the kids from Egypt? The lawyer explained about the Hague convention. Egypt hadn't signed it. My sister would not be breaking any laws. And because this was about the safety of her children she would be protected.

I didn't get a lot of sleep those couple of weeks before my sister boarded her plane. I would go over the plan in my head. Over and over again. Was there something that I was missing? The biggest risk was my dad finding out that something was happening and contacting Youssef. Even something as simple as Youssef emailing him and asking if he was enjoying his time with his grandkids was too risky. I knew I had to ask Ezra to help out. I didn't like involving my brothers because there was a big chance they wouldn't agree with what we were doing.

Ezra was shocked at what I told him but said he would help. He took my dad's laptop and changed something in his settings so that any correspondence to and from Youssef would be rerouted to Ezra's email account. Brilliant. We had a lawyer in Sweden who said she would be happy to take on Susanna's case. She helped organise a women's shelter that Susanna could hide in with her children.

On the morning of her flight Susanna had no idea that Elinka had already flown down to Cairo and was waiting for her in the terminal. Susanna was the last person on the flight and collapsed in her seat. She had made it. She had two over excited boys and a baby to look after. Just as she was wondering how she was going to survive the flight a woman wearing a black headscarf and black sunglasses asked her if she needed help. She went on to say,

Don't worry Susanna, everything has been looked after. Everything will be okay.

She took of her glasses and Susanna realised it was Elinka sitting next to her! She couldn't believe it. Elinka has this way with children and kept them all occupied for the whole flight so that Susanna could calm herself down and try to process what had just happened.

She got to spend three days with our dad. Enjoying seeing him with his grandkids. Wondering if this would be the last time she would be with him. It was only once she had arrived in Jerusalem that Susanna was told the rest of the plan. Abigail would fly with her to Sweden so she didn't have to be alone. Abigail had quit her job in Madison and asked her housemates to pack up her belongings and put them into storage. She was not coming back. Andrew had not complained once when I said we had to buy five tickets from Tel Aviv to Copenhagen. He had meant it when he had told me that he would do whatever he could for my sister to be safe.

After many years of living in the Middle East, Susanna was now back in Sweden to start a new life. She had her three children and her youngest sister with her. Her first night back in Sweden was spent in a women's shelter. There were not enough beds so her daughter had to sleep in a baby bath that night. It was so far from anything she had ever thought she would experience. But she was safe. She was finally safe.

Only a few days later I got married. My new friend Astrid had felted my hair into dreadlocks. Bright colourful dreadlocks. I had a white peasant top and white fishermen pants on. Last minute I crocheted a little, white skirt to go over my pants. Another friend made a gorgeous dragon fly out of metal wire and string for my hair. I looked over at Andrew holding Sage. His hair long and his beard bushier than ever. We sure looked like a couple of hippies. The sun was shining. The garden in full bloom. Our friends sitting on blankets around us. Platters full of fruit and cheese being passed around. We had wanted something relaxed and informal and this was perfect.

Andrew and I eventually stood up in front of our friends. Each of us with a toddler in our arms. Asher and Tikvah between us. We told our story. Explained how we met and why we were together. We wanted this to be as genuine as possible. So instead of gushing about what we loved about each other we had decided that we would say what we didn't like about each other and explain that we still wanted to be together despite that. Andrew said his three or four things that he didn't like about me. When he stopped I reached into a bag next to me and pulled out a receipt roll. In a very dramatic gesture I unravelled metres of it and started to read my list. Everyone laughed.

We didn't want to exchange rings. Neither of us were into jewellery. Andrew especially hated rings. Said they looked silly on his fingers. We wanted to exchange something though. And we wanted it to involve all of us since it wasn't just me and Andrew getting married. We were uniting as a whole family. So instead of rings we exchanged badges. We had spent an afternoon decorating badges for each other. Two each for me and Andrew. Andrew got one from me that said Hubby. And one from the kids that said Dad. I got two as well, Wife and Mamma. The kids got one each with our nicknames for them. It was quirky but it worked.

The ceremony was totally out of the box but heartfelt. Our friends hugging us and saying how special it was to be there and witness the love we had for each other. No one wanted the magic to end, so once the garden got too cold we walked up the street to our friend's house and hung out there, and when everyone started to get hungry again we ordered pizza.

20

Domestic Captivity in Suburbia

The first couple of months after our wedding my focus was still very much on my sister. Going into hiding in Sweden was not as straightforward as we had hoped. Abigail was not allowed to stay with her and ended up returning to Jerusalem while trying to figure out what to do next. It was incredibly hard carrying the burden of making sure that my older sister was all right. Thankfully my mother was helping out with financial support, but she was living in a different part of Sweden so it was really up to Susanna to make it on her own now and it weighed heavily on me.

Her escaping from Egypt had not gone down well with my dad. After a couple of months I had a call from him. He hardly ever called me. A few emails from him had shown me that he thought that Susanna had done the wrong thing by leaving. Breaking her marriage covenant. As a man, her husband had the right to treat her whichever way he wanted. He was the head of the family. All the same crap I had heard in bits and pieces growing up. Now he was calling me and his voice was getting louder and louder. Did I realise what I had done to our family? Could I not see what this meant? I explained that I had helped my sister get away from a dangerous man. That three kids didn't have to live in fear anymore. My dad roared like a wild animal at me.

You've brought a curse into our family. You've cursed us!

My face was burning.

When you left your husband you brought a curse into this family. The curse began with you, you then spread it to your mother so she left me and now ... NOW you have spread it into your sister's life! She was married to a minister. A godly man. And your curse has broken them apart.

Curse? I've brought a curse?

You've cursed our family.

Dad, I don't know what curse you are talking about.

It's a curse from the women in the family. It's the Andersson curse!

He was referring to my mother's maiden name. Morfar's last name. Who knew he had a curse named after him? And a curse only pertaining to women? It was ludicrous. My face was still burning but my dad was sounding crazier and crazier. I held the phone and listened to him rage. He was seriously nuts. He kept going and I just sat there waiting for him to run out of things to say.

Once he settled down somewhat, his breathing still heavy, I very calmly told him that I was incredibly sad that he could not see that his daughter and three grandchildren were now safe. That he was so focused on what was right and wrong that he had lost sight of his daughter's safety. I told him that his children being safe had never been his priority as a father and obviously nothing had changed. I explained that I only had so much energy. I was giving it all to my own family as well as helping Susanna. I had nothing left. If he couldn't be supportive as a dad right now I didn't want to hear from him.

I reminded him that he would only send me emails if he was trying to preach at me for living in sin with the father of my children, or to tell me his latest health gospel. I didn't want it. None of it. I wanted a dad and if he couldn't be a dad to me I didn't want to hear from him. I asked him to not email or call me again. I would love to hear from him when he could be my dad. I would no longer be in contact with a preacher or a health guru.

I needed to make that break. My energy levels were running on empty and at least this was one way to preserve whatever was left. It didn't go down well in the family. My brothers were furious with me. So was Carla, Sam's wife. How could I do that to my father? I was acting like a spoilt brat. It's so disrespectful. Not one of them understood that I couldn't engage with a father who chose danger for his kids. I didn't even want to try to explain myself. I was so over the whole family drama.

I felt it on such a deep level inside my body that as a family we had it so wrong. I couldn't even explain it exactly. I just knew we were so wrapped up in some warped value system that allowed for women to be mistreated in the name of God or Christianity or maybe it wasn't even that? Somehow I had done something wrong in helping my sister. I had done something against my family for leaving my husband. I was to blame for my parents splitting up.

There was no point in me trying to get my dad or even my brothers to see things from my perspective. The thing was, I never heard from my brothers anyway. It wasn't as if we had this connection that was now damaged because of what I had done. They had showed so little interest in my life and it was very clear they didn't know me.

The last time I had spoken to Raphael I realised he didn't even know the names of my children and he had made some comment about me smoking pot and drinking alcohol. Maybe he had seen a photo from my wedding with me having dreadlocks. I had laughed it off by explaining that Andrew and I might be the only couple in Australia who have never been drunk. I had never even been tipsy. In fact, I couldn't remember the last time I had even tasted alcohol. And pot? Again, never even tried it. Neither had Andrew.

It wasn't even about that though. It was realising how little my brother knew about me and the assumptions he could make based on random snippets of information and photos that would be emailed out. If he wanted to be angry at me for not letting my dad rage at me about some Andersson curse I had brought into the family, then so be it. It's not as if I would all of a sudden miss out on a weekly roast with my brothers and their families.

Sam was angry at me as well, but he took a different approach. "Dad is so sick and weak, how can you do this to him? It will break his heart." He had a point. Dad was sick and weak but that wasn't stopping him from saying awful things about me and not taking the opportunity to patch things up with his daughter. If anything his weak heart was making him bolder and more judgmental. I had zero interest in catering to my dad or to my brothers.

Things in my own home were tricky enough to deal with. Both me and Andrew were getting restless with our day-to-day existence. Andrew was working four days a week, which meant he could spend more time with the kids than most dads. I was starting to toy with the idea of maybe getting some work. I knew that Andrew struggled a lot with the way I spent money. He especially struggled with the money I spent on food. Money was becoming more of a hot topic for us and I thought that maybe I could start contributing in some way. I had never actually worked before, besides being a waitress, and what I really wanted to do was counselling. I had recently started going along to the Jewish School in Adelaide. They had an International Playgroup and I loved taking the girls there because it meant being exposed to different languages and interesting people.

I was struggling so much with the level of conversation among our friends and my weekly playgroup meant I could get away from chatting about new Tupperware designs and kitchen extensions. I loved it. The school was small but it had kids from around the globe. My heart went out to them because I knew so well how hard it is to be a Third Culture Kid. Coming from one culture, living in another, not really fitting into either, and belonging to this subculture of misfits. That was me. And I knew that a lot of the kids at this school would be feeling the same and dealing with similar pressures.

What if I offered to come and do some volunteering here as a counsellor? It would be great experience for me and would give me something to put on my very, very empty resume. I would be contributing to something I felt strongly about and hopefully down the track it would mean that I could get some employment out of it.

The more I thought about it the more it appealed to me. I was excited to tell Andrew because it would show him that I had heard him about the money spending and that I did want to help out. I wasn't just planning on leeching off him forever. He was just as capable as me in the home, so leaving the kids with him wouldn't be an issue.

When we eventually had a chance to chat I brought it up as an option. I explained how on Fridays when he was home I would go out and do counselling for a few hours at a school. Andrew shot it down immediately. "Why would you do that? Fridays are our family time. The whole reason I stay home on Fridays is so that we can be together as a family. If you go out and work that totally defeats the purpose of me being home."

Here it was, Andrew dismissing something that was important to me and totally missing what I was saying. We had family time. We had Saturdays and Sundays like most other couples. Yes it was great having Fridays as well, but surely me going out for a few hours wasn't such a big deal. I explained that I was hoping to get some work out of it.

I shouldn't have bothered. Andrew went into great detail about how much he earned per hour and that it would take me years to match that. If we wanted more money then it was a lot more logical for him to work. He could earn in a couple of hours what I could make in a day. I knew he was right but he was missing the point. This was me trying to contribute something outside of the home. Expand my world a bit. Take some steps at making our dynamic more balanced so that Andrew didn't have to carry the financial burden completely. I wanted to show him that I respected his role with the kids. That we didn't have to have traditional roles as husband and wife. I really thought he would like the idea. He didn't.

Andrew and I were both hungry for something to change in our life. Once the kids were in bed we would talk about how we could bring more meaning into our existence. We kept coming back to the idea of communal living. It seemed like the best way to live the values we had. We could cut costs down by sharing our belongings, we loved the idea of sharing meals, not just cooking for our own family, raising our kids with other kids of different ages. I was constantly trying to meet with friends but it was getting harder and harder.

My style of homeschooling fell into the 'free-range' bracket so we didn't follow any time schedule. This meant we were constantly free to pop down to China Town for lunch or to the beach to collect shells or find a playground to explore. It was a lot more fun to do with others. Sadly our homeschooling friends were locked into their routines and our other friends didn't have kids our age. It was getting harder to do things in the evenings as well. We didn't have any family to watch our kids so it either meant we brought our four kids along or just one of us went out. Initially we would bring the kids everywhere but I was starting to realise that this wasn't really appreciated by our friends who either didn't have any children or they had just one little one who could sleep in a side room. Our kids were out and about, chatting away to our friends and happy to interact. I knew our friends liked our kids but they weren't so happy to have them there for the evening events. I could also tell that it was getting a bit tedious with our friends, and that me and Andrew were constantly bringing up communal living as the answer. We were becoming a bit of a broken record.

We had moved into a gorgeous house in Bridgewater that felt way too big for us. Initially we had hoped to share it with friends but then we thought it might be great to have some asylum seekers come and live with us instead. We put the word out and after quite a long time we were told we would have a young Kenyan man move in. We were all very excited since it had taken a lot more effort to organise than we had anticipated.

Andrew went off with our car and trailer to finally collect our new friend who had already come up for dinner a couple of times to get to know us. Once the trailer was loaded I got a call from Andrew. Our search would have to continue. Our Kenyan friend wasn't moving in. It turned out that Andrew had gone into his living room to help load boxes into our trailer when he had seen a whole bunch of porn DVDs and magazines. It had shocked Andrew to see that this guy wasn't even trying to hide the stuff. There was no way Andrew was comfortable with having a guy with that sort of stuff come and live with us.

It was really disappointing but at the same time I was thankful that Andrew had been so proactive about it. It would have been very hard to do this with the trailer already half loaded and ready to go. It meant a lot to me that Andrew had the integrity to do that.

It took us a few more weeks to find someone else and we ended up having two ladies from Iran move in with us. I was embarrassed at how naive I had been with the Kenyan guy and how I hadn't even considered that there might be something like porn to consider. At least with these Iranian ladies we didn't have to worry about that. It was a mother and a daughter. The daughter was in her fifties and the mother in her seventies.

I was looking forward to learning how to cook Iranian food and hearing about their culture. Instead we spent most of the time wondering what we had done wrong. They both seemed angry to be in our house. Upset to be so far away from the city. They kept to themselves as much as possible and when they did talk to me they liked to remind me how much they didn't like my husband. I struggled with him as well but I didn't need two house guests to add to that. I don't like people who are ungrateful at the best of times and here were two women being so critical while living in our home. The kids didn't warm to them at all which was no surprise really. The older woman was the only one who showed them any attention and with her not being able to speak a word of English she would just shriek really loudly when they did something cute. With two very cute toddlers in the house the shrieking was pretty much constant whenever the women came out of their room.

Susanna's court case was coming up in Sweden and I flew over to support her. It had been an incredibly hard year for her and I knew this court case was pushing her to her limits. I wanted to sit with her because I knew that having Youssef in the same building was scaring her. We weren't sure if Susanna had to be in the same room as him, and even just the thought of that was making her shake. Both Ezra and Abigail flew over from Jerusalem to be there as well which was so wonderful.

It meant a lot to me that Ezra showed his concern in such a practical way. I knew that he was caught in a hard spot with my dad so opposed to what had happened with Susanna, and Ezra and my dad were really close. So for him to come and support his sister was a beautiful gesture. My mother wanted to help as well. She had been amazing with helping Susanna financially the past twelve months and she offered to do whatever she could to help out on the day.

We were told to sit in a small room and wait while the lawyers discussed the case. It seemed to be taking a long time with our lawyer coming back to our room for clarification every few minutes. I could see that it was taking its toll for Susanna so I offered to go into the room with the lawyers and see if I could help out.

It only took a few minutes. Youssef's lawyer was very grateful for my help, and he was surprised I was saying that we were open for him to see his children. I explained that as long as there was someone supervising the visits, to make sure the children were safe, we were happy for him to have access. The lawyer seemed to be expecting us to deny Youssef any access. I explained that once the children were older they would be able to decide for themselves if they wanted to see him more or less, but for now we were suggesting three times a year. Youssef's lawyer agreed straightaway and thanked me for our generosity. I had expected the lawyer to be opposing our requests but that wasn't the case at all. I wasn't sure if it was a Swedish thing for lawyers to be so respectful and positive but the whole exchange was very straightforward and they seemed genuinely concerned for Susanna and her children's safety. They didn't say it outright but I did get the feeling they knew that Youssef could not be trusted without supervision.

I walked back to our little waiting room and told Susanna what had happened. It was a huge relief to have the long day over with and we just needed to try to leave the building without meeting Youssef in the corridor. Ezra offered to find out where he was and returned to say that Youssef was pacing up and down the street in front of the entrance to the building.

We had organised for my mom to drive past and pick us up from the side of the building but that wouldn't work now. We called her and explained that we needed to find another way out and we asked her to wait for instructions. After a few minutes of debating what we should do if Youssef didn't leave we were told by the caretaker of the court house that they were locking up and we would need to leave.

We explained that we had this giant Egyptian man pacing up and down in front of the building waiting for us and we were hoping to avoid him. The caretaker stepped outside to have a look for himself and agreed that it was best if we found another way out. He took us through the building. Down corridors and through the dark basement. Eventually we got to a tiny door that he said led to a side alley.

Ezra called mom and told her which street to wait at. Then we ran out, ducking through the door, across a wet town square, trying not to slip on the cobbled street. Mom's little car screeched to a stop and we all hopped in and drove off. I looked over at Susanna and asked if she thought we could get Sally Field to play mom in the movie.

Susanna's lawyer asked me to be there for Youssef's first supervised visit with his children. Thankfully Youssef didn't say a word to me. I wasn't surprised. The last interaction I had had with him was over the phone. He had called me a few days after Susanna arrived in Sweden. Screaming at me and demanding to know where his wife was. Cursing and praying that God would punish me. I had been expecting his call so when he quietened down for a moment I pretended that his son was next to me and I said in a stage whisper "ssshhhh... don't speak, your dad might hear you". Youssef fell for it and demanded to speak to his son.

This meant that for those first few weeks before Susanna was able to get legal protection, because of the Christmas season in Sweden, Youssef thought she had flown to Australia to hide with me and it meant he didn't fly to Sweden to look for her. He was definitely not happy to see me here for his first visit with his children.

I had only been gone for about ten days but when I returned Andrew informed me that our Iranian house guests had left after a big blow up. I was relieved. The last thing I needed was more drama. Especially in my home. With the court case behind me, and now having our home back to just us, our life got back into some sort of rhythm.

I was starting to spend more time with Astrid, my friend who had made the felt dreadlocks for my hair. She was now teaching me how to crochet in her bus. I would go one morning a week, drink chai and eat bliss balls, and learn how to crochet beanies and gloves. I loved it. I had never met a woman who was skilled in so many areas. It seemed as if there was nothing she couldn't do.

She explained that she had done all her schooling in a Waldorf Steiner school, which meant that she was taught how to create beautiful things from wool and wood. I was very impressed. It also explained why she started each day barefoot and made sure she stood under the sun each day for energy. I noticed that she often mentioned the moon. She would work it into the conversation so effortlessly, as if she was talking about a friend. "Things have been really hard at the moment, I just had to go and sit under Luna for a bit last night to clear my head" or "I'm going to wait until the full moon to start my next project, it seems silly to start without Luna's help".

I would just go along with it even though it was so foreign to me. I knew we spoke the same language but her reality seemed so different to mine. She was so in tune with the sky and the seasons. She had an energy about her that was so vibrant. She was the most creative person I had ever met and her eyes were lit up with imagination. I loved that.

I was craving friends so much that I was willing to overlook a lot of beige in order to have someone to hang out with, but with Astrid it was different. She was so full of life and always creating something. Her feet always seemed dirty and her hands looked as if she had been working in the fields, yet she would be able to weave the most beautiful baskets as we sat under a tree with our kids playing around us. Her hands busily making row after row.

Whenever she came over to my house she would dig through my recycling and shriek with joy when she would find an orange netting or shower scrubber. How could I throw out such treasures? She would then weave them into her baskets and create the most delicate creations from these scraps. I once went along to an exhibition she had, and I recognised items from my house and bits and pieces of wool and fabric from clothing I had given her.

When I couldn't handle my itchy scalp anymore from the dreadlocks I chopped them off in a heated moment seeking relief. As I looked at the colourful dreadlocks in my hands I knew they would make a beautiful basket. I was starting to see the world through Astrid's eyes.

One of the other great things about Astrid was that she also had four kids so she understood the intensity of the constant chaos. She also had a very hands-on dad to her children and they seemed to have similar tensions between them as a couple like me and Andrew. This constant power play going on. We didn't talk about it much but when it came up Astrid would always ask me where I was in my cycle. My cycle? It took me a while to realise she was asking me about my period.

I found it pretty confronting. Mainly because I never talked about my period, and secondly because I had no idea where I was in my cycle. I hardly bled at all since having a contraceptive device implanted. A doctor had recommended it to me when I asked him about getting my tubes tied after Sage was born. He explained that there are a lot more risks involved with tube tying that they initially realised and he recommended I try this other thing called a Mirena. I wasn't really interested because I knew that I reacted badly to anything hormonal in my body. He insisted that it was worth looking into since it would only affect my uterus and not my whole system.

In the end I decided to try it since I could easily have it removed if it started to cause any issues. It didn't. I loved it. It made my periods so light I hardly noticed them. It was the perfect contraception as far as I was concerned. Astrid was horrified when I told her. How could I have a foreign object in my body like that? Surely it will create friction as my body tries to reject it? It didn't. It was great and I was so thankful to have something so easy to manage. I didn't have to think about it at all. So when Astrid asked me about my cycle, it was hard to know where I was at. I knew I was horny when I ovulated. I knew it was easier for me to start crying in the week leading up to my period. But that was about it.

Crying was pretty common for me these days. Andrew and I were having so many arguments over nothing and I felt as if he was constantly criticising me over things. He claimed I was doing the same to him so we were in this constant stalemate situation that was so incredibly draining. I felt misunderstood and so confused about where we were at as a couple. Every so often I would write Andrew a letter and try to explain myself, but I had to save those for when I really needed them, otherwise I would be writing letters weekly.

I was also meeting with women once a month who home birthed. It was a great mix of women. There were obviously the more alternative ones that didn't like to follow the system. Hairy legs and armpits and babies wrapped to their chests. I had kind of expected mothers like that. What I really liked was that there were more and more mainstream women coming along to the meetings. Many of them had had traumatic experiences in the hospital system and wanted to make sure that when giving birth the next time they were listened to and treated with respect. We would sit in a circle and often the tears would flow as the women shared their stories. And not just women, sometimes dads would come along as well. It felt good to be part of something like that. Not a lot of my friends had understood why we had chosen to birth at home so it was good to be with like-minded people.

I knew that my midwife Lisa was getting a lot of negative attention from the media so I really wanted to make sure she felt supported as well. It was a tough time for her and she had given so much to us in our two homebirths that this felt like a chance to give back something to her.

In many ways I felt trapped in two worlds. My mainstream friends were referring to me more and more as a hippie. We didn't have a TV or a microwave, we were homeschooling, homebirthing, and talking about communal living. On the other hand, to my alternative friends I was mainstream with our very big house, two cars, engineer husband, eating meat and quite conservative views on life.

Asher and Tikvah weren't spending much time with Paul anymore. He was only asking to see them for about a couple of hours at a time. He was angry at me for not letting him drive them anywhere and said he didn't want them at his house if he couldn't take them places in his car. He didn't seem to understand that his drinking, and more importantly his lying about his drinking, was making it very hard for me to trust him with the kids. He had arrived to collect them for a family event and I could smell the alcohol on his breath. He insisted that he hadn't been drinking but I just couldn't get past the smell. I wanted to believe him, and I didn't want my kids to miss out on a family event at their grandparents house but I decided to keep them with me. Paul got back in the car and drove off. I found out later that he had collapsed shortly after and ended up in hospital.

The kids were becoming more uncomfortable with his behaviour as well. Telling me that he seemed strange. I assumed it was his medication making his speech slurred. He had become very overweight the past couple of years and his body movements were slower. I agreed with the kids, he did seem strange but at the same time he was still their dad and as long as he didn't drive them I felt as if he was safe.

Then out of the blue I got a call from Marg. Paul was in hospital. He had gotten into a fight at the pub. Someone had mentioned the date and Paul let them know that they were wrong. He thought it was February 2001. They laughed at him and said he was years off. Supposedly it got aggressive enough that the police were called and Paul was taken to a psychiatric hospital. He was totally convinced it was February 2001 and that he had a wife and two children. Marg wanted to know if I could bring the kids into the hospital to show

Paul that they weren't the two and three year old kids he claimed to have. Maybe seeing them all grown up would bring him to his senses.

Bring my kids in to a psychiatric hospital to get their dad into the right year? No. I wouldn't do that. I wouldn't even consider it. They already thought he was strange and felt uncomfortable around him. There was no way I was going to use them as some sort of a trigger to get Paul back to 2009. Even as an adult psychiatric hospitals were disturbing, there was no way I would take them there. I was shocked she even asked. I said I would be happy to help and come down to talk to him. Or if the doctors needed any more information that I might be able to help with I could talk to them on the phone or in person. But that was it, the kids would not be part of the offer until Paul was in the right time zone again. It felt awful saying no to Marg but I just couldn't have my kids exposed to any more bizarre behaviour from their father.

Asher and Tikvah really saw Andrew as their dad. They would hardly ever even ask about Abba anymore. They adored Andrew and loved to ask him about the planets and the stars and he still loved telling them about his trip to India. He was even suggesting that we move there as a family. He had started to learn Hindi and was really good at it. I knew he loved it there and I tried to look into some places that might work for us. Maybe Andrew teaching in an International School in the foothills of the Himalayas? I could counsel Third Culture Kids. Could that work? Or maybe Andrew as an engineer in Pune? It sounded like a nice option when I researched Indian cities.

I tried to get my head around it but the more I thought about it the less comfortable I felt about bringing three beautiful girls into a country where girls were openly mistreated on the streets. I didn't want to have to be one of those expat families that were locked away from the locals. Another thing that was really concerning me was our health. We seemed to be getting lots of tummy bugs and I couldn't understand why. All of us were taking turns getting Giardia, with eggy burps, bad stomach cramps and diarrhoea. If we were getting that in the Adelaide Hills then surely we wouldn't survive in India.

I was mainly concerned for Summer. Out of all of us she seemed to be the one getting sick the most. She was such a content and happy girl, with these gorgeous blonde spiral curls around her face. She was happy but exhausted. She seemed to be getting tired even between her naps. I tried to bring it up with Andrew but he dismissed it as me being hyper-vigilant yet again. He was pretty fed up with my constant quest for health. Frustrated with me spending money on supplements and constantly tweaking what I was eating to get healthier. I could understand that it would be hard for him but I was getting desperate. I had never felt this exhausted before and I was getting sick pretty often. If it wasn't my tonsils it was a tummy bug. And I was starting to feel sick after eating certain foods too and my hay fever was worse than ever.

I went to a doctor who specialised in natural health. She started telling me that I needed to cook broths for my gut and to stop eating dairy. It didn't really make sense and seemed so strict. I had tried a lot of things over the years and I found it hard to stick to anything for very long. Asher's skin had improved on his face when he had acupuncture but his body was still covered in eczema and we were spending a lot of much money trying to find ointments that would help soothe his rashes.

I knew Andrew hated hearing about our ailments, so when I saw a lump on Summer's belly I dreaded saying anything. When I did show him, he tried to convince me it was nothing. I agreed that it was tiny but it had looked bigger when Summer had strained while reaching for something. Eventually I convinced Andrew that we needed to get it checked. I also got him to agree to a blood test for her. I was getting really concerned about how lethargic she was. She was reminding me more and more of a rag doll. I knew she loved the library and the day she begged to go to the library only to lie on the floor the whole time sucking her fingers, too tired to even look at any books, I knew something was wrong.

Our doctor agreed that some tests were needed. Not only did Summer have a hernia, her blood tests showed that she was very likely coeliac. That would explain her bloated belly and her exhaustion.

Because of my Swedish heritage the specialist explained we wouldn't really need a biopsy because it was so likely to be coeliac as it's a common disease in Scandinavia. Andrew wanted the biopsy done, he needed proof that his little girl really needed to have gluten removed from her diet for the rest of her life.

Thankfully the surgeons agreed to work together so that Summer could have the hernia fixed the same time the biopsy was done. Only a few days later the results came back. She was well and truly a coeliac. Her stomach lining was damaged from the gluten we had been feeding her. It was so upsetting. I had been expecting the results but it was still incredibly hard to have someone say that our daughter had a lifelong condition to deal with. Andrew was upset as well and I was really hoping he would acknowledge that I was right in seeking help for our girl, or in some way tell me that maybe I wasn't a hypochondriac after all and thank me for being in tune with my kids. It never happened.

The hospital offered us a training session for people diagnosed with coeliac disease. We were told how critical it is to not have any contamination with gluten. Even one crumb can cause weeks of damage. A crumb? I pictured my kitchen. I was constantly baking and cooking. There were crumbs everywhere. There was no way we could try to keep things for Summer gluten-free and continue as we were. Thankfully Andrew agreed that it would also make Summer feel left out if we didn't all go gluten-free at home.

I was so daunted by the thought of cleaning up my kitchen. Wiping every shelf. Removing any remnant of gluten that might make my little girl sick. I asked Andrew if he could take the kids for three days. I didn't care where. I just needed to go through my kitchen from top to bottom and start afresh. I cried as I thought about how things would be so different now. Could we even eat at China Town anymore? What could I bake for the kids? All my recipes were based on wheat flour.

So many times when I was out with the kids we would just stay longer than expected so I would buy pita bread and hummus as a snack. That would have to stop now. And what about when we met up with friends? Would I need to keep Summer away from the food so she wouldn't grab something that would make her sick? It all seemed so hard. So antisocial. We were free spirits and now we had to become those anal people who couldn't eat what was offered. Paul's parents had struggled so much with me not letting the kids drink soft drink and eat chocolate when they were toddlers. This was a hundred times worse than that. Thankfully Asher and Tikvah seemed to understand and we explained to them that we would eat gluten-free in the house but when we were out they could eat gluten as long as they did it discreetly and didn't eat Summer's favourite foods in front of her.

I decided that I would become gluten-free as well to see if it would improve my health. I felt unwell but couldn't exactly define in which way. I was heavier than I had ever been before. Exhausted. I was either constipated or had diarrhoea. My lower back was sore. Nothing was right but I couldn't put it into words. I had a blood test that showed my estrogen levels were way too high. The doctor recommended a progesterone cream for me to rub into my belly but it cost about $60 a month. I knew that would be too much money to expect Andrew to pay for something that wasn't exactly medicine as such. With all our other expenses it seemed like a luxury.

The unease in my body was matching my unease in my relationship. Andrew was becoming more and more interested in politics. Middle East politics to be exact. He was quickly becoming an expert on the topic. He was about four chapters into his first Noam Chomsky book when I noticed him bringing it up at any opportunity. I didn't mind. It was definitely more interesting than him talking about engines and machines. I did struggle though with his need to sound as if he had the answers. And he really wanted me to have opinions on things that related to Israel. What exactly did I think about the occupation? He really wanted to know. I tried to explain to him that it wasn't as easy as that. I actually didn't know how I felt about it. I was confused. I had classmates who told me they wouldn't be happy until all of the Jews were in the sea. At the same time I had Israeli friends who told me that killing Palestinians mothers was okay because they were just giving birth to terrorists anyway.

Andrew insisted I have an opinion. Couldn't I see that Israel was the oppressor? Well, I could. But I also knew that reading one book on the topic was very different to stepping onto a bus in Jerusalem and wondering if it was going to blow up. Or having a friend describe what it's like to step over body parts after missing a bomb by a matter of seconds. Andrew wanted me to have black and white answers. Well, he wanted me to agree with him and Chomsky. I couldn't. For me it was more complex than that.

I tried to explain to Andrew that there were people who tried to stay clear of the politics and instead focus on the people. Friends like Jess who was part of a group trying to create bridges between the two people groups. Find ways for them to connect. Remove the political language and try to reconcile. Focus on our shared humanity. If I had to be anywhere in the conflict, that's where I wanted to be.

But really, I didn't even want to have this conversation with Andrew at all. Why talk about the Middle East when we had our very own conflict to deal with? Why read Chomsky when our marriage needed all the help it could get? It amazed me how much time and energy Andrew had to discuss anything that he felt passionate about yet when it came to the matters of the heart it felt as if there was this NO GO zone. I would only get a few words in before Andrew would accuse me of something or highlight that I was even worse of a spouse than him.

I finally told Andrew that he needed to keep Chomsky out of the bedroom and he needed to get a friend to fill that need. I had already said the same about engines. I was not the person to talk to about engines. This had genuinely upset Andrew and he said it hurt him that he was married to someone who couldn't share that part of his life. I tried to explain that it was the equivalent of me talking about crochet patterns and different types of wool as he tried to make love to me. It's not the time or the place, or the right person for that matter. With four kids to raise there isn't much time to talk, I didn't want to use up that precious space with engines and Chomsky. Surely that wasn't so hard to understand? It was.

On one of the rare nights when Andrew and I were trying to be proactive about our future, by coming up with a solution instead of just going around in circles, we decided to make a list of our options. What was actually feasible? What about moving to Queensland and joining a community up there? Buying some land with a wind farm and trying to live off the grid? Managing a school camp? Buying a bus and travelling around Australia?

All our options meant lots of money was needed. And lots of money meant Andrew needing to work. And that meant him being away from the kids and the whole point was for him to spend more time with them and me.

What about us moving to Bali for six months? Andrew was really surprised. Would I really move to Bali he wanted to know. He assumed it was off the list since India was off the list. I said that India seemed so extreme but I might be able to handle Bali. Andrew's face lit up as he wrote 'six months in Bali' on the list.

One of the girls called out from bed so Andrew went to settle her and I quickly jumped on the computer. Megan was online. A new friend of Andrew's. He had met her a few times at 'Engineers Without Borders' events. It was one of the things he had gotten involved with recently since becoming more aware of social justice issues. She was an incredible woman. Possibly the most intelligent woman I had ever met. Her mind constantly buzzing. This wonderful combination of intelligence, social justice, eclectic dress sense and red lipstick. I really liked her. I hardly ever saw her but would bump into her occasionally on Facebook. I decided to ask her what she thought. *Where do you think we should move to as a family, anywhere in Australia or in the world?*

She answered immediately.

Cambodia.

That's all she said.

Cambodia? I didn't even know where that was. Somewhere in Asia.

Why Cambodia?

You will love it, it's perfect for you guys.

Andrew came back from the bedroom and I told him that Megan thought we should move to Cambodia. He looked at me.

Would you move to Cambodia?

The walls were closing in on me. My Tupperware containers were making me go insane. The conversations about tiles versus splash backs in the kitchen were giving me a rash. Library books that went missing in action no matter what I tried. I had to get out. Suburbia was killing me. Yes, I would move to Cambodia. I really would. I would move pretty much anywhere right now. Okay, not India. But anywhere that my kids would be safe and we could eat gluten-free food.

The next day we had a letter in the mailbox. It was from our real estate agent. They were not renewing our lease. We had six weeks to move out. Our answer had come. We were moving to Cambodia.

It was an incredible feeling. I couldn't wait to get rid of all our stuff. This was the most beautiful home I had ever lived in. We had a magical garden with a creek running through it. A train would go past and there was a tunnel under the train tracks that the kids would love to play in. We had a basketball court. A basketball court! Massive trees to climb. And I just couldn't wait to leave. I had had enough of it all. We organised a garage sale where we hardly asked for any money. We were practically begging people to take our things. The only items I wanted to keep were photos, some of the kid's sentimental stuff and Mormor's paintings.

Andrew's dad was getting remarried in four weeks so we decided to spend our last two weeks in Melbourne. We had bought a house over there with money from Andrew's mum so it was a good chance to check how that was going, as well as spend some time with Andrew's sister, and of course go to the wedding.

A couple of days later we had our trailer packed and we waved goodbye to our lovely home in the Adelaide Hills. It was July 2009. Our two weeks in Melbourne were fairly busy. It was good to check out the house we owned and to remind ourselves what it looked like.

We had made a point of renting it out to people we thought would struggle to find other rentals. So our first tenant was a family with five kids. And now we had a single mother with three kids and her mum in there. It was good to be able to come for the wedding and see Andrew's dad happy. I really didn't know much about Melbourne at all. Andrew grew up in the north-eastern suburbs and there wasn't much there besides a big, ugly shopping centre, lots of trees and about 25 minutes away a weekly hippie market. The most important thing for me was that we had family there, and that meant that we could hopefully get some help with the kids and get away for a night. I really wanted a chance to spend some time with Andrew alone. It was so rare that we had the chance. His sister agreed to have the kids for a night so that we could get away. It was our last weekend in Australia. We had been out and about doing errands when I had a phone call.

The caller asked if I was driving, I said yes, and said they would call back. They called again a few minutes later and I explained it was fine to talk. I wasn't driving. Was I sitting down? Yes, I was sitting down. I looked over at Andrew and gave him a look. This sounded weird.

Was I Lillian Good? The wife of Paul? Yes and no. I was Lillian Good but no longer the wife of Paul. They apologised and explained that they were calling from the South Australian Police. According to their records I was still listed as Paul's wife. They were sorry to inform me that Paul had passed away. Did I know of anyone that needed to be informed?

Paul had passed away? My eyes welled up. Oh no! Paul was dead. Dead! I had felt this coming for so many years but it was still such a shock. And here I was in Melbourne. I had always pictured getting this call and then driving straight to his parent's house to be with them if they got the news. Or at least call someone who they were close with to sit with them as they were told. This was horrible. For them to get a knock on their door from the police with no warning. I started to cry as I thought about how Marg had been dreading that knock for years. Knowing that her son was such a troubled soul. The police went on to say that they had found his body in his house. He had been watching TV as he died. They didn't have many details but it didn't look like suicide.

Oh wow. Paul had died. He had died while watching TV. It was hard to digest the news. I gave the police the address of Paul's parent's house and told them to please be really gentle. This would be very hard for them.

The funeral was booked for the day after we left Australia. I asked Asher and Tikvah if they wanted to fly back to Adelaide with me and go to the funeral. They didn't. I told them to really think about it but they insisted. They really didn't want to go. They agreed that next time we were back in Adelaide we would go to his grave and bring a little gift.

Three days later we got on a plane for Cambodia.

21

White Elephant Palace

The flight from Melbourne to Kuala Lumpur was the worst flight I had ever experienced. Sage screamed almost the whole way there. Eight hours of her throwing herself around in my arms screaming as loud as she could. She was so upset and there was nothing that could be done and she refused to go to Andrew. She slept for maybe twenty minutes at a time when she collapsed from the exhaustion of shrieking. It was horrible. I felt so bad for her but even worse for the passengers around us. I told myself I would never complain again about another child screaming on a plane. We had for sure broken the record for the loudest and angriest toddler on board a plane ever.

We realised when we landed that Sage had intestinal worms. Thankfully I had packed medication. In fact, I had packed medication for pretty much anything I could think of. We all had a bag each for the trip. Mine was mostly medicines and supplements. Thankfully the worm medication worked quickly and Sage and I got to sleep for the short flight between Kuala Lumpur and Phnom Penh. I woke up just as we were about to land so I only caught a few moments of the view. The landscape beneath us looked flooded. There was water everywhere. Tiny huts surrounded by water. In some places you could see patches of fields, but it was mainly water. It reminded me a bit of movies I had seen about the Vietnam War. Thankfully we landed peacefully with no soldiers shooting from the wet rice paddies. We were off to a good start.

I had asked Megan to recommend a place for us to stay in Phnom Penh for our first few days. She said there was a guesthouse that a lot of volunteers stayed at that would be clean and affordable. That had sounded good and, thankfully, they had offered to pick us up from the airport. The drive to the guesthouse made my head hurt. There was so much to take in. Too many new sights for my tired brain to register. Was that really a mother holding a tiny baby attached to an IV drip on the back of a motorcycle? And did we just have to swerve because a cow stepped in front of our car? And when we swerved did we nearly knock a guy off a motorbike who was holding onto a large pane of glass with his bare hands? And was that a man with no legs manoeuvring himself between cars and motorbikes? Wooden boxes were lined up on the side of the road covered in fruit and vegetables and when I had a closer look I realised there were big chunks of meat as well. All out in the middle of the fumes. People were walking in between the cars and motorbikes. Not slowing down or waiting for a lull in the traffic. This was Phnom Penh.

It was a relief to get to the guesthouse. It was very simple with the first floor an open space for tables to eat at, and three levels of rooms above. Everyone was very kind to us and excited that we had children. The guesthouse mainly had volunteers in their twenties staying there so we were a bit of a novelty. Two old, American guys lived there as well. John and Roger. In the eleven days that we stayed at the guesthouse I don't think I saw them move away from their table once. They always had a few beers in front of them even when I would come out first thing in the morning to get hot water for the girls' bottles. A TV was always on, usually showing movies with more blood and guts than I had ever seen before. Or worse, Cambodian video hits. The menu options were endless and as long as I didn't peek into the kitchen and watch them cut the meat on the floor, or focus too much on the giant rat I saw scuttling under the fridge, the food was quite enjoyable.

We knew nothing about Cambodia. Andrew had followed Megan's recommendation of applying for an Engineering job as a paid volunteer. We were sure he would get the position. He was perfect for it. We found out only days before our flight that the job had gone to someone else. We were pretty shocked. The position would have given us a starting point in Cambodia. Without it we were pretty much free-ranging it.

So here we were in a guesthouse with not much to do besides chatting to the volunteers and telling our kids not to look at the TV in the corner. The volunteers were mainly young, British people who paid a lot of money to fly to Cambodia to help out in orphanages. We had arrived only a couple of days after a fresh batch of volunteers. They were horrified to have just found out that they were not actually helping in an orphanage but instead were taken to a school and told to teach a class full of kids. They had no teaching experience and no teaching supplies. Just a room full of smiling kids.

They would come back after a day of 'teaching' and tell us about how crazy it had been. That they had no idea what these kids knew, what the volunteer who had been there before them had taught, and how they were meant to get forty kids to learn anything when there was nothing to write on or with. And what had happened to the thousands of pounds they had paid for the experience? Who was getting that? It obviously wasn't the school or the kids. In the evening the dining area would become noisier as it filled up with more locals and travellers who were happy to drink the night away. We would get the kids back up to our rooms before things got too loud.

They were very basic rooms with the tiniest toilets and showers you could possibly imagine. You could sit on the toilet and have the shower running over you and spit your toothpaste into the sink at the same time. And in order to get back out, you had to manoeuvre yourself around the door so you didn't get trapped between the sink and the toilet. We paid extra so that we could have windows for both our rooms. It meant they were noisier but it also meant we could look outside at everything that was going on below us on the street. We would watch as monks draped in orange robes would come and pray and be handed food to put in their metal trays. I had no idea how much bicycles were able to carry until I moved to Phnom Penh. With just a piece of string one bicycle could have a three metre high pile of baskets strapped to it. It seemed impossible but somehow these young men were able to balance the load and go from street to street selling their goods.

Every few hours we would be visited by a lady selling eggs. She had a special chant that we could hear from down the street. John's special lady friend encouraged me to try one of the eggs. "You try, they give you POWER!!" I had a closer look. There was something poking out of the egg. A beak! She was eating a baby chicken out of an egg. I could hear her crunching the bones and wings. She laughed as I covered my mouth trying not to gag.

We spent most of our time at the guesthouse so we were starting to get to know all the people there quite well. There weren't many places to go with the kids and it was so hot that no one seemed to want to leave the relative comfort of the guesthouse anyway. Sometimes we would just all squeeze into a tuk tuk and ride through the streets to watch all the madness around us. Andrew had found a tuk tuk driver that he really liked so we would try to ask him to be our driver as much as possible. His name was Nara and, like everyone else in Phnom Penh, he had a wide smile. He genuinely seemed friendly though and unlike a lot of the other drivers he seemed fair with how much money he asked for each trip. He also seemed to be very careful with his driving and not take as many risks as a lot of the other drivers.

Andrew was loving every moment of being in Phnom Penh. I had never seen him this happy. He would go for long walks in the afternoons and come back and tell us what he had seen. Construction sites where the builders were balancing on rickety branches while pouring cement. Women washing babies in puddles of water on the side of the road. A family of six fitting onto a motorbike by using a plank of wood as extra seating. He loved it. In the evenings he would run upstairs to the roof so he could watch the lightning. Storm watching was one of his favourite activities and here in Phnom Penh he had access to some of the most spectacular shows. I wasn't sharing in the enthusiasm in the same way. I was still trying to work out what to do with the kids all day. They were struggling with the heat. Especially Sage. She had heat rash in the folds of her neck and on her chest. She was constantly dripping with sweat. The other three were coping better with the heat but they didn't like the busyness of the streets.

Sometimes they would join Andrew for a walk but they preferred staying at the guesthouse. I eventually emailed Megan and asked her if she knew if there was a place I could take the kids for some space to run around. Some sort of a park. She suggested the Olympic Stadium. A massive cement oval that was crowded with people trying to get their daily exercise. Not exactly what I had in mind for my kids needing space. Andrew started calling about apartments for rent. He thought it was time for us to find somewhere to live that was more permanent than a guesthouse. I was keen to get away from the guesthouse but the thought of living in Phnom Penh with children was so far from what I wanted. I went along with Andrew to have a look at some apartments but kept reminding him that the kids would need space. They couldn't handle being stuck in a tiny apartment all day especially if there was no park for them to play in. Andrew was also looking for work. Contacting places that might be interested in having an engineer work for them. He was also a teacher so he looked into that option as well. We had a bit of money but we would need more if we wanted to stay more than a few months.

I decided I would try to see if there was something I could help out with as well. Maybe my counselling degree could be useful. I started asking around on Facebook and someone recommended I get in touch with a guy called James Pond who had an organisation for girls that were rescued from being trafficked. I spoke with him on the phone about the possibility of helping out. The next day when I was at a market I could hear a man that sounded just like James Pond. I waited for an opportunity to introduce myself but he vanished into the crowd. The woman he had been talking to was still there so I tapped her on the shoulder and asked her if the man she had been talking to was called James Pond. She laughed and said no but she actually knew James. She introduced herself and said her and her husband were missionaries in Cambodia and were just about to move to a small town to start a church. She asked if I was part of a church as well. I explained that we weren't. She wanted to know who we were with. I explained to her that we were just a family who had come to Cambodia to live. She looked surprised. I could tell that she was trying to make sense of what I was saying but it wasn't exactly adding up. It was the first time I realised that we were a bit of an anomaly.

I had been trying to convince Andrew that we needed to see more of Cambodia before we started to rent an apartment. Megan had mentioned the coast. A coastal town called Kep with a tropical island not far away. Let's go there I told Andrew. Anything to distract him from his real estate hunting. Thankfully he agreed and the next day we got into a taxi for the drive south. Once we were on the open road I regretted not insisting on seat belts. We were flying down the highway with the driver honking the whole way to warn other cars that we were approaching at full speed. Sage was on my lap in the front seat and I held her as tightly as I could without her squealing. Asher and Tikvah were yelling out at all the crazy things they were seeing. The lopsided trucks. The cars so packed with people that the driver was sharing a seat with at least two others. Babies being held out of windows to urinate while trucks sped by.

I was so grateful when we finally arrived to our destination. I promised myself that I would make sure we never travelled like that again. We would all need seat belts. The coastal town of Kep was miniscule. The centre of the town was actually just a row of huts selling freshly caught seafood. There were some houses inland but the actual town itself, if you could call it a town, was not even worth mentioning. It was wonderful to have fresh air though and to be away from the hustle and bustle of Phnom Penh. After a couple of days staying at an unfriendly, French guesthouse, we decided to take Megan's advice and go out to the island she had mentioned. Rabbit Island was only a half hour boat trip away, but once I saw the boats

I started having second thoughts. They looked so flimsy and the life jackets were missing buckles.

The island itself was very basic and it was nice to see that it hadn't become too touristy. Well, there were tourists, but there were no fancy buildings. Only simple huts and no electricity. The kids loved playing in the water and digging in the sand. There were hammocks stretched between coconut trees and it really felt as if we were on a tropical island. This was a lot more like we had pictured Cambodia to be. Daytime was lovely but the nights were hard. We were used to sleeping under fans to cool down. These huts had nothing like that and because of all the mosquitoes we had to sleep under nets which made it even hotter. The sheets were polyester so the sweat made us stick to the beds. On our second night I eventually tried to get some sleep in a hammock outside our hut, hoping to get a bit of a breeze from the ocean. Not long after I dosed off a wild boar rubbed himself along my body and once my heart started beating again I scrambled back into the hut. I didn't get any more sleep that night.

The next day we noticed that Summer had a spot on her torso. Just one but it looked unusual. Later that day she had a few more. Andrew sent a text to our friend back in Adelaide who was a nurse and she said it sounded like it might be chicken pox. Sure enough, it was. By the next day she was covered with giant spots that were oozing pus. Much worse than Asher and Tikvah had when they were younger. And no relief with the heat. Poor little girl. We needed to get somewhere comfortable for her. I realised that Sage would be next. So we really needed to find somewhere comfortable for the next two weeks while they were sick. My mind was racing. Where could we go? I didn't want to return to Phnom Penh. The French guesthouse had taught us that even a fancy place is not worth it if the owners are unfriendly and don't like children. Was there even such a thing as a kid friendly place in Cambodia?

I remembered a poster I had seen at the guesthouse in Phnom Penh. It was just a few photos and some handwriting. Not a pretty poster but I had noticed a sandpit with some colourful buckets in it.

Something about that photo had stood out to me. We could go there! If they had a sandpit they must be okay with children staying there.

The poster had said Kampot. Less than an hour away from Kep in a tuk tuk. We found a driver who was happy to take us but he tried to explain in broken English that he couldn't take us the whole way. We couldn't understand why we would need a second tuk tuk to meet us. It turned out to be because the road to the guest house was so incredibly bad that our first tuk tuk was unable to manage the ride. He took us as far as he could. Then a bigger and more robust tuk tuk met us for the last bit.

It was crazy. We were shrieking with laughter as we bounced around. Our bodies crashing down on the hard seats after being bounced up in mid air. We held on as tight as we could but were still being thrown around. Parts of the road were completely submerged in water so it was impossible to know how deep the puddles were. At one stage we got bogged in the mud and the driver got us to climb out to lessen the load. It was absolutely crazy to think that this was a normal way to travel. It was a long road that was running parallel to a river. We could see it between some of the palm trees and houses lining the road. On the other side of the river was a beautiful mountain. It was greenish blue with smaller mountains going off into the distance in different shades of green. It felt as if we had found paradise. Paradise with possibly the bumpiest road in the world.

The guesthouse was stretched out along the river. Lots of green lawn and coconut trees scattered around. A Pakistani man in a turban greeted us. His name was Karim and he was the caretaker while the owners were away. Karim made us feel very welcome and explained to us that they don't have many visitors during the wet season. We would have the place mostly to ourselves. The place was exactly what we needed. Spacious with lots of lawn for the kids to run around under the mango and coconut trees. The river was right there and Karim promised us that there were no crocodiles. We could stay for as long as we needed, and yes of course, the sandpit was there for our leisure. The kids were thrilled.

We settled into our room. It was pretty rustic and at night we could hear the rats trying to get into our suitcases, but there was something about having the river and the mountain just there that made all of us feel like we had finally landed. The guesthouse provided meals because it was too far to go into Kampot to eat with the road so bad. We didn't mind. They had beautiful food. Incredibly the bread rolls they served for breakfast were made from tapioca flour so we could eat them.

A very helpful English speaking Khmer lady had helped us write a little note explaining that we couldn't eat anything with wheat flour in it. She included examples. Soy sauce made with wheat, noodles made from wheat and of course bread made from wheat. A few people had already told us that wheat is very expensive in Cambodia so they would mainly use rice and tapioca flour. The bread was similar to baguettes and Summer loved them. It was such a treat to finally be able to give her some bread. Andrew even joked that we should find out the recipe and go back to Australia and open up a bakery. We would be rich very quickly.

After only a few days there I woke up in the middle of the night with the worst stomach cramps I had ever had. The pain was so severe. I found my packet of Buscopan. It had always helped me in Australia with my mystery tummy ailments. It helped but only a bit. For the next three days I was completely out of action. I was going back and forth between my bed and the toilet. Karim was very concerned as were the owners who had returned for the weekend. There wasn't much that could be done and I was happy that Andrew was able to look after the kids so I could stay in bed and try to sleep as much as possible and wait for the bug to leave my body.

Every few hours I would get an update about what they were up to. They had been for another swim in the river. They had watched a DVD. Andrew was telling me that one of the maids had been especially sweet with the girls. Playing with them and always checking if they needed anything. I was relieved. It was awful being locked away for so long but I got dizzy even from the short walk to the toilet and back.

Andrew was excited because he had been told that there was an English speaking playgroup in Kampot. We had gone through the town on our way here. It was only a twenty minute or so tuk tuk trip away depending on how many times you got bogged in the mud. Andrew happily went off the next morning with the kids and bounced back into our bungalow to tell me the good news. There were some really lovely people in Kampot. He was sure I would like them.

Andrew insisted that we would fit in. It sounded good. It sounded really good. Andrew was so critical of people that for him to be this positive really meant a lot. I told him I would go along next week and check it out.

I really think we could live here Lillian, it's got everything you want.

He was right. It really was a beautiful place and if there were some friendly people as well that we could get to know that was even better. The next couple of days Andrew would tell me more. How these people weren't like the regular expats we had heard about in Phnom Penh. They seemed really down to earth and didn't have flashy western lifestyles.

I was intrigued but my main focus was gaining some strength. I had this massive craving for mashed potato. After three days of being completely depleted my hunger had returned. I decided to head into Kampot and find a café that would have mashed potatoes on the menu. The tuk tuk trip was even worse than I remembered it. Maybe the intense rain we had had each afternoon washed some of the road away?

We eventually got into Kampot and I looked out at this little town that might become my new home. It almost looked like an abandoned movie set. These faded terrace houses that were riddled with bullet holes. A bridge going across the river. It was beautiful yet kind of spooky. In its heyday it would have been a gorgeous town.

I got dropped off at a tiny guesthouse on a side street not even close to the river. It seemed like an obscure place to have a guesthouse but the pamphlet I had seen about places to eat in Kampot mentioned mashed potatoes.

I found a table inside under a fan and told the waiter that I wanted a bowl of mashed potatoes. Nothing else. I could hear a woman talking in the corner. She was really loud so it was hard to ignore her. Typical Americans with their lack of volume control. Her voice seemed familiar. I tried to get a glimpse of her face. It was the lady from the market in Phnom Penh! The lady who I asked if her friend was James Pond. How bizarre to see her here. I remembered she had said she was moving to a small town, but to think we had landed in the same town and now in the same tiny guesthouse. I had to go and say hello. Susan remembered me and introduced me to her much quieter husband. They were having a quick lunch before going to look at some houses to rent. Did I want to come with them?

The first house we looked at was majestic. It looked as if royalty had lived there at some stage. A very wide ornamental staircase took us to the top floor which was just as beautiful as the downstairs. Susan had told me they wanted something big so they could have meetings in their home. This would be perfect. As we stood there admiring the view, her husband told us to be quiet for a moment. He could hear something. He then poked his whole hand through the door. Just like that. Termites. Everywhere. I had never seen anything like it.

The owner who was showing us around just shrugged his shoulders and told us it was no problem. For Susan it was a problem. They had one more house to look at and it was close to the guesthouse I was staying at. They could drive me back in their four wheel drive after we looked at the house. That sounded great. I was starting to worry that body parts were falling out of me on these tuk tuk trips. I had almost instinctively looked down on the floor of the tuk tuk to check if my uterus was lying between my feet after my last trip. A car ride seemed very appealing with my tummy still recuperating.

The house we went to look at was just around the corner from the guesthouse. Less than a ten minute walk up the dirt road. It wasn't exactly on the river but the rice paddy was flooded so it looked like the river and with the mountain in the distance it was striking. The house was huge. I was sure Susan would like it. Once we got inside I could tell that she was disappointed. The outside of the house was fancy but on the inside it was very simple. The man who was showing us the house explained that it had six bedrooms, no toilet and no chicken. No chicken? "It has no chicken but they can put a chicken in."

Susan laughed and explained that Cambodians always confused chicken and kitchen. The house had no kitchen. Aha. Right. They were also happy to put in a toilet. Seemed like a good deal to me. Obviously the owner was willing to cater for these western luxuries. Nothing had to be decided right then but I could see that Susan still wasn't happy about the house. They were both fluent in Khmer and were chatting away to the landlady. They then turned to me and asked if I was interested in renting the house. I looked around. Yes it was simple but it had lots of space. If there was some sort of bench put in next to the tap it could easily become a kitchen. We would only need a gas burner and a fridge. And the landlady had already said that she was happy to install a toilet.

It was way too big for us but I loved the idea of the kids being able to use the space since being outside was too hot most of the day. Besides the medications and supplements in my bag I had squeezed in our exercise ball. Our kids played with it for hours. It was the next best thing to the trampoline, which sadly didn't fit in my bag. With all this space the kids could play around on the ball. And come to think of it, we already had friends who were saying they wanted to come for a visit. We could have the spare rooms set up for them. This could work.

I got back to the guesthouse and told Andrew that I thought I might have found a place for us to rent. It was perfect having Susan and her husband there to help with the translating. Andrew was happy to look around at the house, but as soon as we left he let me know what he really thought. Did I have no shame? This wasn't a house. This was a palace! There was no way he and his family were going to be the rich white arses living in a palace among poor Cambodians. Was I really suggesting we live in such a lavish mansion? Here we went again. Both of us looking at the same thing but having such different interpretations of it. Yes the house was big. And yes that was kind of weird. But it wasn't the biggest house on the bumpy road along the river. The one next door and the one opposite were much bigger. I tried to explain to him about the space for the kids. The exercise ball. The fact that our friends were coming to visit.

Andrew was horrified. He had found a bungalow on the other side of the river and wanted to live there. I went with him to have a look. It was built on stilts in case the river flooded. It was actually quite nice. A wooden bungalow but built by a westerner and very tasteful. In fact, it was actually much fancier than the house I had suggested. Just that it was tiny. A one bedroom wooden bungalow.

I asked Andrew where we would sleep. "Oh, we could get custom made bunk beds that would fit into the bedroom for the four kids." I tried to imagine that tiny room with two bunk beds squeezed in. We wouldn't even be able to fit a fan in there to get some airflow. "And where would we sleep?" We would sleep in the living area of course. We could pull out mattresses each night that could be used as a couch during the day. I looked around. That would mean that we had no space for the tiny dining table in there. "And where would our friends sleep?" Andrew stopped for a moment. "They can sleep on the mattresses on the floor and we can sleep in hammocks on the balcony." Right. Me sleep in a hammock. That would work wonders for my sore back.

It was amazing how Andrew could be such a solution focused man when he wanted to be. This bungalow was designed for a maximum of two people. Two people who spent most of their time at work. Not a family with four kids who were pleading not to go outside because of the heat.

We returned to our guesthouse. Nothing needed to be decided now. I didn't want a fight about where we were going to live. I didn't even think I could live in Cambodia at all. It was all too intense. The poverty we had seen in Phnom Penh was still haunting me. Young mothers pleading for money with babies in their arms. Men with missing limbs grabbing on to me and asking for food. It was so full-on. If it was just me it might be okay. But I had my four children, and with them a my focus it wasn't as if I could do anything about what I was seeing. I was used to being proactive and here I was having to turn away. I had been told not to give money to beggars. That it only makes the situation worse. It was better to give to organisations that could help these people properly. That seemed fair enough. Until I was getting back into a tuk tuk with my four kids all eating ice cream and a young woman who couldn't have been much older than 16 was asking me for money for her obviously sick baby. What was I supposed to do with that?

I really didn't think I could last in Cambodia very long. It was now early September. What was the longest I could last? Another month? Oh that was so embarrassing. Coming back to Australia after only two months? Then again, I had kind of done that once before. With Paul. We had made this dramatic exit from Adelaide. Gotten rid of all our stuff and moved to Jerusalem only to return five months later. It wasn't such a big deal. Shit happens. Maybe I could last longer than a month? Maybe I could make it until Christmas. That was less than four months away.

I decided that I would just go along with the bungalow idea. It was so crazy and I knew I was right about us needing space. We wouldn't last long in that tiny shoe box. We could be back in Australia sooner than I had hoped if we went along with Andrew's suggestion. The next day I told him to let the owner know we would move in. I hadn't met any of the playgroup people in Kampot yet but it was enough for me that Andrew liked them. I could get along with pretty much anyone.

I was happy to move into the bungalow? Andrew was looking at me weirdly. Yes, tell him we want it.

Andrew stopped. This wasn't what he had expected from me. What about the kids needing space?

Nope, we can move into the bungalow. It's fine.

Andrew understood. Us living in a bungalow would mean a very short stay in Cambodia. We wouldn't last long. All of a sudden

Andrew wanted the palace. I was right. We did have friends coming to stay that would need a room. The kids will spend hours indoors with the monsoon rains bucketing down around us. Andrew was rattling off my list as if it was his own. He wanted the white arse palace to be ours. Something had clicked.

We told Karim the good news. We would be neighbours. We were moving into the yellow house up the road. Andrew introduced me to Rosa, the maid that had befriended him and the kids. Rosa. Where had I heard that name before? It took me a few moments to remember. Of course! Paul had befriended a prostitute in Malaysia and brought her back to Adelaide with him while in the navy. She had lasted three months. His parents still rolled their eyes years later when her name came up. Here it was again. The same name. I asked her if it was a common name here in Cambodia.

Oh no. It's not Cambodian name. I have a Cambodian name. Rosa is my name for barang people.

That made sense. She wanted a name that sounded more familiar to westerners. It's easier to connect to someone who has a familiar sounding name. I might have done the same if I was in her situation. She was beautiful. Tiny but beautiful. Long, straight black hair and a pretty face. She didn't look like a lot of the Cambodian girls I had seen. Her features seemed more defined and she was darker. She explained that she was the oldest daughter and she had to stop going to school to earn money. Her eyes were sad but she made up for it with a wide smile. She was incredibly sweet and Andrew was right, she was very kind to our kids.

We were heading back to Phnom Penh to buy some of the things we needed for our new home. We had left some of our belongings up there and Karim told us that it would be much cheaper to buy the fridge and the gas burner in the capital and bring it back down. We also ended up buying thin mattresses, bedding from the markets and some cane furniture.

One afternoon as I headed into the guesthouse John looked up from his beer. Did you say you are moving to Kampot? He still made me think of John Wayne every time he opened his mouth. I started to say that it was a village outside of Kampot when John pointed up to the TV screen above his head. Kampot was flooded. Totally flooded. The monsoon rains had been too much for the river. The town was totally submerged. Only the tops of the palm tree were poking out of the brown water.

When we arrived back a few days later Karim told us all about it. How the cows got washed away. Some being trapped in the mango trees. How they didn't know how high the water would go but it eventually stopped just before the second story of the house where they were all getting shelter. I had seen the footage on the TV in Phnom Penh but it was hard to imagine cows stuck in mango trees. I was very happy that we were moving into a palace and thought we might need to invest in some sort of inflatable boat to go along with the palace in case there was another flood. Thankfully I had bought life jackets for the kids. That seemed like a good start.

Before we left for our shopping spree in Phnom Penh Andrew had told me that Rosa had asked him if she could work for us. She wanted to be our maid. I could tell that Andrew was uncomfortable with the idea. It was hard enough to be moving into a palace, but now a maid as well? Everyone who I had spoken to about us living in Cambodia had said the same thing, make sure you get at least one maid.

I had mentioned to Andrew that everyone seemed to assume that we would be getting a helper. I knew what his response would be so it wasn't as if I was even telling him or asking, merely highlighting that everyone seemed to say the same thing. Susan had explained it a bit better to me and said that it was just expected that everyone had a helper. Even Cambodian families will have one as soon as they can afford it. I hadn't thought about this before but they explained that it was actually a great way to be able to help someone out. If you treat them well then it actually creates a very good job for someone who could otherwise be stuck in a pretty grim situation.

Rosa had already been telling Andrew about her hard working conditions. Six days a week unless it was busy season. Then it was seven. Only one holiday a year. She was earning $40 a month but could eventually earn $70 if she got more responsibilities. No wonder she wanted to work for us. Something had made Andrew consider her request and not just shoot it down straightaway. He was really struggling with the idea. He wanted to know what I thought. It wasn't an easy situation for him. He needed to think it through.

The only other time we had gone into so much discussion over a decision was about donating eggs to my friend. We had hardly discussed the other big events in our life at all. We hardly had time for a conversation before I was pregnant, twice. We pretty much moved to Cambodia on a whim. Even buying the house in Melbourne wasn't as big as this. We had taken time to look around at different houses together, but there was no real agony in the decision excepting that Andrew seemed to hate the concept of being a home owner.

This however, was much harder. Andrew was torn between his values of wanting to live a simple, self-sufficient life, trying to live like one of the locals as much as possible, but also seeing that his status as a westerner could give this young girl some financial security and a safe place to work. If Rosa worked for us she would learn English. That would improve her chances of getting a better job. We could make sure she had weekends off so she could study and finish high school and get her high school certificate. We could take her on trips with us and show her more of Cambodia. Andrew stopped. He really wanted me to hear this. If Rosa was going to work for us, we would never take her with us to Australia. There was no way we were going to taint her by exposing her to the West. I hadn't thought about it like that but I agreed. We would have to be really careful to make sure Rosa didn't get the impression that the West was some incredible place to live.

The girls working in the guesthouse in Phnom Penh could think of nothing better than to find a white man to marry and to move back to his country with him. We had seen these couples everywhere. Young Cambodian girls with older western men. It was both sad and gross. Mainly gross. Andrew in particular couldn't handle it. He despised these men so much that he would practically hiss at them if we passed a couple in a tuk tuk.

No, we would have to be so careful to keep Rosa as untainted as possible. Could I agree to that? I assured him I would and that really it just made a lot of sense having some help. It didn't need to be this complex ethical equation. Why not just say yes to someone working with us? Make sure we treated her well, not expose her too much to western crap, and enjoy the fact that we were helping someone out and getting some domestic help at the same time. Andrew had never been good in the cleaning department. His domestic strengths lay elsewhere. I could clean, but the thought of even attempting to lift a mop with the heat and the humidity was almost laughable. Having Rosa come and work for us would benefit all of us.

Even though Rosa hadn't started working for us yet she had helped clean out our house after the flooding. When we arrived back most of the mud from the walls was gone and the work men where nearly done with putting a bench into our kitchen. I was really grateful for all the work because we were already hosting people that weekend. Megan had told us that the guy that got the job that Andrew had applied for was a really nice man. I let her know that he would be welcome anytime to visit us. Well, he had asked if he could come and bring a friend.

Seb and his friend arrived the next day. I was glad that I had bought extra bedding and plates. Megan was right. Seb was a lovely guy. Softly spoken and he seemed to enjoy being with a family. I noticed that Rosa was being extra attentive to Seb. I didn't blame her. Scoring a western man was a ticket to freedom. Susan had explained to me that Cambodian girls were pretty much brainwashed from birth, even in very subtle ways, to think that everything would be okay for them and their families if they could get a white man to marry. It explained why there were so many beautiful young women with their arms around men so much older than they were.

Along with Seb and his friend we also had a woman from New Zealand come and stay. We had met her at the guesthouse and said she was welcome to stay with us in our new home. She had just returned from visiting the White Elephant Palace in Phnom Penh so she brought us a gift. A white elephant statue. We decided that it was the perfect name for our not so humble abode. The White Elephant Palace was always open for anyone who might want to come and stay with us. A couple of days later we waved our visitors goodbye and told them to come back anytime.

I finally had a chance to go along to the playgroup that Andrew had been raving about. It met on top of a café in Kampot. The café belonged to Epic Arts, a performing arts centre for people with disabilities. Katie and Hallam had started it and it was thriving. The café was one of the most popular destinations for tourists passing through Kampot. The playgroup was strangely familiar since they sang all the same songs we used to sing back in Adelaide. The other children were quite a bit younger than our girls so Mia, the playgroup leader, enjoyed having kids in the circle that she could chat to a bit more. I agreed with Andrew. These were really nice people. Every single one of them. I looked forward to getting to know them a bit better.

Mia was thrilled to hear that we were gluten-free as well and told us where we could find some gluten-free products in Phnom Penh. We asked her if she was enjoying the baguettes from the local bakery. She looked confused. She was sure they weren't gluten-free. We told her they were made from tapioca. Katie chimed in and said she was sure they were made from rice flour. This wasn't looking good. The next day I decided to check for myself. I had been told where to find the bakery in town. They were closed but there was another bakery around the corner so I asked them if they knew when the other bakery was open. They only knew a few English word but they explained to me that they use the same flour. It was tapioca flour. I decided to go back a couple of days later to confirm with the actual bakery. This time they were open. I asked them what flour they used. Rice. They used rice. I explained that the other bakery had said tapioca and that they use the same flour. I could hear my voice start shaking. The owner had better English so it was easier to communicate. He was starting to get frustrated that I wasn't understanding him.

We only use rice flour I show you.

He pulled me into the side room where huge bags were stacked up along the wall. Look, it's rice!

100% WHEAT FLOUR it said on each bag. Fuck! We had been eating this stuff. We had been feeding it to Summer. I almost started crying as I pointed to the words. "It's wheat. WHEAT. Not rice. It's wheat. My daughter will be very sick."

No, no. Rice!

He pointed to the picture. Sure enough. The straw with grains on it did look very much like the rice growing in the fields all around us. But no, it was wheat. I realised that this baker had no concept of different grains. He just knew that the flour he used made perfect bread rolls. Light and fluffy on the inside. Crusty on the outside. The picture looked like rice. He probably couldn't even read English. I threw out my little paper in my wallet that explained we couldn't eat wheat. What was the point of showing that to people who had no concept of what wheat actually was?

It was so frustrating but there was nothing that could be done. We would just have to be more careful and assume that everything was made from wheat. We mostly ate food from the local market anyway. Andrew would go in early and get what we needed for a day or two. It reeked in there. The ground was so wet from the rains that most of the time it was a very tricky balancing act trying to stay dry by walking along planks of wood and the odd piece of cardboard. There were lots of misses when a foot or two would disappear into the mud. Fish guts, animal waste and rotten fruit all mixed in with the rainwater.

Andrew loved it though and would come back and tell us about his adventures. Sometimes I would join him and we would buy a bowl of pork and noodle soup for breakfast. It was a small window of being together without the kids. They hated coming to the market. Asher and Tikvah hated it because of the smell and the girls hated it because they kept getting pinched by admiring locals. The pinching was hard enough to leave marks on their arms and cheeks.

Our friends Caleb and Kaia were coming to stay and we were all very excited to see them. We didn't get a chance to see them that often in Adelaide so it was such a treat to have them come and visit. As I hugged Kaia I noticed the shirt she was wearing. It was exactly what I had been looking for to buy. I needed something light that would cover my arms. T shirts were too hot. This shirt was perfect. I was hoping she had bought it on her way through Phnom Penh, but no, it was from an Indian store in London. It was so perfect. I watched her wear it the next couple of days and decided I would try to get it copied by a seamstress in the market. I hadn't been able to find any good quality fabrics in Cambodia but Katie had told me there was a place in town that sold handwoven cotton fabric. It seemed too good to be true.

After a couple of attempts I finally found the place. It turned out to be a vocational training centre in the middle of Kampot. Similar to what the orphanage I went to in Sri Lanka was trying to set up. A way for young women to train in a skill and to hopefully gain some employment. I walked into a giant shed and looked around. There were about 15 enormous looms. A young woman was sitting in front of each one carefully weaving metres of fabric. The woman in charge spoke no English but I managed to walk out of there with some fabric. It had been tucked into glass cabinets. Rolls and rolls of it. They had a few samples of things they had made from their fabric but most things were tucked away. As I walked out of there I had an idea. Getting a couple of shirts done for myself was easy enough, but what if I was to buy some more fabric and get maybe forty shirts or so made up? I loved the idea of showing these young women that I appreciated all the effort. I felt silly just walking away with a couple of metres with so much handwoven fabric being discarded.

I talked to Andrew about buying enough fabric for shirts and then asking my friends on Facebook if they wanted to buy one when I returned to Australia. I had been on a waiting list for surgery for my legs. The varicose veins that had been hurting me for years were finally being removed at the end of March. I could bring a suitcase full of shirts back. I figured that if Kaia liked the shirt most of our friends would. I knew the quality would have to be good. That was a bit of hit and miss with the sewing ladies at the market. They usually charged about seven dollars per item but it wasn't always that great. I realised that the place that had the fabric for sale also trained girls how to sew. What if I was to pay for one of them to come to my house and sew shirts? I could explain that it was only a short-term thing but I would pay them well.

I asked Rosa to come with me to have a chat to the woman in charge of the centre. She said there was no problem with something like that but when she introduced me to the young woman she had in mind I realised it was slightly more complex than having someone come for a few hours a day. The young woman in front of me looked terrified. Absolutely terrified. She had a scarf around her head showing she was Muslim. I knew the Muslims came from the fishing village outside of Kampot. A very poor area and they had very little contact with the rest of the town. I knew we would be friendly to her but I could see in her eyes that this was incredibly scary for her. It was so hard to not have a shared language so I could try to explain that nothing bad would happen to her. I knew from speaking to James Pond that girls were often told they were going to be given employment only to then be sold off to a brothel. Was she worried about that? I couldn't ask. Instead I told Rosa that I would like two seamstresses. Did this young woman have a friend who would also like to sew at our house? I figured we would just need to sell a few more shirts but at least I didn't have to look at those terrified eyes every day.

A couple of days later the two young women arrived at our house. Rosa had met them in Kampot to show them the way. I had been to the market and bought two sewing machines. They looked antique. Andrew pointed out that it meant we wouldn't have to pay more in electricity. I hadn't even thought about it but because they were manual it meant that we didn't have to worry about the constant power cuts we were having. Andrew was good at thinking about stuff like that. Our two shy seamstresses seemed happy with the task I gave them. Rosa did a very good job in translating. Her English was very basic but still it was much better than any other local girl that I had met. And most importantly, she was very keen to learn so anything that she didn't understand she would check with me and we had plenty of funny moments with me using body language as a way to describe a concept or a word.

By the end of the week I was asked by the now not-so-shy sewing ladies if they could bring two friends to join us. I was thrilled to see that we were obviously making them feel comfortable and that they liked working here. Another two ladies though? It was hard to say no. I wasn't sure how many more friends I could get to buy a shirt in Adelaide. Was there anything else I could make that my friends would buy? I knew the ladies had been taught how to sew these cute little hats for babies and toddlers. Lots of my friends had babies. The handwoven fabric would be too rough to use for the hats. I knew parents would be put off by the texture of the fabric before it got washed a few times. I had an idea though.

Just a couple of days earlier I had been to a different part of the markets. It was even more run down than the main area. There were women squatting in front of big piles of fabric. I had a quick look and saw that some of the prints were actually quite nice. Most of the pieces of fabric were torn and some had stains on them. I decided to ride my bike back for another look. After digging through the piles I managed to find quite a few pieces of fabric that were actually great. These vintage patterns my friends would go nuts over. I filled quite a few baskets and rode back home trying to dodge the puddles. It was getting easier to do that now that the rains were easing off.

After the fabric was washed and dried I had to admit that they would look great as little hats. Come to think of it, I wanted some of those fabrics for myself. What if I had some shopping bags made? I could never find one that was the right size. The straps were either too short to hang over my shoulder or there was no pocket for my phone or the bag was way too wide so it looked clumsy. I would design my perfect bag.

By the start of the next week we now had four sewing ladies showing up on their bikes in the morning. I realised that we needed to have some sort of a chat. I needed to make sure that we were on the same page. I had this fear that they would assume that this was long-term. I needed them to understand that I had originally just planned on making forty shirts. I was now adding some things to the list but it was all very short-term. We were flying back to Australia in March and I would be selling the things we made to my friends. This was just a very small project that would end in March. I made sure that Rosa checked that they understood.

Within a couple of weeks we had twelve ladies sewing away downstairs. I found it impossible to say no. I kept having more ideas of things that we could make. I figured that as long as I made sure we were making things that friends, or by now friends of friends, would buy then things would be fine. With six of us travelling back to Australia we actually had quite a lot of luggage that we could fill up. Not all the sewing ladies came from the Muslim fishing village. We now also had some local girls from our tiny village. I just couldn't say no to them. I knew what their homes looked like. I knew how desperate they were for a bit of money.

My days were getting fuller and fuller. I had lots of interest on Facebook about what I was doing. People wanted to come to Cambodia to help out. It took time to respond. It also took time to dig through the piles of fabric. Some days I would return empty handed, and other days I paid a man on a moto to drive the giant bags home because they were too heavy to balance on my bike. Whenever I had to go to Phnom Penh for something I would start looking around at the markets there as well. My face would be dripping with sweat as I tried to find pieces of fabric that would suit. The vendors would yell out at me, showing me fabrics they thought I would like. Never understanding that I wanted cotton or silk, not the bright polyester that they prefered. Rosa explained to me that they couldn't understand why I wanted all the ugly fabric.

I also needed to check on everything that was being sewn. I really wanted our items to be known for their good quality. I hated buying a beautiful Thai shirt at a market only for it to fall apart after a couple of washes. I wanted our things to last. It was easier said than done. I was expecting a lot from Rosa. She was a lot more than a translator. Everything that happened went through her. I had no other way of communicating without her help. It was too much to expect her to carry the load of the cleaning as well as being available for the sewing ladies.

I knew we had to ask someone else for help but wasn't sure how to go about it. Rosa said that her cousin had just found out she was pregnant. She was a teenager and her husband was away most of the time and when he returned home he was often drunk and would beat her. I had seen the bruises myself. She was very happy to come and clean for us. Asher groaned as I told him. He hated having so many women in our house. It was bad enough with the sewing ladies all giggling every time they saw him, but now he had to get used to someone else going upstairs where our bedrooms were to clean.

We had been invited to a wedding that was to be held a few houses down. I really didn't want to go. I'm sensitive to sounds at the best of times, and to have to sit through hours of horrible music blaring while dripping with sweat was not how I wanted to spend half a day. I knew I should though. We had so little contact with the people in our village. Going to one of their weddings was surely a good sign of them warming to us. Rosa explained that it really wasn't about that. They would just like having white people at their wedding and we would be expected to give money. Even less of a reason to go.

Rosa also told me that I would need to wear a traditional dress for the wedding. This was getting worse and worse. How on earth would I find anything that would fit me? I was a giant compared to the tiny Cambodian ladies. I was reminded of how big I was whenever I stepped outside. Tom means big in Khmer. As soon as I left our gates I would hear this rhythmic 'tom tom' echoing around. Kids pointing and women giggling at the tom tom lady.

I managed to have a silk jacket and skirt made. Rosa informed me it wasn't enough. I would need makeup as well, and have my hair done. It was the Cambodian way. I never wore makeup. And my hair? Really? I reluctantly went off to one of the many beauty salons in Kampot. I tried to zone out as much as I could and just take the opportunity to have a quiet moment. However my eyes flung open as I felt something sharp over my eye. A razor blade was quickly pulled away. Thankfully they had only removed part of my eyebrow before I realised what was happening. They had assumed I wanted my eyebrows shaved off and then pencilled in for the big day. I let them continue with the makeup but made sure not to fall asleep and risk anything else happening to my face.

When they finally finished with me I looked at my reflection and saw Tammy Faye Bakker staring back at me. I couldn't believe how I looked. I had this enormous hairdo going on, thanks to hair extensions. Blue eye shadow, and the longest false eyelashes I had ever seen. My skin was hidden beneath a thick layer of something that smelled pretty bad. I had to laugh. Rosa was still being worked on so I decided to run across the road to buy some office supplies. I walked into the shop and heard a Canadian woman speaking to the owner.

I tried to get my supplies without being seen but we bumped into each other at the counter. We introduced ourselves and I apologised for looking like a TV evangelist. Shraps told me she thought it suited me. I liked her immediately. She explained that she worked at a tiny little school outside of Kampot where they helped kids learn English so they could hopefully break out of the poverty cycle. I had heard about the school before and told Shraps I would come and check it out. She was there every day so she would be easy to find.

The wedding lasted all night. It wasn't that bad, another family was there with English speaking kids. I was really excited at the thought of Asher and Tikvah making some friends. In our few months in Cambodia they hadn't met anyone their age who they could talk to. We kept being asked to pose for photos, which was fine until we got asked to stand in front of a pig's head displayed on a fruit platter. The stench from the rotting and now actually melting head was so bad that the girls and me started to gag. We said our goodbyes and made a quick exit.

I had been consistently sending updates about our life in rural Cambodia to friends and family, using email and Facebook. They were just snippets about things we were observing and experiencing. It was great sharing about our life on Uterus Road as I started calling it. Checking each time I got off the tuk tuk that my uterus was still intact. Andrew decided that he wanted to write an update as well. I didn't get a chance to read it until after it got sent out. I had expected him to write something about how much he enjoyed the freedom we had. He just loved living in a place that didn't seem to have any rules. In Australia he was often stopped by the police for looking suspicious, especially when he would drive around in his old Kingswood station wagon. He was such an easy target. Andrew was practically on a high living in Cambodia. I figured he would write about that. Or maybe about the people getting kicked off their land in the name of progress. We were hearing more and more stories of families being forced to leave their home so a road could be widened or the existing train line improved.

I did not expect his update to be about sex. More specifically his observations about sex in Cambodia. How it was so good to be in a country that seemed to have the right idea about sexuality. I tried to keep reading but I was feeling so uneasy. There was something so off about his writing. I felt as if I was seeing into a small part of him that he hadn't allowed me into before. It's not as if anything he wrote was personal as such. It was very much topical and an observation only. Yet I had this feeling I couldn't shake. I was hoping it would change its tune, that somehow it would redeem itself. It didn't. It only got worse.

I started to read the fourth paragraph "*... now - there is undoubtedly a seedy tourist sex trade here - old hideous western men with more cash than dick who have crossed the line from masturbating to porn to paying for prostitutes and who find the cheap sex and huge control that their money brings them while they are here appealing. It is horrible - especially to see how comfortable some of them are with their clearly depraved pastime. One of the more hideous abuses of the privilege of growing up in a rich country ...*"

I had to stop. He had sent this out to our friends and family. Would they feel the same way as I did? I couldn't keep reading. Hopefully this would just be another update for them. An interesting take on life in Cambodia. For me it was something else. I couldn't put my finger on it. We hadn't really talked much about the topic at all. I had once joked about how I would throw a party the first time I saw a handsome Cambodian man. I just didn't find them attractive at all. Andrew had groaned.

You think you have it bad! I'm in a country with women without breasts!

It was true. Cambodian women were tiny. It was impossible to buy a bra that didn't have a thick layer of foam inside to add some sort of a curve to the flat chest. I had even seen underpants with a thick foam layer to give an illusion of curves. To sit there and read Andrew's take on things in Cambodia felt so off, and some of the comments he had made really showed he had no idea about the sex industry in his utopia. Did he really think that the karaoke bars were just that and not brothels? That the beer girls in dimly lit bars were not paid for sex? Sure the local markets didn't pulse with testosterone like the shuks in Cairo, and he hadn't seen a woman's breasts get fondled like he saw on his trip to India, but this was not some puritan country. Yes, pathetic western men came here and felt powerful because of their financial status, he was right about that, but did he really have to word it the way he did? Masturbation and porn, not exactly what our friends and family needed to read about. It was hard to ignore the unease I felt inside.

I was trying really hard to get some friends for Asher and Tikvah. They would occasionally play with the kids in our village but it was sporadic, and they needed kids they could connect with. The family that we had met at the wedding had lots of kids. The dad was Khmer and had managed to survive the Pol Pot years. The mum was American. They were missionaries who had adopted two children with disabilities to add to their own four children. Their life was incredibly busy giving the youngest two kids therapy for hours each day to help them learn to walk and talk. They didn't have much time to play but occasionally we would see them.

It was hard to explain to Andrew how much I craved for our kids to have friends. He didn't seem to understand that they needed more than the local kids to play chase with. I decided to invite Stephanie and her family over for New Year's Eve. There was another missionary family in town that we never got to see at all so I decided to invite them as well. They all said they would come. So would Susan and her husband. I hadn't expected everyone to say they would come. I would have a house full of missionaries for my first New Year's Eve in Cambodia. I called Shraps and invited her to come along as well. I told her I needed someone to balance out the dominant missionary status in the house and to rescue me if anyone tried to convert me. She wanted to know what they would be converting me from. I wasn't exactly sure but I just knew I needed someone normal to usher in the new year with.

Shraps and I had become friends since our serendipitous meeting in the office supply store. She was very busy during the week but often on Sunday mornings we would meet for a long bike ride. We would start early before it got too hot. Ride through Kampot and then out past the railway. We would follow that for a while, passing bright green rice paddies. We would then ride through tiny villages with kids lining up to wave at us. "Hello hello what is your naaaaaame?" Over and over again. We would keep riding and go past temples and shrines. Monks walking alongside us for part of the way. Some mornings we would go past the salt fields and watch the farmers with their heads wrapped in kramas bending down to collect the salt. Other times we would ride down to the fishing villages and watch as the fishermen fixed their nets after a night out in the ocean. After our bike ride we would buy a coconut to drink. It became our little Sunday morning ritual and I loved it. It was a highlight in my otherwise mad week. I was so grateful that Shraps had agreed to be there for New Year's Eve.

The kids had an absolute blast. They spent hours in the river and then came back for a water balloon fight. I loved seeing them so happy. It was good to get to know our guests a bit better. Stephanie was an amazing woman with so much to give her six children. I asked her about the therapy she was doing for her two youngest kids. She explained that it's a very time consuming role but she had only this week been reminded of how it was paying off. They had met a twelve year old boy who had nearly drowned when he was two years old. That was ten years ago and he was now so severely deformed, and his legs so twisted, that his feet were in his face. When Stephanie had first seen him it had taken her a while to register that the dark shape in the back of the house was actually a human and not an animal.

According to Stephanie, this boy could have been able to overcome most of his disability if he had been offered therapy after the near drowning. Years of neglect meant that his muscles had contracted and severely deformed his legs. His family had money but they kept him in the back of the house and were ashamed of him. Now that he was reaching puberty he was starting to get violent and they were thinking of giving him to an orphanage.

Stephanie went on to say that she really believed that things could improve for this deformed boy if he could get some surgery on his legs. I asked her what was stopping that surgery from happening. It would be a very difficult operation and cost a lot of money. She didn't know anyone with that kind of money. I didn't either. But I figured that someone I know might know of someone. Surely it was worth asking. Did she know about Facebook? She had heard of it but didn't use it. I looked over at Shraps. I could tell she knew what I was thinking. Surely between the two of us we could find someone.

Three days later we had. It was ridiculously easy. We didn't even need to find someone rich. It was as simple as getting the word out on Facebook and almost immediately we were told that there was a doctor coming in from the States to do volunteer surgery in Phnom Penh. If this boy called Da could be brought up there he would be operated on for free. It seemed too good to be true. I passed the details on to Stephanie and, sure enough, a few weeks later Da was operated on.

Shraps and I were thrilled that our offer had paid off. Stephanie and her family decided that they would help Da and allow him to have therapy at their house with their two children. He would still need more operations, but this first one meant that it wasn't long before Da was able to have his legs stretched out. One of his legs was much longer than the other though so Stephanie made a foam base for one of his sandals to help him balance.

A few weeks later Stephanie told me that word had spread about Da's miracle. Parents were coming to their gates with children in their arms. Most of them floppy, unable to speak. Could Stephanie fix them? They had no money but they were desperate. I decided to ride my bike over and see what was happening over there.

Their home had been transformed into a therapy centre. It was so full-on. Kids with severe disabilities were smiling up at me from the floor. Giant grins on their faces. Others were on the kitchen table crying as their limbs were manipulated in rhythmic motions. I tried to count how many children I could see. On top of Stephanie's own six children, two of which needed hours of therapy daily, they now had Da as well as about eight others. It was crazy.

My heart went out to Stephanie who just couldn't turn anyone away. I asked her what I could do to help. I had tried asking her before but she was one of those very shy women who hates to be a bother and didn't want to be a burden. I insisted she could tell me at least some items I could provide to help lessen the load. I explained that it wouldn't be me buying the things and that I would put the word out on Facebook.

Sure enough, next time I was in Phnom Penh I was able to buy the bits and pieces that she had asked for. Things like foam squares to put on the floor so the kids didn't have a hard surface to lie on. Bags of rice so they could feed the kids. It was such a humble list of items and I really wanted to give more, and my friends on Facebook seemed happy to give a bit of money towards the cause.

There were so many needs everywhere. It was so hard to know which ones to help and which ones to let slide and hope someone else would do something. I had already decided that any of the profit we made from the items we were sewing would go towards these different stories that I was being drawn into. Initially, when it was just a few shirts, I figured that we might make enough profit to pay the university fees for a young man who had pleaded for my help.

I had gone to have a massage in Phnom Penh. Massages are so cheap in Cambodia. I kept hearing about 'Blind Massage' and was intrigued. Supposedly it was a way for blind Cambodians to get an income. They were trained in Shiatsu massage and charged five dollars an hour. It was somewhat confronting. I wasn't sure what to expect but if I ever had a massage in Australia it would be from one of those no-frills Chinese places at the market. I liked the simplicity of it. I could still wear my clothes. There were no water features or soft music playing. No one talked to me. It was just in and out and they seemed to know exactly where to press.

This was very different. A girl with glazed over eyes handed me a pair of blue cotton pyjamas to change into. Then she guided me to a table. Once I was there a young man with eyes that darted back and forth started talking to me. Well, at me. A million miles per hour.

What is your name? How many kilos you have? What country you are? Then the list of observations.

You tom tom. You have many kilos. You have a lot of money.

Then he started telling me about himself. I had tried to switch off because I really couldn't handle someone poking me and telling me how tom tom I was. His story was hard to ignore though. He grew up in a village outside of Siem Reap. When he was 17 years old he got the measles. Within days he was blind. His family didn't want him to live with them anymore and he got sent to Phnom Penh. Here he was taught how to massage people and he would be paid thirty dollars a month for his work. He hated it. All he wanted was to go to university. That's all he had ever wanted. I asked him what he wanted to study. He didn't care. English, business, anything. His words were flying out of him. It was possibly the worst massage I had ever had. He clearly didn't want to be a masseuse.

There was something about him that connected with me. He was so incredibly annoying but at the same time I could hear how desperate he was. I'd like to think that if my son became blind at 17 and was forced to become a masseuse he'd pester his clients until they gave in and paid for university. I liked his drive. It was annoying as hell, and I really just wanted to get away from his hands that were bruising my body, but I knew I had to help him. I asked him for his phone number and told him I would try to help.

After a few phone calls I learnt that it only cost $300 a year for the university fees. Obviously he would need help with books and other supplies. That was doable. I called him and asked if he had anyone he could live with while he studied and he said yes. On my next visit to Phnom Penh I met with my annoying new best friend and went with him to the university to pay the fees. It wasn't a lot of money but with all our other expenses it was adding up, and our bank savings were very quickly depleting. That's why I thought the money from the shirts would be able to cover his next year's fees, as well as some money to live off each month. Now with more items being made I realised it was a way to help with some of the other needs I was coming across.

My days were full with everything needed for the sewing project. I was often at the markets finding fabric or at home trying out new ideas that could work. I was always on the look out for inspiration. So much so that when Seb came for a visit, and brought his friend Sally with him, I wouldn't let her leave before getting her to take off her dress so one of the sewing ladies could make a pattern from it.

Sally was more than happy to oblige, she was volunteering in Cambodia and loved the idea of contributing to the cause. In the midst of everything that was needed for my own little sweatshop, as I had started to call it - only because I was constantly dripping with sweat as I would look through our products and check for mistakes - I still had to be a mum. The older kids were struggling with not having friends. Asher especially. Tikvah was able to stay busy with her own sewing. She was so good at it and if she ever had any issues she would just tap one of the sewing ladies and point to the problem and they would quickly help. We ended up buying a sewing machine for her as well.

Tikvah was also helping out in the noodle shack that was a minute down the road. She would get up as the sun rose and run over to help our neighbour with serving the soup. It impressed me because most of the village would come through this tiny little hut every morning and I knew she hated the attention. Helping with serving the soup meant that she was starting to learn Khmer though and each day her vocabulary seemed to be growing. When I would go over there myself I loved seeing my blonde haired, blue-eyed daughter ladling hot broth over noodles and placing the slices of liver and solidified blood into the bowl. She was so confident and I could hear her starting to make a few comments in Khmer. She didn't seem to mind the skinny dogs sneaking in looking for scraps of meat or the hens between her feet. I was really proud of her. I knew it was harder for Asher and he was starting to make more and more comments about needing friends.

Mum, I pretty much read, draw, play with the cats and look in the fridge, that's my whole day.

I knew he was right. Every Phnom Penh trip to the doctor, and we had many thanks to endless tummy bugs, I would go to the second hand bookstore and try to find more novels for him. His drawings were amazing but there were only so many hours a day he could do that. I needed to spend time with him, as well as Tikvah. The girls seemed happy to occupy themselves and Andrew put a lot of his energies into them.

It was great to be able to share the cooking duties with Andrew, most nights we either had pork or seafood. My Jewish ancestors would not have approved. There just wasn't much else to eat. The beef was ridiculously dry. Cambodians used their cattle for the manure and their organ meats. Not their flesh. The cows in Cambodia looked nothing like their fat cousins in the western world. They were skinny and their hip bones poked out. Much more like an Indian cow but not exactly the same. The seafood was great but it was hard to find a way to cook it so that the kids would like it.

After dinner I would go upstairs and spend a lot of time on the computer. We still had lots of black outs but I still managed to spend a lot of my time online. Andrew hated it but he also knew that I needed to in order to stay in touch with everyone back home about the upcoming sale. I really needed people to be on board and the only way to ensure that was by staying in touch online and giving regular updates on the growing pile of creations.

Andrew would sometimes take the kids out to Kampot in the evenings for a smoothie from one of the street vendors. I would stay home and listen as the village dogs turned demonic as the moon rose. These skinny dogs that would sleep most of the day or just wander around looking for something to eat would transform at dusk. They would begin howling and then join in the chorus with the rest of the dogs, you could hear them from so far away. It was an awful sound and I always had to warn our visitors about it because it really felt as if something was amiss when it happened. Like these dogs knew something bad was going to happen and had to howl to each other as warning.

I very quickly learnt that I had to ride my bike home before it got dark because the dogs were so ferocious after the sun set. My fear of dogs had only increased since coming to Cambodia but I kept being told that the dogs were harmless during the day. Supposedly they just sounded scary but if you threw a rock at them they would quickly run off. Throw a rock at them? It seemed crazy but I very quickly became used to having rocks in my bicycle basket for my many rides into Kampot. At night the rocks were useless and I would make sure I was in a tuk tuk if I ever had to go out, and even then dogs would often try to bite the poor driver. There wasn't much to do at night as a family anyway so it was simpler to stay home.

I tried to find time to be alone with Andrew but it was easier said than done. On one of our grocery trips to the market I noticed that my throat was just a little bit sore. Nothing major but enough that I suggested we have some hot soup and hopefully that would help anything that might be brewing. I didn't really think much of it for the rest of my busy day.

The next morning I woke up and realised I was struggling to breathe. My throat felt completely blocked. It was only 4:00am but I woke Andrew up and whispered that I was finding it hard to breathe. A cup of tea didn't help much but I tried to just lie in bed and hope that things would improve, but unfortunately they didn't.

It was starting to scare me. I really wasn't getting enough oxygen. I woke Andrew up again and told him I needed to get some help. It was hard to breathe so I was trying to not use a lot of words.

Andrew decided to call our travel insurance company and ask them what they suggested. I tried to keep calm and focus on my breathing. The phone call took a long time and I motioned to Andrew that I needed help. Surely the phone call could wait? We had a really good insurance company who would compensate all the costs after the event. They didn't need to be informed now. Andrew brought a fan over to blow air across my face. It didn't help. I needed oxygen and I needed it now.

The combination of trying to stay calm as well as not use my air for talking meant that I was saying very little, only motioning to Andrew that we had to go. When he finally got off the phone I whispered that I needed oxygen now or I might pass out. My body was burning up and I was feeling light headed. Andrew said he would call Rosa to stay with the kids and then take me into Kampot on our motorbike. On the moto? Was he crazy? I couldn't sit on the back of the moto like this! I whispered that he needed to ask our neighbour to drive us. He was the only one in our village with a car. Andrew didn't want to wake him this early.

It wasn't really that early anymore. Cambodians get up at the crack of dawn and he was a farmer. He would be fine. And really, I wasn't breathing, so even if he did have to wake someone up to keep me alive I would really appreciate the gesture. Our landlady was a nurse and lived next door so she came over to help. She started pinching my arms and my face. I already had so much pain going through my feverish body and now my landlady was pinching me. She helped Andrew guide me down the stairs. Her grip around my arm distracted me from the pain in my throat. Thankfully I eventually managed to convince Andrew with my limited talking to ask the neighbour to drive us into Kampot.

By the time I got into the Medical Clinic I was finding it hard to walk and collapsed on a bed they had for me. A nurse got an IV into my hand. My doctor back in Adelaide had warned me about going to a local clinic in case they used unsterilised equipment. In that moment I didn't care. Every step was closer to me getting oxygen. I had been asking for it as much as my breath would allow me to but I still no one had made sure I got some. I grabbed Andrew's hand and begged him to ask for me. He told me that the doctor had said I didn't need it. Didn't need it?? My lungs were burning. Each breath hurt so much. I kept feeling like I was going to pass out. I NEEDED oxygen.

I couldn't believe that I was even having this moment with Andrew at all. It had only been a few days earlier that Sage's birth came up again in conversation. Andrew mentioned something about how peaceful I looked and he just didn't have any idea of how serious it was for me. I reminded him that I had no control over my facial expressions at the time, not even my hands. But that I had asked for oxygen and really needed it. I had gone on to say that if I ever asked for oxygen again, he needed to make sure I got it no matter what. Even if I didn't look upset or I didn't make a big fuss about it, he needed to believe me. I even clarified that I would never ask for oxygen if I didn't think it was important, and so even if I said it ONCE he needed to make sure I got it. And now here we were, less than one week later, and I was pleading for oxygen, when I had enough strength to speak, and he wasn't taking my request seriously. It was terrifying.

The doctor looked in my throat and said I needed to go to a bigger hospital in Phnom Penh. They would call an ambulance for me. I said I wouldn't go unless they gave me oxygen. The doctor looked pissed off but I finally got my oxygen. My lungs stopped burning. My head stopped pounding. My body relaxed. It still felt as if I had a knife going through my throat but I was okay. I was going to be okay. Once the crisis was over and I could finally get the air I needed the tears started to flow. How had Andrew allowed this to happen?

The first time was bad enough, but back then he really had no idea how severe things were. But to have it happen again? And when I had been so clear about what he needed to do. There was no excuse.

I felt so neglected. I didn't feel safe. Andrew tried to tell me that he could see for himself that I was getting enough oxygen. The clip on my finger was showing numbers on a screen. My oxygen levels were fine. They might have been fine. Except that for me, I needed air and I needed it right then and I needed him to trust me.

Andrew called Mia and asked her if she could go with me to the hospital in Phnom Penh. I was so relieved. I didn't want Andrew to go with me. I needed someone who cared. I didn't know Mia that well but she had come over to our house a few times to enjoy a gluten-free meal with us. It was such a treat for her to not only spend time with a family, but to also eat a home-cooked meal that was safe for her to eat. Now she was sitting in a van, that was meant to be an ambulance, with me.

I was so grateful she had come. It was still early in the morning and she only had a couple of minutes to get to the local clinic but she hadn't even considered not helping me for a moment. It meant a lot.

The four-hour trip to Phnom Penh was hard. I tried to sleep but the sharp pain in my throat was agonising. It felt impossible to swallow. I could feel that my body was burning up and the only thing I could do was try to remain as calm as possible. When we arrived at the Phnom Penh hospital a doctor came out to greet us. A beautiful, older lady with her silver hair pulled back in a tight ponytail. She had a very strong accent. I tried to pick it. Was it Russian? No, she smiled. Bulgarian. She had a quick look in my throat and rushed me inside. She asked for nurses to gather around and check out the IV in my hand.

Eveeeeeen eeeeen Etheeeopia zey have better IV zen dis.

I liked her already. She had spunk. She told me I would need the strongest antibiotics available to try to get the infection under control. She showed me with her thumb how big my tonsils were. She was impressed. Over twenty years in Ethiopia and she was impressed with my tonsils. She also gave me strong painkillers and told me I had to sleep. She was so forceful but incredibly kind at the same time. I knew I was in good hands. After a couple of hours in emergency I was taken to the ward. The hospital was set up in an old mansion.

It didn't have the regular look of a sterile hospital. It had more of a personal feel to it. Again I was so grateful for the travel insurance we had which meant that we didn't have to pay for the stay. My doctor came to visit me once I had settled in.

You vill stay for as long as you neeeeeed. Your body is veeeeery seeeek.

How long did she mean? I needed to be back home as soon as possible. I told her I was thirsty but I couldn't swallow.

Forgeeeeet ze freeeeedge! What was she saying?

Forgeeeeeet ze freeeeeedge, eeef you do not like to beeee sick, forgeeeeeet ze freeeedge!

She went on to explain that having cold drinks is one of the worst things we could do for our health. We were not designed for refrigeration. Our glands would get shocked each time we drank something cold. It was much better to drink a hot drink, even a lukewarm drink. In Cambodia? A hot drink? She almost sneered at me.

Wat do you zink zey drink in ze Sahara desert? Zey drink tea. HOT tea!

She had a point. I knew the Bedouins in Israel drank tea. She told me my throat would thank me. Also I needed to always have something on my feet. The cold tiles in our house were not good for my run down system. And on top of that I needed to keep my neck covered. She suggested a thin silk scarf. Now this was something I knew about but hadn't realised that it was so important, especially in a hot country. My glands needed to be kept in constant temperature. They couldn't handle being exposed to cold. It was why my throat would start hurting even in a short taxi trip with air conditioning. I loved the cool on my body but my throat always protested. She was too scary not to obey. I promised her that I would forget the fridge and not ever have ice in my drinks ever again. She smiled. She felt more like a mother than a doctor. She really seemed concerned for me.

The next morning I was expecting my doctor to return but instead two male Cambodian doctors walked into my room. Neither of them introduced themselves and were discussing my notes as if I wasn't there. After a while they started to rattle off some questions for me. Just standard personal details as well as my medical history. When they asked if I had any surgeries in the past I mentioned that I had a breast reduction. There was a moment of silence until the older doctor burst out laughing. Seconds later the younger doctor exploded with laughter too. They couldn't stop.

They laughed so hard they were holding onto each other. After a while they tried to contain themselves but it would burst out again as soon as they would try to talk. Like two little schoolboys. The giggling continued as they tried to finish the questions on their form. It was hard for me to mention my breast reduction. It was still not something I really ever talked about. Hardly any of my friends knew about it. And here they were wiping the tears away from laughing so hard. I decided to ask them what was so funny. Cambodians had this way of pissing me off on a regular basis. Their pinching, laughing at me when I was obviously upset, saying they understood when they obviously didn't, and so on. This was new grounds though. I wanted to know what was so funny. After many attempts the older doctor finally managed to explain while cupping his hand to his chest, that in Cambodia ladies want to be big. And now barang lady wants to be small. Hilarious.

I had to spend a week in the hospital. Thankfully Mia would come and sit with me. I wasn't able to eat but she would bring me cups of tea. Just having her there was so reassuring. Sally, Seb's friend who I forced the dress off for my sewing ladies to copy, also came to visit me. We had only had a very short time together when she came to my home but here she was in the hospital to see me. Sally spoke from her heart and told me she could see that I wasn't getting the support I needed. Her gentle way of speaking was exactly what I needed.

Despite being in hospital I felt as if I had to be on guard the whole time. The nurses were insisting I took painkillers that would then make me hallucinate. I could see myself floating above my bed back home. The mosquito net making it hard to see clearly, but I could see Andrew in our bed. I floated above him watching him lie there. John Denver was singing in the background. It was so bizarre. I asked what the medicine was that they were giving me. Cold & Flu Tablets. I said I didn't want them. The nurses insisted saying it was doctor's orders. In the end I would just pretend to take them and then throw them out. I felt much better without them. After a few days they asked me to do a urine sample. I couldn't quite understand why but went along with it just to show that I wasn't going to fight them on everything. The results came back saying that I needed further investigation. I was wheeled down to the basement of the hospital and a different doctor told me she had to give me an internal. An internal? Really?

She got me to lie down on her table and put my legs into stirrups. I have always made sure to have pap smears every two years no matter how much I hate them. This was nothing like that. The doctor was scrubbing me clean. Inside and out. Roughly. Very roughly. I asked her to be more gentle which only made her go harder. My thigh muscles started to spasm and I could see them twitching as she pushed and prodded. It hurt so much and nothing I said would slow her down. She had hardly said anything to me since she started and now she was telling me to be patient. All I could do was try to stay calm and wait it out. I couldn't get my legs out of the stirrups so there really wasn't much I could do.

She was so aggressive that I started to wonder if she would pull my contraceptive device out. It had a little string attached to it hanging out of my cervix and it felt as if she was now tugging around there. She eventually stopped. Wiped me with disinfectant and told me to climb off the table. It took a long time for me to get my legs to move. The muscles had seized up. I couldn't believe what had just happened. I got back to my room and cried. More from the shock than from the pain. I told the nurses that night that my back was really sore and that I had throbbing pain in my pelvis. They told me not to worry and just offered more painkillers.

The next day the pain had intensified so I asked for my doctor to come. She was shocked to hear what had happened to me and sent me off for an ultrasound. I had to go to a different hospital for that.

The ambulance driver smoked the whole way there. Sure enough, the internal ultrasound showed that the Mirena had been lodged into my uterus wall. No wonder I was in pain. An infection had started around it and I would need more antibiotics and have it removed. Great. I go into a hospital with a throat infection and come out with a uterus infection. Only in Cambodia. I couldn't wait to get out.

Once I got back home to our village I still needed to recuperate. My body felt incredibly weak. I knew I needed to eat but all that I was craving was chicken stock and stewed apples. Nothing else. I would make up a massive batch every few days or ask Rosa to help me. The thought of any other food made me cringe. I would make my own yogurt, so after a few days I added that into my stewed apples. I ate the same thing for a few weeks. It was all I wanted.

Thankfully things had been fine at home without me. The ladies were still busy sewing and Andrew had everything else under control. It was pretty impressive. The heat exhausted me so much that everything seemed like a massive effort. Not for Andrew. He could manage in the humidity no problem. The kids were happy to have me back though and didn't seem to mind that I needed to rest a lot.

In the meantime there were a lot of expenses. Even though things were cheap in Cambodia it still added up. All the sewing machines, the fabric, the wages, the trips to Phnom Penh for more supplies. Andrew would give me updates on how things were looking in our bank account. Thankfully he was just as committed as I was to the sewing project and we would take turns reminding each other that once we sold the items we would have money to reimburse ourselves, as well as use any profit to help others out. It felt good to be able to do something, nerve-racking in many ways, but good. I was concerned though. Would our items sell? Surely a few shirts wouldn't be hard to sell but the items were starting to pile up. We had so many things now. Would people like the shopping bags as much as I did? What about the hats? Where they just cute to look at or would people actually buy them. I had some nice comments on Facebook but I couldn't say that I was getting an overwhelming feeling of support from our network back home in Adelaide. They were all into social justice stuff so I figured they would spread the word in their own group of friends and the shirts would be snatched up.

Maybe I was expecting a bit too much from my friends having so many items that needed to be sold? I decided I needed to have some sort of event where we could have all the items displayed and try to get as many people to come as possible. Was there a way we could advertise to the broader community? Again, I needed Facebook to help me.

A friend, who just happened to have contacts in the Adelaide media, sent me a list of email addresses from the industry. She told me I had a good story and that I might as well try to get the media on to it. It was worth a shot. I emailed all of them. Giving a bit of a blurb about our life in rural Cambodia and the sewing project we had going. Would they be interested in a story? Sure enough, the Editor of the Adelaide Advertiser said he was intrigued and could I write something for him? After a few goes, because the power kept shutting off, I finally wrote my piece. Roy, the Editor, was very happy with it and said he would like to advertise the sale of our items at the bottom of the article. Perfect!

Now we just had to get everything ready for our trip to Australia and hope for the best. The kids asked if Rosa was coming with us. She had really become part of the family. Like a sister to the kids. Even though she had the weekends off she would often join us for a trip to Kep where we could swim in a pool for a few hours. She would also join us when we went to Phnom Penh or on any other outing. It made sense for the kids to ask if she was coming with us to Australia.

Andrew explained to them that we didn't want to expose her to life in Australia. We didn't want her to think that Australia was this amazing place to live and have her come back to her rural life and feel dissatisfied. And anyway, she struggled enough with our trips to Phnom Penh. She found the noise of the traffic very hard to deal with, the food tasted wrong, the people were not as friendly, it really was a bit of a culture shock just to spend a few days in the capital, let alone in Australia.

We bought six giant suitcases. Most of them were filled with our newly made items. Newly made, but only using fabric that was either handwoven or recycled from the giant piles at the markets. It felt good. I knew we had some great things to sell and I was making sure that the prices were low so there was no excuse for not buying them. I used to hate how expensive it was to buy ethically made products in Australia, it felt so good to be able to write out the price tag with a low number.

A friend offered her garden to host our big sale, and then my friend Jo in Geelong said she would have a smaller one for her friends in her home as well. We would arrive in Melbourne and have a day there. Drive straight to Geelong for the first sale, then drive all night to Adelaide to set up for the second sale. It was pretty crazy but we needed to get it all done that weekend because my surgery was booked in for the Monday and I had been told that it might take me a little while to recover.

After a very long dry spell the heavens opened up for my sale in Geelong and it really felt like the Cambodian monsoon had come to join us. We left Geelong at midnight hoping that the weather would improve by the time we arrived in Adelaide eight hours later. We had a quick, early-morning stop in a small country town on the way into Adelaide. We filled up with petrol and grabbed a copy of the paper. Sure enough, there it was. My article had been printed with a giant photo of us in front of the river with my beloved mountain for all to see. The kids were excited and I could see that they were finally starting to understand that our little sewing project was maybe not so little after all.

22

Uterus Road

Adelaide experienced its wettest day in months. Thankfully Andrew was able to rush off to the hardware store and buy a giant tarp to cover the garden. Pretty amazing for a man who only slept about two hours that night. The rains didn't keep everyone away though and we had a constant crowd coming through. As I looked around I realised that I didn't recognise most of the faces there. It was incredible. So many people wanted to chat to me and tell me that they had read the article in the Advertiser.

I was so brave to go to Cambodia like that with my family. They would love to do something similar but would never be able to. I had an old lady grip onto my hands saying she had always wished to help out in a poor country but life had gotten in the way. Others thanking me for the article which had inspired them to contribute on some level in their own local community. I hadn't realised that my article would impact so many people. It meant a lot that they took the time to tell me.

It was also a great opportunity to see friends that we had missed since being away. I got a massive hug from Kaia who was there helping out. Her giant smile saying it all. She knew that it had all started with her shirt only a few months earlier. Now she got to see what had been triggered by her visit. The day was a great success and felt more like a celebration than a sale. We all collapsed into bed that night, totally exhausted but happy.

The next day I was wheeled into theatre for surgery. I had been told that it was a very straightforward operation. My friend who had it done a few years earlier told me it was really just like watching birds pulling out worms from the sand at the beach. I liked that. Just another day at the beach.

It actually hurt more than I expected though. The incisions on my bikini line stretching as I tried to move. My legs were completely bandaged up and I tried to take as few painkillers as possible since my gut doesn't seem to like them. I was still recovering in hospital when I took a call from a popular radio station. Would I be interested in an interview? I sure was. I figured the beauty of radio is that no one needed to know that I was still looking like an Egyptian mummy from my waist down. As it turned out two radio stations wanted me to come in. It was a great opportunity to spread the word a bit wider about our project.

We didn't have much planned for the rest of our five weeks in Australia. We would drive back to Melbourne once my legs were healed enough to last the eight hour car trip. It would be great to spend some time with Andrew's family. I really wanted our kids to have a relationship with their auntie and grandfather. It would also be a good chance for us to get to know Grandpa's new wife Judith a bit better. I was really excited because Andrew's sister had agreed to having the kids stay for two nights. It would mean a mini getaway for me and Andrew. A much needed getaway. The whole point of us moving to Cambodia was to spend more time as a family, and even though we were, things had been so busy and the sewing project had unfolded so unexpectedly that it was hard to make time for just the two of us.

I booked a holiday house a couple of hours drive down the Great Ocean Road. It was simple but perfect for us. Two days alone. Such a treat. It turned out to be a disaster. A total disaster. What had been an incredibly beautiful drive there was now just a blur. The cliffs and the ocean hardly noticed with tears streaming down my face.

Andrew was crying as well. Apologising and crying. He had tried to blame me for something that was totally unrelated to me. His own shit. He tried to make out that it was me and it had back fired. I was so disgusted by his deceit. How he had sounded so convincing in his lies. That's what I couldn't get my head around. The lying. My own husband lying to me. What was it with me and lying husbands? I didn't really care that much about the topic itself. It was how it was kept hidden from me, and then Andrew trying to blame me.

It cut so deep. Our two days away, that were meant to be a chance for us to reconnect, had become the ugliest chapter in our relationship so far. It was devastating. Despite our now empty suitcases I had never felt heavier stepping on the plane going back to Cambodia. Who was this man? I wasn't even sure if I wanted to know. He knew how much I craved truth. Knew that after living with Paul I needed a man who didn't keep things in the dark.

I was at a complete loss as what to do from here. I knew we needed counselling as a couple. We had needed that for years. Something had to change. Andrew's initial response after our two days away was total remorse, but it very quickly changed to him accusing me of being a bad wife. His words hurt. But he insisted he was right. I was uncaring, unloving and obviously didn't need him. Need him? There it was again. He wanted me to need him. I asked him to explain. How exactly was I a bad wife? What was I doing that was so horrible?

He didn't have much to say but reminded me of the article that I had written for the paper. I had hardly mentioned him in it at all. Did he not matter to me? Here I was getting a story published in the paper and having radio interviews and there was now talk about me going on a TV breakfast show as well. I obviously didn't need him. It made my brain hurt. Was it even worth trying to respond to him? Our marriage was a complete and utter head fuck. I so desperately wanted it to work but had no idea if it was possible. In many ways it seemed like it wouldn't take much for us to be transformed into a couple who could communicate without insecurities and judgements always being in the equation. Then at other times it felt like I was wanting the impossible. I couldn't be the needy wife Andrew was wanting me to be. I just couldn't. I didn't need him. I would never need him. I wanted him though, I really wanted him but that wasn't enough.

I was in Phnom Penh for a few days on my own so I decided to do two things. One was make an appointment with a counsellor. If he was any good I would ask Andrew to join me. It was a huge amount of money for the session but I knew we needed someone to help. I wasn't exactly sure how we would be able to get to any future sessions together but we would just have to make it priority. I told Andrew that we needed to get help and transform our marriage or we needed to divorce. I couldn't do this limbo land anymore where we would live in constant tension. One of the hardest things for me was that I really needed dialogue about what was going on. I hated the silence around it.

Andrew on the other hand felt too confronted with that. He thought that me writing emails to him was better so he could take his time responding. That was fine because it meant that I could write and cry and not feel bad that my tears would make Andrew feel uncomfortable. It was so frustrating to not be able to speak from the heart without the crying. However, the emails meant long delays where I had to wait for Andrew to respond. It was so hard to play happy families while waiting for his email to show up in my inbox. It was doing my head in. One day he would be remorseful and tell me how bad he would feel about how he was criticising Asher because of the connection I had with him, only then the very next day he would be mocking me for being too concerned about Asher's feelings. I couldn't make any sense of it.

The other thing that I did in Phnom Penh was buy a book. I had seen an article about it and was intrigued. It was a book about oral sex. I ended up buying another book as well just so I could cover up the one about oral sex. It felt so weird buying a book like that, but I was desperate. Something needed to change. I was craving playfulness. We had been in such a heavy headspace for so long and maybe it was all too complex to try to discuss and come to a resolution. Maybe we could just have some fun and find a way to connect in the bedroom.

Andrew was appalled. A book about oral sex? Why would he want to be told by someone else what to do to his wife? I was practically inviting someone else into our bedroom. After flicking through a few pages of the book he handed it back to me and said he wasn't interested. I was back to square one.

In the midst of us trying to get our marriage to some sort of functional level we decided that we would continue with the sewing project for a while longer since it was getting so much positive attention. When the word spread that I was running a sewing project everyone seemed to ask me if I knew the lady who ran a knitting project in Phnom Penh. I didn't. Besides Shraps who was now living in Phnom Penh I didn't know anyone there.

Once I got a chance to meet Sophie, the lady with the knitting project, I understood why everyone kept insisting I get in touch with her. She was just the person I needed to connect with. She had lived in Cambodia long enough to understand the ins and outs of the place, she not only spoke the language but was also married to a local. On top of all that she was also witty and seemed to understand my quirky sense of humour. What a relief! I was pretty desperate for like-minded people and it felt good to add her to my list of people who could make me laugh. I now had two in Cambodia. Shraps and Sophie. It was a nice change from my ever growing list of people who were making my life difficult.

Sophie had a great knitting project going on. She was teaching marginalised women, as well as a couple of men, how to knit. She would provide all the training as well as the supplies and then pay them a very fair wage. It meant that they were able to earn an income and not have to be away from their children, which was so often the case. I really liked her products but wasn't sure if I would be able to sell them for her. The knitted monsters that she had were adorable, but way too big for me to try to lug back to Australia with my bags already full of goodies. Her finger puppets were super cute as well, but I had always struggled with finger puppets. I could never seem to keep track of them and before I knew it they were lost in the abyss.

I really wanted to support her somehow but it might mean coming up with a new product.

My life was so hectic but there was something about being on a tuk tuk that helped me in my creative process. Most of my ideas were birthed while riding in a tuk tuk behind Nara. On yet another Phnom Penh visit I was mulling over how I could help Sophie out. I felt as if there was an idea ready to come to life, I just couldn't grasp it yet. There was something about the monkey finger puppets that appealed to me. I kept coming back to their cute little faces. What if we used them somehow? Would we be able to get them made into proper little monkeys with long arms and legs?

I knew they would look great but how could I work that into an item to sell with one of my products? Of course! My shopping bags! If we rolled up my shopping bags we could have a monkey grab around it with his arms. They would just need to attach somehow. How could we do that?

I quickly sent a text to Sophie explaining my latest tuk tuk revelation, asking her if she had access to any magnets. She responded straight away saying he didn't have magnets but if I could find some at the market she was sure that they could be knitted into the monkeys.

I called out to Nara over the noise of the traffic that we needed to stop at the large market instead of going to the guest house.

No problem, but first you need a coconut.

Nara knew me well. We ended up spending half a day in the crowded markets on our magnet quest. Each stall holder sending us on a different direction through the dark maze to find these elusive magnets. Nara and I had already been on many of these adventures before trying to source buttons and zippers. I was so grateful to have a tuk tuk driver that was happy to support me in my random requests.

By now it was dark but we drove across town to drop off the magnets to Sophie. There wasn't a moment to spare. I wanted to see these monkeys come to life now!

A week later Sophie told me that the first monkey was ready and she paid for him to be delivered to our house. I was so excited to open up the small package and behold the creation. My kids were surrounding me waiting for the big moment and all burst out laughing when they saw our new little friend. He was cute, but he sure didn't look anything like a monkey!

His arms and legs were so short that he could hardly reach over his head in order for his hands to connect. He was doing a very good impersonation of a chubby bear! I called Sophie and explained that the monkey in my head had much longer arms and legs. A few days later a long limbed monkey showed up at our house and he was perfect!

My mother flew over from Sweden for a visit. Despite the madness it was great to have her come and see us. I loved having a mother who had no concerns about jumping on a plane to Cambodia. She had no questions about safety or illness or anything like that. I wasn't sure how many women in their sixties would be the same.

We decided to use her visit as an excuse to travel up to Siem Reap and check out Angkor Wat. We were constantly being asked if we had been there yet. Cambodians were so proud of their ancient temples and to have lived in their country for almost a year now and still not go there was borderline offensive. Jo had been telling me about her friend in Geelong who had moved to Siem Reap for six months to volunteer at a school for homeless kids. According to Jo I would love Kylie and she was there with her husband and their three daughters. I had promised I would get in touch with them if we decided to travel north. There was no way we were going to Siem Reap without bringing Rosa with us. This was such a great opportunity for her to explore Angkor Wat.

Rosa's younger sister wanted to come as well and if she was coming we figured we might as well invite Mai, the girl who would come most days and sit at our house and watch the sewing ladies. She was the youngest of three sisters. Her dad had died when she was little and now her mum was trying to raise three daughters on her own. They were the poorest family in our village. It would be an amazing opportunity for Mai to travel to Siem Reap and see the beloved temples.

The ten of us travelled up by bus and taxi. The two young girls from our village were excited yet nervous about being away from home. They had hardly ever been to Kampot, the town closest to us. Now they were going to Angkor Wat! We booked three rooms in a guesthouse. It was nicer than the one we had stayed in in Phnom Penh because it had air conditioning. I knew this would be so strange for Mai. Sleeping in a bed. Having a TV. I had never been inside her home but it was a rickety shack on stilts held together with pieces of scrap metal. Bigger holes were covered up with old rice bags. The ground beneath them never seemed to dry out so even in the hottest month they still had to walk in mud to get to their ladder.

Their home was exactly opposite the noodle shack that was open every morning so if they wanted any privacy they would need to go out while it was still dark and do their business behind the small bush next to their shack. What would a week of staying in a hotel room do for Mai? I wasn't really comfortable about it. Andrew was happy to play guide and took the clan out each morning to explore. I tagged along when I could but it was hard for Sage in the heat. I would stay back with her and Summer and enjoy the pool and try to do some shorter outings with them.

It was great to finally meet Kylie and her family. I knew why Jo had said I would love Kylie. We instantly hit it off. I loved her positivity. She had this very calm presence and seemed to have time to draw despite being busy with motherhood. I really liked her drawing style and started to mull over the idea of her helping me out with the sewing project. Rosa had told me that there were two girls from our village who were going to find work in a local factory. They were only 16. I hated the thought of these two girls in a sweatshop. It would very likely be one that made shoes. Most of the local girls worked there. I could smell the fumes from the glue a few streets away. I really wanted to keep them away from having to work in a place like that yet I didn't really know how I could give them any work.

Now that I was watching Kylie draw I started to come up with an idea. What if we could teach the girls how to embroider? That would be much easier to learn than sewing. If we could teach them that we could maybe get some little things made, ornaments of sorts and sell those to pay their wages. I told Kylie I had this image of angels from different cultures. Could she draw some and then I could get them printed onto fabric and the girls could embroider over the lines? Kylie got right to it and asked me what sort of cultures I was wanting. In the end we had an African angel carrying a basket. A Russian angel carrying a star. A Cambodian angel with a sarong holding a lotus flower. And I couldn't resist having one from Israel. We had her wearing sandals with a baby wrapped to her chest. They were gorgeous. Kylie had totally understood what I wanted and I was so excited to get the images printed out. It was great to add these to my collection of things to sell. I was going back to Adelaide in just over a month and I would have quite a few new items in my collection.

The other item I wanted to add to my next Adelaide sale was silk scarves. Cambodian markets are full of scarves and I hadn't really been paying attention to them. I was only wanting to sell things that were 'happily made' as I liked to call it. I wasn't able to use the Fair Trade label since it cost money to get that certification, and sadly in Cambodia it didn't necessarily mean anything ethical.

I started referring to my items for sale as 'Happily Made in Cambodia'. I figured that would speak for itself. Only things ethically made, with or without the Fair Trade label. When I first noticed the scarves I assumed they were mass-produced like everything else. However, these weren't. They were designed for the French boutique market and amazingly had the ethical stamp of approval. When I spoke to the young man selling the scarves he invited me to come and visit the village where they were made, just over an hour's drive outside Siem Reap. This was a great opportunity to go and visit them and see for myself.

Rosa wanted to come along which was great because I really needed her for translation. Her English was still very simple but with me not having improved in the Khmer language department at all I was totally at a loss without her. I had tried to learn Khmer but gave up very quickly. I couldn't even form the sounds with my tongue, let alone say them. And maybe I was tone deaf but I couldn't in any way decipher the two words that sounded identical to me but supposedly had different meanings all together. It created a lot of laughter when I attempted to speak Khmer but I could never be understood. I blamed the heat. It was just so hot all the time, so to try to add learning a language into my already full existence was too much for me.

My mother also wanted to come along to the silk village to see how the scarves were made. The trip was much longer than we expected and the road was actually worse than Uterus Road, which I didn't think was possible. We eventually got to the tiny village. It was hard to imagine anything beautiful being made there. It was just a few rows of houses in a very dusty part of northern Cambodia. We were told to come in under one of the houses on stilts. A massive woven tray filled with leaves had all these silk worms munching away.

We looked around, there hanging from the ceiling were bunches of twigs. When we looked closer we could see the cocoons clinging on. Fluffy, bright yellow cocoons. Outside the house this old lady, who really looked like she had celebrated her 100th birthday a while back, was sitting by a spinning wheel. I thought it was a spinning wheel, but when I walked up to her I realised it was a bicycle wheel that was now being used to form the silk thread. An old paint tin filled with water was boiling away with the cocoons in it. Smoke rising up above us. I was in awe of what she was able to do with so little. This golden thread growing longer and longer in front of me.

Under another house two girls were using the bicycle wheels to make balls of string. Young women were using giant rickety looms to weave the most intricate patterns with the silk string. I was speechless. It was all so beautiful and done in such a quiet way. It felt so right to order a whole bunch of scarves from them and be able to sell them in Australia knowing where they had been made. It truly was magical.

Our finances were at a really critical point by now. Andrew had decided to look for some work back in Australia and flew there after our visit to Siem Reap. I didn't like being in Cambodia on my own with the kids but a few weeks later we joined him in Adelaide. It felt good being back as a family. Things were hard between me and

Andrew but I knew that our kids were happiest when all of us were together. Being back in Adelaide meant that I could have another sale and this time I had also organised two movie fundraisers. One in Sydney and one in Adelaide. By now I had been asked to write another article for the Advertiser because there was such a huge response from the first one. People were contacting me asking how they could help.

I had this idea of asking people to host an evening where I could come along and speak about what we were doing in Cambodia. Talk about some of the things we were involved with and see if people wanted to be involved in raising funds for different causes I was mentioning. I had quite a few of these evenings lined up. I would bring along a couple of suitcases full of handwoven scarves and sell them.

I was noticing that my back was getting sorer and sorer. Sometimes it would take me a while to straighten up after sitting and driving in the car was hurting my back. I had struggled with lower back pain since having kids so this was nothing new to me. Having lived in Cambodia for over a year and not driving a car the whole time I could tell that sitting in the car seat was not helping my back in any way. Each drive it seemed to get worse. I was starting to get concerned because I knew I had a flight coming up to Sydney for the next movie night, and I still had a few more scarf parties to speak at. Someone suggested that I go see a kinesiologist. They would be able to help me with my ongoing back issues and get to the source of the pain.

My appointment was scheduled for a few days later and I arrived hoping to finally get some relief. The lady seemed nice and explained that she taught kinesiology at the local college. She asked me to lie down on her table. She felt my hip bones and straightaway told me that one of my legs was shorter than the other. I was impressed she could tell. It was something that others had needed an x-ray to confirm. She started feeling my pulse. A bit strange but I thought I would just let her do her thing. She asked me if I was sensitive to smells. Yes, both me and my dad are very sensitive to smells. She kept going. Asking me more bizarre questions. Telling me that I had a very strong connection to both of my grandmothers. One in particular. How weird!

She asked me to look from side to side and blink over and over while she gently moved my knees from side to side. Then I had to take deep breaths while she straightened my legs one at a time. Everything she did was slow and gentle and nothing hurt. I was more focused on the strange questions or comments she had. She went on to tell me that I wasn't getting the support I needed and that my body was very much in flight or fight response. The session finished and I drove back to where we were staying in the city.

I felt consumed with sleep and collapsed on our mattress as soon as I got home. I woke up a couple of hours later after a very heavy sleep. As I tried to get up I realised I couldn't use my legs. This severe pain shot down from my pelvis to my feet. I laid back down thinking it might go away. After about twenty minutes I tried again. Still the same. I was in total agony. For three days I needed help to drag myself to the toilet.

Eventually Andrew and Asher helped me down the three flights of stairs so I could go to a doctor and get some pain relief. It was so scary. I had no idea how the gentle movements at the kinesiologist could have in any way triggered this to happen. After a couple of visits to Adrienne, my chiropractor, and lots of ice packs I was back to walking again, but still in pain.

I had to cancel my trip to Sydney and so couldn't go to the fundraiser there. I was at a total loss as to what I could do. Thankfully my friend Isy stepped in and offered to help me with the Adelaide movie night that was coming up. She was a relatively new friend and I was so touched by her help. Her daughter, Violette, and Tikvah had met while learning to fire twirl with Astrid a couple of years earlier. On our last visit to Adelaide the girls had come up with an idea for how they could raise some money for kids in Cambodia. They started selling these little jars of 'perfume'. A concoction of leaves and flowers that supposedly smelled amazing. They decided to call their project 'Three Jars Full' and had thankfully moved on from selling homemade perfume to now selling baked goodies and treats.

Despite how young they were they were actually very good at baking and all their items sold. They decided to use the money to buy educational toys for preschools in Cambodia. Mia, our playgroup teacher in Kampot, had told Tikvah how she volunteered for an organisation that ran preschools in poor villages and how the kids didn't have anything to play with. It was great being able to use the money from Violette and Tikvah to buy wooden blocks, puzzles and other educational toys. We knew from how much our sewing ladies liked playing with our puzzles that it was such a treat to have something so basic that we took for granted. Having Isy take over from me with the movie night was a massive relief. I loved her easy nature and how she really seemed to want to help. I didn't get that response from many friends and it meant a lot to me when I was in such a difficult spot with my back not cooperating.

As well as Isy offering to help I had a message from someone on Facebook called Claire. She said she knew about me from friends that we had in common and that she was really keen to help out with anything I might need. Was there anything she could do? Yes! There was so much that needed to be done. I organised to meet with her at a café late one night once the kids were asleep. Claire asked if she could bring her housemate Liv who was also really interested in what we were doing. Here were these two chicks who didn't know me but were totally willing to help out. I liked them straightaway.

Not only did I need lots of practical help for everything I was trying to do, but more than that I really needed friends. My time in Adelaide felt so incredibly lonely. Things with Andrew were so damn intense. I needed distraction. They knew my back was bad so we mostly spent time watching crappy TV shows and drinking tea. A mindless exercise, and the perfect escape for my complex life.

It was disappointing to have to cancel the rest of the scarf parties. I really enjoyed the opportunity to speak to women directly about the sewing project. Most of them mothers. Most of them juggling so many things yet so many of them feeling helpless when it came to the poverty around the world. I loved sharing with them simple ideas of how they could do something from the comforts of their own life.

It really didn't take much to change someone's life in a third world country. I encouraged them to find their own way of contributing. In their work place or schools, to have a tin for everyone to put a dollar in once a week. That tiny amount could easily pay for a student in Cambodia to go to school. Often it's something as simple as a bike that's needed to get them there, or a uniform.

For everyone who was renovating or extending their house, I would encourage them to spend a fraction of what they spent on their kitchen, for example, and use that money to pay for a community garden to be set up and in turn that would help feed a village. I really wanted people to see that it wasn't huge amounts of money that were needed, just a spare few coins on a regular basis. The message was getting through and I started receiving emails from these women about what they were changing in their lives. One woman asked all her family and friends to give some money instead of a gift for her son's first birthday. Another woman said that when she had her weekly coffee with her group of friends they all put in two dollars to pay a teacher's wage. No one had to pack up their house and move to a poor country, no one had to really make any sacrifices, yet so much goodness could come from people understanding that a lot of people doing very little can make a huge difference.

Andrew and I had agreed that once we got back to Adelaide we would get some counselling together. Andrew would start while I was still in Cambodia with the kids. Then I would join him later. Thankfully Andrew really connected with the counsellor and enjoyed his sessions with her. Once I met with her as well I realised that I was very much stepping in on his territory. Their sessions together were very productive and it was probably best if they continued with Andrew going alone. I did go along to a couple of sessions despite the ongoing issues with my back. I had intended to go more but the pain really made it difficult to be there.

I struggled listening to Andrew talking about our marriage. He seemed to think that he was a victim somehow. That he was married to this cold-hearted woman who yelled at him. It really stung. After our disastrous weekend away I had told Andrew that

I could no longer initiate conversation about our marriage. I just couldn't anymore. I felt numb and the waiting game was too hard for me. Andrew agreed that he needed to be the one who started the dialogue and promised he would.

I was exhausted from being in Cambodia on my own with the kids. I hated being a solo parent there. The responsibility was enormous. The kids were still getting sick a lot and it terrified me that I didn't have the back up of another adult. I needed to put the marriage stuff to the side and just let Andrew initiate when he was ready. Of course he didn't. When I finally asked him why, he told me it was because I was being cold. Cold? I wasn't being affectionate enough with him. Not tender. Not soft. I tried to explain that I was hurt. I was numb. That was very different from being cold. He had agreed that he needed to drive the communication and then when he didn't I was blamed for it. Was there no room for me to just crash and burn somewhat? Could he not in any way see that I needed him to show that this was just as important to him as to me? How dare he call me cold? I was numb, and for very good reasons too. And only a couple of months before he had acknowledged that, yet now to our counsellor he was making me out to be a heartless bitch.

The one thing that really made the counselling sessions worth it for me personally was that I was finally validated in my communication style. Andrew accused me of yelling at him when I spoke from the heart, despite the fact that I didn't raise my voice. The intensity scared him and he called it yelling. Thankfully our counsellor was married to a Croatian man and she explained to Andrew that it was very common for Anglos, who had spouses from other cultures, to feel intimidated by the intensity. It wasn't anger and it wasn't screaming, it was just someone being passionate.

I wasn't sure if Andrew accepted what she said. His mother was the most meek and mild woman who never spoke about her needs. In the little time I knew her I saw her on so many occasions biting her tongue instead of speaking out. She didn't feel like she could say what she wanted to say. Andrew hated that about her. It was something that attracted him to me. That I wasn't like his mother.

He liked a strong woman. Yet, now that he had an outspoken woman, he despised me for it.

The plan was that I was going to return to Cambodia with the children after the movie fundraiser. I tried to tell Andrew that I couldn't go back. It scared me. Really scared me. My back was still so delicate and the thought of the plane trip alone was enough for me to say I just couldn't do it. Andrew tried to tell me that Asher and Tikvah could help with the luggage while I handled the girls. I wasn't quite sure how he imagined that would work. Just me putting our luggage into the overhead compartment on the plane could trigger my back pain. Not to mention me handling Sage on my own if she had one of her many tantrums. All that aside. I was scared of being in Cambodia with the kids on my own. They were still getting sick a lot and I hated to be the only parent there for that. We also kept having all these mysterious ailments where the girls would wake up with sharp pain during the night and just scream and scream. I couldn't do that on my own anymore.

Thankfully Andrew agreed that we could stay on in Adelaide for longer, at the same time reminding me that it was going to cost a lot more for our family to be there than in Cambodia, and the whole reason he was in Adelaide was to make some money. I knew that, but I also knew I couldn't travel. It was unfortunate but I couldn't do it. I was sorry. But we had to wait until at least my back was stronger.

Andrew seemed frustrated at my weakness and I was hurt by his lack of concern. We had been living with a young couple in the city but with us now staying longer we needed to find another place. Incredibly a woman that I didn't know that well offered for us to stay with her and her family in Henley Beach. Just down the road from where I had gotten married all those years earlier. We had met each other from the homeschool network and she knew we needed a place to stay. I was so touched by her hospitality. She was a busy woman with three of her own children. One still being breastfed. Here she was inviting a family of six to live with her. Trisha and her husband felt very strongly about the importance of community and I was in awe of the integrity they had in that. I couldn't think of too many couples with three children who would feel comfortable about a family of six coming to live with them. A family of six with lots and lots of suitcases.

Our belongings were overflowing. All the items we were selling as well as the bits and pieces we needed for our daily life. Trisha seemed to take it all in her stride. I was so aware that we were not the easiest house guests. So many of us. Me with my dodgy back, which meant lots of resting and not being able to help with much. Andrew away at work for the day. Trisha didn't seem to mind. She kept doing her thing. She had all these concoctions going in her kitchen and her pantry. I would watch her pound cabbage into a jar, explaining that she was making sauerkraut because it was so good for the gut. The gut? I remembered something my doctor had said about eating foods to heal the gut. She had wanted me to cook broths for Summer. Supposedly the bones were exactly what the gut needed to heal. I did it once and the house stank and the kids didn't like it. It was something I kept meaning to do again but it never happened.

Here was Trisha making sauerkraut, and when I asked her about it she went into her pantry and returned with a strange looking drink. She asked me if I had ever heard of kombucha. Of what? No, I hadn't. I had a sip. Later when Andrew got home he tried some too and said it tasted like the bottom of the compost bin. He was right. That's exactly what it tasted like. Trisha laughed and said that maybe it was a bit neglected and a bit too potent but it was still good. She tried to drink it daily.

Along with that her kids didn't seem to eat any fruit. It really intrigued me. Here I was making sure my kids had an endless supply of fruit. Apples, oranges, grapes and bananas were being devoured. Trisha's kids seemed to eat cucumbers between meals. Or expensive tins of sustainable fish. If they ever mentioned that they were hungry Trisha would get them to drink milk. Raw milk. So much of it every day. It went against everything I knew about being healthy. Surely fruit was the best thing for kids to eat as a snack? And milk? I thought it was best to avoid it. Trisha explained to me how she was trying to have her kids avoid sugar, even the sugar in fruit. And raw milk had so many nutrients and good fats that were essential for kids. What she said made sense but I felt like it was something too hard to even contemplate doing while in transit. I was very much just trying to keep my head above water and introducing a new way of eating seemed way too complex.

Claire was starting to ask me more details about some of the things that I was involved with in Cambodia. She was really interested in coming back with us and helping out somehow. She was an occupational therapist who specialised in children with disabilities. I told her about Stephanie and her children and how she had been thrown into the deep end with giving therapy to all the kids who were being carried to her house. To have someone like Claire come along to help out would be incredible. After a few emails back and forth between Claire and Stephanie it was decided that she would come back with us to Cambodia. I was more than happy to have her come and live with our house and then she could ride a bike across to Stephanie's home and help there for a few hours a day. I was thrilled that Stephanie would get some professional help and relieved that I would have someone else in my house with Andrew away so much.

I still felt incredibly intimidated about being in Cambodia without Andrew. My back had improved but it was still flaring up from just the tiniest triggers. Our girls were going to a little pre-school that had been set up with some of our friends from the playgroup. Rosa would take them on Andrew's moto each morning. The girls asking to sit side-saddle like the locals.

Asher and Tikvah were not happy to be back in Cambodia. Asher missed his friends in the Adelaide Hills, two homeschooled brothers that he would spend hours in the backyard with. Making traps and climbing trees. He would spend days at a time with his friends and when I picked him up I could see the disappointment in his face. This was one place where he could have friends. Tikvah was also enjoying spending time with the friends she had in Adelaide, she adored Alice's kids that felt more like cousins than friends. And of course there was Violette as well. Now they were back in Cambodia and I could feel their loneliness. I had to find them some friends and I had to be more available to them.

As much as this sewing project was great, and over time it could probably become something quite amazing, I was no longer able to do both. I couldn't be a mother as well as run this non-profit sewing project without the support of others. Once I realised that the project was becoming bigger than just selling items, on our first Australia trip in March 2010, I had asked Rosa to tell the sewing ladies that if they wanted to continue with the sewing I would support them in making it their own project. I would love for one of them to step up to be trained to take over from my roll. I could teach them what sort of fabrics to look for in the markets. We could figure out who the best sellers were and stick to those. I was happy to do the marketing and sales but it would be wonderful for these women to have a bit more ownership and have it run more like a business for them to grow. Not one of them was interested. They liked it the way it was. They could come in the morning. Sew. Have lunch. Sew. And go home. They would often come early so they could play with our puzzles on the floor. They loved that. But nothing more. They had no desire to work for themselves. It made me feel uncomfortable. I didn't like being the white lady boss who had a room full of Cambodians working for me. I really wanted it to be a joint project, and eventually something of their own.

That uncomfortable feeling had started to grow. It kept growing as I realised that these women coming into my home each day were behaving like young children. Taking food and then blaming Mai, the girl that came with us to Siem Reap. I asked Rosa to call for a meeting and we all sat in a circle on the floor. I explained that this was a home. I lived here with my children. I had invited them to come to work here but it was also my home. Not a factory. I needed to be able to trust them. If they needed food they could tell me that and I would be able to buy them food but I couldn't have them taking things from my home.

Each one of them insisted that Mai had taken the food. It wasn't just one occasion. The other times I had assumed that I was just imagining things. This time I had returned from yet another medical visit in Phnom Penh to an empty fruit bowl and we had nothing else to eat until the next morning. I looked at Rosa trying to tell these women that it wasn't good what they were doing. That was one of the few things I could say in Khmer.

Ot Lao. No good. I was saying it all the time.

When my kids were getting pinched. When our neighbour kept smacking her toddler for no reason. Just laughing and smacking this tiny child. I had yelled it at a tuk tuk driver in Phnom Penh who had promised me he knew where the medical clinic was when Summer had gone floppy in the middle of the night. She could hardly breathe and the hotel insisted that they would not be able to call an ambulance. A tuk tuk would be faster. I made sure they asked the driver if he knew where the clinic was. He assured us he did. I had jumped in the back of the tuk tuk with Summer in my arms. I had to leave my three kids in a hotel room by themselves. Tikvah agreeing to lie down next to Sage in case she woke up. I was still really unfamiliar with Phnom Penh but when we arrived at the River I knew that this bastard of a driver had lied to me. When he asked a man walking past where the clinic was I just lost it. OT LAO!! OT LAO!! That was all I could say. I jumped out of the tuk tuk, Summer still totally pale and floppy. Thankfully I found another tuk tuk with a driver who could speak English and knew where to take us.

Poor Rosa, I knew she was out of her depth. It shouldn't be her role to discipline these women. Most of them were older than her. She was just a young village girl. It was not in her place to show any authority to someone older than her. I knew she was approached by women in our village who wanted to work with us. I knew it was so hard for her to say that they couldn't. Even though I was the white lady boss, I was a mute. I had no language so Rosa became my mouthpiece and these women would take their aggression out on her. Not me. How much was her role with us screwing things up for her down the track?

Once we left Cambodia what would the long-term implications be for Rosa? When I talked to her about it she insisted that it didn't matter. She was okay. She wanted me to know though that it wasn't just stealing of food that was going on. Any time I left the house the sewing ladies would start turning on all the lights around the house. Like school children being naughty they thought it was some sort of revenge at authority to get our power bill as high as possible. I knew that Cambodians were young for their age. Andrew and I would talk about it all the time. Even Rosa who we both adored and cared about was so incredibly young. She was 21 in actual years but really had the maturity of a 12 year old. Andrew and I would roll our eyes at so many of the things she said.

When I had emailed Andrew and told him something that Rosa had done that had bothered me his response was what would you expect from a 13 year old? I really didn't like having to put her in a place where she would be getting grief from people in her village. It wasn't right. I might have felt different if Andrew was there to help with the load but I just couldn't do it all. I had to pull back. My kids needed their mother. Lots of people could step in and do the work I was doing for the sewing project. In fact, it probably needed quite a few people for the many hats I was wearing. But no one else could step in to be my kid's mother. The sewing project would have to finish up. I had nothing more to give.

In many ways I loved doing it but it just got too much. My role as the 'rich white lady' in our village was drawing more attention. I tried to explain that it wasn't the case at all. In fact, our money was at rock bottom. Of course no one could see that with us living in a massive house and me arriving back from shopping trips with huge bags. We must be loaded. Just me having white skin meant that I was rich. So for me to live the way I did meant that I obviously had lots of money. It meant lots of visits from the local police hoping to get bribes from me. A whole bunch of them would come and visit and say that I needed to pay money for running a business. I tried to explain that I wasn't making any profit at all. They insisted they needed money. I had been told from some friends in town that even giving them office supplies would help. A block of A4 paper for their printer and more staples. Unfortunately I didn't have any.

They police men would sit on our front step for ages. Smoking, playing footsies, giggling and pushing each other around like little primary school boys waiting for their class to begin. Only they were man sized and had cigarettes. They eventually went on their way when I asked Rosa to go and buy them all an ice coffee each and some fried rice. The ice coffee lady was only a few houses down. She had this tiny room with blackened walls. Old ceramic pots that had obviously been around before the war. And possibly not washed since before the war. It was the ugliest little space you could imagine and she made the most incredible coffee in the world. This thick syrup that tasted like magic. I had never been a coffee drinker until I was stuck in Cambodia on my own with four kids. Rosa had one every day and in a moment of desperation I had asked her to buy one for me as well. That was it. I couldn't stop. It was the highlight of my day. If I resisted waiting till later in the day I would have two. This stuff was incredible. I was sure I was only getting through my crazy life because of this dark brown elixir. So it seemed like the obvious thing to buy for the police, as well as the fried rice from the medical clinic on Uterus Road. Conveniently the village doctor also sold fried rice between waiting for patients.

I thought that it would be hard to stop the sewing project. That I would miss it after working on it for a year. I didn't. Not for one moment. I hadn't realised how much it had been bothering my kids. I had been so happy making a difference, feeling like I was contributing, being part of the solution, having a purpose, that in the midst of that I had been turning away from the comments from the kids. I realised that I could probably be a better help if I just supported projects that were already up and running. I had no idea how to run a business. And even if this was non-profit, it was still a business and I was clueless. And I was too nice about it. Wanting to pay wages that were too high and make the prices too low. Also, I had to be honest with myself, I was finding it too hard to deal with the locals. They were driving me nuts. I could blame the heat. Or my exhaustion. Or not having Andrew there. But really, they were driving me crazy.

One of the dads in the pre-school had tried to warn me. He had lived in Cambodia for a long time and initially I really struggled with his cynicism. He seemed so cold-hearted in a way. I vowed I would never become like him. When I first met him he had told me that westerners who decided to live in Cambodia can be divided up into three categories. Merchants, Missionaries or Misfits. I had thought to myself that surely there were more categories. But the more time I spent in Cambodia I realised that Lee was right. Every ex-pat I came across could basically slot into one of those.

I knew that Andrew and I well and truly landed in the Misfit box. No matter how much we wanted to fit in with our friends back in Adelaide we never would. We were too opinionated, our soapbox made people feel uncomfortable, but really the main thing was that we would always be seen as newcomers. Our friends had known each other since birth. Their parents knew each other. Heck, some of them were even related a few generations back. Andrew and I couldn't compete with that. We would never be part of the inner circle. We would hover around the edges hoping to be allowed in. Here in Cambodia we would never fit in either. We would forever be the white people. But it was more defined. There was something comforting about that. At least for me.

Letting go of the sewing project was such a relief and a huge burden off my back. It had obviously taken its toll on me and I hadn't even realised how much. There had been so many dramas unfolding that it was hard to tell what was what. At one point, not long before, I had been accused of child trafficking. It was outrageous. I received a phone call warning me. Through a series of very innocent events I had been seen as a child smuggler and the police were very likely coming to my house to bring me in for questioning at the local station. I was horrified that my actions could be interpreted that way and that there was a chance of me ending up in jail, and very likely not being released without some exorbitant amount of money being handed over. Apparently it happened a lot in Cambodia. I had called up Andrew crying, not knowing what I should do. If I got in a taxi with the kids and fled to Phnom Penh it would look as if I was guilty. If I stayed my kids might not have a mother and would be stuck without a parent until Andrew flew back from Australia.

All that had happened was that a man who rode his bike through our village every few days selling ice cream had told Rosa that a young woman up the road was going to sell her baby after she fell pregnant to a barang. Was I interested in buying the little boy? I was horrified at the thought of this young mum being so desperate that she would sell her baby to a stranger. I told the ice cream man to tell the young woman that she shouldn't sell her baby. There were other ways of getting help. A couple of days later he returned saying that she had decided she would sell the baby. She had been offered $300 from someone. I asked Rosa to take me there. I got on the back of the moto. Rosa's long hair whipping me in the face. We often travelled like this, I knew it would look hilarious with the tom tom white lady behind this tiny Cambodian girl. Me sitting like a man and not side-saddle like women should. Uterus Road was way too bumpy for me to even attempt side-saddle.

We arrived only a few minutes later. Their hut was small but still nicer than many that I had seen. They were cooking on an open fire and had a chicken cut up ready to go into a soup. They couldn't be that poor if they could afford meat. A baby was asleep in a hammock. He was absolutely gorgeous. Rosa helped me talk with the young mother. I introduced myself and explained that I couldn't buy her baby but if she insisted on giving her baby away she should go through a proper organisation. There were even places in Kampot that would take her baby and she could come and visit whenever she wanted. That way her son would still have a mother. She explained that she wanted money. If her baby was a girl she would keep her but not a boy. A boy was a waste of money. Eventually he would marry and go and live with his wife's family. She hadn't heard about organisations that took babies but unless she would be paid to put him there she wasn't interested.

Did I want to hold him? No, I didn't. I wasn't exactly sure why but I felt that I needed to keep my distance somehow. I wanted to help this little boy so much but at the same time I had to be careful.

Not just that, if I held him I would probably not ever want to put him down. How could anyone possibly discard a beautiful little boy like this?

I asked if I could take some photos. I explained that if she did decide to give him away I wanted him to have some images of where he came from. I wanted him to see how his mother held him. I thought back to the orphans in Sri Lanka and how much they would value having photos of themselves as babies being cared for by their birth mother. The baby boy was being breast fed and he was holding on to his mother's hair. I wanted him to know that when he grew up. I wanted him to see how his grandmother would swing the hammock back and forth to rock him to sleep. The chickens pecking beneath.

Would she please give him to an organisation in Kampot instead of selling him and then I could go there and give them the photos for him to have when he was older? We left without me really knowing what she would do. I felt that I couldn't say anything else. I had tried. The only other thing I could think of was asking a couple in Phnom Penh who wanted a baby if they would consider adopting him. I knew that adoption laws were tricky but maybe they could figure out a way to do it. I didn't really know them well but they had seemed so lovely.

If this mother was wanting to get rid of her baby, then at least he could go to a family that would adore him. A few days later I got the call that I had been reported for child trafficking. The ice cream man had told someone that I was taking photos of the baby. I was obviously trying to sell him. It was things like this that were making me lose my sanity. The heat mainly, but with things like this on top of the heat, it was enough to send me loopy.

Andrew was coming back from his time in Australia and he couldn't be happier. He bought himself another motorbike. Funny how we seemed to have enough money for certain luxuries. His first moto was good for trips to the market and dropping the girls at pre-school but it wasn't enough to satisfy his itch to explore Kampot. He bought this huge bike and would ride around exploring. He would then come back and tell me how he rode to up the mountains around

Kep, the village by the sea that we had visited when we first arrived in southern Cambodia.

He would also ride up to Bokor, a resort on top of a mountain not far from us. It had been destroyed by the Khmer Rouge and was now in ruins. He also rode up Uterus Road and then make his way up the hill to see where a Chinese company was building a giant dam. It was a huge project. Andrew loved checking it all out. He was just so happy to be back. Telling the kids how great it was to be away from Australia with all its rules. He hated it so much. Hated feeling oppressed by the system.

In Cambodia there was none of that. He could do as he pleased. The only issue as far as he was concerned was us needing to make money. We had to generate some sort of funds in order to stay there. I had felt that our time was up in Cambodia for a while. I had tried to talk to Andrew about it. Now that he had been away for so long I felt bad saying something. It had been so hard for him in Australia and he deserved some time in his utopia. I couldn't bring up the kids needing friends again. Surely he would see that for himself. It was so obvious by now.

When we discussed ways of making an income that meant Andrew being able to stay home, we had come up with an idea of making our own coconut oil. I knew how amazing the stuff was from listening to my friend Naomi telling people about it at the Stirling market while I gave people hand massages. Her dad, Dan, was trying so hard to sell the stuff but was struggling to make Australians see how healthy it was. Things were changing however. His coconut oil was now being sold all over Europe and the US. People were starting to take notice. More and more Aussies were buying it. It was still early days but the message was getting through.

What if we started producing it and sold it to tourists coming through Cambodia looking for an ethically made product? Could we do that? Would enough people want it? After lots of talking it through, and emails back and forth with Dan and his company Niu Life, we felt that we could go ahead with our idea. I had admired Dan's integrity in the coconut oil production. It felt right having him as our connection and buying the extractor from him. Cold pressed coconut oil was a pretty simple concept. Grate the flesh out of the coconut. Heat it a little bit to dry it, but not enough to damage any of the nutrients. Then press it through an extractor and the oil would ooze out ready to be consumed.

We quickly realised it was slightly trickier than that. We had rented the shack next door to us and fitted it out with a long brick bench. A small fire would be lit underneath. Just enough flame to make the stainless steel plate on top warm through to heat the coconut. We started with getting the coconut shredded at the market but realised it would be much better to shred it ourselves. We bought this crazy contraption that would grate a coconut in a matter of seconds, and possibly make you lose a couple of fingers at the same time if you didn't pay attention.

As it turned out nothing is straightforward in Cambodia. We were surrounded by coconut trees so the least of our worries was sourcing coconuts. It turned out that wasn't the case. We needed mature coconuts. The ones growing around us were mainly sold while still green. The amount of coconuts we needed would need to be imported from Vietnam. And no, they wouldn't be as cheap as we had been told. Everyone wanted to profit from barangs trying to start a business. It was frustrating and slow.

Andrew would keep trying different batches of oil. Letting them sit for a few days so see if he had got the coconut dry enough to not have any moisture left in it, if it did, then the coconut oil would be cloudy and go rancid. If he dried it too much the coconut oil was too dark and lost its healing properties. It was hard for Andrew. We had paid a lot of money for the expressor. We needed this to work. We didn't have a plan B for how to make a living in Cambodia.

Andrew was becoming more and more frustrated. His patience was running low. He had already been giving Asher a hard time for a couple of years but it was intensifying. Asher seemed an easy target for Andrew. He was jealous over the connection that Asher and I had. Andrew knew that each nasty comment to Asher hit me deep. He couldn't stop himself. I begged him to be more careful with what he said to Asher. It was taking its toll on my son. Andrew even acknowledged to me that he was doing it but didn't seem able to stop himself.

Since Asher and Tikvah were born I had wanted to do something special for them for their 'coming of age' birthdays. It was a Jewish tradition that really appealed to me. For boys it was 13 and for girls 12. I loved the idea of acknowledging this really important milestone. I had been mulling it over. I didn't want anything religious as such, but I did want the kids to have a 'before and after' moment that they could look back on. I wanted the opportunity to talk to them about the deeper things in life. I had always had a really good connection with them and it felt right to do something special for the occasion.

Asher's 13th birthday was coming up and I really wanted Andrew and him to have a connecting experience together. I felt so sad about how things were going between them. To send them away together in a negative headspace was pretty confronting for me. I just had to set my worries aside and trust that Andrew would handle the situation with care. I knew that when he set his insecurities and pride aside he could be the most wonderful dad I had ever hoped for with my kids.

He seemed keen to take Asher away. Andrew also asked his friends to each give a letter to Asher about reaching manhood. Write some things that they wished they had been told when approaching this important age. I was so grateful that Andrew hadn't shot the idea down when I suggested it to him. And thankfully his friends had come through. So many of them had taken the time to write to Asher. Heartfelt letters. Even my brothers had done it. It meant a lot to me.

My wish was that the guys who wrote these letters would over time be a bit of a mentor to Asher and he would feel as if he could approach them with concerns or issues. I loved that Asher had these letters to refer back to, and even though I didn't read them myself I knew that the things written came from the heart. Along with the letters, Asher and Andrew went to Laos for an adventure.

Once again it was Megan who had told us about this amazing place in the jungles of Laos. It was called the Gibbon Experience. Zip lines stretched for kilometres high above the jungle. Tree houses were built on stilts that connected each line. Andrew and Asher spent a few days speeding across the jungle sky. Going from tree house to tree house. It was initially terrifying but after a few goes Asher could enjoy the thrill. It was a great experience and the boys came back telling us of their adventures.

Tikvah knew that her time away with me was only six months down the track. Her twelfth birthday was in October. I was going to surprise her with a trip to England and Sweden. I had found tickets online that would cost less than $1,000 for both of us to fly there and back. It was so cheap. Tikvah had been asking me for years to go back to Sweden. She couldn't remember being there as a toddler but felt a connection to the place. For me it was a chance to have her meet with women who were important to me from my childhood. It was a perfect way to celebrate her coming of age.

I didn't want to tell her though. I thought it would be an amazing surprise. I was thinking through how I could pull it off. We were going up to Phnom Penh for regular dental appointments with Asher. He was getting his teeth straightened with a retainer that needed regular tweaking. Andrew was completely opposed to our kids getting their teeth straightened, saying it was so unnecessary and vein. I disagreed. For me it was really important. I had a retainer as a kid in Sweden and having straight teeth was more than having a pretty smile. It meant dental hygiene. For Andrew this was ridiculous and he was happy to remind us that when he was offered braces as a teenager he had refused. Why would we spend cash on something as shallow as that? I had eventually convinced him when I said we could use the money from Paul's inheritance to pay for it. It meant regular trips to Phnom Penh though, and I thought that on one of those trips in October I would surprise Tikvah, and only tell her once the tuk tuk got to the airport. It would be a wonderful surprise.

Unfortunately I couldn't wait that long. Tikvah was struggling so much in Cambodia. My normally happy daughter was incredibly lethargic. She didn't want to leave the house. It felt as if she was walking through deep water and couldn't quite surface. I felt for her. I knew she needed more than what life in rural Cambodia could offer her. I decided to tell her about her twelfth birthday present. I asked her to just try to hold on to that. Focus on the fact that she would have this wonderful trip in a few months. Could she do that?

She promised me she would try and it seemed as if her mood improved somewhat. I felt incredibly stuck. Andrew had been away from his idyllic life in Cambodia and he was needing to recharge his batteries in this lawless country. My kids on the other hand, my older kids specifically, were over it. Well and truly over it. My only solution was to try once again to find them some friends. I ended getting in touch with a homeschooling UN family in Phnom Penh with similar aged kids. Being homeschooled they didn't seem to have that bratty expat attitude that we had come across in our travels. Incredibly wealthy kids living the high life in Cambodia. They almost seemed liked royalty. I knew it could happen so easily when you grow up with maids, cleaners, drivers and guards. Thankfully this family was very different to that and our kids got along straightaway.

Not only were they friendly, they were hospitable and as desperate as us for friends. We got invited to extend our dental visits to Phnom Penh and spend the night at their house. We played in their pool for hours. We would share large spontaneous dinners, with their family being as big as ours. Rosa would normally travel with us to Phnom Penh and she got along with their helper so it really was a perfect match. It was so overdue and exactly what our friendship-starved family needed.

Once we were back in our village it was hard to keep the kids in a positive frame of mind. I tried to tell Andrew that I was really concerned for them but he seemed to think I was exaggerating. He was still very frustrated with the amount of time I spent online. For me I needed both. I needed time during the day with the kids but I also needed to connect with the rest of the world.

In many ways it became my sanity. I didn't have many friends that I could be with in Kampot. Everyone was busy with their own lives and I tried as much as I could to invite people over for meals or ask if they wanted to join us down by the river. I really enjoyed spending time with Katie and Hallam. Hallam was often busy away on trips, helping Cambodians who were getting kicked off their land in the name of 'progress'. Katie, as well as being a mother, was running Epic Arts. They often had their shack on the river full of young deaf people for a lunch and swim and we would be invited to join in on the fun. I had a lot of respect for both Katie and Hallam and the work they were doing in Cambodia. We would try to have cups of tea as often as their busy schedule would allow and they would ask me all about parenting, feeling out of their depth in their new venture. It was so refreshing to see two people who were genuinely contributing to Cambodia but not living a lavish lifestyle. They were truly passionate about what they were involved in, and even though they could have easily cashed in on the attention they were getting, neither of them had. I wished I had more chances of catching up for cups of tea in their garden but it was still a rare treat. Instead I would escape into Facebook land in the evenings. It wasn't as if I was watching YouTube clips about cats. By now I had quite a large group of people following our story.

Mai's older sister had just given birth. She had been one of my embroidery girls. I decided to go over and give her a gift for the occasion. They only lived a few metres down Uterus Road. Opposite the noodle shack. In a mud pit. It was monsoon season so I had to walk through a deep puddle to get to their tiny hut. I had never really had a close look before but as I started climbing the rickety ladder I was very much paying attention. It felt as if I was going to make the whole thing collapse. As if I was trying to get into one of the forts that Asher and Tikvah used to build in Adelaide. It was held together with rusty metal, pieces of plywood and palm branches.

As I poked inside I could see the new mother on the floor. Her baby girl next to her. Both of them wet from the rain that had poured in that night. The grandmother boiling something in a blackened tin. The smoke from the tiny fire going into the hut. It was so tiny. So ridiculously tiny. I couldn't even imagine how they fit everyone in at night to sleep. Three sisters, their mother, the new father of the baby and of course the baby as well. There wasn't enough floor space for that many people. Summer had come with me and she knelt down to kiss the baby girl. I remained by the door hoping the shack wouldn't collapse from my weight. It was absolutely insane. A young mum having to live like this. I knew how going to the toilet is so delicate after birth. How did she get down that ladder? And then wade in the deep puddle? Not just that, but both the mother and the baby were getting rained on! I had to do something.

I asked Rosa to help me talk to a builder. How much would it cost to replace their shack with a proper structure? It would cost less than $1,000 and would only take a couple of days. Too easy! I got on Facebook and told my now big group of friends about what was happening. I showed a couple of photos of the shack we needed to replace. The money started to come in immediately. It was incredible.

I went to tell Rosa that we had the money only a few hours after we had spoken to the builder. Instead of looking pleased she seemed troubled. Word had spread about their home being replaced. Did I know they were living on illegal land? The village chief would not approve of a structure going up there. He had turned a blind eye to this rickety shack but even then had recently told the family that they would need to leave. Our road was going to be widened and the space they were in would be swallowed up. Damn! It was so frustrating. This family needed somewhere to live.

The only solution was to buy them some land. Buy them something that they couldn't be kicked off. Rosa told me that we could buy a segment of a rice paddy close to her house. It was only a few hundred metres away from where this family lived so they wouldn't feel disoriented. Buying land was more expensive than building a house though.

I didn't need to worry. Yet again my Facebook peeps came through. Within a couple of days all the money needed for the land was covered. Incredible! Friends who I hadn't heard from in years. Friends who I knew struggled financially. It felt so good to know that all these people around the world were understanding how critical it was for this family to have a home.

While their house was being built, and the rain was pouring down, I invited them into our home. They seemed somewhat terrified at the concept of living with us but I assured them through Rosa that they could still cook their food on an open fire and they didn't need to use the rest of our house if they didn't want to. They could all just snuggle up in our smallest room and pretend they were home. And they did. Because of the heavy rain it took longer than expected but after two weeks this little family finally had a home. A proper home. Rosa told me that they wouldn't need a chicken. They would be able to cook their meals under the house.

I was trying to find things to do with Asher and Tikvah to keep their minds off how lonely they were. I had been suggesting a bike ride for a while. I wanted to show them the places that Shraps and I would ride to on our Sunday mornings. Asher was keen but Tikvah seemed hesitant. I couldn't quite figure out why. Eventually she agreed.

We rode past the submerged rice paddies. Past huts and kids waving to us and asking us what are names were. Past temples and salt fields. I was so happy to finally get Tikvah out of the house.

Just as we were finishing our adventure we had to cross a road. The highway coming into Kampot. As I crossed I could see Tikvah following me. Assuming it was safe to cross when I crossed. It wasn't. Just the couple of seconds of delay meant that a speeding moto crashed right into her. I saw her fly off her bicycle and skid across the road. At the same time the moto toppled to the ground and two monks went flying into the air. Their orange robes unravelling as they came crashing down. It was surreal.

I looked over at Tikvah. I couldn't believe that we hadn't been hit by an oncoming truck. Normally there was one every few seconds at this time of day. We had somehow managed to have this all happen in some sort of a truck lull. Once I got Tikvah off the road I checked her for injuries. She had skid across the road yet I couldn't see any marks on her body. I kept checking. She was shaking and crying.

I could see the monks in their tiny undergarments that looked like women's slips. They were standing in the middle of the road gathering metres of fabric into their arms. A crowd of onlookers were now surrounding us. All the traffic stopping to look at the barang family. It was such a close call. I couldn't believe that Tikvah was unharmed. Her only injury was a sore wrist. How could she have landed like that and not be hurt? It took me and Asher a few days to stop asking each other.

The trip to Sweden couldn't come fast enough. Tikvah was counting the days until she could get on the plane. The trip turned out to be so much more than we could have hoped for. We spent a week in England with my cousin who I hadn't seen since I was a child. Who knew that we were so connected? I felt as if I was with a long lost sister. In fact, she almost felt more than a sister. We had the same humour. The same intensity. Her poor husband just shook his head that there were two of us. One was more than enough. We were giddy with joy at being together. Tikvah was lapping it up. She loved seeing me so happy. But it was more than that. I couldn't quite put my finger on it.

We spent a few days with my teachers from my school in Jerusalem. Miss Johnson, was now Amanda. Last memory I had of her was Raphael throwing her into the pool at high school graduation. Now she was a vicar in London. Totally spoiling us she took us around London to see the sights. A ferry ride to Greenwich Village where we stumbled across Sherlock Holmes being filmed. A day at a castle. Tikvah loved anything medieval and this was the ultimate outing for her.

We then went off to Oxford where we got to spent time with my favourite teacher from school, Miss Payne. Who I now had to call Helen. I had adored her in high school. She was kind and seemed to understand more than the other teachers did. It was great to see her after so many years. We didn't get as much time with her as we did with Miss Johnson but we made the most of it. I was thrilled to have her give me her book about Third Culture Kids. After finishing teaching in Jerusalem she had furthered her studies and now had a doctorate on the topic. I loved that. The more that was researched about this growing breed of people who didn't really belong in any culture, the better.

We then flew to Sweden for Tikvah to finally spend some time there. It was so good to see my mother again. She lived a very short bike ride away from where I had moved when I saw seven. She even worked at the school that I had gone to with Magdalena all those years before. The two of us walking around feeling proud about our ugly clothes because it meant we were going to Heaven. Now the school had been converted into a school for adults. Immigrants mainly. Teaching them Swedish so they could find jobs quicker. My mother was a counsellor there. Doing so much more than her job description asked of her. Inviting lonely immigrants to her home. Baking for their special occasions. Bringing them gifts when they had babies. They loved her for being so kind and warm.

I had always marvelled at people who still lived in the same city that they were born in. For me it was incredible to be able to build layers of memories in the same place. I had never experienced anything like that. We only had a couple of days with my mother but we were able to go down to Falsterbo and walk through the beautiful graveyard where Mormor and Morfar were buried. We could hear the sound of the waves crashing in as we placed shells on their memorial stone. In the evening Tikvah cooked with her Grandma. Something so rare and so precious. I longed for my kids to have rituals with their grandparents, so deeply sad that my children had missed out on priceless childhood memories.

One of the surprises I had for Tikvah was that I had asked all the women in my life that I respected to write a letter for her. I had the letters bound together so on her actual birthday evening I presented her with the book. The cover was a beautiful mandala that Claire had drawn for her. As well as that I had asked if each person that we were going to visit could spend some time with Tikvah cooking one of their favourite recipes, that had a bit of a story attached. I would then make her another book that included all the recipes as well as the stories, and maybe even a photo of Tikvah and this woman cooking together. It was simple but it gave our trip a bit of a storyline.

We then caught a train to see Susanna and her kids for a weekend. Again, a miniature visit but so worthwhile. Seeing my nephews and niece, now fluent in Swedish and English, was so wonderful. Another train trip and we got to see my friend Magdalena. Now a mother of three. Still a force to be reckoned with. She was now working in a school trying to empower immigrant students by encouraging them to become political activists instead of using violence as a way to be heard. Many of them had been living in oppressed countries. Violence was their form of communication. It didn't have to be like that in Sweden. Racial tensions were increasing in southern Sweden and Magdalena felt that so much of it could be avoided if these immigrants were able to gain a voice in the political realm. It was working. Her pilot program had just received funds so it could be introduced to other schools across Sweden. I was so proud of her.

Our next stop was Gothenburg. We had Swedish friends who had lived in Adelaide for a couple of years that had returned home. Their house backed on to a forest. Tikvah and her friend Siri would be gone all day. They would come in once it got dark. Their faces flushed by the excitement. Stories of getting stuck in deep mud, pretending to be running away from an orphanage. Finding berries and mushrooms. The two of them were so similar and they were bursting with excitement. Who was this girl? I hardly recognised my daughter.

Tikvah was pleading to stay out longer. She didn't care if it was dark. She was dirty from sliding down boulders. A shoe missing, apparently still stuck in deep mud. I looked at her and realised she was still a little girl. A little girl desperate to have fun. So starved of play. She begged to stay. Could she please live with Siri and her family? She didn't want to go back to Cambodia. She begged me. I couldn't believe how ignorant I was. I had assumed that a lot of her wanting to stay indoors was her getting older and hitting puberty. I knew that was so common in those in between years. I was so wrong. So utterly wrong. Tikvah was still a kid. Desperate to squeeze some more years out of her childhood. I could see the desperation in her eyes.

Mamma, please let me stay here.

Tears rolling down her face. I knew it was too much to ask this family to host my daughter who had just turned twelve a few days earlier. She needed her Mamma. She needed her Mamma to stop worrying about pulling Andrew away from his utopia. She needed her Mamma to put her kids needs first. I promised Tikvah I would talk to her dad. I didn't know what I could do but I would talk to him.

We then caught yet another train to Uppsala. Our friends Ronia and Aaron now lived here. It was Ronia's mother that I had met at the Central Markets in Adelaide when I was selling bread. Both Tikvah and I adored them and were excited to see what their life in Sweden looked like. We felt as if we stepped into an Astrid Lindgren book. Their red house. Their barn. Their giant apple tree. It was an idyllic spot and we soaked up our few days with them Ronia was still able to paint despite having three boys to look after. She had always been amazing like that. Being able to create art in the midst of chaos. Aaron was busy writing yet another book. I had lost count. Was this his third? I was pretty sure that when I first met him he was just about to finish his first book. The one he was writing sounded fascinating. Telling the story of driving to Poland with his dad and oldest son to find a treasure that his grandfather had spoken about his entire childhood. They had escaped Nazi Europe. Aaron was raised in Sweden as a Jew. We spent many evenings laughing at how similar the characters in our families seemed despite them living on opposite sides of the globe. That Jewish anxiety and hyper caution, especially around food and new experiences, knew no boundaries. We seemed to share the same aunties and grandparents.

Tikvah spent most of her time picking apples or riding a bike down to the forest. I pretty much spent the whole visit sitting at their kitchen table talking to whoever happened to sit down next to me. How were they able to attract such fascinating friends? The conversations were vibrant. So many different languages spoken. Cups of tea being refilled as breakfast became lunch and lunch became dinner.

The one character that stood out the most to me that visit was a friend of theirs who was an asylum seeker from Iran. He had lived in Sweden for seven years. His Swedish was almost fluent. Only a slight accent gave him away. He was working as a teacher at a school. Helping immigrant kids absorb into Swedish culture. He told me that he and his brother had fled at the same time. Both fearing for their lives. They were separated along the way. His brother ended up in Australia. Seven years later he was still in detention. Still locked up. Still waiting to hear if Australia would accept him as a genuine refugee.

This man on the other hand, who landed in Sweden, only spent three weeks waiting to be processed. He needed to sleep in the accommodation provided for him but was able to come and go as he pleased. He was never treated as a criminal. He was able to start learning Swedish straightaway. He was now earning money as a teacher and contributing back to the country that had welcomed him. How different to the men that I had helped teach English in Murray Bridge. The years they spent being imprisoned. How they were traumatised from their experience. One of them even committing suicide not long after being told he had to return to Afghanistan. How could they be treated so differently in the two countries? My heart ached for this man's brother.

We arrived back in Phnom Penh and had hardly put our suitcases down when Tikvah burst out crying. Not just crying, but hyperventilating. She was having a panic attack. It went on for ages. I wrapped her in a blanket and just cradled her. She would try to speak but the words wouldn't come out.

A couple of hours later, when she had finally settled with her head in my lap she started to speak between the sobs. She couldn't live in Cambodia anymore. She just couldn't. Even the trip from the airport to the guesthouse had been too much. It had brought everything back. She hated it here. She had hated it for so long. She had tried to like it because she knew it was important for me and dad. But she couldn't pretend anymore. She was pleading with me.

I just want to be a girl Mamma. I just want to be a girl. They look at me as if I'm grown up. I'm only twelve. They think I'm a woman.

I had no idea. I hadn't even considered it. Tikvah was tiny. In Australia she was often mistaken for someone two or three years younger than her actual age. But she was right, in Cambodia she was the size of a grown woman. Rosa was only a tiny bit taller than Tikvah, and her body smaller.

No wonder men were looking at Tikvah. No wonder she hadn't wanted to leave our house. No wonder she had become a kid as soon as we landed in England, and then in Sweden she had disappeared into the forest with her friend Siri. She was a kid. A little kid with men ogling her. She had done what I had asked her. More than six months earlier I had asked her to hold on until we went on our trip to Sweden. She had. It had taken everything in her but somehow she had held on. Now she had tasted the freedom of being a kid for a month and arriving back to reality was too much. I knew our time in Cambodia was up. I had known for a long time but I had tried to push the thought away. It was too hard to face.

I knew Andrew would be devastated. For me the idea of suburbia was terrifying. As much as I struggled with the heat and the annoying habits of the locals who saw me and the kids as endless entertainment, it was still better than suburbia. Starting and ending my day in a car. Library fines. Endless comments about the weather. For Lillian there was nothing worse. But in this moment I had to be a mother. I couldn't base my decision on what Lillian wanted. And anyway, I couldn't do what I wanted to do in Cambodia at the same time as being a mother. It just didn't work. Someone had to miss out and unfortunately in Cambodia that would be my kids. I couldn't do it. I just couldn't. We had to go back. Back to suburbia.

The reality was starting to sink in as Tikvah continued to lay in my lap, the occasional sob still coming to the surface. I needed to talk to Andrew. I needed to let him know our time was up. Andrew had started a new job not long before we left on our trip to Sweden. After almost two and a half years Andrew had been employed to work in Cambodia. No more trips to Australia. The only issue was of course that the job was based in Phnom Penh and often required him to go out to the countryside for a few days at a time.

It was a dream job for Andrew. Just not for the rest of us. I was happy that he had this opportunity but reminded him that having his family in a village in southern Cambodia while he spent the weekdays in Phnom Penh and beyond, was not in any way fulfilling our desire to spend more time together as a family. Andrew reminded me that it would be too expensive to live in Phnom Penh as a family and I reminded him that I would never want to live in Phnom Penh even if we had the money.

And no, me living in our village with the kids for the week was not the solution. Andrew was coming back exhausted on the Friday and then leaving Sunday night to start his week in Phnom Penh on Monday morning. It was nuts. How long was he expecting us to survive with this new set up that obviously suited him perfectly and scared the shit out of me? When was he going to understand that my nerves were not coping with us living apart?

We decided that we would talk about it properly when he came up with the rest of the kids the next day. We took the big kids and Rosa to watch a movie while the girls played in an indoor playground. It was our one chance to talk. I was totally straight with Andrew. I explained again what had happened with Tikvah. Explained that this had been going on for a while now. That we needed to act. And we needed to act soon.

Andrew agreed that Cambodia was no longer best for our older kids. That they needed to feel safe. They needed to feel normal. He knew it was best for them to leave. But where exactly was I suggesting? Andrew knew that I had been googling places to live in Australia for a while. On one of our trips we had flown to Queensland for two nights to check out a commune. Was I suggesting there? He knew I had been searching for the place in Australia that was most bike-friendly so we didn't need to base our life around our car. My search had come back with options that just wouldn't work for us. We would need a place that could provide a job for Andrew and I was thinking that I might have to get some study done to upgrade my much-neglected counselling degree. I couldn't expect to get work with my empty resume.

I knew Andrew was opposed to me volunteering at a school but maybe he would be more open-minded about me studying. Even if it was just one day a week. I had spent so many nights lying awake trying to think of what options we had if we ever did move back. I always came back to the same thing. Our kids needed family. They needed relatives. They needed to belong. The only place that even remotely offered that was Melbourne. A city I really knew nothing about. I had been to St Kilda a couple of times, and to the Aquarium. That was it. I could probably get used to liking the hippie market half an hour from where Andrew grew up. That was all I knew about Melbourne. Except the glaring truth that it was the only place in Australia that we had family. Andrew's dad and sister. Not a huge amount but it was a start.

Andrew was horrified when I told him.

Melbourne?? Melbourne?? Why would we ever move there??

He was shocked. I explained to him about our kids belonging somewhere and it just wouldn't happen without relatives. We had learnt that the hard way in Adelaide. Andrew was furious. To him the only option was Adelaide. He wanted to be with his friends. If he had to live a miserable life in Australia the least I could give him was his friends in Adelaide.

I couldn't bite my tongue anymore. He was acting like a spoiled teenager. This wasn't about him. This wasn't about me. This was about the kids. If we were making a decision based on them there was no other choice but Melbourne. He wanted to know where I was suggesting we live? I reminded him that we owned a house in Melbourne. A four bedroom house that we had picked based on something we could consider living in if we ever had to, both of us hoping it would never come to that. We could live there.

Andrew thought I was kidding. "It's the worst house ever. It's pokey. It's in the most boring part of Melbourne. The rooms are so small." His list went on forever. This was ridiculous. The house was fine. Totally fine. It had a great view. If anything it was me who had said when we bought it that if we ever did move in I would want to change the flooring. The beige tiles were awful and the worn out carpet a horrible dusty pink. That would have to go. It was me who had been complaining about it. Two and a half years in Cambodia had changed all that. I couldn't care less about the beige tiles anymore. The carpet was no problem. It was a house. Our house. It had showers with actual pressure to them. No more risk of being electrocuted from dodgy wiring. Yes the area seemed boring. But our kids would have a grandpa and an auntie. Surely we could overlook some beige things in exchange for that? I could feel Andrew's rage. He knew it was the right decision. But he just couldn't get passed the fact that he felt forced into it by me.

The next few weeks were a whirlwind. Andrew was still working during the week but would come home on the weekends. I wasn't scared of him but I kept my distance. His loathing for me was palpable. I had done the unforgivable. Forced him away from his utopian life in lawless Cambodia. We had so many things that needed to be done and it was hard to talk to Andrew about them with his anger so close to the surface.

I let him know that my friend was happy to lend us some money to help us pay for the trip home. I hadn't seen her since I lived in Portland as a teenager but here she was sending me messages on Facebook telling me to get the hell out of that jungle. She was one of the few people who I had opened up to about how bad it had become. I didn't feel as if it was something I could share freely. It was too woven into the complexity of our marriage. She understood my desperation though and told us that she would transfer money across asap.

My mother helped as well. So relieved that we were going back to Australia. Andrew's dad was helping out as well. It meant a lot that we had these people stepping up at such a delicate time. Andrew had got every job he applied for in Australia. He was incredibly good at being an engineer and it was pretty obvious in his interviews that he would be an asset to any company that hired him. Within a very short amount of time he landed a job with Ford in Melbourne. He could start in the new year. Our tenants agreed to move out. We had dreaded asking them but they were hoping to find something a bit cheaper anyway so the timing was actually good for them. That had been our biggest hurdle. Pretty much everything was in place. We only had a few more weeks to go.

Our tickets were booked for December 20, 2011. We would arrive back just before Christmas. In the meantime we had to pack up our house and celebrate the girls birthdays. I wasn't sure how we would make it all happen since it was an enormous job to get our house packed. We didn't want to bring alot of things back to Australia but we still needed to sort all our belongings and declutter. It really was a mammoth task.

I ended up asking Rosa to spread the word in our village that anything that we put on the porch was free to take. I had already allocated the bigger items to Rosa and Mai's family. We didn't have anything of value but for them our $7 wicker bookshelves were a treasure. We had so many to give away that each family member could have their own set of shelves. Not just that, but our thin mattresses as well. These cheap foam mattresses that were starting to go mouldy from the humidity were welcomed with open arms. Rosa wanted the bed linen and the kitchen utensils. I told them it would be handed over on our last night. It felt so good to get rid of our stuff. Once most of our belongings were gone I tried to map out our last few days there.

I still had some money left over from Tikvah's and Violette's Three Jars Full venture. I had been trying to think of something we could do for the two families I felt were the most desperate in our village. Mai's family who now had their house. As well as Rosa's cousin, who was struggling with her little boy and her husband who wouldn't share the money he earned while away. I had been asking about this for a while and finally decided to go ahead and buy them each a calf. It was the closest you could come to being financially secure in rural Cambodia. It meant money for the future. It was the ultimate thing to own. It wouldn't cost much to impregnate the cow once she was old enough and then they could sell off each calf that was born. And the manure could be used to grow vegetables. I knew how much the cow owners in our village loved their cows. We often had a young man spend a few hours in our backyard chopping grass for his beloved cow. At night a small fire was made to keep the mosquitoes away. These cows would eventually bring a lot of money into a family if they took care of her and made sure she didn't get sick.

I had started using the same taxi driver for my trips to Phnom Penh. He had the winning combo of speaking English as well as having a seat belt for each passenger. He promised me he would find me a couple of calves. And he did. It wasn't as straightforward as I had hoped. But after a few visits we finally had the money paid and we were promised the calves would be delivered the next day. It was a big occasion and I asked the village chief to take part in the proceedings.

I wanted the new cow owners to really understand that I was serious about what I said. I figured that maybe with the village chief as witness they would go ahead and act on my wishes. My only request from them was that the second female calf that was born from their cow, they would give to a family who was poorer than them. No payment. Just a gift. And they would be told to do the same thing once that calf grew up.

The idea I had was that if this actually worked, there would be a lot more cow owners a few years down the track in southern Cambodia. It was my attempt at a long-term plan. Possibly my only long-term plan ever. I really wanted it to work. The village chief seemed to like the idea. So did my taxi driver. They were busy holding hands while watching the calves being untied from the back of the moto. I tried not to cringe at how roughly these poor calves were treated. I tried to focus on the fact that they were still alive after travelling upside down on the back of a moto all the way down Uterus Road. My taxi driver had picked strong cows.

I knew Andrew was really struggling with this move and I was trying to think of something nice he could do before we had to leave. I suggested he take the kids to Rabbit Island for a night. It would not only be great for them to have one last chance to visit there but it would also give me a chance to get some cleaning done with no kids in the house. The electricity wasn't working which meant no DVDs to distract the kids with, as well as no fans which made it extra hot. It would have made sense for Rosa to stay with me and help clean the house. After all she was technically our maid.

Instead I decided that it was probably her last chance to go to Rabbit Island, at least for a long time. I doubted that her new employers would be as kind to her as we had been. The likelihood of her having time away like that seemed pretty far-fetched. I was happy to wave them all off on a tuk tuk as I got back to cleaning the house on my own and cursing the fans for not working.

I received a text from Andrew the next day. They were having such a great time, they would stay a bit longer. It was so good to hear anything remotely positive from Andrew. I told him to enjoy his time away. I stayed at the house, part of me wondering if Rosa would return to help me with the packing and cleaning.

I knew there was going to be a lunar eclipse that night and I had pictured sharing the moment with my family. Instead I walked through the streets of Kampot. Something I never did. I was always on a bike or a tuk tuk. It felt so different to walk. I sat down to watch the eclipse that was about to begin.

This was new for me. I never really paid attention to the moon. Sometimes I would notice that it was full. Or that it was low on the horizon. Or think to myself that a crescent was almost more beautiful than a full moon. There was something about giving it my full attention. It tapped into a part of me that I didn't recognise.

I wondered what my life would look like by the next full moon. It seemed too crazy to even think about me back in Australia. Far, far away from Kampot. As I continued sitting there I had this eerie feeling that it wasn't so much about me sitting there looking at the moon. In fact, it felt as if the moon was looking down at me. All of a sudden I could see me from the moon's perspective. This woman sitting in the middle of a road. The tiny town around her. The river not far away. Behind the river the beautiful mountain. Then the rice paddies stretching off into the horizon with the occasional sharp mountain peak poking out. In that moment it was just me and the moon. Me and the Cambodian landscape stretching around me. The moon was now completely hidden.

I thought about Andrew. I knew he would be watching the moon as well. Rosa would be with him. Probably Asher and Tikvah as well. The girls hopefully asleep, exhausted from two days of playing in the ocean. I loved knowing that they were all enjoying themselves. It had been a hard couple of days cleaning the house but I had made the right decision. Andrew had already sent me a text to say that they were extending their visit yet again. They must be having a really good time. What a relief.

All I longed for was harmony for my family. Meaning for myself. A better life for others. Our time in Cambodia was over. Melbourne was waiting. I looked up to the silhouette of the moon wondering if she knew what lay ahead. What would our next chapter have in store? I was dreading returning to Australia yet longing for our family to have a fresh start with support around us. My heart ached at wanting to keep helping those less fortunate yet it would have to be done from suburbia so that my children's needs could come first. I had tried so hard and I just needed to trust that better things were on the horizon.